ALL·IN·ONE

CCISO™

Certified Chief Information Security Officer

EXAM GUIDE

ABOUT THE AUTHORS

Steven Bennett, CCISO, CISSP, CISA, is an engineer, sportsman, entrepreneur, and consultant. He has worked in the information technology field for over 40 years helping organizations protect their most important assets from criminal threats. Steve has spent his lifetime studying human and animal behavior in complex systems, the relationships between predator and prey, and offensive and defensive survival strategies and tactics observed in business and nature. Steve's information security consulting career includes supporting clients in healthcare, manufacturing, retail, finance, military, and government.

Jordan Genung, CCISO, CISSP, CISM, CISA, has served as an information security officer and security advisor for public- and private-sector organizations. His experience includes security consulting for Fortune 100 companies and government agencies, building information security programs, and developing information security curriculum. Jordan holds a degree in computer science and information security from the University of Texas at San Antonio, which is an NSA and DHS National Center of Academic Excellence in Cyber Operations, Cyber Defense, and Research.

About the Technical Editor

Michael Lester has worked in the information security industry for over 20 years and currently is the chief technology officer (CTO) of WindTalker Inc. (maker of data-centric security encryption software products). Previously Mike was the chief instructor and consultant for Shon Harris's Logical Security LLC (now Human Element LLC), where he taught and developed courses on CISSP, hacking/pentesting, digital forensics/e-discovery, CISA, and others. Mike also authors and instructs classes for LinkedIn Learning. He holds a master's degree in information systems security from Boston University (a National Security Agency [NSA] Center of Academic Excellence) as well as over 20 industry certifications, including CISSP, CISA, CCE, Security+, MCSE:Security, CCSE+, and ITIL.

ALL·IN·ONE

CCISO™

Certified Chief Information Security Officer

EXAM GUIDE

Steven Bennett
Jordan Genung

New York   Chicago   San Francisco
Athens   London   Madrid   Mexico City
Milan   New Delhi   Singapore   Sydney   Toronto

McGraw Hill books are available at special quantity discounts to use as premiums and sales promotions, or for use in corporate training programs. To contact a representative, please visit the Contact Us pages at www.mhprofessional.com.

CCISO™ Certified Chief Information Security Officer All-in-One Exam Guide

1 2 3 4 5 6 7 8 9   LCR   24 23 22 21 20

Library of Congress Control Number: 2020946895

ISBN   978-1-260-46392-7
MHID   1-260-46392-3

Sponsoring Editor	**Technical Editor**	**Production Supervisor**
Wendy Rinaldi	Michael Lester	Thomas Somers
Editorial Supervisor	**Copy Editor**	**Composition**
Janet Walden	William McManus	KnowledgeWorks Global Ltd
Project Manager	**Proofreader**	**Illustration**
Parag Mittal,	Rachel Fogelberg	KnowledgeWorks Global Ltd
KnowledgeWorks Global Ltd	**Indexer**	**Art Director, Cover**
Acquisitions Coordinator	Ted Laux	Jeff Weeks
Emily Walters		

In memory of Shon Harris.

CONTENTS AT A GLANCE

CONTENTS

ACKNOWLEDGMENTS

Steve would like to thank his incredible wife, Debby, for her unyielding support throughout the book-writing process. I love you, hon. Now maybe things can get back to normal around here. Warmest thanks go to co-author Jordan, who put up with my obstinance and made this project fun.

Jordan would like to thank his family and friends for their continued support and encouragement. A special thanks to Steve for the invitation to collaborate on this book. Your expertise and guidance were invaluable in this undertaking. It was an honor and a pleasure.

Both authors wish to thank Wendy Rinaldi, Emily Walters, and the extraordinary team at McGraw Hill. Your professionalism, insight, and advice were instrumental to the success of this project. A big thanks to our friend Mike Lester for his excellent technical editing, savvy, and guidance. Other friends who counseled us and deserve our thanks include Tom Conkle, Ray Gabler, David Goldstein, and Greg Witte. And finally, a thank you to all of the CISOs who must remain unnamed but who shared with us their stories, advice, and experiences that helped us describe the life and challenges of the CISO in the real world.

INTRODUCTION

Security is mortals' chiefest enemy.

—Hecate, from *Macbeth* by William Shakespeare

As we put the finishing touches on this book, Twitter is busy recovering from the latest very public and newsworthy cybersecurity incident widely reported in the media. For every one of these highly publicized breaches there are hundreds of other damaging cyber-attacks experienced by businesses and government entities. To help organizations protect themselves against and respond to information security incidents, many of them turn to the chief information security officer (CISO) for leadership. The CISO is becoming the guardian of the modern business, charged with protecting the organization against security threats in the digital world.

Twenty-five years ago, the role of the CISO didn't even exist, yet now over 60 percent of Fortune 500 businesses have a CISO. Although that may seem like rapid adoption, it shows that 40 percent of large companies have not seen fit to turn to CISOs to be the guardians of their organization. Proliferation and development of the role of the CISO are driven by questions such as these:

- Where does the CISO sit in the organizational structure?
- What is the relationship between the CISO and the other C-level leaders?
- What qualifications are required to be a successful CISO?
- What does having a CISO mean to the business?

The answers to these questions are evolving as more organizations adopt and fill the role of CISO.

Like many industries, the information security field includes professional organizations and standards bodies that establish criteria and certify people in industry-specific skills. Sometimes these groups merely reflect the current industry trends and practices, while other times they take a leadership role and shepherd the industry to new places. EC-Council, the governing body of the CCISO certification, seems to be edging toward the latter. The very existence of the CCISO certification breaks new ground. While there are a few other organizations offering CISO certification programs, none have gained much traction. The EC-Council CCISO is the only CISO-specific certification that is included in the US Department of Defense's approved baseline certifications contained in DoD 8140/8570.

For the aspiring CISO, the EC-Council CCISO program provides a template that defines the core knowledge and skills every CISO should have. For organizations seeking to create a CISO position or hire a CISO, the certification provides not only a picture of what skills a good CISO should possess but also a means to independently validate the qualifications of a given candidate.

An argument can be made that certifying CISOs is a fallacy because there is no one-size-fits-all when it comes to CISOs. It is true that the role of the CISO varies widely based on the industry in which the CISO operates, the size and nature of their organization, and their own personal background and personality. The CISO of a software product vendor may have a vastly different focus from that of a CISO who works for a public utility supplier. However, there are core skills that both CISOs—and all other CISOs—should have. The CCISO certification focuses on those core skills.

Security is not binary, whereby an organization either has security or doesn't. Rather, security is a sliding scale: an organization can have a lot of security and minimize its risk or it can have a little security and have a lot of risk. It is the CISO's job to determine how much security is necessary based on their organization's tolerance for risk.

The CISO's approach is greatly influenced by their own view of the world. One CISO the authors know has a background in law enforcement, which has influenced his approach to his company's information security program. His company's security program emphasizes incident detection and response over other aspects of security. Many organizations' security programs reflect the personality or background of their respective CISO. The CCISO certification does not seek to change that dynamic but instead tries to ensure good security practices are applied no matter who is in charge. If our friend's detect and respond approach fits with his company's business and threat environment, his approach may be entirely appropriate. The CCISO program informs the CISO of the core elements of any security program, which the CISO can then mold based on many factors, including the organization's tolerance for risk and the CISO's own characteristics and experience.

The CCISO certification is reflective of the reality of today's population of CISOs, some of whom come up through the technical ranks but lack business acumen and some of whom are already business leaders but may not have a technical or security background. The CCISO certification establishes core criteria for each. For the technically oriented security professional coming up through the ranks to become a CISO, the CCISO program broadens their skillset beyond technical domains by including topics such as strategic planning, finance, accounting, and resource management. These are topics that are important to the CISO but may not be included in traditional security professional certification programs such as CISSP from (ISC)2 or Security+ from CompTIA. Likewise, for the business leader who does not have a background in information technology or security but has business experience and is assuming the role of CISO, the CCISO program teaches technical topics to the level that most CISOs should understand.

About EC-Council

The International Council of E-Commerce Consultants, known as EC-Council, was founded in 2003 to provide security education, training, and certification programs. EC-Council may be best known for its Certified Ethical Hacker (CEH), Computer Hacking Forensic Investigator (CHFI), Certified Security Analyst (ECSA), and Licensed Penetration Tester certifications. As mentioned, EC-Council is also the certifying body for the Certified Chief Information Security Officer (CCISO) certification, developed to serve as a certification program for security executives.

In 2006, EC-Council established EC-Council University, which offers bachelor's and master's degrees in cybersecurity, with master's specializations and graduate certificates in the following areas: information security professional, security analyst, enterprise security architect, cloud security architect, digital forensics, incident management and business continuity, and executive leadership in information assurance.

Certification Process

This section outlines the EC-Council process for becoming CCISO certified. This process is illustrated in Figure 1. There are three main avenues for certification:

- CCISO certification through self-study
- CCISO certification through EC-Council approved training
- EC-Council Information Security Manager (EISM) certification program for individuals who do not meet CCISO prerequisites

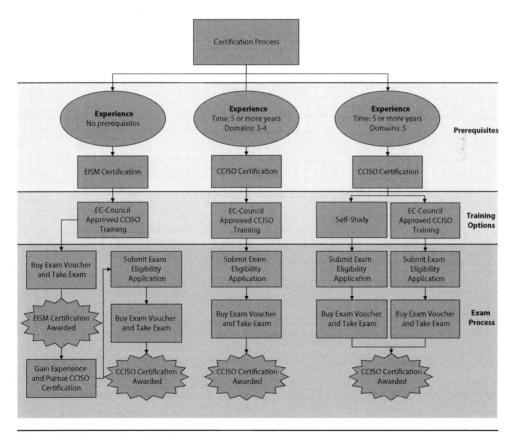

Figure 1 EC-Council certification process

> ## EC-Council Requirements
> The EC-Council requirements for certification change often, so it is important for candidates to check the EC-Council website for the most up-to-date information. The requirements listed in this section are accurate at the time of this writing.

Prerequisites

CCISO exam eligibility is determined based on the number of years of experience the candidate has in the five CCISO domains:

- Domain 1: Governance and Risk Management
- Domain 2: Information Security Controls, Compliance, and Audit Management
- Domain 3: Security Program Management and Operations
- Domain 4: Information Security Core Competencies
- Domain 5: Strategic Planning, Finance, Procurement, and Vendor Management

To be eligible to take the CCISO exam without obtaining official EC-Council training (self-study), a candidate must be able to demonstrate at least *five years of experience in each of the five* CCISO domains.

Alternatively, if a candidate completes an EC-Council approved CCISO training class, the candidate is only required to have five years of experience in *three of the five* CCISO domains.

The EC-Council Information Security Manager (EISM) certification program is a third option for individuals who *do not have the required years of experience* to apply for CCISO certification (through self-study or training avenues). Candidates can take the same EC-Council approved CCISO training course, sit for the EISM exam (a lighter version of the CCISO exam), and then, upon successfully passing the exam, pursue CCISO certification after meeting the minimum experience requirements.

 NOTE Some degrees and certifications count toward the minimum experience requirements for certification. For a list of acceptable experience waivers, visit the EC-Council website.

Training Options

There are two primary training avenues available to become certified:

- **Self-study** The self-study option, such as using this *CCISO Certified Chief Information Security Officer All-in-One Exam Guide*, is available to CCISO candidates with the necessary experience in each of the five CCISO domains.

- **Training**   EC-Council approved CCISO training classes are available from EC-Council and from EC-Council approved training providers. This route may be preferable for CCISO candidates who learn best from bootcamp-style training or for those who do not meet the minimum experience requirements for self-study. In addition, this is a requirement for EISM candidates interested in taking the EISM exam and later pursuing CCISO certification after meeting the experience requirements.

Exam Process

The exam process differs based on the training option and program selected:

- **Self-study**   To qualify to take the exam, self-study candidates must complete the Exam Eligibility Application ($100 application fee at the time of writing) on EC-Council's website and list all of their experience, certifications, and degrees (if applicable) to demonstrate that they have the necessary years of experience in each of the CCISO domains (five years in all five domains). Once a candidate's application has been accepted, verified, and approved, the candidate may purchase an exam voucher ($999 fee at the time of writing) from EC-Council to take the CCISO exam. Upon passing the exam, the candidate is awarded CCISO certification.

- **Training**   At the completion of an EC-Council approved CCISO training class, CCISO candidates are required to submit the Exam Eligibility Application demonstrating five years of experience in at least three of the five CCISO domains. Once a candidate's application has been accepted, verified, and approved, the candidate may obtain an exam voucher from EC-Council to take the CCISO exam. Upon passing the exam, the candidate is awarded CCISO certification.

- **EISM program**   At the completion of the EC-Council approved CCISO training class, EISM candidates may obtain an exam voucher from EC-Council to take the EISM exam. Upon passing the exam, the candidate is awarded EISM designation. Once the candidate acquires the necessary amount of experience to pursue CCISO certification (minimum of five years of experience in at least three domains), the candidate must submit the Exam Eligibility Application. Once the application has been accepted, verified, and approved, the candidate may obtain an exam voucher from EC-Council at half price to take the CCISO exam. Upon passing the exam, the candidate is awarded CCISO certification.

Exam Information

The CCISO exam consists of 150 scenario-based multiple-choice questions. Candidates are given 2.5 hours to complete the exam and must achieve a score of at least 72 percent. The CCISO exam includes three types of questions, listed here in order of increased difficulty:

- **Knowledge**   These types of questions merely test a candidate's ability to recall information. This often manifests in questions that test the candidate's understanding of definitions or comprehension of terms.

- **Application** These types of questions test a candidate's ability to apply a concept. This requires knowledge of the concept as well as an understanding of how to apply the concept.

- **Analysis** These types of questions are the most rigorous. They test the candidate's ability to analyze a scenario and identify the correct course of action.

Similar to the CCISO exam, the EISM exam is 150 questions. The EISM exam is based on the same questions as the CCISO exam without the scenario-based (analysis) questions. In addition, the EISM exam must be completed in 2 hours with a 70 percent passing score. Candidates who become EISM certified can take the full CCISO exam, at a reduced cost, once they have met the experience requirements for CCISO certification.

How to Use this Book

This book is organized by chapters that correspond to the CCISO domains as defined by EC-Council. Each chapter covers the topics required by EC-Council's exam objectives. In some cases, this approach results in overlapping coverage because EC-Council lists some topics in more than one domain. In cases in which a topic appears in more than one section, we have tried to avoid duplicating information in favor of giving a different perspective of the topic. For example, the topic of *securing assets* is discussed in terms of the risk management process in Chapter 1, in terms of asset management in Chapter 3, and in terms of asset security in Chapter 4.

Each book chapter is introduced here:

- **Chapter 1, "Governance and Risk Management,"** covers foundational concepts for the CISO. It focuses on ways the CISO ensures that an organization's security program aligns with the organization's business. The chapter covers information security governance, information security basics, what a typical information security program looks like, and descriptions of laws and frameworks relevant to security.

- **Chapter 2, "Information Security Controls, Compliance, and Audit Management,"** describes how an organization establishes and implements security controls, control frameworks, and the control life cycle. It also includes extensive coverage of information security auditing concepts and processes.

- **Chapter 3, "Security Program Management and Operations,"** discusses how the CISO goes about defining and managing a security program. The chapter addresses program management approaches and processes, as well as resource and budget management. The chapter also addresses security project management, as security programs often include projects in addition to ongoing security streams of work.

- **Chapter 4, "Information Security Core Competencies,"** contains a wide range of topics that every CCISO should be familiar with. Each competency relates to several others, but the relationships between them are complex and therefore have no bearing on the order in which the competencies are presented in the chapter.

The core competencies are arranged in the order in which they can best be explained. The chapter begins with sections describing the most common types and methods of cyberattacks, then sections covering technical security competencies, followed by management- and process-oriented competencies.

- **Chapter 5, "Strategic Planning, Finance, Procurement, and Vendor Management,"** discusses how organizations use strategic planning to establish goals and define plans to meet them. It also describes how CISOs can use strategic planning to define and implement an information security program. This chapter covers management topics important to the CISO, including accounting, finance, and procurement, as well as a section describing ways to manage an organization's third parties and vendors to ensure they do not introduce vulnerabilities into the organization's enterprise.

Each chapter starts with a short outline and text introducing the topics covered, followed by sections corresponding to the outline. Throughout each chapter, supplemental information is provided utilizing the following features to help you understand and remember various topics:

 NOTE Notes appear throughout the book to highlight or reinforce topics or provide advice.

 TIP Tips provide information that saves you effort or time. Tips may include tricks, shortcuts, or advice to help you remember a topic. Tips may also be used to provide real-world examples of a concept or process.

 EXAM TIP These targeted tips provide key information the CCISO candidate should know for the CCISO exam. Exam Tips may include test-taking advice or warnings of exam pitfalls.

In addition to the Notes, Tips, and Exam Tips, you will also encounter shaded boxes, which are used to dig deeper into topic, present a case study, or share an anecdote that illustrates or emphasizes a subject in the chapter.

Like all McGraw Hill All-in-One Exam Guides, this book uses repetition as an aid to reinforce the information presented and to facilitate committing information to long-term memory. The end of each chapter has a "Chapter Review" section that presents a review of the essential themes of each section within the chapter. The chapter review is followed by a "Quick Review" section, which is a bulleted list of key points from the chapter that are important to remember. The "Chapter Review" and "Quick Review" sections combine to reinforce the information presented in the chapter.

Each chapter concludes with questions that test the CCISO candidate's retention and understanding of the topics covered. The questions contained in the book are written as another means to reinforce topics. The answers include short explanations describing why the correct answer is right and, in some cases, why the incorrect answers are wrong.

The Appendix, "About the Online Content," contains instructions for accessing an online testing resource called TotalTester Online. This online tool allows the CCISO candidate to practice questions similar to the ones on the real exam by configuring tests by domain, number of questions, and other customizable options.

Preparing for the CCISO Exam

We recommend preparing for the CCISO exam by using a repetitive sequence as follows:

1. Read this book and try to answer the questions at the end of each chapter to reinforce comprehension of the information.

2. Use TotalTester Online to take practice tests by domain. Write down the topic of every question that you answer incorrectly or have difficulty understanding.

3. Using the list of difficult topics as a study list, go back and reread the applicable sections of the book, taking notes or using study methods that have worked for you in the past.

4. Repeat the cycle of reading, testing, and studying until you are consistently scoring above 80 percent in each domain using the TotalTester Online practice questions.

Once you are regularly scoring 80 percent or greater in each domain, you should be ready to take the CCISO exam with confidence.

Governance and Risk Management

This chapter discusses the following topics:

- Governance
- Information security management structure
- Principles of information security
- Risk management
- Management and technical information security elements
- Compliance
- Privacy
- Laws and regulatory drivers
- Standards and frameworks
- Information security trends and best practices
- Information security training and certifications
- Ethics

This chapter describes how an organization's information security program relates to the business as a whole and discusses the key components and purpose of an information security program. This chapter also discusses how the information security program ensures the organization is in compliance with the laws and regulations that pertain to the business and how frameworks are used to guide the design and implementation of the information security program to result in compliance success.

As security consultants, we commonly hear our clients say, "Our organization is different, so we can't apply security the same way as everyone else. Our (*fill in the blank*) is why we can't do security like other companies." When we hear this "we are different" argument, our response is, "Yes and no." The fact is that every company and organization is unique. While the principles of good security are immutable, the application of these security principles to an organization's specific situation ultimately determines success or failure. The key for every chief information security officer (CISO) is to understand the organization's business, goals, operations, and tolerance for risk so that the CISO can create a security program that is *appropriate for the organization*. This alignment of the organization's security program to the organization's business and operations is the key to the success of any security program and is pivotal to the role of the CISO.

Governance

Any discussion of the role of the CISO starts with a discussion of governance. *Governance* is the system by which an organization defines, implements, and controls the business as a whole (such as organizational or corporate governance) or a specific part of the organization (such as IT governance, financial governance, or information security governance). Proper governance ensures that the organization's strategies are aligned with its business, regulatory, and operating environment.

Corporate governance can be considered from two perspectives: strategy and authority. The *governance strategy* involves defining and understanding the factors that are important to the organization. A typical governance strategy diagram depicts what the organization has determined are the strategic factors that are important. The example diagram in Figure 1-1 shows all the factors that feed into the governance strategy and, therefore, the functions that the strategy should enable. For instance, the organization has decided that *transparency* is important and should be addressed in the organization's organizational structure, culture, business processes, and business operations.

As mentioned, the other perspective of organizational governance is *governance authority*. This perspective depicts the organizational structure and lines of authority, as shown in the example in Figure 1-2.

Figure 1-1
Governance
strategy diagram
showing strategic
factors of the
governance
program

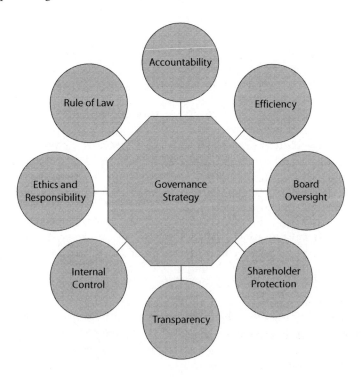

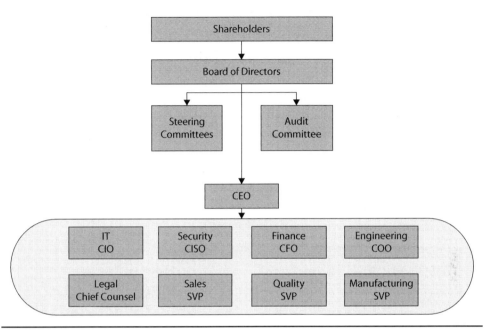

Figure 1-2   Governance diagram showing lines of authority

Every organization has some kind of governance, although some organizations do not have a formal governance program. Whether formal or informal, at some point the leaders of the organization consider the organization's goals and business environment and then define the strategies, processes, controls, organizational structure, and business functions needed to meet those goals.

There are many models for corporate governance. In some cases, laws and regulations drive the governance requirements for an organization. For instance, companies that list their stocks for sale on public securities exchanges must follow the exchanges' requirements for corporate governance. As an example, the New York Stock Exchange and the NASDAQ Stock Market both require member companies to have governance programs that include the following requirements:

- Independent directors
- Auditing
- Reporting
- Annual meetings
- Codes of conduct
- Avoidance of conflicts of interest
- Shareholder approvals

These governance requirements define *what* the corporation must do, but not *how* the corporation must do it.

The International Organization for Standardization (ISO) is in the process of developing ISO 37000, *Guidance for the Governance of Organizations*. This standard is expected to be completed by 2020. ISO 37000 is intended to be used alongside regulatory policies by providing guidance that is based on global consensus of what constitutes good governance.

Information Security Governance

Information security governance is a subset of organizational governance that addresses the strategic direction, leadership, and framework for the information security program. The information security governance framework guides the development and maintenance of the security program. There is no single standard for information security governance frameworks, but the framework should generally include the following elements:

- Definition of the information security strategy aligned with the organization's governance and organizational goals
- Information security organizational structure
- A methodology for *risk management*
- Information security *management directives* (including policies, standards, guidelines, and so on)
- Continuous measurement and improvement of the program

Ideally the information security governance framework aligns with the organizational governance framework and takes into account internal and external factors that shape the security program.

External drivers that shape the security program are

- **Regulatory drivers**   Certain organizations are subject to laws and their corresponding regulations that impact the security program. These should be addressed at the governance level to ensure the organization is in compliance. Examples include the Health Insurance Portability and Accountability Act (HIPAA), which has requirements for protecting patient information, the Sarbanes-Oxley Act (SOX), which has requirements for protecting financial information of publicly traded companies, and the Gramm-Leach-Bliley Act (GLBA), which has security requirements for financial and insurance companies. These laws are discussed in more detail later in this chapter.

- **Industry practices**   Some organizations' security programs are shaped by standards and practices that apply to the industry in which they operate. One example is the Payment Card Industry Data Security Standard (PCI DSS), which defines security requirements for companies that handle or process credit card data or transactions. Another is the National Institute of Standards and Technology (NIST) *Framework for Improving Critical Infrastructure Cybersecurity* (commonly known as the NIST Cybersecurity Framework), which is a voluntary framework that provides guidance for organizations in the following critical infrastructure sectors: chemical, commercial facilities, communications, critical manufacturing, dams, defense industrial base, emergency services, energy, financial services, food and agriculture, government facilities, health care and public health, information technology, nuclear, transportation, and water and wastewater systems. Although originally developed for critical infrastructure organizations, it has been used by noncritical infrastructure entities as well.

- **Risks and threats**   Each organization operates in its own threat environment (more on risks and threats later in this chapter). For instance, a government agency supporting the military faces different threats than a department store due to the nature of the assets requiring protection and the profile and intent of potential adversaries. Each organization must understand its own threat and risk environments and build its security program to address them.

Internal drivers that shape the security program are

- **Leadership understanding and perception**   This could be one of the most challenging aspects of the CISO's job. Security starts at the top of the organization. Therefore, a successful security program depends on the alignment of leadership's understanding of security with that of the CISO. The CEO or head of the organization does not need to be a security expert, but they do need an accurate understanding of the importance of security to the organization. One aspect of the CISO's job is to assess and, if necessary, improve leadership's grasp of security.

- **Management structure**   Where does the CISO, and ultimately the security organization, sit in the management or organizational structure? The answer varies from organization to organization and there is no "right" answer. In some organizations the CISO reports directly to the CEO and has authority alongside that of other C-level executives such as the chief financial officer (CFO) or chief information officer (CIO). In other organizations the CISO reports to another C-level executive such as the CIO or the CFO. In fact, the latter situation is more common that the former. Any approach can be successful; the key is not where the CISO sits in the organization but rather the communication that exists between the CISO and the CEO and leadership. The CEO must have an accurate understanding of the threat and risk environment and there should be a collective understanding between leadership and the CISO on the organization's security strategy.

- **Communication**   Expanding on the first two internal drivers, if the organizational structure, or the personalities or styles of the executives, fosters the exchange of information and ideas concerning the organization's security, the security program has a higher likelihood of success. Sometimes if the CISO reports to another executive and not the CEO, it can result in a firewall preventing alignment between the CISO and leadership. But it isn't the organizational structure that is necessarily the deciding factor—it is communication that is key.

- **Culture and climate**   Companies and organizations exist in order to meet their business goals. The most important thing for an organization is to manufacture products, deliver services, produce sales, and so on. Information security is usually pretty far down the list of what is important. Managers need to run their organization or group to meet its goals; employees want to do their jobs, get a good performance appraisal and raise, and advance their careers. How does security fit into the culture of the organization? Understanding where security is, where it can be, and where it should be in the cultural spectrum are important drivers of the security program.

- **History and lessons learned**   Every security program should have a feedback loop to measure the performance of the program and make changes to it as appropriate, even at the highest (governance) level. There is nothing like a security breach to cause an organization to think differently about security. The lessons learned from formal measurement of performance or real-world events such as security incidents are drivers that impact decisions about the governance of the security program.

Figure 1-3 shows an example of a security governance framework. Based on the information security drivers, *security governance* defines the overall security strategy and the key elements of the program, in this case, the security organization and associated roles and responsibilities, security policies and supporting documents, and the enterprise information security architecture (EISA). The strategy and EISA are discussed in detail in Chapter 5 of this book.

The CISO should define the organization's security governance in a document, sometimes referred to as a *security program plan* or *security charter*. This document, and the governance itself, should be a living doctrine. It should evolve over time and always reflect the current approach. This security charter should show how the security program aligns with the goals and governance of the organization.

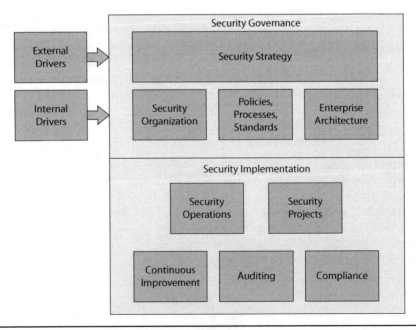

Figure 1-3   Security governance framework example

One key aspect of security governance is measuring and monitoring the governance program itself. Usually these measurements are to support the organization's understanding of the security return on investment (ROI). The organization should know if security spending is adequate and if the security program is meeting its goals. In many organizations the CISO spends considerable time measuring, understanding, communicating, and justifying the economic value of the information security program to the organization as a whole. These measures, which facilitate continuous improvement of the program, are enabled by tools and reporting. These include balanced scorecards as well as a multitude of commercially available applications for the collection, analysis, and presentation of information reporting on a variety of metrics.

Forms of Business and Liability for Security Breaches

There are several types of business forms or entities, differing based on factors including ownership, management structure, liability, and tax responsibility. What is important to the CISO is how the form of the business relates to information security. Since security is all about risk management, each business form has its own characteristics with respect to liability and responsibility for security and privacy.

Sole Proprietorship or Partnership   Sole proprietorships are owned by one person; general partnerships are owned by two or more persons. In sole proprietorships and general partnerships, the owners manage and control the operations of the business, and they have personal liability for the actions of the entity. This means the owners can be found to be personally responsible for security breaches of the organization, and it means that their personal assets may be exposed. This is true even if a given partner was not himself directly involved in the wrongful act, because general partners are liable for the wrongful actions of their partners. Limited partnerships differ from general partnerships in that they are owned by combinations of owner/managers (general partners) and investors (limited partners). The general partners of a limited partnership manage and control the operations of the business, and they have personal liability for the actions of the entity just as general partners of a general partnership do. Limited partners are typically not responsible for the acts of the limited partnership (unless they were personally involved in the wrongful act) and their exposure is typically limited to the amount of their investment.

Corporation   Corporations are owned by shareholders and run by a board of directors and officers that report to the board. Corporations afford a higher level of liability protection than sole proprietorships or partnerships. Individual shareholders, officers, and directors are generally not responsible to third parties, but they can be held personally liable for their own negligent conduct if it can be established that they owed a duty to the claimant (the victim of the negligence).

(continued)

Corporations generally agree to indemnify such individuals (that is, provide a defense and cover any judgment or settlement), provided that the individual acted within the scope of their duties to the company and did not break any laws. The value of a corporation's agreement to provide indemnity depends in part on whether the corporation has the wherewithal to provide (that is, afford to pay for) the indemnity. The corporation itself can be held liable for security breaches and their resulting impacts. Note that there are also small corporations (sometimes called "closely held" corporations) that consist of only a handful of shareholders, or even one. In those instances, the individuals may face greater potential for liability because the company itself may not have the resources to defend or pay for claims.

Limited Liability Company (LLC) LLCs are treated like partnerships for tax purposes (that is, they are generally tax "pass-through" entities) but structured like corporations for management and liability purposes. They are owned by one or more individuals (called "members") based on a percentage of ownership. The liability protection and risk of LLC members is similar to that of corporations.

Nonprofit Organization Nonprofit organizations use their profits for charitable purposes. A nonprofit is a specific type of corporation, or it can be an LLC. In either case the owners are protected from liability resulting from a security breach, again, as long as they personally did not violate any law. And, like corporations, the nonprofit entity is responsible for security breaches and violations. However, one interesting characteristic about nonprofits is that they sometimes have prominent and well-known donors who expect the nonprofits to protect their reputations from damage due to a security breach. In one engagement by the authors of this book, security decisions of a nonprofit entity were driven in part by the intent to protect the donors not from personal liability but from potential damage to their reputations and good name.

There are limitations to the liability protections offered by LLCs, corporations, and nonprofits. Liability protection of the board only applies if the board has fulfilled its "duty of care" responsibility. *Duty of care* is "what a reasonable person would do" in a given situation. Consider this situation: A CISO advises the board that the company is vulnerable to an attack and the exposure of customers' personal information unless a particular control is put in place. The board ignores this advice and a hacker exploits the vulnerability to steal customer data. In this case the board may be found to have not fulfilled its duty of care obligation and could be liable to the customers for damages or compensation. Managers, officers, and directors of these entities may assert the protection of the *business judgment rule*, which generally shields them from liability if they can establish that they exercised their business judgment in taking the action in question, even if it was wrong. This affords the individuals greater flexibility of action than the simple duty of care standard, but the rule is usually hotly contested in litigation and involves the testimony of competing expert witnesses.

Information Security Management Structure

The CISO's job is to create and lead the right management and organizational structure to enable security functions. If *governance* defines the strategy of the information security program, the *organizational structure* enables its implementation. The structure is composed of departments, staff, resources, assigned responsibilities, and lines of communication. These features can be defined and arranged in limitless ways. It is the CISO's job to create the optimum organization to meet the goals of the security program. This section discusses the size and management of the information organization. Roles and responsibilities, staffing, and other details of the information security program organization are discussed in Chapter 3.

Sizing

How big or small should the information security organization be? How much security is the right amount? Many C-level executives like to compare their organization's or company's size and spending to other similar organizations in their industry. In fact, there are third-party and industry groups that conduct surveys of information security leaders and managers to obtain sizing information and then publish the results. Comparison to other organizations provides interesting data points but should not be used as the driving factor for sizing the security organization. Instead, the organization should be sized based on the organization's tolerance for risk. This is discussed in more detail in the section on risk management discussed later in this chapter. The basic principle is that the annual spending for security should be that which is required to protect the organization's information assets.

Some of the third-party groups that publish industry trends on security spending are PwC, Gartner, Forrester, and InformationWeek, although there are many others. These organizations publish data on how security spending compares with other organizational metrics as well as how those numbers change over time. Here are some widely published sizing numbers and trends:

- One industry source reported that average annual security spending per employee in 2018 was $1,178 (as compared to $584 in 2012).
- Information security spending can range from $1,000 to $3,000 per full-time employee.
- Information security spending as a percentage of IT spending ranges from 1 percent to 15 percent depending on the reporting source and the industry being analyzed. Many surveys report 6 percent as an average and some report information security spending as a percentage of IT spending as high as 30 percent.
- Information security spending can range from .2 percent to .9 percent of company revenue.

As this list demonstrates, information security spending varies greatly; therefore, comparisons to other organizations have limited value. In spite of this, many CEOs or leaders ask their CISO, "Why is our information security spending X when our industry is spending Y?" The CISO better know the answer. The factors that can impact security organization spending and sizing are extensive, but here are a few:

- The value of assets, especially the assets most important to the organization
- The type and frequency of risks and threats
- The current state of the organization's security posture
- Regulatory requirements

Management Structure

The structure of the information security organization should be the one that best fits the organization as a whole. Regardless of the exact structure chosen, the management structure should have the following elements:

- **Clear lines of authority (chain of command)** The information security organization should have clearly defined lines of reporting and authority. Each function, department, and role should have a clear designation of who is in charge and a path for reporting to higher levels of authority. This provides proper oversight.

- **Situational awareness** The structure should provide the CISO with a view of the performance of the entire security program so that the CISO has an understanding of the security posture of all assets and the current state of all aspects of the program.

- **Internal and external communication and reporting** The structure should provide ways of reporting the most essential information within the security organization as well as outside of it. Key to this is communicating with corporate leadership and with all of the departments and groups outside of the security organizations.

There are many types of organizational structures and frameworks that can be utilized to implement a security organization. Here are a few of the most commons types:

- **Hierarchical (tiered)** Organizations that have a chain of command from top to bottom are hierarchical. Therefore, every entity in the organization is subordinate to one (and only one) other entity, except for the CISO, who sits at the top of the information security organization. The hierarchy provides clear lines of reporting, tight controls, and well-defined roles. However, hierarchies can also be bureaucratic, causing slow decision making and added costs.

- **Flat (horizontal)** Also called organic organizations, flat organizations are the opposite of hierarchical in that entities can have more than one higher-level entity. This creates a flat network of entities. Flat organizations impart more responsibility onto entities (or individuals) and require more collaboration. Flat organizations require fewer layers of management than hierarchical organizations and may be best suited for smaller organizations, because the larger the organization, the more difficult it is to maintain a flat structure.

- **Matrix** The matrix structure can be thought of as a hybrid of hierarchical and flat. Reporting relationships are more of a grid than a tier or a network. As an example, in a matrix organization, an engineer may be a member of the engineering department and report to the engineering manager, while at the same time the engineer may be part of a product team and report to a product manager. Matrix structures can be a good way to share resources and use them more efficiently. However, matrix organizations can also create confusion and even conflict since there are a lot of managers with potentially competing goals and priorities.

Most information security organizations that we encounter are hierarchical. These organizational structures can be built around top-level entities that are functional (such as Security Engineering, Security Operations, Incident Management, etc.), divisional (such as Americas, Europe, Asia, etc.), or product-based (such as planes, trains, automobiles, etc.). The majority of the information security organizations we are familiar with are functional. A typical example is shown in Figure 1-4.

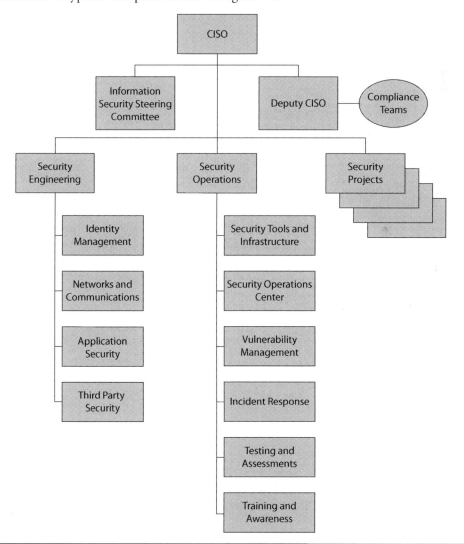

Figure 1-4   Example information security organizational chart

Principles of Information Security

This section describes core principles of information security that serve as the foundation of all information security programs. Although most readers of this book may already be familiar with these concepts, we include them to establish the terminology used throughout the book as well as to review these essential information security elements. Key information security principles include the following:

- The CIA triad
- Security vulnerabilities, threats, risks, and exposures
- Cyberattack elements
- Defense-in-depth

The CIA Triad

The three basic principles of information security are

- Confidentiality
- Integrity
- Availability

These are referred to as the CIA triad, illustrated in Figure 1-5. Information security controls are designed to address any or several of these principles.

Confidentiality refers to the protection of data to ensure the data is only accessible by the people authorized to see it. An example of a breach of confidentiality is when an attacker steals credit card data. Confidentiality protections ensure that the necessary level of secrecy is enforced within the data processing system and prevents unauthorized

Figure 1-5
The CIA triad

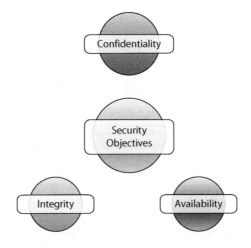

disclosure of confidential information. This level of confidentiality should exist while data resides on systems and devices, as data is transmitted, and once it reaches its destination.

Integrity refers to the accuracy of the data. Examples of integrity attacks are when an attacker defaces a website or changes the content of a file. Integrity protections ensure that data is accurate and reliable and that unauthorized or unintended modifications are prevented. Hardware, software, and communication mechanisms must work in concert to maintain and process data correctly and to move data to intended destinations without unexpected alteration. The systems and network should be protected from unauthorized interference and contamination.

Availability refers to the protection of systems to ensure reliable access to data and resources. An example of a compromise of availability is when an attacker disrupts the operation of a website to prevent access, known as a *denial of service (DoS)* attack. Network devices, computers, and applications should be available to do their job. They should be able to recover from disruptions in a secure manner so that productivity is not negatively affected. Necessary protection mechanisms must be in place to protect against inside and outside threats that could affect the availability and productivity of all business-processing systems.

Security Vulnerabilities, Threats, Risks, and Exposures

An important concept is the relationship between vulnerabilities, threats, risks, exposures, and countermeasures.

- **Vulnerability**   Any weakness that could potentially be exploited. The weakness could be software, hardware, process, or human. Examples include application vulnerabilities, unpatched systems, misconfigured network devises, and unlocked doors.

- **Threat**   A potentially damaging event associated with the exploitation of a vulnerability. Actors that exploit vulnerabilities are called *threat agents*.

- **Risk**   The likelihood that a vulnerability could be exploited and the corresponding impact of such an event. Risk ties the vulnerability, threat, and likelihood of exploitation to the resulting business impact.

- **Exposure**   The potential that a security breach could occur. For instance, an unpatched system *exposes* the organization to a potential loss.

- **Countermeasure**   A control that is put in place to mitigate a risk. Controls include the use of access control lists, deployment of firewalls, enforcement of strong passwords, and the use of encryption.

EXAM TIP   CCISO candidates should have a practical understanding of foundational information security terminology such as vulnerability, threat, risk, exposure, and countermeasure.

Cyberattack Elements

Cyberattacks are deliberate actions by bad actors to gain access to or disrupt information systems with the intent of causing damage or harm. Cyberattacks generally involve the following steps performed by the attacker:

1. Reconnaissance
2. Enumeration
3. Exploitation
4. Action on objectives

Reconnaissance

This first step in an attack is the gathering of information about the target organization by the attacker. The attacker conducts research to learn about the target by performing web searches, examining social media accounts of the organization and its employees, reading press releases and media articles, attending conferences, symposia, or trade shows, or even physically observing the organization's employees or facilities. The attacker attempts to uncover as much information as possible about the target, such as:

- Domain names
- Corporate information
- Network diagrams
- Names of employees and key managers
- E-mail addresses and phone numbers
- Social media activity and friends
- Facility location and layout
- Ingress/egress details

Once this information is gathered, it forms the basis of the next step in the attack.

Enumeration

During this phase the attacker tries to identify the organization's information assets and corresponding vulnerabilities to exploit in the next phase. Based on data gathered from reconnaissance activities, the attacker analyzes reconnaissance results to attempt to identify specific targets such as people, organizations, departments, facilities, capabilities, data, vendor names, and information systems. The attacker may conduct scans of the environment to produce lists of systems and then probe further to discover vulnerabilities that could possibly be exploited. The primary goal of this phase is the enumeration of the organization's systems and data to identify vulnerabilities to exploit in the next phase.

Exploitation

Once the assets and vulnerabilities are enumerated, the attacker can design and execute their attack. This phase involves probing and exploiting specific vulnerabilities with the goal of gaining unauthorized access to the enterprise. Many times, this involves *weaponization*, which is designing and creating tools to aid in the attack. Here are some weaponization and exploitation tools and methods commonly used by attackers:

- **Phishing**   Obtaining sensitive information by disguising oneself as a trusted entity, usually via e-mail
- **Fake websites**   Used for harvesting sensitive information (credentials)
- **Malware**   Software that intentionally is harmful or malicious
- **Virus**   A type of malware that is usually hidden inside another application
- **Trojan**   A virus disguised as something useful
- **Worm**   A virus that propagates itself to other systems
- **Rootkit**   A virus that hides itself by modifying the operating system
- **Social engineering**   Tricking someone to do something that is not in their best interest
- **Scripting**   Manipulating data entered into fields to produce unintended results
- **Vulnerability-specific attacks**   Exploiting buffer overflows or other software defects

The ultimate goal of the exploitation phase is to gain unauthorized access to systems and data.

Action on Objectives

Once the attacker gains access, they can exfiltrate or steal data (a compromise of confidentiality), modify data (a compromise of integrity), or destroy data and otherwise disrupt the environment (a compromise of availability). Usually the attacker attempts to expand access laterally throughout the network to explore and discover more systems and data to gain deeper access and perform more attacks. Frequently, the attacker attempts to cover their tracks to avoid detection by the victim or their organization.

Defense-In-Depth

Defense-in-depth is the concept that an organization should not rely on just one control for protection, but instead should use layers of controls to increase the work factor of potential attackers. Defense-in-depth is the coordinated use of multiple security controls in a layered approach. A multilayered defense system minimizes the probability of successful penetration and compromise because an attacker would have to get through several different types of protection mechanisms before gaining access to critical assets.

Figure 1-6 Risk management includes choosing the appropriate controls and achieving the right balance of security versus cost.

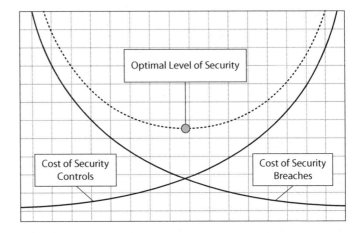

Risk Management

Risk management is the process of identifying and assessing risk, reducing it to an acceptable level, and implementing the right controls to maintain that level. Some organizations use risk management to strike a balance between the value of an asset and the cost of the controls to protect the asset, as shown in Figure 1-6. It may be unwise for an organization to spend $1 million to protect a $100,000 asset. Risk management ensures the *right controls* are chosen that are appropriate to the asset and the business of the organization.

Risk Management in the Real World

In the real world, risk management programs vary widely (or wildly) in their formality and structure. Some organizations follow structured risk management frameworks and spend considerable time, effort, and resources performing risk analysis, threat modeling, and implementing risk management programs. However, other organizations (maybe even the majority of them) approach risk management in a less disciplined or even casual fashion. There are many organizations that do not perform any kind of risk analysis to determine a target level of acceptable risk for the organization and instead make those decisions based on the gut feel or experience of one or two key decision makers. In this book we describe what goes into a successful risk management program. However, the *extent to which* the functions described herein are implemented in a given organization is driven by many factors, including leadership's experience and judgment, the organization's culture, business, and operating environment, and the organization's history with threats and events, if any, that have harmed the organization. The extent to which an organization performs risk management is in itself a risky decision that has prominence in the CISO's journey.

In practice, risk management can apply to an entire organization or to a specific asset. It can even apply to groups of assets. NIST Special Publication (SP) 800-39, *Managing Information Security Risk*, proposes a holistic approach whereby risk management is applied to an entire organization holistically in three tiers:

- **Organizational tier**   Addresses risk at the organizational level by defining and implementing a holistic risk management program that applies to the entire organization or business entity
- **Mission/business process**   Addresses organizational risk using "risk-aware" business processes or addressing the enterprise architecture as a whole
- **Information system**   Addresses risk as part of the systems development life cycle (SDLC) of a given information system

Whether risk management is addressed in tiers or not, the organizations that have the best handle on information security address risk both at the organizational level and on a system-by-system basis.

Risk management is an attempt to predict the future. It involves trying to figure out all the bad things that might happen to the organization or system for the purpose of deciding how to best allocate resources. There are a large number of variables to take into consideration. This includes trying to identify possible threats (such as hurricanes, fires, burglars, hackers, and so on) and propose solutions to defend against them or mitigate their impact. Risk management also deals with a variety of unknowns, such as "How often is a hurricane going to hit our facility?" As a result, the risk management prediction includes some amount of uncertainty. Also, the prediction attempts to quantify things that may be inherently qualitative. That means putting a dollar sign or a number to something that isn't easy to quantify, such as the organization's reputation. These are some of the challenges that are involved in risk management.

Risk Management Program

Information security risk management programs generally have three components: Approach, Process, and Method. Depending on the organization, these components may not be formally defined and implemented, but each component is usually employed to a certain extent. Note that we use the terms Approach, Process, and Method in this book to explain risk management, but these exact terms aren't necessarily used in industry risk management standards and frameworks. These components are illustrated in Figure 1-7.

Many organizations choose to follow an industry-standard risk management framework for their risk management program. The risk management frameworks commonly used today may encompass one, two, or all three of the components. For instance, the NIST Cybersecurity Framework covers Approach and Process but leaves the choice of what type of risk method to use up to the organization. We discuss some of the more popular risk management frameworks later in this chapter.

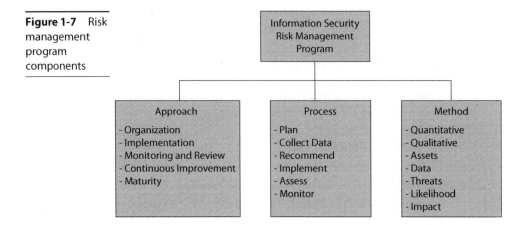

Figure 1-7 Risk management program components

Information Security Risk Management Program

Approach
- Organization
- Implementation
- Monitoring and Review
- Continuous Improvement
- Maturity

Process
- Plan
- Collect Data
- Recommend
- Implement
- Assess
- Monitor

Method
- Quantitative
- Qualitative
- Assets
- Data
- Threats
- Likelihood
- Impact

Risk Management Program: Approach

The Approach component encompasses all the activities and factors that go into managing, implementing, and improving the risk management program. Industry frameworks can be used as guidance, but the Approach must be tailored to how the organization is governed and operated. Like any organizational program, the risk management program is often implemented following a Plan, Do, Check, Act (PDCA) cycle. Here are some factors that should be considered in the risk management approach:

- **Organization**   Information security risk management may be addressed as part of an existing organizational risk program, which may be under the direction of a chief risk officer (CRO), a risk committee, or a similar entity. The organization must establish a responsible party for managing the risk management program and, just as important, who is responsible for risk in the organization. Whether it is the CISO, CRO, CEO, or someone else, the responsible person or group will ultimately approve the products of the program. These products include establishing the acceptable risk levels for the organization and assets, choosing the risk mitigation approaches, and approving the mitigation results and the results of risk assessments. It is important that the responsible person or group performs this task in close collaboration with leadership and stakeholders throughout the organization to ensure the risk decisions are commensurate with the business goals and operating environment of the organization.

- **Implementation**   The risk management program is defined by a program charter, plan, and risk management policy that define the scope, goals, and requirements of the program. The plan should define the required resources including staff, equipment, and budget. The program is implemented in accordance with the plan and in close collaboration with all organizational entities that have a stake in the risk results. This usually includes departments and functions within the organization and external drivers as well. The risk management program is implemented following protocols consisting of procedures, rules, reporting requirements, and so on.

- **Monitoring, reporting, and continuous improvement**   Reporting should include gap analysis of identified risk levels compared to defined acceptable levels. There should be, at a minimum, an informal review cycle to monitor the program. Depending on the maturity of the organization, there may be formal or informal means to establish goals and measure the performance of the program based on well-defined success factors. There should be a defined process for reporting and escalating any material risks discovered during risk assessments. In fact, for US publicly traded entities the US Securities and Exchange Commission (SEC) requires reporting of material risks and associated mitigations to the shareholders.

- **Maturity**   Hopefully, an organization's capability to perform risk management improves over time. Improvement can be enabled if the organization adopts a formal process improvement methodology such as ISACA's Capability Maturity Model Integration (CMMI) or other similar models. The goal is to raise an organization's capability through incremental improvements. For instance, CMMI's maturity levels are

  - **Initial**   Processes are reactive and not based on any form of structured planning.

  - **Managed**   Processes are executed according to a plan.

  - **Defined**   The organization has adopted standards and is operating proactively to address goals.

  - **Quantitatively Managed**   The organization takes advantage of well-defined metrics and quantitative data to drive its processes and decisions.

  - **Optimizing**   The organization has evolved to the point that it is able to apply innovation, agility, and flexibility to its very mature processes.

As discussed earlier in the sidebar "Risk Management in the Real World," many organizations never move beyond the Initial capability level. For these organizations, decisions about how best to handle risk may not be based on sound research and analysis and, therefore, they may be missing the mark and leaving themselves vulnerable. But for every organization, maturity of any capability, including risk management is a business decision which itself comes with its own risks.

Risk Management Program: Process

Although there are countless variations to this process, generally, the risk management process includes the activities shown in Figure 1-8 and described next.

Plan   Risk management planning involves the following activities:

- **Identify the team**   Due to the importance of risk management and the fact that the risk management decisions impact the entire business, the team should include representatives from as many parts of the organization as practical— not just the IT or security departments, but other major functions and roles as well. For instance, auditors tend to have a very unique perspective on the organization, so they should be involved. Leaders from different business units should have a voice at the table. The organization's legal function should be

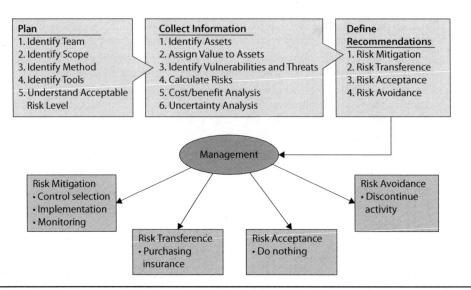

Figure 1-8 Risk management process

included, not simply because of regulatory drivers involved (although that would be a good reason), but because security and risk management frequently requires defending against actions that are illegal and involve the commitment of some kind of crime. In addition, the organization privacy function may reside in the legal department. Since employees are involved, HR representatives should be included, and, of course, management must be involved as they are going to make the big decisions.

- **Define the scope** The next step is to define the scope of the risk management project. The organization defines the subject of the risk assessment, analysis, and mitigation. For instance, is the effort going to cover one facility or multiple facilities; a certain region; or enterprise wide? Scope can be defined by a

  - System or other asset
  - Business process
  - Function, region, or department

In practice, most organizations view the environment, for the purpose of risk management, as a collection of systems. Risk management is then applied to each system.

Defining scope should also consider the types of variables that are included in the chosen model. If the model includes consideration of the types of threats, a decision should be made concerning the types of threats that are included. For instance, are manmade threats such as burglary or riots in scope? Or are natural disasters, like hurricanes, wildfires, and so on, in scope? Are technical threats, like hackers or perhaps loss of some kind of data connectivity, in scope? These decisions define the scope of the effort. Models are discussed in more detail later in this chapter.

- **Define method or model**   The next step is to define what risk method will be employed. When it comes to risk analysis, there are essentially two approaches: *quantitative analysis* and *qualitative analysis*. Quantitative analysis seeks to identify how much money it will cost the organization if a risk is realized. For example, an organization may value an asset at $100,000 and estimate that the asset would lose 50 percent of its value if it were to catch fire, making the Single Loss Expectancy $50,000. The organization may also estimate that the chance of the asset catching fire per year (Annualized Rate of Occurrence) is 1 percent, and therefore calculate the Annualized Loss Expectancy to be $500. That's an illustration of quantitative analysis. Qualitative analysis is a bit more touchy-feely. Organizations commonly frame a qualitative analysis of an asset using a risk scale such as 1 to 10 or low/medium/high. Both quantitative analysis and qualitative analysis are discussed in more detail later in this chapter. In practice, we typically see some kind of combination of the two because some things can't be easily quantified, such as reputation or brand.

- **Use of tools**   Depending on the complexity of the risk management program, collecting all data and properly interpreting the results can be overwhelming if done manually. There are several automated risk management tools available that can help this process complete faster and with more accuracy. While the intent of these tools is to reduce the amount of manual work, their real value is the ability for the user to quickly change parameters and run various scenarios. This allows the risk management team to try different what-if scenarios and choose the best ones after reviewing the results. A single integrated tool sounds ideal, and there are some out there, but many organizations use an integrated solution that provides several tools that each perform a part of the task. Classes of tools include configuration management databases that provide a repository to list and track the assets in the environment; threat intelligence platforms that collect and disseminate information about current external threats; and entire risk management suites that automate the process of running quantitative or qualitative models.

- **Understand acceptable risk level**   The goal of this activity is to establish the minimum acceptable level of risk for various types of systems or assets in the environment. All systems are then assessed and compared against this criteria and, ideally, an asset should not be approved to be operational unless it meet this criteria.

  The risk acceptance level is the maximum overall exposure to risk that should be accepted by the organization. The risk we are talking about here is the *residual risk*, which is the risk that remains after controls or countermeasures are put in place. As a result, the organization must define what level of risk is acceptable.

  Note that some organizations skip this step altogether and instead determine the acceptable level of risk based on judgments by management.

Collect Information   The exact information to be gathered during the risk management process is specified by the Method used. A quantitative model may require collecting detailed financial information, including labor and materials costs or even estimates from outside vendors, in order to determine asset value. Qualitative models require information about assets, threats, vulnerabilities, and the probability of occurrence of different events. Once this information is collected, an analysis is performed to capture what the threat represents to the business.

Define Recommendations   As part of the risk analysis process, the possible approaches for handling specific risks are considered and recommendations are made to the decision-making authority, which we refer to as "management." The definition of who "management" is in this instance varies depending on the organization. In some organizations it is the CEO, but in others it may be the CISO, the board of directors, or even a risk committee. The key is that someone in every organization must make the decision regarding how to best handle risk for a given asset or the organization as a whole.

Once the risk handling decisions are finalized, they can be implemented by applying the corresponding controls. Generally, there are four choices for how risk recommendations are made and how they are implemented:

- **Mitigate** or reduce the risk by putting some kind of control in place.
- **Transfer** risk and make it somebody else's problem.
- **Accept** the risk, which means that as long as it is within acceptable risk levels, the organization can "live with" the risk and take their chances.
- **Avoid** the risk entirely by stopping the related activity or shutting down a system entirely.

With management's approval, risks are handled using appropriate mitigations and controls that are deployed, measured, monitored, and continuously improved.

EXAM TIP   CCISO candidates should understand the different risk treatment options and be able to select a method given a scenario.

Risk Management Program: Method

Risk management *methods* generally fall into two categories: quantitative and qualitative.

Quantitative Methods   Quantitative methods are used to calculate the monetary loss associated with a given threat. This is accomplished by assigning numeric values to each factor in the analysis. Factors may include

- Asset value
- Threat probability
- Vulnerability
- Impact of loss
- Cost of countermeasures or controls

Two frequently used quantitative methods are Single Loss Expectancy and Annualized Loss Expectancy.

Single Loss Expectancy (SLE) is the potential value of a loss for a single threat event. Note that the event can apply to a single asset or a group of assets. The formula is

$$AV \times EF = SLE$$

- *Asset Value (AV)* is the cost of the asset or assets that are subject to the event. The AV can be simply the replacement cost of the asset or it can include other costs that may be incurred if the asset were lost, such as labor and installation costs, costs to the business due to downtime, or even costs due to loss of business.

- *Exposure Factor (EF)* is the percentage of loss that would likely occur for the subject event. For instance, if the threat being modeled is a *theft* and the asset is a *laptop*, the EF might be 100 percent since nobody steals part of a laptop. Alternatively, if the threat is a fire and the asset is an entire datacenter, the EF may be 40 percent as an estimate for the potential loss. The EF is a prediction that should be backed up by data, research, or some documented reason.

Annualized Loss Expectancy (ALE) brings in the element of time. ALE is used to predict the potential value of a loss on an annual basis. The formula is

$$SLE \times ARO = ALE$$

- *Annualized Rate of Occurrence (ARO)* is an estimate of how many times the event is estimated to occur in a given year.

The ALE quantitative analysis allows an organization to predict loss in terms of dollar amounts for particular events on an annual basis. It may be used to establish tolerance levels for the organization; for instance, the organization may find, after analysis, that any asset that has an ALE greater than $1M has the highest risk priority and should have the highest level of mitigating controls. An organization may also use the ALE to determine spending, as it may not make sense to spend $100K annually to protect against an asset and threat combination with an ALE of $10K.

Qualitative Methods   Qualitative methods do not use dollar amounts (although they may still involve calculations). Qualitative analysis may be as simple as an executive saying "System X is really important to us, so I designate it as high risk" or it may be a highly complex analysis with many variables. Qualitative analysis may take into account a variety of factors including

- Severity of threat
- Likelihood of threat occurrence
- Severity of impact to the business (also known as *consequence*)
- Effectiveness of controls

In most cases qualitative risk analysis is used to determine the risk of a given threat applied to a given asset, such as the risk of the organization's warehouse flooding or a

		Impact				
		Negligible	**Minor**	**Moderate**	**Significant**	**Severe**
	Highly Likely	Low	Medium	High	High	High
	Likely	Low	Medium	Medium	High	High
Likelihood	**Possible**	Low	Low	Medium	Medium	High
	Unlikely	Low	Low	Medium	Medium	Medium
	Highly Unlikely	Low	Low	Low	Medium	Medium

Table 1-1 Using Impact vs. Likelihood to Determine Risk Levels

denial of service attack against the organization's web server. The following three tables provide examples of qualitative analysis methods.

Table 1-1 is an example of risk analysis using likelihood versus impact to establish risk levels. An organization might use this method to determine the risk of different threat and asset pairs, using a separate table for each pair.

Table 1-2 illustrates how an organization might determine risk levels for compromises of confidentiality, integrity, or availability of a specific type of system in the enterprise. The overall risk is usually the highest risk of the three event types. In this example the overall risk is High.

The next example in Table 1-3 shows how an organization might model the risk before (inherent risk) and after (residual risk) the application of mitigating controls.

Risk assessment teams may use specific techniques to help them use the selected models most effectively. Here are a few best practice techniques:

- **SWIFT**   The Structured What If Technique is a structured process for group collaboration. It involves conducting brainstorming sessions using guidewords and other elements to describe systems, identify and assess risks, and propose actions to reduce risk to acceptable levels.

- **Delphi**   The Delphi method was developed by the RAND Corporation as a means to predict technological change. It is now used to facilitate discussions among subject matter experts to achieve consensus. It uses a tiered, iterative process to pose questions to the group, with each iteration delving more deeply into the topic.

System Type: Internal database with Sensitive data			
Event Type	**Likelihood**	**Impact**	**Risk**
Compromise of Confidentiality	Likely	Severe	High
Compromise of Integrity	Possible	Significant	Medium
Compromise of Availability	Unlikely	Minor	Low
		Overall Risk:	High

Table 1-2 Modeling the Risk of Compromise Types

Threat	Asset	Impact	Probability	Inherent Risk	Control	Residual Risk
Data exfiltration	Web servers	Critical	40% (Medium)	High	Disk encryption	Low
Fire	Datacenter	Critical	10% (Low)	Moderate	Upgrade fire suppression system	Low

Table 1-3 Inherent and Residual Risk Example

- **Bowtie** The bowtie method is so named because the diagram that represents it is shaped like a bowtie. At the center or knot of the bowtie is an event. The left side (sources) and the right side (consequences) are larger than the center because, for a single event, there may be many sources and consequences. The bowtie technique provides a structured way to model and analyze threats, their effects on an organization, and evaluate mitigations.

- **Decision tree analysis** This technique is used to help people choose the best option from a number of possible choices. It uses a visual model to help illustrate and understand the relationships among the variables that are considered in the risk analysis. It also facilitates the understanding of how changes to one aspect of the problem impacts others.

 EXAM TIP CCISO candidates should be familiar with quantitative and qualitative risk management and be able to identify which method is being used given a scenario.

Best Practice Frameworks for Risk Management

The following is a brief summary of some of the frameworks that have been developed to help organizations perform information security risk management.

- **OCTAVE (Operationally Critical Threat, Asset, and Vulnerability Evaluation)** OCTAVE was originally developed by Carnegie Mellon University's Software Engineering Institute. There are now three instances: OCTAVE, OCTAVE-Allegro (a more streamlined framework), and OCTAVE-S (for small organizations). OCTAVE relies on the idea that people working in the organization are best suited to understand and analyze risk. It addresses assets, threats, vulnerabilities, and what is needed to address them. OCTAVE is a qualitative risk management framework with associated models.

- **FAIR (Factor Analysis of Information Risk)** FAIR is a quantitative risk framework. FAIR provides a risk taxonomy that breaks risks down into specific factors and subfactors. It includes very specific types of losses, threats, and vulnerabilities and includes ways to measure them and derive quantitative analysis results.

- **ISACA Risk IT Framework**   ISACA Risk IT is an IT-oriented framework rather than one that is exclusive to information security. Risk IT includes three domains: Risk Governance, Risk Evaluation, and Risk Response and includes specific implementation models for accomplishing analysis using a hybrid of quantitative and qualitative methods.

- **ISO/IEC 27005**   ISO/IEC 27005, *Information technology – Security techniques – Information security risk management*, is a high-level framework that supports application of information security as part of the ISO/IEC 27000 family of guidance. It implies a continual process for performing quantitative or qualitative risk analysis but does not contain a specific model. ISO 31000, *Risk management – Guidelines*, is a more robust risk management framework that includes three elements: Principals, Framework, and Processes for implementation. However, ISO 31000 does not suggest either a quantitative or qualitative approach.

- **FISMA/FIPS/NIST RMF**   The collection of standards and special publications used to meet US Federal Information Security Modernization Act (FISMA) requirements provide a framework, processes, and models for performing qualitative risk analysis. These standards also provide libraries of security controls, resulting in an end-to-end framework for risk management and implementation.

Management and Technical Information Security Elements

A good information security program has numerous management and technical elements, as shown in Figure 1-9. Every security program should have these elements, although every organization has its own way of naming and organizing them.

The following sections introduce each element. They are discussed in more detail in Chapter 4.

Security Program Plan

Many organizations have a security plan that defines the complete information security program. This plan defines all security roles and responsibilities, specifies strategic goals for the program, and identifies security activities. The plan identifies all regulatory and business drivers and ensures the program presented in the plan is risk-based. An example security program is illustrated in Figure 1-10 and shows the relationship between the program components. Each component from the example is discussed next.

- **Security streams of work**   Streams of work are activities that are executed to implement the core subject areas, or domains, of information security. Example streams of work may include intrusion detection and monitoring, access control and identity management, vulnerability management, and change control. The streams eventually must all be implemented throughout the enterprise to have a complete security program.

Figure 1-9
Key elements of
an information
security program

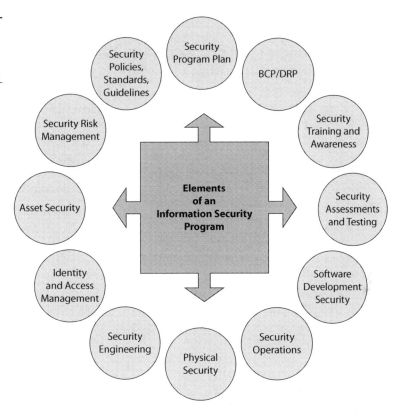

Figure 1-9
Key elements of
an information
security program

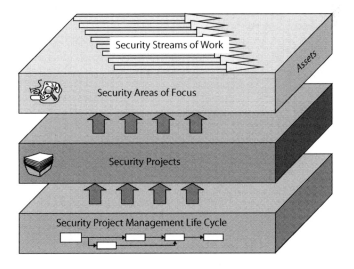

Figure 1-10
Example security
program
components

- **Assets** Assets are systems, data, business units, departments, or critical areas of the enterprise to which the streams of work are applied. The asset-related activities address what security should get applied where and when, based on factors such as the asset's relative priority, risk, or resources.

- **Security areas of focus** There are aspects of the security program that require focus due to external drivers—usually regulatory drivers. For instance, PCI DSS requires that all credit card data be mapped across the enterprise and that specific security controls be put into place based on where the data resides. Examples of areas of focus are PCI DSS, HIPAA, Sarbanes-Oxley, and internal drivers such as the ISO/IEC 27000 series. The areas define what security activities are required to be applied where. Areas of focus may apply to one or many assets.

- **Security projects** Projects are specific activities that result from the application of streams of work against targets and/or areas of focus. Examples of security projects might be implementation of single sign-on (SSO), deployment of a particular intrusion detection system (IDS), or the design and implementation of a security dashboard.

- **Security project management life cycle** All security projects should be managed following a defined life cycle. The life cycle ensures that security projects are well defined, properly documented, and executed with a beginning, middle, and an end. The life cycle defines how security projects are managed and provides for the proper control of resources, quality, and results.

Security Policies, Standards, and Guidelines

The security program typically has a collection of management security directives, as shown in Figure 1-11. These directives form a library of rules and practices that the program personnel are to follow. The top-level documents are the security policies, which define hard-and-fast rules (requirements) that govern what will be done (but not necessarily how to do it). Examples include the access control policy, password policy, incident handling policy, and so on—essentially, every information security activity or domain (core competency) should have its own policy.

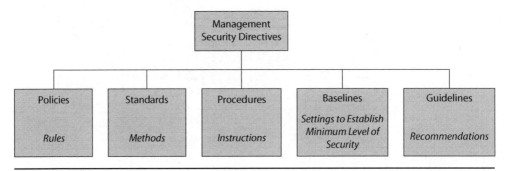

Figure 1-11 Management security directives

Other documents include the following:

- **Standards** Standards establish specific methods for meeting the requirements defined in policies. For instance, standards may be used to define specific encryption tools or products or the types of controls to be used in specific situations in order to meet an organization's data encryption policy.

- **Processes or procedures** Processes or procedures are step-by-step workflows or instructions that define how certain security functions are performed. They define who is responsible for the activities and how they are carried out.

- **Baselines** Baselines are sometimes lumped in with the standards and establish specific configurations for implementations of hardware or software. They may include Windows registry and other types of settings required to ensure the correct and repeatable security implementation of assets in the enterprise.

- **Guidelines** Guidelines provide general direction or recommendations without specifying a requirement. An example might be a guideline to describe how users can use *passphrases* to meet password policy requirements. In this example, the use of a passphrase isn't a requirement, but it's a good suggestion and is best communicated using a guideline.

 EXAM TIP CCISO candidates should understand the difference between policies, standards, procedures, baselines, and guidelines, including which are mandatory and which are recommendations.

Asset Security

Asset security is the concept of identifying what assets the organization has and determining what types of controls are appropriate for each. The types of assets in the environment and the types of controls used for each are identified and addressed in the organization's policies, standards, and procedures.

Often asset security focuses on data (information assets). Asset security addresses implementing security throughout the data life cycle, as shown in Figure 1-12.

The asset security program defines and implements controls for protecting access to data at rest and during transmission and uses technologies such as access controls, encryption, and digital signatures.

Figure 1-12
The data life cycle

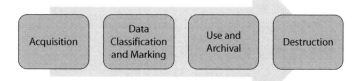

Acquisition · Data Classification and Marking · Use and Archival · Destruction

Identity and Access Management

Access controls are security features that control how users and systems communicate and interact with other systems and resources. They protect the systems and resources from unauthorized access and include components that participate in determining the level of authorization after an authentication procedure has successfully completed. Although people usually think of a "user" as the entity that requires access to a network resource or information, there are other types of entities, such as other systems, that require access to resources that are subject to access control.

Identity and access management uses concepts including identification, authentication, authorization, and accountability. It uses models such as discretionary access control (DAC), role-based access control (RBAC), and mandatory access control (MAC). It includes the use of identity management systems such as Microsoft Active Directory and Kerberos, protocols such as Lightweight Directory Access Protocol (LDAP), and security controls such as biometrics and passwords. All of these items are explained in Chapter 4.

Security Engineering

Security engineering is a vast domain that addresses the secure design and implementation of information systems. The key concept is that security should be an integral part of the design of the enterprise. Security engineering involves including all aspects of the computing environment such as:

- Computer architecture components
- Operating system security and protection mechanisms
- Information systems architecture and protection mechanisms
- Network security design
- Enterprise security solutions (such as firewalls, anti-malware, data loss prevention, endpoint security, and secure gateways)
- Remote connectivity
- Wireless connectivity
- Cloud computing
- Cyber-physical systems
- Database security
- Mobile device security
- Security models
- Security assessment and authorization
- Cryptography

Figure 1-13
Physical security
layers of defense

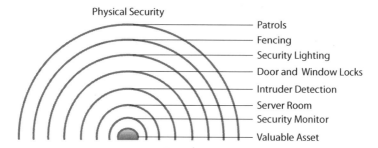

Physical Security

Patrols
Fencing
Security Lighting
Door and Window Locks
Intruder Detection
Server Room
Security Monitor
Valuable Asset

Physical Security

Physical security addresses the understanding of threats to the physical information systems, facilities, and personnel as well as the controls to combat those threats. Physical security is not always within the domain of responsibilities of the CISO. Sometimes physical security is managed separately from information security, depending on the practices of the organization. Physical security includes the following:

- Facility location

- Facility construction

- Physical security risks, threats, and countermeasures

- Personnel security

Just like IT security, physical security also has the concept of defense-in-depth, using layers of defense, as shown in Figure 1-13.

Security Operations

Security operations focuses on actively performing day-to-day functions to prevent, detect, and respond to security risks and threats. Those functions include the following:

- **Vulnerability, configuration, and patch management**   All IT assets have vulnerabilities. These assets include desktops, laptops, mobile devices, servers, network and storage appliances, operating systems, application software, and so on. It's a fulltime job to keep track of all the assets in an organization and whether or not they have the latest patches and the correct versions of software. A good vulnerability, configuration, and patch management program should give the organization "situational awareness" or an accurate picture of all the assets and their configuration and patch status.

- **Monitoring and logging** This critical function involves capturing all significant events within the IT enterprise to detect malicious activity and to support investigations of previous or ongoing security events. This function is performed by configuring systems in the enterprise to capture activity such as logins and access to assets, data read/write/modify, data exfiltration, access to external and internal systems, login attempts, and so on. Capturing these activities and monitoring them in real time supports *intrusion detection*. Capturing these events for future analysis supports *forensic investigations*. Monitoring and logging covers deciding what events to log and monitor based on business risk and available resources. Capture too much and you have the high costs of storage and network traffic. Capture too little and you won't capture enough data to be useful. Mature organizations continually tune their logging and monitoring capabilities to best fit their business.

- **Incident handling** The time to figure out what to do in response to a security breach is not after one occurs. Incident handling is all about planning for various types of security incidents and defining what to do ahead of time. Usually incident handling follows a six-step model, as shown in Figure 1-14.

These six steps are followed in response to significant security events. The *preparation* phase is performed ahead of time. In this phase the security organization attempts to predict the types of events that could occur. For each type of event, the remaining steps are planned out and sometimes rehearsed. The goal is to be able to *identify* what type of event happened, *contain* the damage from spreading, *eradicate* what is causing the problem, *recover* from the event and return to normal operations, and finally, conduct a *lessons learned* activity to determine what actions could or should be undertaken to prevent reoccurrence of the event or improve how the response was handled. One key aspect of the incident handling process is knowing when to escalate the issue to management or the board, or notify law enforcement agencies.

Figure 1-14
Six steps of
incident handling

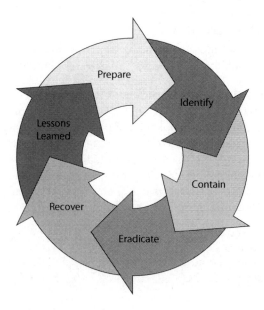

- **Forensics and investigations**   Some security breaches may be an indication of a violation of law or company policies. Such events may require a computer forensic investigation to fully reveal all information about the event. Such events may also require contacting and cooperating with law enforcement organizations. All of this needs to be planned accordingly so missteps are not made that could cause further damage to the business or individuals involved.

- **Security operations center**   All of the security operations activities are usually staffed and performed by personnel in the organization's security operations center (SOC). The SOC usually operates the organization's security incident and event management (SIEM) system, which provides 24/7 monitoring of network, computer, and user activity to detect, prevent, and respond to security events.

Software Development Security

Many organizations develop their own software or build custom applications for their own use. Such software must be built in a manner that ensures it does not contain security vulnerabilities. Software and applications must be built in concert with security expertise to ensure the developers define, build, test, promote, and maintain secure applications. In addition to preventing vulnerabilities, software and applications must be built using the key concepts that underpin access control and identify management, such as *least privilege* and *separation of duties*.

Security Assessments and Testing

All security programs must have an ongoing *assessment and testing* component to continuously assess and verify all aspects of the security program. The administrative, technical, management, and operational controls developed and implemented as part of the security program are assessed using audits and checklists to determine compliance with stated goals. In addition, there should be an ongoing *vulnerability management* activity that includes vulnerability testing to ensure the successful performance and management of vulnerability remediation activities. Testing usually involves a combination of vulnerability assessments and penetration testing. *Vulnerability assessments* are comprehensive tests using tools that scan the entire computing environment, internal and external, to discover and enumerate known vulnerabilities. The results of this testing feeds into the *vulnerability and patch management* set of activities to report and track remediation activities. *Penetration testing* is usually performed by engineers posing as hackers. These engineers seek to exploit vulnerabilities to gain access to systems and data. While vulnerability testing is comprehensive, penetration testing is limited and serves as a demonstration of what could happen if vulnerabilities are left exposed.

Security Training and Awareness

All employees should be made aware of the organization's security policies and processes as well as good security practices in general. Security awareness and training should be focused on the organization's entire user population. It should contain training delivered in a variety of forms, especially practices, drills, and exercises to provide users with reality-based experience dealing with cyberattacks, including social engineering. The best training programs take advantage of a combination of off-the-shelf training to teach general concepts and customized training to teach concepts that are unique and specific to the company or organization.

Business Continuity and Disaster Recovery

Every organization should have plans and procedures in place to be able to ensure that the organization can continue to operate in the event of a security breach or other disaster. To accomplish this, organizations create business continuity planning and disaster recovery (BCP/DR) plans (or continuity of operations [COOP] plans) that focus on recovery of those systems and services that support critical business functions within the time frame specified by the business. The BCP/DR plans define the extent to which the organization can recover from a breach or disaster based on the organization's risk tolerance. Sometimes, but not always, BCP and DR come under the auspices of the CISO.

Compliance

Earlier in this chapter, we covered many of the governance practices the CISO is responsible for, including understanding the organization's business drivers and creating and maintaining a security program that facilitates these drivers. A critical aspect of developing these drivers is understanding the compliance requirements of the organization. *Compliance* is an approach to governance designed to ensure alignment with applicable laws, regulations, standards, organizational policies, ethical conduct, and other business goals. The discussion around compliance often focuses on regulatory compliance because the consequences of noncompliance (fines, reputational damage, and so on) are potentially steep. However, compliance with regulations is not the only form of compliance. There are both internal and external compliance requirements, as outlined in Figure 1-15, that drive the organization to implement policies, standards, and procedures to support compliance.

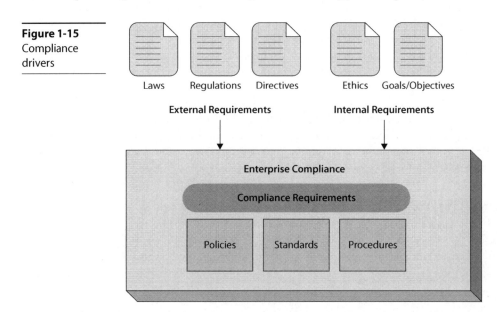

Figure 1-15 Compliance drivers

Chapter 1: Governance and Risk Management

35

External compliance focuses on complying with external laws, regulations, standards, or other industry mandates. Maintaining compliance with the long list of legal and regulatory requirements is a major concern for executives. Compliance with legal, regulatory, contractual, and statutory requirements is achieved through the implementation of controls, regular audits, and legal awareness. There are many types of external requirements to consider:

- Industry regulations or directives
- State regulations
- Federal regulations
- Local laws and regulations
- International standards

Internal compliance focuses on internal business practices that enable and protect people, processes, and technology. These practices are intended to ensure compliance with internal policies, ethical conduct, or other business rules and objectives. These activities generally focus on good business practices that do not directly stem from an external legislative mandate, regulation, or directive. These activities include ensuring

- Alignment with internal codes of conduct, policies, standards, and procedures
- Ethical employee behavior
- Alignment with other key organizational rules or objectives (reputation, image, preventing financial loss, and so on)

In this section, we discuss the compliance team and walk through the compliance management process.

Compliance and Security

A common misconception among executives is that being compliant means an organization is secure. Being compliant does not necessarily mean an organization is secure and, conversely, a good security program isn't necessarily compliant with its drivers. For example, an organization may be required to be compliant with PCI DSS or the General Data Protection Regulation (GDPR). PCI DSS compliance requires operating in a manner that meets the PCI DSS specifications for processing credit card information, while GDPR compliance requires protecting EU citizens' data. As is the case with many external compliance factors, these are very specific. In this case they are focused on a particular type of data. However, an organization that focuses on securing this data exclusively can leave itself open to other attack vectors.

Security is ever evolving to address changes in threats, technologies, and protection measures. Compliance requirements change but not usually at the same pace to adequately address security challenges. While compliance may not holistically address security, compliance is an important business enabler, and an organization that is not compliant with external factors such as industry laws and regulations can't operate in its chosen business for long.

Compliance Team

The compliance team is typically involved in providing guidance on internal policies and procedures as well as evaluating current processes and technology to determine ways to improve compliance. Depending on the organization, the team may focus solely on internal compliance, focus solely on external compliance, or be responsible for both. Responsibilities of the compliance team may include the following:

- Identification of external compliance requirements (for example, laws and regulations)
- Development and management of internal compliance requirements (for example, ethics)
- Development or guidance on policies, standards, and procedures
- Managing the organization's privacy program
- Oversight and execution of compliance training initiatives
- Monitoring the program for violations and efficiency

Not all organizations have dedicated compliance resources. Smaller organizations often take a shared-responsibility approach to compliance management or have a single dedicated compliance resource such as a compliance officer. Large organizations typically have a compliance department that reports to a senior compliance official, such as a chief compliance officer (CCO). Enterprises with specific or complex compliance requirements may even have separate teams for specific compliance factors, such as a PCI DSS team or a HIPAA team.

The reporting structure for the compliance team varies from organization to organization. Again, in larger organizations, the compliance team typically reports to a CCO. The CCO may report to the legal department's general counsel (because they have expertise regarding compliance with laws and regulations) or may report directly to the CEO, board of directors, or audit/compliance committee. Similar to the reporting structure for the CISO, there is no one-size-fits-all solution. Ultimately, the reporting structure for the head of the compliance team is effective if it facilitates communication and reporting that keeps the CEO and/or board of directors aware of compliance risk.

Compliance Management

Compliance crosses all aspects of the business and, like any other program, must be appropriately managed to ensure alignment. *Compliance management* is the process by which an organization plans, implements, and maintains the activities that support compliance. Compliance management enables organizations to put into place governance, policies, systems and processes, and reporting and measurement. Every organization engages in some kind of compliance management activities, but not all organizations have a formal compliance program, a dedicated compliance team, or follow a defined compliance management process.

All organizations must comply with a mix of corporate policies, standards, laws, regulations, and internal requirements that govern their business conduct. An ad hoc approach to compliance management may work for small organizations with limited compliance obligations. However, organizations with many compliance drivers must properly manage and maintain compliance to ensure the accuracy and completeness of their compliance efforts. There are many processes and methodologies for managing compliance. The process covered in this chapter is based on ISO 19600:2014, *Compliance management systems*, and focuses on a cyclical approach similar to the Plan, Do, Check, Act (PDCA) cycle (also known as the Deming cycle or Shewhart cycle). The steps are as follows:

1. Plan

2. Implement

3. Evaluate

4. Maintain

The process is illustrated in Figure 1-16. The external and internal requirements (laws, regulations, directives, ethics, goals, and objectives) serve as input into the compliance management process.

 EXAM TIP   The CCISO exam will not contain questions pertaining to the exact steps for compliance management outlined in this section. The goal is to conceptually understand the general process for managing compliance and be able to distinguish scenarios where a specific compliance approach is applicable.

Plan

The first step in the compliance management process is to determine the scope of the applicable internal and external compliance requirements in order to understand the full compliance landscape. This requires having a thorough understanding of the internal business requirements, the industry that the organization operates in, the types of information that the business deals with, and the geographical areas in which the organization operates. There are different laws and regulations at the local, state, federal, and national level and these laws and regulations are often applicable to specific data types. An inventory of applicable legal and regulatory drivers as well as internal requirements should be produced to identify compliance risk that affects the business. The goal is to develop a strategy for identifying, measuring, and correcting instances of noncompliance.

Implement

After the strategy or plan of action has been developed, steps must be taken to address instances of noncompliance. Implementation often requires a cross-departmental effort and can manifest in many different activities, including requirements to

- Develop and maintain a specific policy, procedure, or documentation

- Implement a particular control

- Enforce disciplinary action for noncompliance or violation of internal requirements

- Assess competence and administer training

- Communicate compliance expectations to the organization

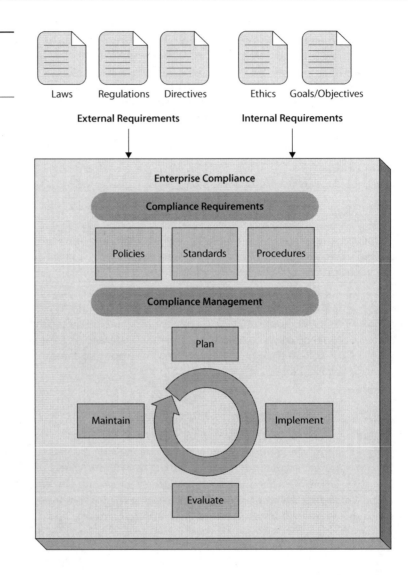

Figure 1-16
Compliance
management
process

Laws   Regulations   Directives   Ethics   Goals/Objectives

External Requirements   Internal Requirements

Enterprise Compliance

Compliance Requirements

Policies   Standards   Procedures

Compliance Management

Plan

Maintain   Implement

Evaluate

Ultimately the implementation step requires the organization to connect the regulations and requirements to specific policies, procedures, and controls. As part of addressing the findings there needs to be some way to track the progress and implementation of the remediation. Some organizations utilize software tools to assist in the tracking and remediation process. Other organizations with needs and requirements that are less complex may use something as simple as a spreadsheet or checklist. You don't always need a sophisticated tool. Sometimes the simplest solution can be the most effective.

Evaluate

The next step is to evaluate or assess the compliance program controls and measure the findings. Compliance assessments are used to identify and measure compliance risk due to missing controls. In some cases, a compliance assessment may cover multiple laws, regulations, and business requirements. In other cases, an organization may have an assessment performed against a specific compliance obligation such as a PCI DSS, HIPAA, ISO/IEC 27001, or an internal ethics survey. Compliance assessments can be both internal and external.

Internal compliance assessments are performed by internal staff to measure the organization's compliance risk and determine actions that need to be taken to comply with laws, regulations, and other compliance requirements. They are also used to determine whether the organization is following internal objectives, policies, standards, and best practices. The internal assessment may be performed by the internal audit team, the compliance team, or another internal resource depending on the structure of the organization and distribution of compliance responsibility.

External compliance assessments are performed by an independent third party and evaluate an organization's alignment with a specific law, regulation, or standard (for example, PCI DSS or HIPAA). External compliance assessments result in a report being issued measuring the organization's compliance. Depending on the type of assessment, the resulting report may be used by regulators to assess noncompliance to determine whether to impose a fine or other penalty. External compliance assessments can also result in certification. For example, some organizations may pursue ISO/IEC 27001 or PCI DSS certification. In order for an organization to become certified, a comprehensive audit must be conducted by an accredited third party (for example, a Qualified Security Assessor [QSA] for PCI DSS). Upon successful completion of the audit, and given that all the requirements are met, the organization will be certified as compliant. Compliance is an ongoing process of ensuring alignment with requirements, while certification is attestation of compliance for a specific period of time.

CISOs can use the results of compliance assessments to improve the maturity of the organization and as a basis for a request for funding for the implementation of controls to mitigate risk and address findings.

Maintain

To effectively ensure compliance, the organization must remain vigilant to ever-changing compliance requirements. Compliance is like any other program and requires ongoing maintenance, monitoring, and reporting. New laws are established, new regulations are imposed, and new internal organizational requirements are developed as the organization evolves. As an organization's technical infrastructure, business processes, or scope changes, new laws and regulations may govern the business that previously were not applicable. The goal is for the program to be able to address new compliance risks, identify and examine instances of noncompliance, and adapt to the evolving landscape on an ongoing basis.

Privacy

Many of the laws and regulatory drivers discussed later in this chapter have a common theme of a focus on privacy. Data privacy is an important aspect of compliance. Organizations must understand the privacy, legal, and regulatory requirements for the industry they operate in. It is crucial to document how privacy-related information is processed;

this includes collection, use, sharing, archival, and disposal. Some key things to think about to begin maturing privacy efforts are the following:

- What data does the organization have?
- How is the data used?
- Where is the data stored and processed?
- What privacy laws or regulations govern the business?

Privacy Impact Assessment

A risk assessment carried out to assess privacy is called a *privacy impact assessment (PIA)*. A PIA focuses on analyzing data collection, use, dissemination, archival, and destruction for the following:

- Compliance with applicable laws and regulations
- Determining risk and effect of data handling
- Evaluating data protection measures and processes to mitigate privacy risks

Many organizations have a data privacy officer and departments with the specific responsibility of ensuring privacy and compliance with privacy laws. Often the privacy department is attached to the legal department. Ultimately, privacy should be a multifaceted effort between the legal, compliance, audit, and security departments. The security department has the expertise in the technical requirements and controls required to implement privacy, while the legal team has the expertise in complying with laws and statues.

Privacy and Security

Often privacy and security are lumped together, but it is important to remember that these are different practices. *Privacy* indicates the level of control an individual should expect to have over their own sensitive data. This is typically focused on the authorized collection, use, sharing, archival, and destruction of personal information that the organization has been entrusted with. For instance, HIPAA requires health organizations to protect the privacy of their patients' personal information. *Security* refers to measures to guard against a threat and is generally focused on protecting the data from unauthorized access and ensuring the data is appropriately destroyed when no longer needed. Organizations accomplish privacy goals by implementing good security practices.

Laws and Regulatory Drivers

This section focuses on some of the key laws and regulatory drivers a CISO should be aware of. Some organizations are not legally mandated to be compliant with these laws. However, if an organization conducts business with other entities that are legally mandated to be compliant, those businesses may require compliance from their suppliers, partners, or vendors as part of their compliance or risk management program. The laws and regulatory drivers covered in this section are listed here:

- FISMA
- DFARS 252.204-7012
- Clinger-Cohen Act
- PCI DSS
- Privacy Act
- GLBA
- HIPAA
- FERPA
- SOX
- GDPR
- NERC-CIP

 EXAM TIP CCISO candidates should be familiar with the provisions of laws that affect organizational information security.

Federal Information Security Modernization Act

The *Federal Information Security Management Act of 2002 (FISMA or FISMA 2002)* is a US law enacted as part of the E-Government Act of 2002. The intention of FISMA is to help US federal agencies implement minimum security requirements in order to reduce the risk of data loss. FISMA requires US federal agencies to build, document, and implement an agency-wide information security program to support agency operations. This includes the following:

- Following key security best practices
- Assessing their compliance with these practices
- Reporting their findings to the Office of Management and Budget (OMB)

The *Federal Information Security Modernization Act of 2014 (FISMA or FISMA 2014)* amended FISMA 2002 to provide new requirements intended to modernize federal security practices to focus on risk-based security versus a checklist-style approach. These new requirements include changes to the responsibility of federal security oversight agencies, updated security reporting requirements, and steps to promote the use of automated tools.

Who does FISMA apply to? FISMA compliance is mandatory for US federal agencies but also applies to anyone who handles federal government information. Federal contractors, state agencies administering federal programs, and private-sector companies with government contracts must comply with FISMA. Failure to comply can result in loss of federal funding.

How does compliance impact an organization? In accordance with FISMA requirements, NIST is responsible for developing standards, guidelines, and other publications that represent security requirements to be applied to US federal agencies. These include Federal Information Processing Standards (FIPS) and NIST Special Publications (SPs). These publications are covered in greater detail later in this chapter. The key requirements of FISMA include the following:

- **Inventory of information systems** An accurate system boundary must be identified, including a complete inventory of assets.

- **Security risk categorization of information systems** Information systems must be categorized using guidance in FIPS 200 and NIST SP 800-53.

- **Security controls** Security controls must be implemented based on the system's risk categorization. Guidance implementing security controls is provided in FIPS 200 and NIST SP 800-53.

- **Risk assessment** A security risk assessment must be performed to assess system risk and criticality.

- **System security plan** A system security plan (SSP) must be developed using the guidance in NIST SP 800-18.

- **Certification testing** The system must be authorized based on guidance in NIST SP 800-37.

- **Continuous monitoring** Systems must be monitored for compliance with controls and baselines.

Defense Federal Acquisition Regulation Supplement 252.204-7012

The *Defense Federal Acquisition Regulation Supplement (DFARS)* is administered by the US Department of Defense (DoD) and is a supplement to the Federal Acquisition Regulation (FAR). DFARS provides specific acquisition regulations that DoD contractors and subcontractors must follow as part of the procurement process. DFARS 252.204-7012 outlines the minimum-security requirements for the protection of Controlled Unclassified Information (CUI) in nonfederal information systems.

Who does DFARS 252.204-7012 apply to? DFARS 252.204-7012 applies to DoD contractors and subcontractors that process, store, or transmit CUI in nonfederal information systems. If an organization is working with DoD CUI, the organization must comply with DFARS 252.204-7012 requirements and must bring its business into compliance.

How does compliance impact an organization? Guidance for the security controls that must be implemented is provided in NIST SP 800-171, *Protecting Controlled Unclassified Information in Nonfederal Systems and Organizations.* NIST SP 800-171 is essentially the cybersecurity framework that organizations handling CUI must implement. If a DoD contractor fails to comply with DFARS 252.204-7012/NIST SP 800-171, the contractor risks a range of potential criminal, civil, administrative, or contract penalties, including contract termination and breach of contract damages.

Clinger-Cohen Act

The *Clinger-Cohen Act of 1996* is a US federal law that applies to federal agencies focused on improving the acquisition, use, and disposal of information technology. It is intended to improve IT acquisition, investment, and expenditures to reduce waste.

Who does the Clinger-Cohen Act apply to? The Clinger-Cohen Act applies to US federal agencies.

How does compliance impact an organization? The Clinger-Cohen Act is composed of two laws that were passed together: the Information Technology Management Reform Act (ITMRA) and the Federal Acquisition Reform Act (FARA). Some of the key requirements of the Clinger-Cohen Act include the following:

- Enforce accountability of the agency head for IT management and investment as well as information security
- Implement a capital budget planning and investment process
- Develop a plan for evaluating risks and maximizing IT investment value
- Establish the chief information officer (CIO) role in agencies
- Develop standards and benchmarks for IT systems and investments
- Create an enterprise architecture
- Periodically review the budget process

Payment Card Industry Data Security Standard

The *Payment Card Industry Data Security Standard (PCI DSS)* is a control framework focused on the protection of credit card information. PCI DSS is an example of a self-regulation approach to privacy and data security, as it is not a government law or regulation. It is a private-sector industry initiative administered and enforced by the Payment Card Industry Standards Council. The Council was established by the major credit card companies, including Visa, MasterCard, Discover, JCB, and American Express. At the time of writing, the current version of PCI DSS is version 3.2.1, available at https://www.pcisecuritystandards.org/document_library.

Who does PCI DSS apply to? PCI DSS applies globally to any organization that handles cardholder data. This includes any organization that stores, processes, or transmits cardholder data, such as businesses that process credit card transactions.

How does compliance impact an organization? The PCI DSS control framework consists of 12 control requirements organized into the following six categories:

- Build and maintain a secure network and systems
- Protect cardholder data
- Maintain a vulnerability management program
- Implement strong access control measures
- Regularly monitor and test networks
- Maintain an information security policy

The 12 control objectives for PCI DSS are

- Install and maintain a firewall.
- Reset default vendor-supplied passwords and security parameters for systems.
- Protect stored cardholder data.
- Encrypt cardholder data when transmitted across open or public networks.
- Implement and maintain up-to-date antivirus software or programs.
- Develop applications and systems with security in mind.
- Restrict access to cardholder data based on business need to know.
- Assign a unique ID to each individual with system access.
- Restrict physical access to cardholder data.
- Track and monitor access to cardholder data and network resources.
- Test systems and process security on a regular basis.
- Maintain an information security policy.

Failure to comply with PCI DSS can result in fines from the credit card companies, loss of customers, reputation, and brand image, and lawsuits from customers. In addition, credit card companies may revoke the organization's ability to accept credit cards.

Privacy Act of 1974

For many years there has been great concern regarding the US federal government's involvement in surveillance and investigation of individuals as well as the potential for abuse of personal data the government maintains. The *Privacy Act of 1974 (Privacy Act)* is a US federal law developed to help address these concerns by focusing on striking a balance between the government's need to collect and maintain an individual's personal information and the privacy rights of the individual.

Who does the Privacy Act apply to? The Privacy Act of 1974 applies to records and documents maintained by specific branches of the US federal government. Similar to many laws, there is a list of exceptions in the legislation for exempted agencies and circumstances.

How does compliance impact an organization? The Privacy Act requires that agencies protect certain records maintained by the US federal government. The legislation focuses on four main policy objectives (see https://www.justice.gov/opcl/policy-objectives):

- To restrict disclosure of personally identifiable records maintained by agencies
- To grant individuals increased rights of access to agency records maintained on themselves
- To grant individuals the right to seek amendment of agency records maintained on themselves upon a showing that the records are not accurate, relevant, timely, or complete

- To establish a code of "fair information practices" that requires agencies to comply with statutory norms for collection, maintenance, and dissemination of records

Violations of the Act can result in civil action including fines, damages, and criminal penalties.

Gramm-Leach-Bliley Act

The *Gramm-Leach-Bliley Act (GLBA)*, also known as the Financial Services Modernization Act of 1999, requires financial institutions to protect individual's nonpublic personal information. This includes disclosing to customers how their private information will be protected and whether it will be distributed to third parties.

Who does the Gramm-Leach-Bliley Act apply to? GLBA is mandatory for financial institutions, including banks, mortgage brokers, real estate firms, insurance companies, and other organizations engaged in providing financial services or products.

How does compliance impact an organization? There are three major provisions of GLBA that protect customers' information: the Financial Privacy Rule, the Safeguards Rule, and the Pretexting Rule.

The Financial Privacy Rule requires financial institutions to provide each customer with a privacy notice that outlines the following:

- The types of data collected
- How the organization will use, share, and protect the data
- The customer's rights regarding the data

The Safeguards Rule requires financial institutions to develop an information security plan that includes

- Designating an employee to manage the information security program
- Developing a risk management program to identify risks to customer information
- Ensuring service providers are safeguarding customer information
- Designing, implementing, testing, and monitoring controls to mitigate identified risks
- Continuously monitoring the information security program

The Pretexting Rule requires financial institutions to implement controls to defend against pretexting, also known as social engineering, which can include someone impersonating an account holder by phone, mail, or e-mail to collect their private data. (Social engineering is covered in greater depth in Chapter 4.) GLBA makes it illegal to attempt to obtain or disclose customer information by pretexting. To meet GLBA requirements in this area, an organization must develop a security awareness training program that includes recognizing social engineering and phishing scams.

Failure to comply with GLBA can result in severe consequences, including fines, criminal penalties, reputational damage, and imprisonment.

Health Insurance Portability and Accountability Act

The *Health Information Portability and Accountability Act of 1996 (HIPAA)* is a US federal regulation covering the handling of protected health information (PHI). HIPAA provides a framework for protecting the security and privacy of health information.

Who does HIPAA apply to? The rules in HIPAA apply to covered entities and business associates. A covered entity is defined as a health care provider, health plan, or health care clearinghouse. A business associate is an entity that provides services to a covered entity that involves the use or disclosure of PHI.

How does compliance impact an organization? HIPAA is enforced by the US Department of Health and Human Services (HHS) Office for Civil Rights (OCR). Noncompliance with HIPAA can result in severe penalties based on the level of perceived negligence. Noncompliance can result in civil and criminal penalties, including potential fines and imprisonment. The most common HIPAA compliance issues include the following:

- Unauthorized use or disclosure of protected health information
- Failure to protect protected health information
- Failure to provide patient access to their protected health information when requested
- Disclosing more protected health information than necessary

Some of the key components of HIPAA include the following:

- **Privacy Rule**   Establishes standards for the privacy of PHI, including authorized use and disclosure, and gives patients rights over their information.
- **Security Rule**   Establishes administrative, technical, and physical security standards for the protection of PHI.
- **Breach Notification Rule**   Establishes specific reporting requirements for covered entities when breaches of PHI occur.

To help ensure HIPAA enforcement, the US government passed the *Health Information Technology for Economic and Clinical Health Act (HITECH)* as part of the American Recovery and Reinvestment Act of 2009 (ARRA). HITECH applies to business associates and covered entities under HIPAA. Subtitle D of the HITECH Act expands the scope of security and privacy requirements under HIPAA for the protection of health data in part by strengthening the legal penalty for noncompliance.

 NOTE   Covered entities and business associates that create, use, transmit, or store protected health information must comply with both HIPAA and HITECH.

Family Educational Rights and Privacy Act

The *Family Educational Rights and Privacy Act of 1974 (FERPA)* is a US federal law focused on protecting the privacy and confidentiality of student educational records. FERPA does not require the implementation of specific information security safeguards or controls. However, FERPA does require the use of reasonable methods to protect student records.

Who does FERPA apply to? The law applies to all educational agencies and institutions that receive funding from programs administered by the US Department of Education.

How does compliance impact an organization? FERPA requires educational institutions to be responsible for the privacy of student personally identifiable information. Some of the key provisions of the act include the following:

- Providing parents and students with access to the students' educational records
- Providing parents and students the ability to request amendments to educational records
- Requiring schools to receive written permission from the parent or student to disclose student educational record information

Noncompliance with FERPA can result in loss of funding from the US Department of Education.

Sarbanes-Oxley Act

The *Sarbanes-Oxley Act of 2002 (SOX)*, also referred to as the Public Company Accounting Reform and Investor Protection Act of 2002, is a US federal law focused on holding board members and executives accountable for the accuracy of the financial statements of their organization. SOX was passed as a result of many large-scale scandals where executives intentionally misled the public about their financials (for example, Enron), which resulted in the loss of billions of investor dollars.

Who does SOX apply to? SOX applies to all publicly traded companies doing business in the United States. This includes any company publicly traded on US markets.

How does compliance impact an organization? The goal of SOX is to reduce fraud and hold board members and executives accountable for the accuracy of financial statements. A majority of the law has to do with accounting practices, with the exception of Section 404 of the law, which applies to information technology. Section 404 of SOX is a driver of internal control assessment activities by requiring

- Management responsibility for establishing and maintaining adequate internal controls for financial reporting
- Assessment of effectiveness of internal controls by a public accounting firm

These requirements for internal controls are often achieved through the implementation of an industry security framework for the organization that is customized for its specific needs.

Failure to comply with SOX can result in negative publicity, lawsuits, and fines and imprisonment. Executives can be jailed if is discovered that their company submitted fraudulent financial reports to the Security Exchange Commission (SEC).

General Data Protection Regulation

The *General Data Protection Regulation (GDPR)* is a European Union (EU) privacy law that regulates the processing of EU citizens' personal data.

Who does GDPR apply to? GDPR applies to EU organizations that process personal data as well as to organizations outside the EU that provide services into the EU that involve processing EU citizen data. This means that if a business located outside the EU has an Internet presence and collects EU personal data in the course of providing services, the business needs to comply with GDPR regardless of where it is located. Therefore, US firms may need to be compliant with GDPR if they want to conduct business with EU businesses or have customers within the member states of the EU.

How does compliance impact an organization? The legislation aims to put control of the individual's personal data into the individual's hands. Some of the key provisions in GDPR include

- **Consent**   Requires the organization processing personal data to obtain informed consent from the data subject for processing of their data outside of specific legitimate purposes. Also requires that the terms and conditions statements be clear and concise, with no blanket consent.

- **Breach notification**   Companies must notify data subjects of security breaches within 72 hours of discovery.

- **Right to access**   At the data subject's request, companies must confirm their personal data is being processed, including where and for what purpose. Companies must also provide a copy of the data to the data subject at no charge. Companies have one month to respond to data subject access requests.

- **Right to be forgotten**   Companies are required to erase personal data when requested by the data subject.

- **Data portability**   Companies must provide data subjects with a method to receive data about themselves in a commonly used machine-readable format. The data subject also has the right to request that their data be transmitted to another company at no charge.

- **Privacy by design**   Data protection and privacy must be a consideration from the start of the design process and only data absolutely necessary for processing should be collected.

- **Data protection officer**   Organizations that meet certain criteria will be required to designate a data protection officer (DPO) to oversee GDPR compliance.

GDPR imposes substantial fines for noncompliance based on the nature of the infringement. Fines can be as large as €20 million or 4 percent of annual global revenue, whichever is greater.

NOTE Post Brexit, the withdrawal of the United Kingdom (UK) from the EU, the UK will still be subject to EU law, including GDPR, for a transition period from January 31, 2020 to December 31, 2020 unless an additional extension is agreed upon. This means that UK citizens are still protected under GDPR during the transition period. Following the transition period, a UK amended version of GDPR will be followed, known as UK GDPR, which will cover protection of UK citizen data. However, the UK organizations will still be subject to EU GDPR if they collect personal data of EU citizens.

North American Electric Reliability Corporation Critical Infrastructure Protection

The *North American Electric Reliability Corporation (NERC)* develops standards for energy system operation and monitoring and enforces compliance with these standards. These standards are mandatory for all North American bulk power systems. NERC's authority is granted by the Federal Energy Regulation Commission (FERC), which designated NERC as a national Electric Reliability Organization (ERO). NERC developed the *Critical Infrastructure Protection (CIP)* standards, known as *NERC CIP*, a set of cybersecurity standards for the security of North America's power grid. NERC CIP provides a framework for the protection of critical systems for North America's bulk power systems.

Who does NERC CIP apply to? NERC standards outline controls for the protection of the electric utility infrastructure of North America. This includes NERC CIP, the cybersecurity family of standards. Previously, NERC standards were voluntary. This changed as a result of the Energy Policy Act of 2005, which authorized FERC to make NERC standards mandatory. These standards are now mandatory for all North American bulk power systems. This means that organizations involved in electric transmission, generation, and interconnection of power systems in North America must comply with NERC standards. This is a condition of doing business in the electricity industry sector.

How does compliance impact an organization? The NERC cybersecurity standard, NERC CIP, is composed of 11 standards as of this writing. According to https://www.nerc.com/pa/Stand/Pages/CIPStandards.aspx, the standards currently subject to enforcement are as follows:

- **CIP-002** Cyber Security – BES Cyber System Categorization
- **CIP-003** Cyber Security – Security Management Controls
- **CIP-004** Cyber Security – Personnel & Training
- **CIP-005** Cyber Security – Electronic Security Perimeter(s)
- **CIP-006** Cyber Security – Physical Security of BES Cyber Systems
- **CIP-007** Cyber Security – System Security Management
- **CIP-008** Cyber Security – Incident Reporting and Response Planning
- **CIP-009** Cyber Security – Recovery Plans for BES Cyber Systems
- **CIP-010** Cyber Security – Configuration Change Management and Vulnerability Assessments

Law/Regulatory Driver	Who It Applies to
Federal Information Security Management Act (FISMA)	US federal agencies and anyone who handles federal information or manages federal programs.
Defense Federal Acquisition Regulation Supplement (DFARS) 252.204-7012	DoD contractors and subcontractors that process, store, or transmit CUI in nonfederal information systems.
Clinger-Cohen Act	US federal agencies.
Payment Card Industry Data Security Standard (PCI DSS)	Companies handling credit card data.
Federal Privacy Act of 1974	Specific branches of the US federal government.
Gramm-Leach-Bliley Act (GLBA)	Financial institutions, which includes banks, mortgage brokers, real estate firms, insurance companies, and other organizations engaged in providing financial services or products.
Health Insurance Portability and Accountability Act (HIPAA)	Covered entities and business associates. A covered entity is defined as a health care provider, health plan, or health care clearinghouse.
Family Education Rights and Privacy Act (FERPA)	Educational agencies and institutions that receive funding from the US Department of Education.
Sarbanes-Oxley Act (SOX)	Companies publicly traded on US markets.
General Data Protection Regulation (GDPR)	Any business that collects personal data from citizens of EU member states in the course of providing services.
North American Electric Reliability Corporation Critical Infrastructure Protection (NERC CIP)	Companies involved in North America's bulk power systems.

Table 1-4   Summary of Affected Industries for Laws and Regulatory Drivers

- **CIP-011**   Cyber Security – Information Protection
- **CIP-014**   Physical Security

NERC CIP standards are enforced through regular CIP compliance audits, so it is crucial for bulk power system organizations to be able to demonstrate compliance. Failure to comply with NERC CIP can result in significant fines.

Summary of Laws and Regulatory Drivers

Table 1-4 provides a high-level summary of the regulatory drivers covered in this section.

Standards and Frameworks

There are many nonregulatory standards and best practice frameworks available to assist organizations in structuring their information security programs. While there may not be a legislative requirement to implement these standards, they can serve as a foundational tool for building a security program, establishing a baseline for compliance, and allowing the CISO to identify gaps in current strategies. In addition, aligning practices with an industry framework demonstrates a certain level of commitment that may be valued by customers, partners, and stakeholders. The standards and frameworks discussed in this section are listed here:

- ISO/IEC 27000 series
- ISO/IEC 27001
- NIST Cybersecurity Framework
- Federal Information Processing Standards (FIPS)
- NIST Special Publications
- Privacy Shield
- COBIT

 EXAM TIP   CCISO candidates should be familiar with common information security standards, frameworks, and best practices.

ISO/IEC 27000 Series

The International Organization for Standardization (ISO) and the International Electrotechnical Commission (IEC) develop joint international standards. The *ISO/IEC 27000 series*, known as the information security management systems (ISMS) family of standards, serve as industry best practices for managing security holistically. Here are some of the key standards in the ISO/IEC 27000 series, with our abridged versions of their titles:

- **ISO/IEC 27000**   ISMS overview and vocabulary
- **ISO/IEC 27001**   ISMS requirements
- **ISO/IEC 27002**   Code of practice for information security controls
- **ISO/IEC 27003**   ISMS implementation guidance
- **ISO/IEC 27004**   ISMS monitoring, measurement, analysis, and evaluation
- **ISO/IEC 27005**   Information security risk management
- **ISO/IEC 27006**   ISMS certification body requirements
- **ISO/IEC 27007**   Guidelines for ISMS auditing
- **ISO/IEC 27008**   Guidelines for auditors on information security controls
- **ISO/IEC 27014**   Governance of information security
- **ISO/IEC 27017**   Information security controls for cloud computing services
- **ISO/IEC 27018**   Protecting PII in the public cloud
- **ISO/IEC 27031**   Technology readiness for business continuity

- **ISO/IEC 27032**   Guidelines for cybersecurity
- **ISO/IEC 27033**   Network security
- **ISO/IEC 27037**   Digital evidence handling guidelines
- **ISO/IEC 27799**   Health information security management

The following are some of the publications that have been drafted but not yet published:

- **ISO/IEC 27030**   Security and privacy in Internet of Things (IoT)
- **ISO/IEC 27099**   Public key infrastructure
- **ISO/IEC 27100**   Cybersecurity overview and concepts
- **ISO/IEC 27101**   Cybersecurity framework development guidelines
- **ISO/IEC 27102**   Guidelines for cyber-insurance
- **ISO/IEC 27550**   Privacy engineering for system life cycle processes

ISO/IEC standards are highly respected and useful; however, they are not free, which has limited their adoption compared to other standards. They may be purchased from https://www.iso.org.

ISO/IEC 27001

ISO/IEC 27001, *Information technology – Security techniques – Information security management systems – Requirements,* is the best-known framework in the ISO/IEC 27000 series family. ISO/IEC 27001 contains guidance on establishing a wholistic ISMS. The key requirements that make up ISO/IEC 27001 are organized into the following ten sections in the publication:

- Scope
- Normative references
- Terms and definitions
- Context of the organization
- Leadership
- Planning
- Support
- Operation
- Performance evaluation
- Improvement

Figure 1-17 outlines the core components of an information security management system according to ISO/IEC 27001.

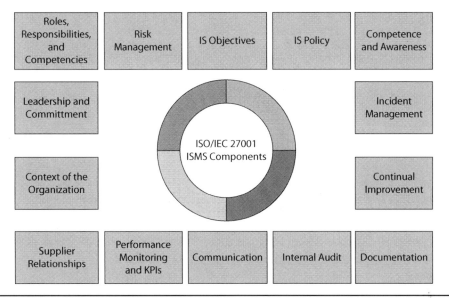

Figure 1-17   ISO/IEC 27001 ISMS components

Organizations may seek ISO/IEC 27001 certification by an accredited third party. The third party will assess the organization's ISMS based on the requirements in ISO/IEC 27001 and attest to the organization's compliance level.

NIST Cybersecurity Framework

The *NIST Cybersecurity Framework (NIST CSF)* is a risk-based cybersecurity framework customizable to an organization's needs and business requirements. The framework was designed for critical infrastructure but is applicable to any organization. The CSF is used by many organizations looking for a baseline for their security program. The three main components that make up the CSF are illustrated in Figure 1-18 and outlined here:

- **Framework Core**   The Framework Core is made up of five functions: Identify, Protect, Detect, Respond, and Recover. Each function is composed of categories (control family), which are made up of subcategories (controls) and references (mappings to other control frameworks).

- **Framework Implementation Tiers**   The Framework Implementation Tiers range from Partial (Tier 1), Risk Informed (Tier 2), Repeatable (Tier 3), to Adaptive (Tier 4). While the tiers appear to be maturity levels, they are meant to be contextual references for communication around risk appetite, mission priority, and budget.

- **Framework Profiles**   The Framework Profiles represent an organization's alignment of resources, requirements, and risk appetite with the desired outcomes of the Framework Core (functions, categories, subcategories, and references). Profiles are used to evaluate the "Current" sate of an organization with a "Target" state.

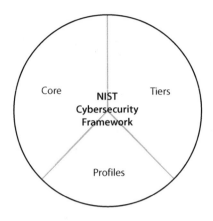

Figure 1-18
NIST
Cybersecurity
Framework
components

Federal Information Processing Standards

Federal Information Processing Standards (FIPS) are standards and guidelines issued by NIST for the security of US federal information systems. Not all FIPS publications are mandatory for federal agencies. The "Applicability" section of each FIPS document indicates if the standard is applicable and mandatory. While these documents are developed specifically for the US federal government, they can be useful for organizations looking for industry best practice guidance. In addition, FIPS are also mandatory for government contractors and vendors doing business with federal agencies. Federal agencies are mandated by FISMA to implement FIPS. The following are the current FIPS as of this writing:

- **FIPS 140-2**   Security Requirements for Cryptographic Modules
- **FIPS 180-4**   Secure Hash Standard (SHS)
- **FIPS 186-4**   Digital Signature Standard (DSS)
- **FIPS 197**   Advanced Encryption Standard (AES)
- **FIPS 198-1**   The Keyed-Hash Message Authentication Code (HMAC)
- **FIPS 199**   Standards for Security Categorization of Federal Information and Information Systems
- **FIPS 200**   Minimum Security Requirements for Federal Information and Information Systems
- **FIPS 201-2**   Personal Identity Verification (PIV) of Federal Employees and Contractors
- **FIPS 202**   SHA-3 Standard: Permutation-Based Hash and Extendable-Output Functions

NIST Special Publications

A *NIST Special Publication (SP)* is a document published by NIST, often to support FIPS publications or developed as part of NIST's responsibility under FISMA. The *NIST SP 800 series* are publications specific to computer security. Many private-sector organizations use NIST SP 800 series documents in the development of their security program and strategy. Following is a list of some of the most commonly used standards from the NIST SP 800 series:

- **NIST SP 800-18** Guide for Developing Security Plans for Federal Information Systems
- **NIST SP 800-30** Guide for Conducting Risk Assessments
- **NIST SP 800-34** Contingency Planning Guide for Federal Information Systems
- **NIST SP 800-37** Risk Management Framework for Information Systems and Organizations
- **NIST SP 800-39** Managing Information Security Risk
- **NIST SP 800-40** Guide to Enterprise Patch Management Technologies
- **NIST SP 800-53** Security and Privacy Controls for Federal Information Systems and Organizations
- **NIST SP 800-53A** Assessing Security and Privacy Controls in Federal Information Systems and Organizations
- **NIST SP 800-55** Performance Measurement Guide for Information Security
- **NIST SP 800-60** Guide for Mapping Types of Information and Information Systems to Security Categories
- **NIST SP 800-61** Computer Security Incident Handling Guide
- **NIST SP 800-66** An Introductory Resource Guide for Implementing the Health Insurance Portability and Accountability Act (HIPAA) Security Rule
- **NIST SP 800-70** National Checklist Program for IT Products
- **NIST SP 800-88** Guidelines for Media Sanitization
- **NIST SP 800-114** User's Guide to Telework and Bring Your Own Device (BYOD) Security
- **NIST SP 800-122** Guide to Protecting the Confidentiality of Personally Identifiable Information (PII)
- **NIST SP 800-124** Guidelines for Managing Security of Mobile Devices in the Enterprise
- **NIST SP 800-125** Guide to Security for Full Virtualization Technologies
- **NIST SP 800-137** Information Security Continuous Monitoring (ISCM) for Federal Information Systems and Organizations

- **NIST SP 800-160**   Systems Security Engineering
- **NIST SP 800-171**   Protecting Controlled Unclassified Information in Nonfederal Systems and Organizations
- **NIST SP 800-181**   National Initiative for Cybersecurity Education (NICE) Cybersecurity Workforce Framework

The 800 series covers a wide range of topics. Specific NIST SPs are discussed in greater depth in later chapters.

Privacy Shield

The EU-US and Swiss-US *Privacy Shield* Frameworks exist to regulate exchanges of personal information from the European Union and Switzerland to the United States. The frameworks were developed by the US Department of Commerce in conjunction with the European Commission and Swiss Administration with the goal of enabling US companies to receive personal data from the EU while complying with EU privacy laws. To join either the EU-US or Swiss-US Privacy Shield Framework, organizations are required to self-certify and publicly commit to compliance to the Privacy Shield principles. Once a company self-certifies, the commitment is enforceable under US law. The Department of Commerce maintains a public list of US organizations that have self-certified at https://www.privacyshield.gov/list.

As of this writing, the Privacy Shield is composed of 7 principles and 16 supplemental principles, listed at https://www.privacyshield.gov/eu-us-framework as follows:

Principles:

- Notice
- Choice
- Accountability for Onward Transfer
- Security
- Data Integrity and Purpose Limitation
- Access
- Recourse, Enforcement, and Liability

Supplemental Principles:

- Sensitive Data
- Journalistic Exceptions
- Secondary Liability
- Performing Due Diligence and Conducting Audits
- The Role of the Data Protection Authorities

- Self-Certification
- Verification
- Access
- Human Resources Data
- Obligatory Contracts for Onward Transfers
- Dispute Resolution and Enforcement
- Choice – Timing of Opt Out
- Travel Information
- Pharmaceutical and Medical Products
- Public Record and Publicly Available Information
- Access Requests by Public Authorities

Failure of participating organizations to comply with Privacy Shield can result in fines or sanctions. Persistent failure to comply will result in the organization's removal from the Privacy Shield list and require the organization to return or delete personal information collected under the agreement.

COBIT

The *Control Objectives for Information and Related Technology (COBIT)* is a best practice framework for governance and management of IT developed by ISACA and the IT Governance Institute. The most recent version at the time of this writing is COBIT 2019. COBIT 2019 is made up of five governance and management domain objectives, shown in Figure 1-19. These domains are made up of 40 objectives.

The core publications for COBIT 2019 are available from http://www.isaca.org/resources/cobit for a fee. The publications include the following:

- COBIT 2019 Framework: Introduction and Methodology
- COBIT 2019 Framework: Governance and Management Objectives

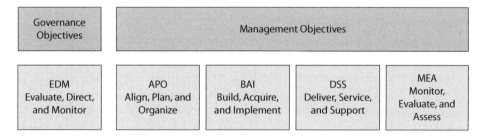

Figure 1-19   COBIT governance and management objectives

- COBIT 2019 Design Guide: Designing an Information and Technology Governance Solution
- COBIT 2019 Implementation Guide: Implementing and Optimizing an Information and Technology Governance Solution

Information Security Trends and Best Practices

This section presents several sources of information for security trends and best practices for information security professionals. There are many organizations focused on providing resources to improve the information security industry. This section does not provide a comprehensive survey of these organizations, but it does introduce some of the more notable security best practice organizations in the industry. These organizations provide a range of benefits to the community, including tools and security best practice resources. It is important for the CISO to be aware of best practice organizations as both a resource and to stay up to date on the industry.

Open Web Application Security Project

The *Open Web Application Security Project (OWASP)* is an international organization focused on enabling organizations with the skills and tools to plan, develop, acquire, operate, and maintain secure applications. OWASP develops tools, guides, and best practice documents and organizes conferences focused on application security. Additional information regarding application security is covered in Chapter 4.

Cloud Security Alliance

The *Cloud Security Alliance (CSA)* is a nonprofit organization focused on promoting best practices for the use and adoption of cloud computing. CSA provides tools, research, frameworks, and best practice documents on cloud security, governance, and compliance. The Cloud Security Alliance provides training on cloud security and cloud governance and compliance, as well as certification for the following:

- Certificate of Cloud Security Knowledge (CCSK)
- Certificate of Cloud Auditing Knowledge (CCAK)

Center for Internet Security

The *Center for Internet Security (CIS)* is a nonprofit organization focused on developing best practice tools, frameworks, and resources for information security. CIS develops the CIS Controls and CIS Benchmarks, which are global standards for information security best practices. These standards are covered in greater depth in Chapter 2 and Chapter 4. CIS also hosts the Multi-State Information Sharing & Analysis Center (MS-ISAC) and the Elections Infrastructure Information Sharing and Analysis Center (EI-ISAC). These information-sharing and analysis centers provide critical resources and discounted services to state, local, territorial, and tribal governments.

Information Security Training and Certifications

This section covers some of the well-known vendor-neutral information security certification bodies. These certification bodies provide a range of benefits to the community, including forums, conferences, networking opportunities, and security best practice resources, as well as certifications and training for continuous learning. It is important for CISOs to be aware of continuous learning opportunities to identify training opportunities for themselves and their teams.

International Information System Security Certification Consortium

The *International Information System Security Certification Consortium (ISC)²* is a nonprofit organization specializing in certification and training for information security professionals. (ISC)² organizes regular conferences, provides research and best practice material, and offers a variety of certification and training programs. The (ISC)² certifications include the following:

- Certified Information Systems Security Professional (CISSP)
  - Information Systems Security Architecture Professional (CISSP-ISSAP)
  - Information Systems Security Engineering Professional (CISSP-ISSEP)
  - Information Systems Security Management Professional (CISSP-ISSMP)
- Systems Security Certified Practitioner (SSCP)
- Certified Cloud Security Professional (CCSP)
- Certified Authorization Professional (CAP)
- Certified Secure Software Lifecycle Professional (CSSLP)
- HealthCare Information Security and Privacy Practitioner (HCISPP)

ISACA

ISACA, previously known as the Information Systems Audit and Control Association, is a nonprofit professional association for advancing the field of information security, assurance, risk management, and governance. ISACA provides members with access to best practice frameworks, documentation, conferences, and training programs. ISACA may be best known for developing COBIT, previously discussed. ISACA provides training and certifications for the following:

- Certified Information Systems Auditor (CISA)
- Certified in Risk and Information Systems Control (CRISC)
- Certified Information Security Manager (CISM)
- Certified in the Governance of Enterprise IT (CGEIT)
- Cybersecurity Nexus (CSX)

International Council of E-Commerce Consultants

The *International Council of E-Commerce Consultants (EC-Council)* is a professional security organization that provides training and certification on a variety of IT security topics. EC-Council is the certifying body for the Certified Chief Information Security Officer (CCISO) certification. EC-Council also operates several security conferences as well as EC-Council University (ECCU). Some of the certifications provided by EC-Council include the following:

- Certified Ethical Hacker (CEH)
- Certified Network Defender (CND)
- EC-Council Certified Security Analyst (ECSA)
- EC-Council Certified Security Specialist (ECSS)
- EC-Council Certified Encryption Specialist (ECES)
- Certified Secure Computer User (CSCU)
- EC-Council Disaster Recovery Professional (EDRP)
- Computer Hacking Forensic Investigator (CHFI)
- EC-Council Certified Incident Handler (ECIH)
- Certified Chief Information Security Officer (CCISO)
- Certified Application Security Engineer (CASE)
- Certified Threat Intelligence Analyst (CTIA)
- Certified SOC Analyst (CSA)

SANS Institute

The *SANS Institute*, officially the Escal Institute of Advanced Technologies, is an information security training and certification organization. SANS offers a variety of resources, including training/certification, conferences, webinars, articles, and other resources to help develop security professionals. SANS is particularly known for its hands-on training. SANS stands for SysAdmin, Audit, Network, and Security to represent the range of topics their certifications and training cover. Here is a list of several of the SANS certifications:

- GIAC Security Essentials (GSEC)
- GIAC Certified Incident Handler (GCIH)
- GIAC Certified Forensic Analyst (GCFA)
- GIAC Penetration Tester (GPEN)
- GIAC Certified Intrusion Analyst (GCIA)
- GIAC Web Application Penetration Tester (GWAPT)

- GIAC Certified Forensic Examiner (GCFE)
- GIAC Security Leadership (GSLC)
- GIAC Reverse Engineering Malware (GREM)
- GIAC Information Security Fundamentals (GISF)
- GIAC Certified Enterprise Defender (GCED)
- GIAC Systems and Network Auditor (GSNA)
- Global Industrial Cyber Security Professional (GICSP)
- GIAC Certified Windows Security Administrator (GCWN)
- GIAC Continuous Monitoring Certification (GMON)
- GIAC Network Forensic Analyst (GNFA)
- GIAC Exploit Researcher and Advanced Penetration Tester (GXPN)
- GIAC Certified Perimeter Protection Analyst (GPPA)
- GIAC Information Security Professional (GISP)
- GIAC Critical Controls Certification (GCCC)
- GIAC Mobile Device Security Analyst (GMOB)
- GIAC Assessing and Auditing Wireless Networks (GAWN)
- GIAC Certified UNIX Security Administrator (GCUX)
- GIAC Cyber Threat Intelligence (GCTI)
- GIAC Secure Software Programmer-Java (GSSP-JAVA)
- GIAC Certified Web Application Defender (GWEB)
- GIAC Python Coder (GPYC)
- GIAC Law of Data Security and Investigations (GLEG)
- GIAC Strategic Planning, Policy, and Leadership (GSTRT)
- GIAC Advanced Smartphone Forensics (GASF)
- GIAC Response and Industrial Defense (GRID)
- GIAC Certified Detection Analyst (GCDA)
- GIAC Secure Software Programmer-.NET (GSSP-.NET)
- GIAC Defending Advanced Threats (GDAT)
- GIAC Certified Project Manager (GCPM)
- GIAC Security Expert (GSE)
- GIAC Critical Infrastructure Protection (GCIP)
- GIAC Defensible Security Architecture (GDSA)
- GIAC Enterprise Vulnerability Assessor (GEVA)

Computing Technology Industry Association

The *Computing Technology Industry Association (CompTIA)* is a nonprofit organization focused on continuous training in the information security and technology industry through training and certification. In addition to training, CompTIA releases research studies to track trends and changes in the industry. Following is a list of the CompTIA certifications:

- CompTIA IT Fundamentals (ITF+)
- CompTIA A+ (A+)
- CompTIA Network+ (Network+)
- CompTIA Security+ (Security+)
- CompTIA Cloud+ (Cloud+)
- CompTIA Linux+ (Linux+)
- CompTIA Server+ (Server+)
- CompTIA Cybersecurity Analyst (CySA+)
- CompTIA Advanced Security Practitioner (CASP+)
- CompTIA PenTest+ (PenTest+)
- CompTIA Project+ (Project+)
- CompTIA Certified Technical Trainer (CTT+)
- CompTIA Cloud Essentials+ (Cloud Essentials+)

International Association of Privacy Professionals

The *International Association of Privacy Professionals (IAPP)* is a nonprofit organization focused on providing a forum for privacy professionals to network, gain access to resources, and pursue privacy certifications. IAPP certifications include the following:

- Certified Information Privacy Professional/Asia (CIPP/A)
- Certified Information Privacy Professional/Canada (CIPP/Canada)
- Certified Information Privacy Professional/Europe (CIPP/E)
- Certified Information Privacy Professional/US Private-sector (CIPP/US)
- Certified Information Privacy Manager (CIPM)
- Certified Information Privacy Technologist (CIPT)

Offensive Security

Offensive Security is a security company focused on providing penetration testing professional services, training, certifications, and tools to the security community. Their courses focus on hand-on penetration testing and ethical hacking. Offensive Security developed the Kali Linux distribution with preinstalled penetration testing and forensic tools. Their certification programs include the following:

- Offensive Security Certified Professional (OSCP)
- Offensive Security Certified Expert (OSCE)
- Offensive Security Web Expert (OSWE)
- Offensive Security Wireless Professional (OSWP)
- Offensive Security Exploitation Expert (OSEE)

Ethics

Organizational ethics are the principles that govern the behavior of the organization, with a focus on acting with integrity, accountability, and responsibility. Ethics starts with the moral compass of the individual employee. However, companies and organizations cannot always trust employees to do the right thing. Therefore, many organizations have a code of ethics, ethics policies, and an ethics program in place. This sets the tone for the expected behavior of the board, executives, employees, and the organization as a whole. Ethics initiatives are sometimes tied into an organization's compliance initiatives and are a focus for internal compliance. Ultimately organizational ethics should mature beyond simply distributing a code of conduct to creating a culture of transparency, integrity, social responsibility, and sound governance.

The CISO is not usually responsible for the ethical conduct of the entire company or organization. However, many of the ethical decisions of the CISO and the security organization impact the company as a whole. Therefore, ethical polices, standards, and decisions must be well-coordinated between the CISO and the board and leadership.

The CISO is responsible for his or her own ethical conduct and that of their information security organization. The CISO must set the ethical standards for the information security program and staff. The CISO role in particular is one that must foster trust and credibility in the organization.

Ethics is sometimes considered in terms of the stakeholders involved. Typically the stakeholders are employees, customers, and owners/shareholders. These stakeholders are the recipients, or beneficiaries, of ethical conduct. Here are some examples of how ethics impacts information security operations and the role of the CISO:

- In conducting vulnerability and penetration testing, the information security staff discovers a previously unknown security flaw in a commercial product. In this case the security professionals are not under any legal obligation to report the flaw to the product manufacturer. However, reporting the flaw to the manufacturer would be the responsible thing to do. In this case ethics plays a role in the staff's behavior.

- The security staff believes that customer data may have been compromised, but they are not sure. Should the customers be notified? This is an ethical decision that should not be made on the spot—there should be policies and guidelines to follow that address the situation.

- A government agency requests that the organization disclose information related to a customer. If your organization is not required by law to comply, should it do so anyway? What is the ethical responsibility in this case, and to which stakeholder: the customer or the government agency?

The CISO should define and implement an ethics program within the security function, similar to the organization's compliance program, to ensure that ethics is well managed and that the conduct of the employees and the company meets the goals of the organization. An ethics program should have the following components:

- Set standards for ethical conduct within the information security organization
- Define ethics-related policies, standards, and guidelines
- Conduct ethics training for the information security staff
- Evaluate the performance and effectiveness of the program
- Maintain and improve ethical performance by applying lessons learned to the improvement of all aspects of the ethics program

CCISO candidates should be aware of the EC-Council Code of Ethics (https://www .eccouncil.org/code-of-ethics/), which is applicable to EC-Council certification holders and members. As part of the process of becoming a CCISO, the candidate must agree and adhere to the EC-Council Code of Ethics. The Code of Ethics outlines specific requirements for conduct as an information security professional.

Chapter Review

Organizational governance is the top-down definition of the strategy, organizational structure, and lines of authority of the organization. Likewise, information security governance is the definition of the goals and organization of the information security program. To be in alignment, both corporate governance and information security governance must take into account external and internal drivers such as regulations and industry practices. Key to the success of organizational and information security governance is good communication between the leaders of the organization, such as the CEO and the board, and the leader of the information security program, the CISO.

The information security program should be built to ensure that all three aspects of the confidentiality, integrity, and availability (CIA) triad are fulfilled, taking into account the organization's vulnerabilities, risks, threats, and exposures. This is accomplished by implementing defense-in-depth based on a risk management approach to ensure that the appropriate controls are selected to achieve the right balance of security versus cost. Information security programs generally include the following elements:

- Security program planning
- Security policies, standards, and guidelines
- Security risk management

- Asset security

- Identity and access management

- Security engineering

- Physical security

- Security operations

- Software development security

- Security assessments and testing

- Security training and awareness

- Business continuity and disaster recovery

Forms of business structures include sole proprietorships, partnerships, corporations, and LLCs. These forms of business provide some form of liability protection for the officers of the company in the event of a security breach or event. However, this protection is enabled only if the leaders fulfill their duty of care obligation and follow the business judgment rule in making information security–related decisions.

The information security program organizational structure can take many forms but it should provide clear lines of authority, situational awareness, and good internal and external communication and reporting.

The information security program is the mechanism to ensure compliance with external and internal business drivers. Many, but not all, organizations have a compliance program and a compliance team (or teams) to implement good compliance management. Compliance management can use industry models such as ISO 19600:2014 to help ensure compliance.

Quick Review

- Alignment of the organization's security program to the organization's business and operations is the key to the success of its security program and pivotal to the role of the CISO.

- Governance is accountability, authorization to make decisions, and oversight. Proper governance ensures that the organization's strategies are aligned with its business, regulatory, and operating environment.

- Information security governance is the framework for reducing information security risk to the organization.

- External drivers that shape the information security program include regulatory drivers, industry practices, and risks and threats.

- Internal drivers that shape the information security program include leadership understanding and perception, organizational structure, culture and climate, history, and lessons learned.

- The basic principles of information security are confidentiality, availability, and integrity.

- A vulnerability is a weakness that could potentially be exploited.
- A threat is any potential danger that is associated with the exploitation of a vulnerability.
- A risk is the likelihood of a threat agent exploiting a vulnerability and the corresponding business impact.
- An exposure is an instance of being exposed to a loss from a threat. A vulnerability can expose an organization to possible damages.
- A countermeasure (or a control) is put into place to mitigate a potential risk.
- Defense-in-depth is the concept that an organization should not rely on just one control for protection, but instead use layers of controls to increase the work factor of potential attackers.
- Risk management is the process of identifying and assessing risk, reducing it to an acceptable level, and implementing the right mechanisms to maintain that level.
- Organizations use either qualitative or quantitative methods to analyze risk.
- The security program typically has a collection of management security directives (policies, standards, guidelines) that form a library of rules and practices that the program personnel are to follow.
- Asset security is the concept of identifying what assets the organization has and determining what types of controls are appropriate for each.
- Access controls are security features that control how users and systems communicate and interact with other systems and resources.
- Security engineering is a vast domain that addresses the secure design and implementation of information systems.
- Security operations focus on actively performing day-to-day functions to prevent, detect, and respond to security risks and threats.
- Software must be developed in a manner that ensures it does not contain security vulnerabilities.
- All security programs must have an ongoing assessment and testing component to conduct vulnerability testing and ensure the successful performance and management of vulnerability remediation activities.
- All employees should be made aware of the organization's security policies and processes as well as good security practices in general.
- Every organization should have a plan and procedures in place to be able to ensure the business can continue to operate in the event of a security breach or other disaster.
- An information security organization should be sized based on the organization's tolerance for risk.
- The structure of the security organization should have the following elements: clear lines of authority, situational awareness, and internal and external communication and reporting.

- Compliance is an approach to governance designed to ensure alignment with applicable laws, regulations, standards, organizational policies, ethical conduct, and other business goals.

- Being compliant does not necessarily mean an organization is secure, and a good security program isn't necessarily compliant.

- The compliance team is typically involved in providing guidance on internal policies and procedures as well as evaluating current processes and technology to determine ways to improve compliance.

- Compliance management is the process by which an organization plans, implements, and maintains the activities that support compliance.

- Privacy indicates the level of control an individual should expect to have over their own sensitive data.

- The Federal Information Security Modernization Act (FISMA) requires US federal agencies to build, document, and implement an agency-wide information security program to support agency operations.

- The Clinger-Cohen Act of 1996 is a US federal law that applies to federal agencies focused on improving the acquisition, use, and disposal of information technology.

- The Gramm-Leach-Bliley Act (GLBA), also known as the Financial Services Modernization Act of 1999, requires financial institutions to protect individuals' nonpublic personal information.

- The Health Information Portability and Accountability Act (HIPAA) is a US federal regulation covering the handling of protected health information (PHI) and provides a framework for protecting the security and privacy of health information.

- The Family Educational Rights and Privacy Act of 1974 (FERPA) is a US federal law focused on protecting the privacy and confidentiality of student educational records.

- The Sarbanes-Oxley Act of 2002 (SOX) is a US federal law focused on holding board members and executives accountable for the accuracy of the financial statements of their organization.

- Organizational ethics are principles that govern the behavior of the organization, with a focus on acting with integrity, accountability, and responsibility.

Questions

1. Which of the following is the best way to determine if an information security program supports the organization's business objectives?

   A. Determine if the information security program plan or charter is consistent with the management strategy

   B. Determine if the information security program is adequately staffed

   C. Determine if the information security program is utilizing its people and equipment efficiently

   D. Determine if the information security program is able to easily adapt to change

2. A student compromises a system that contains test grades and changes her grade on a recent test from a D to A. Which of the following has been compromised?

   A. Integrity

   B. Availability

   C. Confidentiality

   D. Both availability and confidentiality

3. Which of the following is the most correct?

   A. A countermeasure is usually intended to reduce a threat.

   B. Risks, threats, and exposures are generally the same.

   C. Vulnerabilities are the result of poor password management.

   D. A countermeasure is a control that is put into place to mitigate a risk.

4. A CISO must define the rules by which the organization will meet its security objectives. Which document or set of documents is the best mechanism to accomplish this?

   A. Security program plan

   B. Security policies

   C. Security guidelines

   D. Security standards

5. Which of the following is most important when defining the organizational structure of an information security program?

   A. Ensuring the CISO reports directly to the CEO

   B. Showing clear lines of authority

   C. Using a matrix organization to ensure situational awareness

   D. Sizing the organization similar to other companies in the industry

6. Which of the following laws is focused specifically on the handling of protected health information?

   A. GLBA

   B. SOX

   C. HIPAA

   D. FISMA

7. An e-commerce site that accepts online payment is expanding and hires a CISO to ensure that the organization is complying with industry regulations and standards. Which of the following frameworks is of greatest concern to the CISO for ensuring compliance?

   A. SOX

   B. FISMA

C. ISO/IEC 27001

D. PCI DSS

8. An organization has a business need to receive personal data from citizens of the EU and needs guidance from the CISO on how to comply with EU privacy laws. Which of the following frameworks would be a good place for the CISO to start in order to fulfil this requirement?

A. Privacy Shield

B. FISMA

C. FIPS

D. SOX

9. An organization is looking for best practice guidance to secure its web applications. Which of the following organizations would be the best resource for the organization?

A. CSA

B. OWASP

C. CIS

D. IAPP

10. A publicly traded company collects cardholder data in the course of business operations. The organization's CEO recognizes the importance of information security and hires a CISO. Which of the following must the CISO ensure the business is compliant with?

A. GDPR and FISMA

B. PCI DSS and GDPR

C. PCI DSS and SOX

D. GDPR and SOX

Answers

1. **A.** While many of these answers might demonstrate the information security program's alignment with business objectives, the best way to determine if the information security strategy supports business objectives is to review the information security program plan or charter for consistency with the management strategy.

2. **A.** Integrity of a system is maintained when only authorized changes are permitted. In this case the student is not authorized to modify her own grade.

3. **D.** A countermeasure is put into place to mitigate a potential risk. Also called controls, countermeasures are features such as devices, configurations, or products that reduce the likelihood that a vulnerability could be exploited.

4. **B.** Security policies define the hard-and-fast rules that must be followed. The security program plan describes the overall security program and organizational structure, while guidelines and standards are supporting documents that are important but do not define requirements.

5. **B.** The organization should prioritize having clear lines of authority. The CISO does not always need to report to the CEO as long as there is good communication. A matrix type of organization is just one of several viable approaches. The organization should be sized according to its tolerance for risk, not based on comparisons to other companies.

6. **C.** The Health Information Portability and Accountability Act (HIPAA) is a US federal regulation that focuses specifically on the handling of protected health information (PHI). HIPAA provides a framework for protecting the security and privacy of health information. The rules in HIPAA apply to covered entities and business associates.

7. **D.** The Payment Card Industry Data Security Standard (PCI DSS) is a control framework focused on the protection of credit card information. PCI DSS applies to any organization that handles cardholder data.

8. **A.** The EU-US and Swiss-US Privacy Shield Frameworks exist to regulate exchanges of personal information from the European Union and Switzerland to the United States. The goal of Privacy Shield is to enable US companies to receive personal data from the EU while complying with EU privacy laws.

9. **B.** The Open Web Application Security Project (OWASP) is an international organization focused on enabling organizations with the skills and tools to plan, develop, acquire, operate, and maintain secure applications. OWASP develops tools, guides, best practice documents, and organized conferences focused on application security.

10. **C.** The CISO must ensure that the organization is compliant with PCI DSS and SOX. The Sarbanes-Oxley Act (SOX) applies to all publicly traded companies doing business in the United States. The Payment Card Industry Data Security Standard (PCI DSS) applies to any organization that handles cardholder data. Since the organization is both a publicly traded company and handles cardholder data, the organization must be compliant with both.

Information Security Controls, Compliance, and Audit Management

This chapter discusses the following topics:
- Information security controls
- Information security control life cycle frameworks
- Information security control life cycle
- Exploring information security control frameworks
- Auditing for the CISO

Chapter 1 introduced the concept of risk management, in which an organization performs a risk analysis of the entire enterprise to understand each asset's importance to the business. An asset is an information system, a facility, data, or any component (hardware, software, or data) used to support operations. This chapter explores how an organization goes about selecting and auditing security controls for a given asset. *Security controls* are processes or technologies put into place to address risks. Implementing a strong password policy, encrypting data at rest, and capturing events using logging are just a few examples of security controls. For a given information system or asset, hundreds of controls may be put into place. Organizations can develop their own definitions of controls; however, an approach that is simpler and less resource intensive is to use existing industry standard frameworks that provide libraries of controls along with guidelines for how to select them. The frameworks are typically used in a similar manner and generally follow the same process:

1. The first step is to categorize the asset or system using a model of defined categories. Usually the categories are defined by simply rating each security characteristic (confidentiality, availability, and integrity) of the asset with a security rating, which may be as simple as low, moderate, or high.

2. Based on the category of the asset, select the corresponding set of security controls that can be put into place to achieve the correct security. Frameworks often provide a method to map categories to suggested lists of controls.

3. Sometimes the organization tailors the set of controls suggested by the framework to the organization's specific needs and operational and business environment.

4. Once the controls are selected, they are then implemented, assessed, audited, and monitored for the life of the asset.

This chapter explores security controls, the security control life cycle, commonly used security control frameworks, and the auditing of controls.

Information Security Controls

This section introduces foundational details about information security controls, including control classes, control functionalities, and types of control frameworks.

Control Fundamentals

A security control, also known as a safeguard or countermeasure, is a mechanism put in place to mitigate risk and protect the confidentiality, integrity, and availability (CIA) of an asset. This section reviews fundamental terminology such as control class and control functionality.

Control Classes

Controls can be grouped into *classes*, the names of which vary depending on the framework used. In practice, the three classes that are most often used are *administrative*, *technical*, and *physical*. However, NIST uses a different set of classes, *management*, *operational*, and *technical*. Different organizations use different terminology. Here is a description of the terms used most often:

- **Administrative** Management-oriented controls such as policies, procedures, guidelines, training, risk management, and employment practices (hiring, firing, and so on). Administrative controls are also referred to as soft controls or managerial controls.

- **Technical** Hardware or software components that provide security control functionality. Examples include encryption, password enforcement, multifactor authentication, intrusion detection systems (IDSs), intrusion prevention systems (IPSs), and firewalls. Technical controls are also referred to as logical controls.

- **Physical** Tangible controls put in place to protect people, assets, and facilities against physical threats. This includes protecting people, assets, and facilities. Examples include fencing, lighting, locks, bollards, server room doors, alarms, and security guards.

As discussed, NIST defines a different set of classes. FIPS 200, *Minimum Security Requirements for Federal Information and Information Systems*, and NIST SP 800-53 Rev. 3, *Security and Privacy Controls for Federal Information Systems and Organizations* (and prior versions), use the control classes *management*, *operational*, and *technical*. Each of these classes are defined by NIST as follows:

- **Management**   The security controls (i.e., safeguards or countermeasures) for an information system that focus on the management of risk and the management of information system security.

- **Operational**   The security controls (i.e., safeguards or countermeasures) for an information system that are primarily implemented and executed by people (as opposed to systems).

- **Technical**   The security controls (i.e., safeguards or countermeasures) for an information system that are primarily implemented and executed by the information system through mechanisms contained in the hardware, software, or firmware components of the system.

There is not a one-to-one mapping of the general control classes (administrative, technical, and physical) to the NIST control classes (management, operational, and technical), with the exception of the technical classes. Some controls, such as risk management, are administrative and management controls. Other controls, such as employee termination, are administrative and operational controls.

Table 2-1 shows NIST SP 800-53 security control classes and their corresponding families of controls. A *control family* is a grouping of controls that typically address the same security domain or function. For example, controls that address access control reside in the Access Control (AC) family of NIST SP 800-53. EC-Council's view is that

	Control Class	**NIST Control Family**
Table 2-1 NIST SP 800-53 Control Classes and Corresponding Control Families	**Management**	Security Assessment and Authorization (CA) Planning (PL) Risk Assessment (RA) System and Services Acquisition (SA) Program Management (PM)
	Operational	Awareness and Training (AT) Configuration Management (CM) Contingency Planning (CP) Incident Response (IR) Maintenance (MA) Media Protection (MP) Physical and Environmental Protection (PE) Personnel Security (PS) System and Information Integrity (SI)
	Technical	Access Control (AC) Audit and Accountability (AU) Identification and Authentication (IA) System and Communications Protection (SC)

CCISO candidates should be familiar with the mapping shown in the table. However, the latest version of NIST SP 800-53 (Rev. 4) does not contain this mapping because, in practice, many controls in a control family map to more than one control class.

 EXAM TIP CCISO candidates should be familiar with NIST control classes and control families.

Control Functionality

The terms administrative, technical, and physical address the class of the control but not how the control operates and functions. Security controls can be broken down based on their makeup and functionality. Security functionality of controls describes what the controls do for the organization. Functionalities of controls include the following:

- **Preventive** These types of controls prevent or stop the occurrence of an adverse event or incident. Examples include mandatory background checks, firewall access control lists (ACLs), door locks, fences, bollards, and IPSs.

- **Detective** These types of controls discover, detect, or identify a potential adverse activity, event, intruder, or incident. Examples include IDSs, security log review, mandatory vacations, and reviewing events captured on surveillance cameras.

- **Deterrent** These types of controls deter or discourage a potential adversary from performing an attack or engaging in unwanted behavior. Examples include system warning banners and warning signs.

- **Corrective** These types of controls correct adverse events that have occurred by fixing a system, process, or activity. Examples include IPSs, terminating an employee after an offense, antivirus that quarantines malicious software, using a fire extinguisher to extinguish a fire, and implementing a business continuity plan or incident response plan.

- **Directive** These types of controls are typically administrative controls that communicate expected behavior by specifying what actions are or are not permitted. Examples include security policies, standards, and procedures.

- **Recovery** These types of controls restore an environment or operations back to regular functionality. They are similar in function to corrective controls but are thought of as having advanced capability. Examples include restoring a system from backup, removing malware from an infected system, and utilizing a watchdog process that can determine that a service has stalled and restart it.

- **Compensating** These types of controls serve as an alternate or secondary control implementation to a primary control. These are often used when the primary control is not feasible to implement due to cost, complexity, or other business constraints. Examples include implementing network isolation of business-critical applications that cannot be patched and installing fences, locks, and alarms after a determination that a full-time security guard is too expensive.

EXAM TIP A control can be associated with more than one control functionality. For example, an IPS could be considered both preventive and corrective and fencing could be considered both preventive and deterrent, depending on the context and how the question is presented.

Control Frameworks

A *control framework* is a catalog of controls used to provide a foundation to aid in the implementation of a comprehensive information security program. Control frameworks are useful in assessing, planning, implementing, and documenting how and what security controls are implemented in the organization. Without a control framework, additional time and effort would need to be spent designing controls and developing a methodology for implementation.

Types of Frameworks

Many different types of frameworks are used by security professionals, but there are three fundamental types:

- **Process model** Describes how to implement security controls (examples include NIST RMF, ISO/IEC 27001, and NIST CSF).

- **Determinant** Describes what to implement, such as a library of controls (examples include NIST SP 800-53, ISO/IEC 27001/27002, CIS Top 20, and NIST CSF).

- **Evaluation** Describes how to assess the implementation and can therefore be used for auditing (examples include NIST SP 800-53A, ISO/IEC 27007, and ISO/IEC 27008).

Some frameworks may consist of only one of these characteristics while others may consist of all three or may utilize or reference other frameworks to achieve other functions. For example, the NIST Risk Management Framework (process model framework) utilizes NIST SP 800-53 (determinant framework) and NIST SP 800-53A (evaluation framework) as part of the life cycle process steps.

EXAM TIP The terms process model, determinant, and evaluation are used here simply to discuss and categorize the different types of control frameworks; these terms might not appear on the actual CCISO exam.

Selecting a Control Framework

The following are some of the most common control frameworks selected by organizations that are interested in utilizing a framework instead of building one from scratch:

- NIST SP 800-53
- NIST Cybersecurity Framework (CSF)
- ISO/IEC 27001/27002

- CIS Critical Security Controls/CIS Top 20
- CSA Cloud Controls Matrix

Each of these frameworks is discussed in greater depth later in this chapter.

Organizations select a framework based on a variety of organizational drivers and factors, including the following:

- Laws and regulations
- Industry vertical (for example, US federal government, critical infrastructure, and so on)
- Compliance requirements (for example, PCI DSS, SOX, GDPR, and so on)
- Competitive edge (for example, ISO/IEC 27001)
- Breadth of framework coverage
- Prior experience of security team (for example, comfort with or preference for a specific framework)
- Other business objectives or requirements

For example, a security professional working in the US federal government will eat, sleep, and breathe the NIST Risk Management Framework (process model) and NIST SP 800-53 (determinant framework). A security professional in the private sector may be utilizing a framework based on the organization's industry or compliance requirements or simply because that was the framework the organization previously chose. Part of the CISO's job is to evaluate the framework the organization is using or considering to determine if it is the best fit for the organization and enables the achievement of key business goals and objectives.

Information Security Control Life Cycle Frameworks

Security professionals select the right controls by following a life cycle that typically includes risk assessment, design, implementation, assessment, and monitoring. Using a life cycle framework helps an organization by defining a formal control implementation process. Without a defined process, control implementation is typically done in an ad hoc fashion. This may work for small organizations. However, as an organization grows larger and its control requirements and environment become more complex, a structured control life cycle process becomes more important. The best practice is to use a formalized process regardless of the size of the organization. This section explores some of the most well-known life cycles from process model frameworks.

NIST Risk Management Framework

One example of a control life cycle is the NIST Risk Management Framework (NIST RMF or RMF). The RMF is used primarily by US federal government agencies for the implementation of controls in accordance with FISMA (introduced in Chapter 1). Documented in NIST SP 800-37, the RMF is a process that integrates risk management and information security into the security control selection and implementation process. The RMF is a cyclical six-step life cycle with an additional prepare component:

Prepare.

1. Categorize the information system.

2. Select the applicable security control baseline.

3. Implement and document the security controls.

4. Assess the security controls.

5. Authorize information system operation.

6. Monitor the security controls in the information system.

NIST Cybersecurity Framework

The NIST Cybersecurity Framework (NIST CSF or CSF), discussed in Chapter 1, is a risk-based cybersecurity framework that was originally designed for critical infrastructure but has been adopted by many different organizations. The CSF has a specific methodology for implementing the framework that consists of seven steps:

1. Prioritize and scope.

2. Orient.

3. Create a current profile.

4. Conduct a risk assessment.

5. Create a target profile.

6. Determine, analyze, and prioritize gaps.

7. Implement action plan.

ISO/IEC 27000

ISO/IEC 27000 series publications, known as the information security management systems (ISMS) family of standards, use the Plan, Do, Check, Act (PDCA) life cycle for the implementation of security controls as part of an ISMS.

- **Plan**   Establish an ISMS.
- **Do**   Implement and operate the ISMS.
- **Check**   Monitor and review the ISMS.
- **Act**   Maintain and improve the ISMS.

Information Security Control Life Cycle

The previous section discussed several established security control life cycle frameworks. Some organizations tailor their own life cycle by combining concepts from several different frameworks and methodologies as part of their information security program. Here we walk through a life cycle derived from NIST RMF, NIST CSF, and ISO/IEC 27000. The process consists of five steps:

1. Risk assessment

2. Design

3. Implementation

4. Assessment

5. Monitoring

 NOTE Part of the CISO's role is to oversee and supervise the control life cycle process to ensure that objectives are met and projects are executed within the defined budget, scope, and timeline. The CISO is also responsible for ensuring that progress is communicated to key stakeholders with a vested interest in the project (for example, system owner, executive team, board of directors, and so on).

Step 1: Risk Assessment

The first step is to perform a risk assessment to gain a wholistic perspective of the risks associated with an asset that needs to be protected. The risk assessment may be guided by previous risk assessments or by the organization's risk management process. The risk assessment provides the organization with an understanding of the threat landscape for a particular asset. This includes the following:

- The perceived value of the asset
- Threats and vulnerabilities
- Likelihood and impact of security compromise

Without a proper risk assessment the organization may end up implementing controls that do not address the actual threats, implement a control that costs more than the asset that is being protected, or fail to provide the level of security appropriate for the asset based on the organization's risk appetite. The risk assessment identifies risks, thereby allowing for informed decisions to be made regarding the design of the right controls for the job. While risk assessment is part of the control life cycle, the formal risk management process is covered in detail in the "Risk Management" section in Chapter 1.

NIST Security Categorization

The NIST Risk Management Framework uses FIPS 199, *Standards for Security Categorization of Federal Information and Information Systems*, as part of the risk assessment to determine the level of security required for the information or information system based on potential impact. This occurs during the "Categorize" step of the RMF process life cycle. Table 2-2 provides an overview of the potential impact definitions in FIPS 199 for each security objective. In the RMF, the potential impact is used to determine the level of security required for the information systems (low, moderate, or high). This determines the security controls that the organization will implement from NIST SP 800-53.

Security Objective	Potential Impact		
	Low	**Moderate**	**High**
Confidentiality	The unauthorized disclosure of information could be expected to have a **limited** adverse effect on organizational operations, organizational assets, or individuals.	The unauthorized disclosure of information could be expected to have a **serious** adverse effect on organizational operations, organizational assets, or individuals.	The unauthorized disclosure of information could be expected to have a **severe or catastrophic** adverse effect on organizational operations, organizational assets, or individuals.
Integrity	The unauthorized modification or destruction of information could be expected to have a **limited** adverse effect on organizational operations, organizational assets, or individuals.	The unauthorized modification or destruction of information could be expected to have a **serious** adverse effect on organizational operations, organizational assets, or individuals.	The unauthorized modification or destruction of information could be expected to have a **severe or catastrophic** adverse effect on organizational operations, organizational assets, or individuals.
Availability	The disruption of access to or use of information or an information system could be expected to have a **limited** adverse effect on organizational operations, organizational assets, or individuals.	The disruption of access to or use of information or an information system could be expected to have a **serious** adverse effect on organizational operations, organizational assets, or individuals.	The disruption of access to or use of information or an information system could be expected to have a **severe or catastrophic** adverse effect on organizational operations, organizational assets, or individuals.

Table 2-2 FIPS 199 Potential Impact Definitions for Security Objectives

Step 2: Design

The risk assessment enables the organization to design the proper security controls based on the risk identified as well as the operational needs and goals of the organization. The primary goals of the design phase are as follows:

- **Control selection**   Select controls to address risks identified in the risk assessment that align with the goals, objectives, and needs of the organization.
- **Control design**   Identify resources required for control implementation and maintenance (for example, financial, staffing, architectural, and so on).
- **Control testing**   Test controls before they are implemented in production to ensure control efficacy.

Control Selection

The organization may elect to design a control from scratch or utilize a control framework. The control frameworks provide lists of the specific controls that should be implemented based on the risk assessment of the asset. Instead of, or in conjunction with, control frameworks, controls may be selected based on best practice recommendations, experience, judgement, or budget requirements in order to mitigate identified risk.

Consideration should also be given as to whether the control will be automated or manual:

- **Automated**   Control exercised by an automated system with limited to no human interaction. Examples of tools and techniques for control automation include automated fire suppression, security information and event management (SIEM) alerts, and IPSs.
- **Manual**   Control exercised by a person without direct use of automation. Examples include policies, standards, procedures, training, and visitor logs.

Most information systems use a combination of both manual and automated controls. In addition, while some control processes may be manual, such as updates to security policies, there may be automated techniques that can assist such as the use of a governance, risk management, and compliance (GRC) system to automate policy review and approval workflows and send reminders to perform annual reviews.

Control Design

A critical part of the control design process is determining and planning the resources required to implement and operationalize the control. Even when a control framework is used, there are still many design factors to consider and document, including the following:

- Budget and scope
- Personnel and staffing requirements
- Infrastructure and architecture requirements (for example, OS, applications, hardware, tools, and so on)

- Ongoing control costs and maintenance (for example, maintenance, support, monitoring, and so on)
- Staff responsible for design, implementation, assessment, and monitoring of the control
- Communication plan to inform stakeholders of project status
- Development of metrics for measuring control success

Control Testing

Part of the control design process should also include testing the control before it is put into production to ensure the efficacy of the control and that it will not have negative impacts to the environment. In addition, a backout plan should be developed in case control implementation has a negative impact on the environment. While the assessment phase of the life cycle occurs after the implementation phase, this does not negate the need to test as part of the design process prior to implementation. The assessment phase of the life cycle is an ongoing phase that ensures the control is continuously assessed.

Step 3: Implementation

The next step is the implementation of the controls in order to mitigate risk identified in the risk assessment. Once controls are designed, it is time to execute on the projects outlined in the design phase. Implementation may be simple or complex depending on the control in question. For example, developing a password security policy is much less time and resource intensive than standing up a vulnerability management program. Depending on the control in question, implementation may require changes to the following:

- Policy, standards, and procedures
- Business process or workflows
- Information system or software architecture

When multiple controls are being implemented, it is necessary to prioritize control implementation. Prioritization should be determined using a risk-based approach to ensure that the appropriate assets are being protected and that priority is given to assets that are important to achieving the goals of the business. As part of implementation, it is crucial to maintain documentation of the control to ensure appropriate detail exists for control design, development, implementation, and expected behavior.

 NOTE A key responsibility of the CISO role is oversight of the security program, which includes supervising the control implementation process to ensure that the controls are implemented and documented in a timely manner, are within budget and scope of the project, and address the intended purpose. In addition, communication is a key component of implementation, as the proper stakeholders should be kept up to date on the status of project implementation.

> ## Documentation Example
> One of the methods used for control documentation is the development of a system security plan (SSP), which describes and documents how controls are implemented for a given system. An SSP typically contains, at a minimum, the following:
>
> - **Description**   A description of the system, including name, purpose, information owner, custodians, security categorization, data flows, and so on
> - **Environment and boundaries**   A description of the boundary of the system environment, including description of the architecture, topology, hardware and software assets, ports, protocols, services, and so on
> - **Security control implementation**   A description of how each applicable security control is implemented as well as the implementation status of each control

Step 4: Assessment

Control assessment is an ongoing phase of the life cycle. Controls must be assessed to ensure that they are effective, implemented and operating correctly, addressing their intended purpose, and operating in accordance with the organization's policies, standards, and procedures. The assessment phase consists of three main components:

- Assessment and testing
- Reporting
- Remediation

Assessment and Testing

There are different types of assessments, including the following:

- Internal audits
- External audits
- Control self-assessments

The fundamental techniques to assess a control include examination, interview, and testing. The following definitions for these terms have been modified from NIST 800-53 to make them applicable to any control framework:

- **Examination**   Reviewing, inspecting, observing, or analyzing a process or control to ensure that it performs and executes as expected and aligns with the control objective.
- **Interview**   Holding discussions with key individuals or stakeholders within an organization to facilitate understanding or obtain evidence of how a process or control is operating.

- **Testing**   Exercising one or more control objectives to compare actual results with expected behavior. Testing consists of "hands-on" assessment of a control.

An organization will utilize one or more of these methodologies in the assessment of its controls.

Reporting

After an assessment has been completed, any deficiencies discovered should be documented and analyzed. The findings should state what aspect of the control was not operating as expected and how the implementation differs from what was planned or expected. The findings produced by the assessment are used to determine the overall effectiveness of the controls associated with the asset that was evaluated. Assessment results typically are reviewed by the information owner and senior management (CISO, executive leadership, and so on) to determine the appropriate course of action to remedy the situation in a timely manner. The results of the assessment should include the following:

- List of applicable controls
- Assessment and test plans for the controls
- Report indicating pass or fail per control tested
- Identification of corrective action and mitigation required for deficiencies

Remediation

Remediation begins after findings have been documented and a process to remedy the situation has been identified. The remediation activities and methodology are typically determined by many vested stakeholders (information owner, custodian, system maintainers, CISO, and others as required). Remediation is typically prioritized based on a variety of factors, including the following:

- Resources required for remediation
- Risk and severity level of the asset
- Risk associated with the finding
- Scope of the finding
- Type of assessment (internal versus external audit)
- Visibility of the finding internally and externally to the organization

Depending on the criticality or risk associated with the finding, the organization will typically have a policy outlining the expected remediation window. The remediation window may also be provided if the finding was the result of a regulatory audit.

 NOTE   When making any changes to the environment, it is important to have a backout plan in place. This should be created and documented before undergoing remediation implementation efforts. Always have a backout plan in place before making any changes in case remediation efforts go south.

> ## NIST Security Assessment Procedure Example
> Assessment and testing methodologies may be outlined in the control framework the organization has chosen to utilize. For example, an organization using NIST SP 800-53, *Security and Privacy Controls for Federal Information Systems and Organizations* (a determinant framework) can utilize NIST SP 800-53A, *Assessing Security and Privacy Controls in Federal Information Systems and Organizations: Building Effective Assessment Plans* (an evaluation framework). Figure 2-1 shows an example of a control and assessment procedure from NIST SP 800-53A Rev. 4 for the CP-9 Information System Backup control.
>
> NIST SP 800-53A contains detailed assessment procedures that include one or more assessment objectives. Each assessment objective is associated with the assessment methods (examine, interview, and test) and defines how the assessment team should assess the control.

Step 5: Monitoring

The final phase of the security control life cycle is continuous monitoring. Controls must be monitored on a continuous basis to determine the following:

- Control performance and effectiveness
- Alignment with organization strategies and objectives
- Changes to information systems and environment
- Compliance with legislation, regulation, and organizational policy and procedures

The focus in this phase shifts from implementing security to maintaining security going forward. It is important to consider the monitoring component in the design phase to ensure that the controls can be monitored, and that consideration is given as to how monitoring will occur. Without proper monitoring, the organization will struggle to ensure that the control is operating and performing effectively. To effectively monitor a control, S.M.A.R.T. metrics should be developed. *S.M.A.R.T.* stands for specific, measurable, actionable, relevant, and timely.

- **Specific**   Metric is clear, well defined, and targeted to the control being measured
- **Measurable**   Metric can be measured and data is accurate and complete
- **Actionable**   Metric data is easy to understand and take action on it
- **Relevant**   Metric must be relevant and provide meaningful data about the control
- **Timely**   Metric data is available when needed

The S.M.A.R.T. methodology aids in the development of meaningful metrics and key performance indicators. A *key performance indicator (KPI)* is a metric that measures

CP-9	INFORMATION SYSTEM BACKUP	
ASSESSMENT OBJECTIVE Determine if the organization:		
CP-9(a)	CP-9(a)[1]	defines a frequency, consistent with recovery time objectives and recovery point objectives as specified in the information system contingency plan, to conduct backups of user-level information contained in the information system;
	CP-9(a)[2]	conducts backups of user-level information contained in the information system with the organization-defined frequency;
CP-9(b)	CP-9(b)[1]	defines a frequency, consistent with recovery time objectives and recovery point objectives as specified in the information system contingency plan, to conduct backups of system-level information contained in the information system;
	CP-9(b)[2]	conducts backups of system-level information contained in the information system with the organization-defined frequency;
CP-9(c)	CP-9(c)[1]	defines a frequency, consistent with recovery time objectives and recovery point objectives as specified in the information system contingency plan, to conduct backups of information system documentation including security-related documentation;
	CP-9(c)[2]	conducts backups of information system documentation, including security-related documentation, with the organization-defined frequency; and
CP-9(d)	protects the confidentiality, integrity, and availability of backup information at storage locations.	

POTENTIAL ASSESSMENT METHODS AND OBJECTS:

Examine: [*SELECT FROM:* Contingency planning policy; procedures addressing information system backup; contingency plan; backup storage location(s); information system backup logs or records; other relevant documents or records].

Interview: [*SELECT FROM:* Organizational personnel with information system backup responsibilities; organizational personnel with information security responsibilities].

Test: [*SELECT FROM:* Organizational processes for conducting information system backups; automated mechanisms supporting and/or implementing information system backups].

Figure 2-1 NIST SP 800-53A Control and Assessment Procedure example (Source: NIST)

how effective the organization is at performing a specific task. In this context, a KPI is a metric that measures the performance of a control. KPIs are also used to measure strategic security program–wide goals and objectives. As part of control monitoring, documenting control performance and metrics is important not only so that reports can be generated showing how controls are performing and meeting objectives but also so that deviations from expected behavior can be addressed. The monitoring phase allows for control status reports to be developed and shared with key stakeholders to support decision making and ensure that the control is meeting the organization requirements and objectives.

Monitoring is an important aspect of the security control life cycle because threats are constantly changing. Organizations must continuously monitor the controls, as well as the environment for new threats, and identify and implement appropriate controls to mitigate associated risk using the control life cycle.

Exploring Information Security Control Frameworks

This section explores the makeup and structure of some of the most commonly used information security control frameworks:

- NIST SP 800-53
- NIST Cybersecurity Framework
- ISO/IEC 27002
- CIS Critical Security Controls
- CSA Cloud Controls Matrix

While this is by no means an exhaustive list, these are some of the prevalent frameworks. Some of these frameworks were briefly covered in Chapter 1 through the lens of governance, compliance, standards, and best practice frameworks. This section dives deeper into the frameworks to explore the control framework structure, including the controls and control families. Control frameworks generally follow a similar structure for how they are organized and may include some or all of the following components:

- **Control family**   A group of controls covering a specific domain (for example, Access Control, Risk Management, and so on). This may be known as a control, control family, control group, or control category depending on the framework.
- **Control family identifier**   Unique identifier for the control family, which may be a combination of letters or numbers (for example, AC, RM, 1, A.1, and so on).
- **Control name**   The name of an individual control that may or may not be part of a control family (for example, Access Control Policy and Procedures, Change Management, Documented Operating Procedures, and so on). An individual control may be referred to as a control, subcontrol, or subcategory depending on the framework.
- **Control identifier**   Unique identifier for the control (which may also include the control family identifier; for example, AC-1, ID.RM-1, ID.RM-2, A.12.1.1, 12.1.1, and so on).
- **Control description**   A description of the control, including its function. Some frameworks may include only a description of the control that is to be implemented and not a control name.
- **Supplemental guidance**   Guidance, references, or addition information for a specific control to utilize as part of implementation.
- **Assessment guidance**   Guidance on how to assess the control.

- **Control mappings** Informative references or sections showing how controls are mapped to controls in other frameworks.

EXAM TIP CCISO candidates should be familiar with commonly used information security control frameworks.

NIST SP 800-53

NIST SP 800-53, *Security and Privacy Controls for Federal Information Systems and Organizations*, is a well-known NIST publication consisting of a catalog of security and privacy controls used to assist US federal government agencies in meeting the requirements of FISMA and serves as a best practice framework for other, non-federal entities.

NIST controls are organized into 18 different control families, listed in Table 2-3. In addition to these control families, a Privacy Control Catalog was added in SP 800-53 Rev. 4 (Appendix J) to address the ever-growing concerns around privacy and to establish a link between the relationship of security and privacy controls.

The controls are further grouped into control baselines based on potential impact (low, moderate, and high) and priority codes used to assist in determining the priority for control implementation (from NIST 800-53: "a Priority Code 1 [P1] control has a higher priority for implementation than a Priority Code 2 [P2] control, a Priority Code 2 [P2] control has a higher priority for implementation than a Priority Code 3 [P3] control, and a Priority Code 0 [P0] indicates the security control is not selected in any baseline"). For US federal agencies, baselines are selected based on guidance in FIPS 199, *Standards for Security Categorization of Federal Information and Information Systems*.

NIST controls follow a specific convention and format. NIST 800-53 controls consist of the following sections, the descriptions for which are from Rev. 4:

- **Control** Prescribes specific security-related activities or actions to be carried out by organizations or by information systems
- **Supplemental Guidance** Provides non-prescriptive, additional information for a specific security control

ID	Family	ID	Family
AC	Access Control	MP	Media Protection
AT	Awareness and Training	PE	Physical and Environmental Protection
AU	Audit and Accountability	PL	Planning
CA	Security Assessment and Authorization	PS	Personnel Security
CM	Configuration Management	RA	Risk Assessment
CP	Contingency Planning	SA	System and Services Acquisition
IA	Identification and Authentication	SC	System and Communications Protection
IR	Incident Response	SI	System and Information Integrity
MA	Maintenance	PM	Program Management

Table 2-3 NIST SP 800-53 Security Control Families

- **Control Enhancements** Provides statements of security capability to: (i) add functionality/specificity to a control; and/or (ii) increase the strength of a control (provide greater protection than the base control)

- **References** Includes a list of applicable federal laws, Executive Orders, directives, policies, regulations, standards, and guidelines that are relevant to a particular control

- **Priority and Baseline Allocation** Provides: (i) the recommended priority codes used for sequencing decision during security control implementation; and (ii) the initial allocation of security controls and control enhancements to the baselines

The example in Figure 2-2 is from the Auditing and Accountability family of NIST 800-53. This figure illustrates the structure of a typical NIST security control.

NIST Cybersecurity Framework

The NIST Cybersecurity Framework (NIST CSF or CSF) is a voluntary security framework to assist organizations in managing security risk and facilitating communication among stakeholders. The three main components of NIST CSF were introduced in Chapter 1 and are summarized here for your review:

- **Framework Core** Composed of five functions: Identify, Protect, Detect, Respond, and Recover. Each function is composed of categories, which are made up of subcategories and references.

- **Framework Implementation Tiers** Range from Partial (Tier 1), Risk Informed (Tier 2), Repeatable (Tier 3), to Adaptive (Tier 4). While the tiers appear to be maturity levels, they are meant to be contextual references for communication around risk appetite, mission priority, and budget.

- **Framework Profiles** Represent an organization's alignment of resources, requirements, and risk appetite with the desired outcomes of the Framework Core (functions, categories, subcategories, and references). Profiles are used to evaluate the "Current" state of an organization with a "Target" state.

The NIST Cybersecurity Framework Core consists of the following components:

- **Functions** High-level cybersecurity activity groupings consisting of five functions (Identify, Protect, Detect, Respond, and Recover)

- **Categories** Subdivisions of each function into control family groupings (for example, Asset Management, Governance, Risk Management Strategy, and so on)

- **Subcategories** Subdivisions of a category into specific activities (for example, ID.AM-1: Physical devices and systems within the organization are inventoried, ID.RM-1: Risk management processes are established, managed, and agreed to by organizational stakeholders, and so on)

- **Informative references** Map each subcategory to other control frameworks (for example, CIS Critical Security Controls, COBIT 5, ISO/IEC 27001: 2013, NIST SP 800-53 Rev. 4)

AU-3	CONTENT OF AUDIT RECORDS

Control: The information system generates audit records containing information that establishes what type of event occurred, when the event occurred, where the event occurred, the source of the event, the outcome of the event, and the identity of any individuals or subjects associated with the event.

Supplemental Guidance: Audit record content that may be necessary to satisfy the requirement of this control includes, for example, time stamps, source and destination addresses, user/process identifiers, event descriptions, success/fail indications, filenames involved, and access control or flow control rules invoked. Event outcomes can include indicators of event success or failure and event-specific results (e.g., the security state of the information system after the event occurred). Related controls: AU-2, AU-8, AU-12, SI-11.

Control Enhancements:

(1) CONTENT OF AUDIT RECORDS | ADDITIONAL AUDIT INFORMATION

The information system generates audit records containing the following additional information: [*Assignment: organization-defined additional, more detailed information*].

Supplemental Guidance: Detailed information that organizations may consider in audit records includes, for example, full-text recording of privileged commands or the individual identities of group account users. Organizations consider limiting the additional audit information to only that information explicitly needed for specific audit requirements. This facilitates the use of audit trails and audit logs by not including information that could potentially be misleading or could make it more difficult to locate information of interest.

(2) CONTENT OF AUDIT RECORDS | CENTRALIZED MANAGEMENT OF PLANNED AUDIT RECORD CONTENT

The information system provides centralized management and configuration of the content to be captured in audit records generated by [*Assignment: organization-defined information system components*].

Supplemental Guidance: This control enhancement requires that the content to be captured in audit records be configured from a central location (necessitating automation). Organizations coordinate the selection of required audit content to support the centralized management and configuration capability provided by the information system. Related controls: AU-6, AU-7.

References: None.

Priority and Baseline Allocation:

P1	**LOW** AU-3	**MOD** AU-3 (1)	**HIGH** AU-3 (1) (1)

Figure 2-2 NIST 800-53 Control example (Source: NIST)

Function ID	Function	Category ID	Category
ID	Identify	ID.AM	Asset Management
		ID.BE	Business Environment
		ID.GV	Governance
		ID.RA	Risk Assessment
		ID.RM	Risk Management Strategy
		ID.SC	Supply Chain Risk Management
PR	Protect	PR.AC	Identity Management and Access Control
		PR.AT	Awareness and Training
		PR.DS	Data Security
		ID.IP	Information Protection Processes and Procedures
		PR.MA	Maintenance
		PR.PT	Protective Technology
DE	Detect	DE.AE	Anomalies and Events
		DE.CM	Security Continuous Monitoring
		DE.DP	Detection Processes
RS	Respond	RS.RP	Response Planning
		RS.CO	Communications
		RS.AN	Analysis
		RS.MI	Mitigation
		RS.IM	Improvements
RC	Recover	RC.RP	Recovery Planning
		RC.IM	Improvements
		RC.CO	Communications

Table 2-4 NIST Cybersecurity Framework Functions and Category Identifiers

Each function, category, and subcategory is assigned a unique ID. Table 2-4 illustrates the breakdown of the functions and categories as well as the corresponding identifiers.

Figure 2-3 provides an illustration of a sample component of the NIST CSF Framework Core using the Risk Management Strategy category as an example. The Risk Management Strategy (ID.RM) category is organized in the Identify (ID) function and is made up of three subcategories (ID.RM-1, ID.RM-2, and ID.RM-3), each of which includes the informative references mappings.

ISO/IEC 27002

As discussed in Chapter 1, ISO/IEC 27001, *Information technology – Security techniques – Information security management systems – Requirements*, is a best practice framework used for implementing an information security management system (ISMS) and determining which controls to adopt. ISO/IEC 27002, *Information technology – Security techniques – Code of practice for information security controls*, is a supplementary standard focused on recommended controls that the organization may decide to implement to address security objectives. A summary of ISO/IEC 27002 controls is included in Annex A of ISO/IEC 27001 but describes each control in only a few sentences. ISO/IEC 27002 on the other hand goes into much greater detail, discussing each control, how the control works, what the control objective is, and how to implement the control. Unlike ISO/IEC

Function	IDENTIFY (ID)	
Category	**Risk Management Strategy (ID.RM):** The organization's priorities, constraints, risk tolerances, and assumptions are established and used to support operational risk decisions.	
Subcategory	**Informative References**	
ID.RM-1: Risk management processes are established, managed, and agreed to by organizational stakeholders.	**CIS CSC 4** **COBIT 5** APO12.04, APO12.05, APO13.02, BAI02.03, BAI04.02 **ISA 62443-2-1:2009** 4.3.4.2 **ISO/IEC 27001:2013** Clause 6.1.3, Clause 8.3, Clause 9.3 **NIST SP 800-53 Rev. 4** PM-9	
ID.RM-2: Organizational risk tolerance is determined and clearly expressed.	**COBIT 5** APO12.06 **ISA 62443-2-1:2009** 4.3.2.6.5 **ISO/IEC 27001:2013** Clause 6.1.3, Clause 8.3 **NIST SP 800-53 Rev. 4** PM-9	
ID.RM-3: The organization's determination of risk tolerance is informed by its role in critical infrastructure and sector specific risk analysis.	**COBIT 5** APO12.02 **ISO/IEC 27001:2013** Clause 6.1.3, Clause 8.3 **NIST SP 800-53 Rev. 4** SA-14, PM-8, PM-9, PM11	

Figure 2-3   NIST CSF Framework Core example (Source: NIST)

27001, an organization cannot become certified against ISO/IEC 27002. It is simply a reference and guidance document for information security controls.

ISO/IEC 27002 consists of 14 security control clauses made up of 35 security control categories and 114 controls. Each security control category consists of a control objective to be achieved and one or more controls that may be implemented to achieve the objective. The security control clauses in ISO/IEC 27002 are as follows:

- Information security policies
- Organization of information security
- Human resources security
- Asset management
- Access control
- Cryptography
- Physical and environmental security
- Operations security
- Communication security
- System acquisition, development, and maintenance
- Supplier relationships
- Information security incident management
- Information security aspects of business continuity management
- Compliance

NOTE ISO/IEC 27002 is a determinant framework (list of controls) and should be utilized with another process framework (for example, process guidance such as ISO/IEC 27001) to implement a wholistic information security program.

CIS Critical Security Controls

The Center for Internet Security Critical Security Controls (CIS CSC), also known as CIS Top 20 and previously the SANS Top 20, is a voluntary framework consisting of a set of best-practice controls used to mitigate risk to information and information systems. The framework consists of 20 "critical" controls that focus on key fundamentals of information security. Table 2-5 lists the 20 Critical Security Controls and reproduces their descriptions from the Center for Internet Security at https://www.cisecurity.org/controls/cis-controls-list/.

Control	Description
1. Inventory and Control of Hardware Assets	Actively manage (inventory, track, and correct) all hardware devices on the network so that only authorized devices are given access, and unauthorized and unmanaged devices are found and prevented from gaining access.
2. Inventory and Control of Software Assets	Actively manage (inventory, track, and correct) all software on the network so that only authorized software is installed and can execute, and that unauthorized and unmanaged software is found and prevented from installation or execution.
3. Continuous Vulnerability Management	Continuously acquire, assess, and take action on new information in order to identify vulnerabilities, remediate, and minimize the window of opportunity for attackers.
4. Controlled Use of Administrative Privileges	The processes and tools used to track/control/prevent/correct the use, assignment, and configuration of administrative privileges on computers, networks, and applications.
5. Secure Configuration for Hardware and Software on Mobile Devices, Laptops, Workstations, and Servers	Establish, implement, and actively manage (track, report on, correct) the security configuration of mobile devices, laptops, servers, and workstations using a rigorous configuration management and change control process in order to prevent attackers from exploiting vulnerable services and settings.
6. Maintenance, Monitoring, and Analysis of Audit Logs	Collect, manage, and analyze audit logs of events that could help detect, understand, or recover from an attack.
7. Email and Web Browser Protections	Minimize the attack surface and the opportunities for attackers to manipulate human behavior though their interaction with web browsers and email systems.
8. Malware Defenses	Control the installation, spread, and execution of malicious code at multiple points in the enterprise, while optimizing the use of automation to enable rapid updating of defense, data gathering, and corrective action.

Table 2-5 CIS Critical Security Controls (continued)

Control	Description
9. Limitation and Control of Network Ports, Protocols, and Services	Manage (track/control/correct) the ongoing operational use of ports, protocols, and services on networked devices in order to minimize windows of vulnerability available to attackers.
10. Data Recovery Capabilities	The processes and tools used to properly back up critical information with a proven methodology for timely recovery of it.
11. Secure Configuration for Network Devices, such as Firewalls, Routers, and Switches	Establish, implement, and actively manage (track, report on, correct) the security configuration of network infrastructure devices using a rigorous configuration management and change control process in order to prevent attackers from exploiting vulnerable services and settings.
12. Boundary Defense	Detect/prevent/correct the flow of information transferring networks of different trust levels with a focus on security-damaging data.
13. Data Protection	The processes and tools used to prevent data exfiltration, mitigate the effects of exfiltrated data, and ensure the privacy and integrity of sensitive information.
14. Controlled Access Based on the Need to Know	The processes and tools used to track/control/prevent/correct secure access to critical assets (e.g., information, resources, systems) according to the formal determination of which persons, computers, and applications have a need and right to access these critical assets based on an approved classification.
15. Wireless Access Control	The processes and tools used to track/control/prevent/correct the security use of wireless local area networks (WLANs), access points, and wireless client systems.
16. Account Monitoring and Control	Actively manage the life cycle of system and application accounts—their creation, use, dormancy, deletion—in order to minimize opportunities for attackers to leverage them.
17. Implement a Security Awareness and Training Program	For all functional roles in the organization (prioritizing those mission-critical to the business and its security), identify the specific knowledge, skills, and abilities needed to support defense of the enterprise; develop and execute an integrated plan to assess, identify gaps, and remediate through policy, organizational planning, training, and awareness programs.
18. Application Software Security	Manage the security life cycle of all in-house developed and acquired software in order to prevent, detect, and correct security weaknesses.
19. Incident Response Management	Protect the organization's information, as well as its reputation, by developing and implementing an incident response infrastructure (e.g., plans, defined roles, training, communications, management oversight) for quickly discovering an attack and then effectively containing the damage, eradicating the attacker's presence, and restoring the integrity of the network and systems.
20. Penetration Tests and Red Team Exercises	Test the overall strength of an organization's defense (the technology, the processes, and the people) by simulating the objectives and actions of an attacker.

Table 2-5　CIS Critical Security Controls

Each of the 20 Critical Security Controls is broken down further into several sub-controls. Each sub-control consist of the following components:

- **Sub-Control**   Unique sub-control identifier.
- **Asset Type**   Type of asset such as devices, applications, users, network, data, or N/A.
- **Security Function**   Security function based on functions in the NIST CSF.
- **Control Title**   Name of control subtype.
- **Control Descriptions**   Description of control to be implemented.
- **Implementation Groups**   Sub-controls are categorized by three implementation groups (IGs) based on the organization profile. The IGs are meant to assist organizations in determining their profile as well as providing a priority for control implementation (IG 1, IG 2, then IG 3) and serve as a process framework. For some organizations IG 1 may be sufficient based on their risk assessment.

CSA Cloud Controls Matrix

The *Cloud Security Alliance Cloud Controls Matrix (CSA CCM* or *CCM)* is a control framework of security concepts and principles for cloud security. It is a tool to be used by cloud customers to assess security risk of vendor cloud implementation or for an organization to assess their own cloud implementation. CCM consists of the following 16 control domains, which are broken down into approximately 100 individual controls, each assigned a unique control ID. CCM is based on a range of industry standards and maps each control to other industry frameworks and regulations, including ISO/IEC 27001/27002, COBIT, PCI DSS, HIPAA, NERC CIP, NIST SP 800-53, and more.

- Application & Interface Security (AIS)
- Audit Assurance & Compliance (AAC)
- Business Continuity Management & Operational Resilience (BCR)
- Change Control & Configuration Management (CCC)
- Data Security & Information Lifecycle Management (DSI)
- Datacenter Security (DCS)
- Encryption & Key Management (EKM)
- Governance & Risk Management (GRM)
- Human Resources Security (HRS)
- Identity & Access Management (IAM)
- Infrastructure & Virtualization (IVS)
- Interoperability & Portability (IPY)
- Mobile Security (MOS)
- Security Incident Management, E-Discovery & Cloud Forensics (SEF)

- Supply Chain Management, Transparency & Accountability (STA)
- Threat & Vulnerability Management (TVM)

Another useful framework tool developed by CSA is the *Consensus Assessments Initiative Questionnaire (CAIQ)*. The CAIQ consists of assessment questions for each individual control in the CCM to provide a means of assessing your organization's or vendor's cloud security against the CCM. It is an example of an evaluation framework for the CSA CCM. A sample of the CAIQ is illustrated in Figure 2-4. The sample consists of

Control Group	CGID	CID	Control Specification	Consensus Assessment Questions	Consensus Assessment Answers		
					Yes	No	n/a
Governance and Risk Management *Policy Enforcement*	GRM-07	GRM-07.1	A formal disciplinary or sanction policy shall be established for employees who have violated security policies and procedures. Employees shall be made aware of what action might be taken in the event of a violation, and disciplinary measures must be stated in the policies and procedures.	Is a formal disciplinary or sanction policy established for employees who have violated security policies and procedures?			
		GRM-07.2		Are employees made aware of what actions could be taken in the event of a violation via their policies and procedures?			
Governance and Risk Management *Business/ Policy Change Impacts*	GRM-08	GRM-08.1	Risk assessment results shall include updates to security policies, procedures, standards, and controls to ensure that they remain relevant and effective.	Do risk assessment results include updates to security policies, procedures, standards and controls to ensure they remain relevant and effective?			

Figure 2-4 Consensus Assessments Initiative Questionnaire (CAIQ) example (Source: Cloud Security Alliance)

assessment questions for two controls in the Governance and Risk Management Control Group: Policy enforcement and Business/Policy Change Impacts. The CAIQ provides an elegant solution to perform a quick, high-level gap assessment against the CCM.

Auditing for the CISO

The CISO and the organization must be aware of the effectiveness of their security program and to what extent it is meeting its compliance goals. This is accomplished through *auditing*, a careful examination of the security function to verify its correctness and effectiveness and to identify any shortcomings. This section examines audit management, the auditing process, control self-assessments, continuous auditing, and specific types of audits.

 EXAM TIP There may not be questions regarding specific auditing terms or techniques. Having a good understanding of auditing practices and processes should be sufficient for the exam.

Audit Management

Security auditing can be accomplished in isolation but is usually managed as part of a larger auditing program that includes examining other aspects of the organization such as the organization's financial or information systems functions.

Some organizations have an audit committee that oversees the organization's audit program (usually for the primary purpose of financial auditing). In a corporation, the audit committee usually reports to the board of directors. The committee ensures that the audit program is in compliance with regulations such as the United States' Sarbanes-Oxley Act or the European Union's Directives. Depending on the organization, the information security audit function may be part of the organization's overall audit program or may be within the security department and under the purview of the CISO.

Internal and External Audits

Audits may be performed by either internal or external entities or a combination of both. Internal audits are performed by employees who know the organization well, including its policies, procedures, people, and threat landscape. The goal is to ensure that the organization is complying with its internal policies and adhering to applicable laws and standards. External audits are performed by an external entity, either a firm or a regulating body. External audits typically involve auditing for compliance with regulation (laws) and industry standards.

Although there is a school of thought that says all audits should be performed by a separate external entity independent of the one being audited, there are advantages and disadvantages to both internal and external auditing. Since internal auditors are employees of the organization under audit, they may be very familiar with the inner workings of the organization. This could present some advantages. For instance, internal auditors, due to their deeper understanding of an organization's systems or processes, may be more likely to uncover issues that may be hidden deep inside. In addition, due to their knowledge of the inner workings of the organization, the internal auditors may be able to complete an audit more efficiently and in less time. Contrarily, internal auditors may lack the independence or objectivity of external auditors and are often subject to internal organizational politics, which could impact their judgement or motivation. For this reason, external audits are sometimes viewed as being the preferred method. Many organizations use a combination of both.

Audit Charters and Engagement Letters

The scope of the audit can be defined in an *audit charter*, which documents the authority, scope, and responsibilities of the audit. The charter helps plan the auditing functions so the audit can be carried out in a well-defined and repeatable manner. Here are some of the questions that may be answered in an audit charter:

- Who are the stakeholders and the asset owners?
- What assets are within the scope of the audit?
- What functions are being audited?
- Who is performing the audit?
- What is the periodicity of the audit activities?
- What is management's responsibility within the auditing process?
- How will things get approved and what is the escalation process?

One key advantage of an audit charter is that it can be used as a benchmarking tool. By clearly defining the audit scope, the results of audits over time can be compared. This can lead to an understanding of trends and a picture of how the security program is changing and, hopefully, improving over time. The audit charter also serves to empower the auditors if there is pushback from business unit leaders.

While the audit charter defines the requirements for an audit, an *engagement letter* is like a service-level agreement (SLA) between the entity being audited and the auditor. Engagement letters are especially helpful when an entity engages an external audit organization to perform an audit. The letter serves to define the terms of the engagement, set proper expectations, and prevent any misunderstandings. The letter may be part of a contract or may serve the purpose of a contract.

Both the charter and the engagement letter are intended to eliminate or reduce the risk that an audit may not produce the desired results because of a lack of understanding. The charter and/or letter establishes management's understanding of what is being audited so they can properly prepare for the audit results, make the best use of them, and respond appropriately.

Audit Planning

Before an audit is conducted, it is important to plan all the necessary activities and identify the resources that will be required. Most audits are quite broad and involve the collection and analysis of large amounts of data. Such an activity can get out of hand if it isn't well planned.

Before audit planning can begin, the auditors must first define the audit universe, which is an important term when describing the scope and size of an audit. The *audit universe* describes all the business processes and assets that are included in the audit. A CISO friend used to say, "You can't boil the ocean"; likewise, you can't audit everything, so one must choose what items are most relevant to support the goals of the organization. The audit universe defines everything that is in scope of the audit.

The first criteria for determining the audit universe is to identify the business processes and associated assets that are essential to meeting regulatory compliance requirements. For instance, if the purpose of the audit is to determine HIPAA compliance, and the company stores patient data in a database, the database and associated security controls would likely be part of the audit universe.

Some organizations determine the audit universe using a risk-based approach. Using this method, the business processes, and corresponding assets, are ranked by risk level (such as high, medium, low). The business processes or functions that present the greatest risk to the business (have the most business impact) would have the highest priority in audit planning.

Audit planning is sometimes captured in two documents: the audit strategy and the audit plan. The *audit strategy* defines the scope, timing, and direction of the audit, whereas the *audit plan* defines the nature, timing, and extent of the audit activities. Figure 2-5 shows an overview of a typical audit planning process. The following provides an explanation of each numbered step in the figure.

1. Understand the business. To gain this business understanding, the audit planner may do the following:

   - Review long-term strategic plans
   - Perform a walkthrough of the organization to understand what each group or department does, how it operates, and what are its key systems, processes, and assets
   - Interview key leadership and personnel to learn about trends, history, drivers, and operations

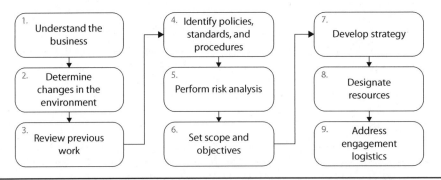

Figure 2-5 Typical audit planning process

- Identify specific regulations that drive business decisions or impact how the business operates
- Identify outsourced activities (are there third parties?)

2. Determine if there have been any changes to the business or environment since the previous audit and, if so, how these changes may impact this audit.

3. Review the work from the previous audit to understand any deficiencies found and recommendations made. Recommendations from the previous audit should be checked in the next one.

4. Review policies, plans, standards, and procedures to understand and identify the controls that are in place to meet the requirements.

5. Perform risk analysis to assess and rank business processes and assets based on their value to the organizations and the impact of loss of confidentiality, integrity, or availability.

6. Set the scope and objectives of the audit based on what is learned from the previous steps. This is defined by dividing the audit into manageable chunks such as categories (based on control types or technologies) or phases (based on time-based activities).

7. Develop and document the strategy for how the audit will be executed. The strategy takes into account all of the data collected during the prior steps in the planning process. The strategy is essentially the answers to all of the questions asked during data collection. It defines what will be done and is the basis for the audit plan, which maps out exactly how the audit strategy will be carried out.

8. Designate the resources required to implement the audit strategy, usually in the audit plan. This includes both internal and external resources.

9. Address and identify any other engagement logistics. These may include a master schedule of all audit activities that identifies resources, priorities, and interdependencies; and acquisition of any required resources such as equipment and software.

Validating the Audit Plan

Before carrying out the audit, the audit plan should be checked to ensure that it will provide the compliance verification that the organization needs. Yes, that means the audit plan should be audited. Checking the plan ahead of time is better than finding out late in the process that the plan doesn't cover what it should.

Gaining Approval of the Audit Plan

If the information security audit is under the scope of an audit committee, the plan requires the committee's approval. If so, this is likely part of an approval process defined by approval (and pre-approval) policies that the committee must abide by. For instance, if the organization must comply with US Security and Exchange Commission (SEC) regulations, there are SEC requirements for how accounting audits are governed and approved. In this instance the audit committee has oversight over the audits.

Audit Process

Auditing cannot be accomplished without a carefully crafted plan. The plan should include documented steps for each activity and the identification and/or creation of a repository for all auditing artifacts to be stored and maintained. The goal is to define a repeatable audit process that can continually evolve and improve. An audit process provides a mechanism to convey the scope and requirements of the audit to ensure the audit is fulfilling its intended purpose. The process should include the following auditing best practices:

- **Checks and balances**   One method for mitigating the risk of auditing errors is to implement separation of duties using checks and balances. In this approach the person(s) responsible for executing a task is separate from the person(s) responsible for verifying the task was done correctly.

- **Two-person rule**   Wherever practical, audit activities should be performed by two-person teams whereby one person does a task and a second person looks over their shoulder to make sure it was done correctly. The key part of a two-person rule is that it is a *rule*, meaning an activity that falls under the two-person rule is *not permitted* to be performed by just one person.

- **Independent validators**   Similar to checks and balances, the idea is that auditing should be performed by individuals that do not have an interest in the audit outcome. For instance, if Joe designed and implemented a security control, he shouldn't be the person auditing the implementation to make sure it was done correctly. Instead, a noninterested party should perform the audit.

- **Checklists**   "Back in the day" auditors carried clipboards with checklists of items to be examined and verified. Nowadays they use spreadsheets and databases, but the concept is the same—create and use checklists of actions with corresponding boxes to check or data to capture. Detailed checklists are the auditor's best friend as they define each audit action aligned with the corresponding result.

- **Establish audit records**   There should always be a record of who checked what and when the check occurred. Audit records permit the organization to look back and verify what was done and that it was performed properly.

- **Securely store audit records**   Audit records are highly sensitive because they contain information about vulnerabilities in the environment. This information could be exploited if shared with the wrong individuals or organizations. Audit records should be properly secured and access to them should be tightly controlled so that only authorized persons are permitted to see the information.

The audit process generally includes these activities, each of which is discussed in the sections that follow:

- Select auditing and control framework(s) for the organization
- Consider and scope special factors such as audit risk, scaling, and sampling
- Conduct audit preparation

- Collect evaluation evidence
- Assess the evidence and determine compliance
- Communicate the audit results to leadership, management, and stakeholders
- Conduct audit closeout activities

Select Auditing Standards and Frameworks

As introduced earlier, in this book we discuss three categories of control frameworks: *process model frameworks*, which define processes or life cycle models that organizations can follow to implement controls; *determinant frameworks*, which contain libraries of controls that can be used or tailored to meet objectives; and *assessment frameworks*, which provide guidance for measuring compliance. Many published control frameworks contain one or more of these categories of guidance, although they do not necessarily use these terms.

This section focuses on assessment frameworks used to support auditing. An organization may define its own assessment framework, but creating a framework from scratch can be a daunting task. Many organizations find that it is better to follow an industry-standard framework. Using an established framework not only saves time but can provide better results, as an industry-standard framework likely has withstood the test of time and has been improved and refined over the years. Assessment and audit frameworks provide a process for auditing controls. Here are a few such standards and frameworks commonly used in practice:

- NIST SP 800-53A
- ISO/IEC 27007
- ISO/IEC 27008

NIST SP 800-53A   The NIST Risk Management framework contains an auditing component outlined in the assessment phase of the process that references NIST SP 800-53A, *Assessing Security and Privacy Controls in Federal Information Systems and Organizations: Building Effective Assessment Plans*. NIST SP 800-53A contains a set of procedures for conducting assessments of security and privacy controls (outlined in NIST SP 800-53) at various phases of the system development life cycle.

ISO/IEC 27007:2017   ISO/IEC 27007, *Information technology – Security techniques – Guidelines for information security management systems auditing*, is a standard that provides guidance for information security management systems. ISO/IEC 27007 advises on how to apply ISO 19011:2018, *Guidelines for auditing management systems*, within the context of an ISMS. The standard covers the following:

- Managing an ISMS audit program (who, what, where, when, and how to audit)
- Performing internal or external ISMS audits (audit process)
- Managing ISMS auditors (skills, competence)

ISO/IEC 27007 is helpful for organizations interested in auditing an ISMS or in standing up an internal ISMS audit function.

ISO/IEC TS 27008:2019 ISO/IEC 27008, *Information technology – Security techniques – Guidelines for the assessment of information security controls*, is a standard focused on assessing information security controls. ISO/IEC 27008 is meant to complement ISO/IEC 27007. Whereas ISO/IEC 27007 is focused on auditing the management aspects of an ISMS, ISO/IEC 27008 is focused on auditing controls within an ISMS.

Consider and Scope Special Audit Factors

Before undertaking an information security controls audit, some special considerations should be addressed. One is the topic of *audit risk*, which is the risk that the audit may produce results that contain errors. These errors may be the result of incorrect audit procedures, inaccurate system documentation, misconfigurations, or other issues. Errors during auditing can produce incorrect results and lead to incorrect conclusions, resulting in wasted time and effort.

Organizations treat audit risk in a manner similar to the handling of other risk—by predicting and categorizing potential risks and deciding on a treatment approach for each item. Here are some of the most common treatment approaches:

- **Mitigate**   Risk mitigation is taking an action to reduce or minimalize the impact of the risk.

- **Accept**   Risk acceptance is making a decision that the activity can proceed either because the risk is determined to be at an acceptable level or because the cost of mitigation is too high in relation to the potential impact.

- **Avoid**   Risk avoidance is making a decision to not proceed with an activity based on a determination that the risk is too high to be acceptable.

- **Transfer**   Risk transfer is transferring the risk to another entity. Risk transfer is most commonly accomplished by purchasing insurance or outsourcing the activity to another entity that assumes responsibility for the risk.

Another audit consideration is determining the correct scale of the audit and if or when to use sampling. The audit should be scaled based on the needs of the business. For instance, spending $10M to conduct an audit of a $1M asset may not make sense. If auditing that asset is essential, then the audit activities for it should be scaled appropriately. One method of audit scaling is sampling. In *sampling*, instead of auditing an entire system or department, a representative sample or subset of the system is examined. Key to this approach is selecting the right samples to provide a good representation of the whole system.

Sampling requires a deep understanding of the asset being audited in order to determine which processes should be selected and which need more sampling than others. There are two general approaches to sampling:

- **Statistical sampling**   Uses a quantitative approach to select the items that comprise the sample. Statistical sampling starts by objectively determining the size of the sample and then using a random or near-random approach to choose the sample items of the required size. Statistical sampling requires mathematical analysis of the results in order to extrapolate how the results reflect the system as a whole.

- **Nonstatistical sampling**   Uses a qualitative approach to select the items to be included in the audit. The items are selected using nonquantitative means based on the judgement of the auditor. Essentially, any method that does not use sample size and randomization to select the items to be audited is considered nonstatistical. Either approach (statistical or nonstatistical) can be valuable if executed properly, but neither is as thorough as auditing all items in the environment.

Conduct Audit Preparation

Auditing is accomplished by comparing something against a defined criteria. Therefore, in order to plan an audit, the first thing that should take place is to determine the criteria. You can't determine if something is good if you don't know what "good" looks like. For any audit, the planning stage must include defining the audit requirements. Requirements are defined and understood in order to create a set of criteria against which the audit data can be compared. Top-level requirements may originate with regulations that the organization must comply with, frameworks the organization has adopted, or both.

Whose responsibility is it to determine the requirements? Ideally, the requirements are determined not by the auditor but by the designers or builders of the systems, processes, and controls being audited. After all, if they didn't know the requirements, how did they know what to build? However, in the real world the requirements are not always well understood by the developers or, in some cases, regulations are enacted after a system or process is in place. Therefore, in practice, often the responsibility falls to the auditor to capture and document the requirements used as the audit criteria.

Requirements for the audit are derived from regulatory drivers, frameworks, policies, procedures, and standards the organization has adopted. These are consolidated and form the basis of the audit planning process. Planning should produce the following artifacts that guide the auditing activities:

- Audit charter and/or audit plan
- Audit procedures
- Audit checklists
- Timelines and schedules

If the audit is used to determine regulatory compliance, planning should start with identifying and documenting the external requirements from the law or regulation. These requirements are then mapped to the systems, processes, and controls that were designed to meet them. This activity is sometimes an extremely large undertaking, as there can be thousands of requirements mapped to a multitude of systems and controls within a large enterprise. Audit planners make extensive use of spreadsheets or feature-rich tools to help them capture requirements, allocate them to systems and assets, map them to derived requirements, assign derived requirements to items to be tested, and capture test results.

Once the requirements are identified and mapped to assets, test or audit procedures are developed to verify compliance. The procedures are often supported by checklists that are used to capture test results. These documents form the basis of the audit planning and enable the audit to proceed.

Case Study: Parent and Derived Requirements

ABC Online is an online retail store that processes credit card transactions and must therefore be compliant with the Payment Card Industry Data Security Standard (PCI DSS). PCI DSS contains the following requirement (PCI DSS Req. No. 6.4): "Follow change control processes and procedures for all changes to system components." ABC has a change control policy that contains these requirements:

- ABC shall develop, document, and publish standardized configurations for all computing assets within the ABC computing environment.

- These standard configurations shall be approved by the IS manager prior to implementation.

- The IS manager shall be responsible for developing and staffing the ABC Change Management Board (CMB).

- The CMB shall be responsible for categorizing and prioritizing the requests for change (RFCs).

- No changes will be made to any asset unless the change has been authorized, tested, approved, and scheduled by the CMB.

In this example, the parent PCI DSS requirement is broken down into several derived requirements that are listed in the policy. It is these derived requirements that are tested by the auditors in order to determine the organization's compliance with the parent requirement.

Collect Evaluation Evidence

Evaluation evidence is data collected by the auditor as the result of audit activities. The evidence is then compared against requirements or analyzed to determine compliance. Generally, the following four methods are used to collect and evaluate evidence:

- **Inspection** Reviewing of data, such as:
  - Reviewing documentation such as policies, procedures, and diagrams
  - Reviewing source code
  - Reviewing configuration setting and files
  - Reading log files
  - Reading file attributes
  - Inspecting serial numbers (hardware) or licenses (software)
  - Observing physical attributes
  - Interviewing personnel (users, employees, technical staff)

- **Demonstration**   Conducting a process, such as a test, that produces results that can be read and compared with a set of expected results. Demonstrations sometimes include making observations, such as observing the response to inputs on a screen.

- **Testing**   Executing a series of steps or examining the results of several different demonstrations.

- **Analysis**   Processing the results of demonstrations or tests. For instance, analysis is usually used to determine performance characteristics such as efficiency, latency, and so on.

Evidence is collected and stored in an audit repository or database. As mentioned previously, evidence can contain sensitive information, such as enumeration of vulnerabilities, so its access should be strictly controlled based on "need to know" principles.

Assess the Evidence and Determine Compliance

Once the evaluation evidence is collected, the next step is to use it to determine compliance or identify areas of noncompliance that must be remediated. In evaluating the evidence, some auditors feel it is important to separate *observations* from *insights*.

- **Observations**   The results of inspection, demonstration, test, or analysis

- **Insights**   The conclusions that can be drawn from observations

The difference between the two is that observations are purely factual, whereas insights are intuitive interpretations that are derived from facts. It's important to separate the two because the auditor may draw insights too quickly, before they have all the facts, and this could skew the audit results.

Here is an example. During an audit, the auditor finds that a large number of user accounts have not been used for over 90 days. This is an observation. What insights can be drawn from this observation? One possible insight is "The user account provisioning policy is not adequate." Other possible insights include "User account provisioning procedures are not being followed" or "User accounts are not being managed centrally." Any or all of these insights may be correct. More data and observations are needed for proper evaluation. Depending on the observation, insights, and corresponding controls, compliance with a specific regulatory requirement can be determined.

Insights are the first step in performing *root cause analysis (RCA)*, an activity that examines audit findings to understand the underlying cause of security compliance issues. Often vulnerabilities or areas of noncompliance are addressed by fixing the immediate problem (putting out the fire) without solving the underlying reason for the problem. RCA is used as a way to uncover the source of the problem in order to prevent its reoccurrence.

Evaluation of audit results should take into account the *materiality* of the findings. A finding is determined to be material if it shows a failure to meet a control objective. Materiality requires the definition of a threshold or pass/fail criteria, although sometimes

Case Study: Root Cause Analysis

An audit of a large health care services company revealed that most of the software applications developed in-house contained security vulnerabilities such as buffer overflows caused by a lack of input error checking. Although these bugs were fixed upon their discovery, ongoing testing of software applications kept uncovering the same types of problems. Upon interviewing the in-house developers, it was found that they had not received any guidance or training concerning secure coding practices. This lack of training and guidelines was the *root cause* of the problem. Because fixing the bugs did not fix the underlying root cause, new software was developed with similar problems. Once the root cause was revealed, the company adopted a training program for developers and assigned a team to create secure coding standards for the organization. These activities addressed the root cause and eliminated the recurrence of the problem in future audits. When analyzing findings or deficiencies, determining the root cause is important because findings often are a symptom of a larger underlying problem. Performing a root cause analysis helps to identify the underlying issue in order to prevent its reoccurrence.

such a threshold is not completely clear. Therefore, determining materiality is sometimes an issue of professional judgement. Here are things that are sometimes considered when determining materiality:

- **Degree of significance**   The degree to which the finding impacts the overall requirement should be considered. The "extent to which" concept applies. The finding may impact a single requirement, but that requirement may be significant enough to the business to be relevant.

- **Stakeholders**   The people that are the "audience" of the materiality should be considered. Such stakeholders include the board of directors, the CEO, government regulatory bodies, lenders, insurers, and so on. It isn't the auditor's view that is important; rather, it is the view of the stakeholders that the auditor must consider.

- **Measurement**   The findings can be determined using a quantitative or qualitative evaluation (or a combination of the two). *Quantitative* is a numerical measure, such as what percentage of systems are impacted by an ineffective control, or how much data is at risk. Quantitative evaluations are based on the establishment of numerical thresholds. Quantitative evaluations may include the cost of the business process or asset impacted or even the cost of penalties for noncompliance. *Qualitative* measurements are based on nonnumerical criteria such as the criticality of the business function or system supported by the control in question.

- **Audit integrity**   The concept of materiality should not be used as a way to get around meeting a requirement. Materiality should not be abused; it should be a way to bring a real-world interpretation to the audit rather than serve as an excuse to skip or ignore a requirement that is hard to implement or test.

For further information, the AICPA publishes helpful guidance on materiality. See AU-C Section 320, *Materiality in Planning and Performing an Audit*, which is available on the AICPA website.

Communicate Audit Results

A crucial part of an audit is how the auditor or audit organization goes about reporting and communicating the findings to key stakeholders. This is usually accomplished with an audit report and an exit interview, both of which are supported by a library of audit records commonly referred to as *audit workpapers*.

The *audit report* is the byproduct of all of the auditing work. It is the final deliverable to management. Sometimes there is a preliminary version of the report presented to management, possibly reviewed at an exit interview (described in more detail a bit later), to discuss the preliminary findings before they are finalized. This is an opportunity to clarify misunderstandings or even resolve issues found prior to the production of the final report.

The auditor should take care to ensure that the final report is easy to understand for both technical and nontechnical audiences. Usually the report contains an executive summary to introduce the audit, define its scope, and summarize the audit findings. The purpose of the executive summary is to outline the scope of the audit as well as the key findings so that management can get a quick understanding of the most important information. The executive summary messaging can be supported by the use of visual representations such as graphs, charts, and so on.

The audit would not be complete without the meat of the material, which is in the body of the document and technical attachments that will be reviewed by the technical staff such as system and network administrators and security analysts.

The exact format of the report is sometimes dictated by policies or procedures and will vary depending on the scope and intended audience. Typically, the audit report includes the following sections:

- **Executive summary**   Summarizes the scope and findings.

- **Statement of purpose, objectives, and the scope of the audit**   Describes why the audit was conducted.

- **Findings**   Describes what the auditors found; specifically, if there's an indication that a control was not in place or was not effective.

- **Conclusions**   Discusses the conclusions the auditors arrived at based on the findings. This includes the insights that could be drawn from the findings or root causes that can be determined.

- **Recommendations**   Provides recommendations on how to remediate findings. Whether this section is included in the report depends on the type of audit. Some audits are focused on simply identifying control deficiencies, leaving it up to the organization being audited to remediate the findings.

In some cases, the auditor or audit organization conducts an *exit interview* or *outbrief* for management personnel. This provides the auditor an opportunity to present findings and conclusions. This is important because it provides management not only the opportunity to correct any misunderstandings but also the opportunity to express any views concerning how the audit was conducted or the audit results. Depending on the type of audit and the scope of the audit, the attendees may also discuss the practicality of the recommendations and timelines for implementation. In general, the auditor performs the following activities at the exit interview:

- Presents preliminary findings and conclusions to management
- Provides the opportunity to correct any misunderstandings
- Allows management to express their views

It is important to document everything about the exit interview, especially key conclusions or concerns. Items to be documented include the location of the outbrief, a list of attendees, a list of the key items discussed, and detailed notes of the meeting.

All of this information should be supported by the *audit workpaper* file. The audit workpapers are a library containing all audit documentation, including the audit plan, procedures, auditor's notes, and artifacts contained in the audit reports. This audit documentation is necessary to demonstrate how the auditor came to certain conclusions, describe what they did, and demonstrate due diligence. These workpapers should be properly handled and stored to preserve integrity.

Close the Audit

At the conclusion of the audit there should be an orderly shutdown of audit activities, preparation and delivery of audit findings, and (sometimes) an outbrief or exit interview to present the audit results to stakeholders such as the board or audit committee.

Audit closing usually includes housekeeping activities to clean up, organize, and store the audit data. Care should be taken to decide what evaluation evidence and working papers should be kept and what should be discarded. Some auditors keep everything, while others only retain the minimal amount of data to support the report and findings. It's always a tradeoff—keep too much and there is a risk of keeping highly sensitive data about the organization's vulnerabilities; keep too little and there may not be enough data to properly support the findings in the report.

Control Self-Assessments

Many organizations have found that the traditional practice of separating the audit function from the other functions of the organization is inefficient. While independent auditing is embraced because of its impartiality and objectivity, separating the auditors from the rest of the operation can be expensive and can cause extra work. Independent auditors are not as familiar with the assets they are auditing as are the developers or operations staff. Likewise, if the developers and operations personnel are not familiar with the goals, methods, and requirements of the auditors, they may be less likely to create systems or processes that are compliant. This situation has led many organizations to adopt control self-assessments (CSAs) to make the organization more efficient by integrating the auditing function within the organization's operations.

Traditional audits are performed by staff who are independent of the organization's operations or development staff. The audit staff may be internal employees of the organization or employees of an outside firm hired to perform the audit (or a combination of both). The traditional audits are usually performed on a periodic basis. In contrast to traditional audits, a CSA is performed by the operations staff of the organization and the audit function is integrated into the operations.

Benefits of CSAs

Without a CSA program, an organization won't know where it stands until an audit takes place. Therefore, problems and security vulnerabilities could be left exposed for long periods of time before they are discovered. The CSA gives the organization a continuous view and enables continuous remediation and improvement of controls.

The CSA also provides an opportunity to merge audit functions into the actual implementation of controls. This provides the opportunity to make the controls stronger. CSAs also enable organizations to assign staff to integrate control implementation and monitoring functions. After all, who is better able to define metrics for measuring the success of security controls than the people that design and implement the controls?

Before CSAs we had silos. Implementers would implement and auditors would assess. This proved to be very inefficient and made the remediation process slow. By allowing assessments to be performed by the operations staff, controls can be better aligned with business and organizational goals. CSAs improve the quality and knowledge of the implementation staff. They make the employees more invested in the quality of controls.

Many regulatory agencies require CSA programs (such as the FDIC). And many organizations use CSAs to help them meet the internal control reporting requirements of the Sarbanes-Oxley Act. Benefits of using CSAs include the following:

- Brings auditing into the organization's day-to-day functions
- Integrates control *implementation* with control *monitoring*
- Allows better definition and use of metrics
- Better enables addressing of problems at their source
- Allows the organization to detect problems earlier

CSA Pitfalls

Some organizations may resist doing CSAs because it is perceived as making more work for the operations staff. In many organizations, the operations staff (and staff in other departments) already have a full plate. However, the concept is that the organization will have to remediate problems found by the auditors anyway, so if the organization identifies them and fixes them internally, the process becomes more efficient and causes less work overall for the operations staff. That's the idea and, in practice, if the CSA program is implemented properly, it can provide this efficiency.

Having the same staff implement and assess can lead to failure to evaluate objectively. This can be due to the employees being too close to the problem or being too invested in the control's creation or implementation. This situation can be addressed by implementing auditing best practices such as using a two-person rule and ensuring that audit processes are peer reviewed prior to implementation.

Another potential pitfall is that operations staff may be reluctant to call out issues created by their own department, peers, or supervisors. To address this, some organizations permit employees to participate in the CSA anonymously or have their names redacted from the audit reports. However, the best way to address this is by management fostering a culture of openness and a spirit of improvement within the workplace.

Implementing a CSA Program

Some organizations find it is best to create a CSA group or function that drives how CSA is conducted throughout the organization. This CSA group should be staffed by auditors that are CSA specialists. Auditors know how to assess and can ensure alignment of the CSA with other auditing goals. Here are the general steps to implement a CSA program:

- **Create a charter**   Just like an audit charter, the CSA charter defines a common set of goals and processes for all departments and groups to follow. It also identifies the staff that are responsible for CSA functions and the level at which CSA occurs in the organization. The charter may also contain a roadmap laying out a schedule of activities for the CSA.

- **Define processes**   The CSA can use the same methods to collect evaluation evidence as those used for traditional audits. However, the CSA can also use collaborative methods such as tabletop workshops and walk-throughs of operational scenarios. If a workshop is used, it is common to have a facilitator who will ensure that a structured process is followed and the right information is gathered. The purpose is to use the best means to gather information about how the organization works.

- **Track remediation activities**   The CSA process involves a constant stream of tasks to collect data, perform analysis, catalog and prioritize deficiencies, define remediation actions, and verify successful remediation. These activities should be tracked in a list, tool, or database. The tools should always provide up-to-date information of the current status of CSA activities.

- **Create situational awareness**   Management and employees involved should always have a view of the status of their compliance with CSA goals. The organization should use metrics, dashboards, and other tools to provide situational awareness of where they are as an organization, department, and company/agency.

Continuous Auditing

Continuous auditing is essentially auditing on a more frequent basis. It is often made possible by technology that can rapidly collect and analyze data. In fact, continuous auditing is typically automated to provide real-time or near real-time results.

Continuous auditing almost always uses an agent such as a piece of software or a hardware sensor built into the business process. The agent operates in real time, pulling information or detecting something and sending the results to a database or data warehouse where it is stored, sorted, and normalized. Then the data is mined to find relationships and draw conclusions. Applications that are transaction-based use transaction logging to feed into the database.

Benefits of Continuous Auditing

Continuous auditing supported by technology can provide the following benefits:

- Automates the data collection process, making the audit process more efficient. Automation also supports the practice of control self-assessments.

- Provides immediate output to detect errors, inefficiencies, and issues as they arise (rather than waiting until next quarter's audit).

- Provides independence and objectivity as the auditor (human) is taken out of the data collection loop.

- Integrates tools and agents, which permits auditing things that couldn't otherwise be easily audited. For example, data or events that are embedded deep inside an application can be exposed by using automated tools.

Where Is Continuous Auditing Applicable?

Continuous auditing is suitable for certain situations, such as the following:

- Where the volume of transactions by processes is so high that a point-in-time audit couldn't capture a large enough sample size to accurately reflect the state of the organization. Instead, the auditors can use an agent that collects data over time and stores it in a database for processing.

- Where periodic sampling is insufficient.

- Where noncompliance must be detected in a timely manner to avoid penalties (situations where the organization can't wait to discover a problem after the fact). If an organization has a situation in which one error can cause noncompliance, having an agent that is constantly looking can shorten the time until the organization is aware of a problem so that it can be fixed sooner.

- Where high efficiency is needed (tuning and maturation). With continuous auditing, the organization can tune and course correct much faster than it could by waiting for the next audit.

Specific Types of Audits and Assessments

This section explores some of the most common types of audits that a CISO should be familiar with. The following types of audits are covered:

- SOC audits
- ISO/IEC 27001 certification audits
- FedRAMP assessments
- Industry-specific audits

SOC Audits

A *Service Organization Controls (SOC)* audit is an audit performed on a service organization (such as a cloud service provider) by a third party who assesses the internal controls of the service organization. These internal controls may include IT controls, security controls, or other systematic controls of the organization. After the audit is completed, the third-party auditor issues a report attesting to the service organization's internal controls. The service organization provides this report to customers, partners, and regulators as an attestation.

The SOC audit matured from the *Statement of Auditing Standards No. 70 (SAS 70)* audit standard developed by the American Institute of Certified Public Accountants (AICPA). In 2010, the SAS 70 standard was superseded by the *Statement on Standards for Attestation Engagements No. 16 (SSAE 16)* standard in the United States and the International Standards for Assurance Engagements No. 3402 (ISAE 3402) outside the United States. In 2017, SSAE 16 was superseded by *SSAE 18*.

There are three types of SOC audits and reports:

- **SOC 1**   Pertains to financial controls.
  - **Type I**   A single point-in-time examination of service organization controls and design. Focuses on determining if controls are designed properly.
  - **Type II**   An audit over a period of time (typically six months to one year). Expands the scope of type 1 to include assessing control effectiveness.
- **SOC 2**   Pertains to trust services (security, availability, confidentiality, process integrity, and privacy).
  - **Type I**   A single point-in-time examination of service organization controls and design. Focuses on determining if controls are designed properly.
  - **Type II**   An audit over a period of time (typically six months to one year). Expands the scope of type 1 to include assessing control effectiveness.
- **SOC 3**   Like SOC 2, also pertains to trust services. SOC 3 is similar to SOC 2 but goes into much less detail and is primarily used as a marketing tool to provide to customers.

SOC audits provide a way for a service organization to demonstrate to customers and partners that strong internal controls are in place. The various types of SOC audits covered are outlined in Table 2-6. In addition, a SOC report can be beneficial for the CISO to assist in assessing the strength of a potential service provider's controls during vendor or service selection.

ISO/IEC 27001 Certification Audits

ISO/IEC 27001, *Information technology – Security techniques – Information security management systems – Requirements*, was introduced in Chapter 1 as a best practice framework that provides guidance on establishing a wholistic information security management system (ISMS). In addition, organizations may become ISO/IEC 27001 certified by an accredited third party. The third party will assess the organization's ISMS based on

	SOC 1	SOC 2	SOC 3
Standard	SSAE 18	Attestation engagements	Attestation engagements
Controls assessed	Financial controls	Security and privacy controls	Security and privacy controls
Report type	Type I or II	Type I or II	Type II
Intended audience	Restricted report (management, customers, and auditors)	Restricted report (management, customers, and other knowledgeable parties)	Public report (anyone)

Table 2-6 Types of SOC Audits

the requirements in ISO/IEC 27001 and attest to the organization's compliance level. In addition, regular internal audits are required to ensure continued alignment with ISO/IEC 27001.

FedRAMP Audits

The *Federal Risk and Authorization Management Program (FedRAMP)* is a US federal government program that provides a standard approach for assessing, authorizing, and continuous monitoring of cloud-based products and services. In order for a cloud service provider (CSP) to sell services to the US federal government, the CSP must be FedRAMP authorized. FedRAMP is essentially a cybersecurity approval process for cloud-based products and services. As discussed in Chapter 1, the Federal Information Security Management Act (FISMA) requires that US federal government agencies authorize the information systems they use (the process used for this is the NIST RMF). FedRAMP is essentially FISMA for the cloud. The goal is to aid in the authorization process using a "do once, use many times" approach so that each US federal agency doesn't need to conduct redundant security assessments.

A CSP becomes FedRAMP authorized by being assessed by an accredited Third-Party Assessment Organization (3PAO). The 3PAO assesses and certifies the CSP's controls. FedRAMP security baselines (low, moderate, and high) are derived from the NIST SP 800-53 controls, with a set of control enhancements to address the unique security requirements of cloud services. FedRAMP documentation and information can be found at https://www.fedramp.gov.

Industry-Specific Audits

Chapter 1 discussed many of the legal and regulatory drivers that may affect a CISO's organization. Many of these drivers contain their own set of control and auditing requirements that must be implemented for compliance. These include but are not limited to

- **PCI DSS** for organizations accepting payment card information
- **HIPAA** or **HITECH** for health care "covered entities" under HIPPA
- **FISMA** for federal government
- **GDPR** for organizations collecting EU customer data

EXAM TIP CCISO candidates should be familiar with industry-specific audits that could impact an information security program.

Chapter Review

Organizations perform risk management to understand each asset's importance to the business. Assets are first categorized to determine the nature of each asset's risk and the sensitivity of the information stored, processed, or transmitted. Organizations commonly use frameworks that provide libraries of suggested controls for each security category. Organizations use or tailor these libraries to determine the set of security controls to apply to a given asset. The organizations can then design the implementation of the controls, implement and test them, and then monitor the asset for ongoing compliance throughout the asset's life cycle.

Auditing is a formal process used to determine compliance with regulatory requirements or an organization's internal policies, or both. Security auditing is usually part of an organization's overall auditing program, which may, or may not, be under the authority of the CISO. Traditional auditing is done periodically using auditors that are independent of the organization or department being audited. Alternatively, some organizations use control self-assessments to accomplish auditing. CSAs are performed regularly and utilize the operations staff to perform the audit to provide audit efficiency. Common security audits include SOC audits, ISO/IEC 270001 certification audits, FedRAMP audits, and other, industry-specific audits.

Quick Review

- A security control, also known as a safeguard or countermeasure, is a mechanism put into place to mitigate risk and protect the confidentiality, integrity, and availability of information or an information asset.

- Controls are selected by first categorizing an asset based on risk and the asset's value to the enterprise and the impact of potential loss of confidentiality, integrity, and/or availability of the asset.

- Controls are classified into three main groups:
  - Administrative controls, also known as soft controls, are management-oriented controls such as policies, procedures, guidelines, training, risk management, and employment practices (hiring, firing, and so on).
  - Technical controls, also referred to as logical controls, are hardware or software components that provide security control functionality.
  - Physical controls are tangible controls put in place to protect against threats in the realm of physical security.

- NIST defines a different set of classes:
  - Management controls focus on the management of risk and the management of information system security.

- Operational controls are primary implemented and executed by people (as opposed to systems).

- Technical controls are primarily implemented and executed by the information system through mechanisms contained in the hardware, software, or firmware components of the system.

- A control family is a grouping of controls in a framework that typically address the same security domain or function.

- Security functionality of controls describes what the controls do for the organization. Functionalities of controls include the following:

  - Preventive controls prevent or stop the occurrence of an adverse event or incident.

  - Detective controls discover, detect, or identify a potential adverse activity, event, intruder, or incident.

  - Deterrent controls deter or discourage a potential adversary from performing an attack or engaging in unwanted behavior.

  - Corrective controls correct adverse events that have occurred by fixing a system, process, or activity.

  - Directive controls are typically administrative controls that communicate expected behavior by specifying what actions are or are not permitted.

  - Recovery controls restore an environment or operations back to regular functionality. They are similar in function to corrective controls but are thought of as having advanced capability.

  - Compensating controls serve as an alternate or secondary control implementation to a primary control. These are often used when the primary control is not feasible to implement due to cost, complexity, or other business constraints.

- A control framework is a catalog of controls used to provide a foundation to aid in the implementation of a comprehensive information security program. The three fundamental types of control frameworks are process model, determinant, and evaluation.

- Common information security control frameworks include the following:
  - NIST SP 800-53
  - NIST Cybersecurity Framework
  - ISO/IEC 27001/27002
  - CIS Critical Security Controls/CIS Top 20
  - CSA Cloud Controls Matrix

- Security professionals select controls by following a security control life cycle that typically includes risk assessment, design, implementation, assessment, and monitoring.

- Security auditing is a careful examination of the security function to verify its correctness and effectiveness and to identify any shortcomings.
- Audits may be performed by internal or external entities or a combination of both.
- The audit charter defines the requirements for an audit, while the engagement letter serves to define the terms of the audit engagement, set proper expectations, and prevent any misunderstandings.
- The audit universe describes all the business processes and assets that are included in the audit.
- Audit planning is sometimes captured in two documents: the audit strategy, which defines the scope, timing, and direction of the audit, and the audit plan, which defines the nature, timing, and extent of the audit activities.
- A method for mitigating the risk of auditing errors is to implement separation of duties using checks and balances.
- Audit records should be properly secured, and access to them should be tightly controlled so that only authorized persons are permitted to see the information.
- Commonly used auditing frameworks include NIST SP 800-53A, ISO/IEC 27007, and ISO/IEC 27008.
- In sampling, instead of auditing an entire system or department, a representative sample or subset of the system is examined. There are two types of sampling: statistical and nonstatistical.
- Evaluation evidence is data that is collected by the auditor as the result of audit activities. The evidence is then compared against requirements or analyzed to determine compliance.
- Evaluation of audit results should take into account the materiality of the findings. Materiality is the concept that just because a test uncovers an error, that does not necessarily mean a control objective is not met. Thresholds should be established to enable the assessment of control objectives; minor errors may be permitted if they do not indicate the failure of a control objective.
- In contrast to traditional audits, a control self-assessment is performed by operations staff of the organization.
- Continuous auditing is essentially auditing on a more frequent basis and is typically automated to provide real-time or near real-time results.
- The following are common types of audits a CISO may encounter:
  - An SOC audit is an audit performed on a service organization by a third party who assesses the internal controls of the service organization.
  - An ISO/IEC 27001 certification audit is a third-party assessment of an organization's information security management system.
  - A FedRAMP assessment is a cybersecurity approval process for cloud-based products and services that support the US government.

- Industry-specific audits include the following:
  - PCI DSS for organizations accepting payment card information
  - HIPAA or HITECH for health care "covered entities" under HIPPA
  - FISMA for federal government
  - GDPR for organizations collecting EU customer data

Questions

1. A security analyst is reviewing the security logs of a web server for indicators of compromise. Which of the following control functionalities is this an example of?

   A. Detective

   B. Preventive

   C. Recovery

   D. Directive

2. The CISO is tasked with determining whether a control is sufficient. Which of the following would the CISO use to determine this?

   A. Business drivers

   B. Regulatory drivers

   C. Assessment results

   D. Determinant framework

3. A newly hired CISO is performing a physical security review of the organization's datacenter. In the process of the assessment, the CISO determines that the organization has implemented server room door locks, fences, and bollards. Which type of control do these controls represent?

   A. Directive

   B. Recovery

   C. Preventive

   D. Technical

4. Under the direction of the CISO, the security team is implementing a preventive technical control to address risks to an information system. At which point in the control life cycle should the control be tested?

   A. Prior to implementation

   B. Prior to implementation and regularly thereafter

   C. After the risk assessment

   D. After implementation

5. NIST SP 800-53 outlines management, operational, and technical classes. Which of the following NIST control families is an example of a management control class?

   A. Risk Assessment

   B. Awareness and Training

   C. Physical and Environmental Protection

   D. Personnel Security

6. The CISO of an organization is looking for an impartial assessment of the information security program. Which of the following would provide the most impartial assessment?

   A. Internal audit

   B. Control self-assessment

   C. External audit

   D. Financial audit

7. Which of the following steps must be completed before the others in the audit planning process?

   A. Set scope and objectives

   B. Develop strategy

   C. Designate resources

   D. Understand the business

8. Which of the following includes the processes, assets, entities, users, and resources that are in scope for an audit?

   A. Engagement letter

   B. Audit review

   C. Audit universe

   D. Audit checklist

9. The CISO is writing an organization security policy. This is an example of which of the following control types?

   A. Administrative

   B. Technical

   C. Physical

   D. Detective

10. An organization has fallen victim to an attack that altered the e-commerce web page on its website so that customers can no longer use it to make a purchase. This has impacted which security fundamental(s)?

   A. Both integrity and availability

   B. Availability

   C. Integrity

   D. Neither integrity nor availability

Answers

1. **A.** Reviewing security logs of a system for indicators of compromise is an example of a detective control, as this type of control is used to identify potential adverse events or activity. Preventive controls stop the occurrence of an adverse event, recovery controls restore an environment to regular functionality, and directive controls communicate expected behavior.

2. **C.** The CISO would use assessment results to determine if a control is meeting its planned purpose and operating as intended. Business drivers and regulatory drivers would serve as the foundation for security strategy and may assist in deciding on a determinant framework and be used as criteria for assessment, but they would not be used to assess control sufficiency.

3. **C.** Server room door locks, fences, and bollards are examples of preventive controls because they serve to prevent the occurrence of an adverse event. Directive controls communicate expected behavior, and recovery controls restore an environment to regular functionality. The controls listed are examples of physical controls, not technical controls.

4. **B.** Controls should be tested, as part of the control life cycle, prior to implementation and should be tested regularly thereafter at an organization-defined interval. While the assessment phase of the life cycle occurs after the implementation phase, this does not negate the need to test as part of the design process prior to implementation. The assessment phase of the life cycle is an ongoing phase that ensures the control is continuously assessed.

5. **A.** The Risk Assessment control family is considered a management control class. Awareness and Training, Physical and Environmental Protection, and Personnel Security are considered operational control classes.

6. **C.** An external audit would provide the most impartial assessment of the security program. Internal audits and control self-assessments are performed by internal staff, who may be influenced by their close association with the organization and tend to be less impartial. A financial audit does not address the impartiality requirement of the question.

7. **D.** The first step in audit planning is to understand the business. The other steps in the audit planning process cannot be completed without an understanding of the business.

8. **C.** The audit universe describes all the business processes and assets that are included in the audit. The audit universe defines everything that is in scope of the audit.

9. **A.** Developing an organizational security policy is an example of an administrative control. Administrative controls are management-oriented controls such as policies, procedures, guidelines, and training. Technical controls, also referred to as logical controls, are hardware or software components that provide security control functionality. Physical controls are tangible controls put in place to protect against threats in the realm of physical security. Detective controls discover, detect, or identify a potential adverse activity, event, intruder, or incident.

10. **A.** Both integrity and availability have been impacted, as the e-commerce site has been altered (which impacts integrity) and the site is no longer accessible for the customers (which impacts availability).

Security Program Management and Operations

This chapter discusses the following topics:

- Security program management
- Security program budgets, finance, and cost control
- Security program resource management: building the security team
- Project management

The CISO carries out the job of protecting the organization's assets by implementing a well-planned and executed information security program. This chapter describes what an effective information security program looks like and how it is managed, staffed, and funded. An information security program generally has two types of activities: *subprograms*, also known as *streams of work*, which are long-term activities or ongoing activities, and *security projects*, which have a defined end state that, when achieved, signals the end of the activity. This chapter describes the management processes used to carry out both types of activities.

Security Program Management

Chapter 1 introduced the components that make up a typical security program. To review, a synopsis of the components follows (see Figure 3-1):

- **Security areas of focus** External drivers that impact the security program, such as PCI DSS, HIPAA, Sarbanes-Oxley, or FISMA, along with internal drivers, such as an IT department's IT service management policy.
- **Security streams of work** Ongoing security activities that are continuous, such as security event monitoring, incident response, vulnerability management, and so on.

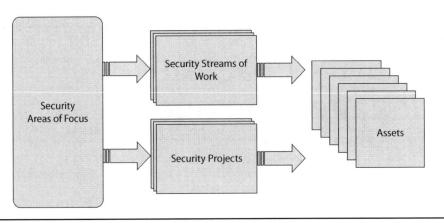

Figure 3-1 Security program components

- **Security projects** Activities initiated and implemented by the security organization that are not ongoing but instead have a defined goal or end product. Examples of security projects include choosing an identity management solution, deploying a specific GRC system (described in the adjacent sidebar), building a security awareness portal, or performing a vulnerability assessment. Projects are implemented following a project management process.
- **Assets** Resources owned by the organization. Within the context of a security program, assets are resources that require protection against threats. Assets most often consist of systems and data.

The CISO's challenge is to manage these elements in a cohesive and coordinated manner.

Security Areas of Focus

Security areas of focus are drivers that impact how the streams of work and security projects are carried out. The areas of focus impact an organization's decisions regarding which security activities are required and where they need to be applied. Areas of focus may apply to specific assets or groups of assets. For instance, PCI DSS requires specific security controls to be put into place based on where in the enterprise credit card data resides. Therefore, PCI DSS impacts the security requirements of the design, implementation, and operation of the assets in the enterprise that store, process, or transmit credit card data. PCI DSS may impact one or more streams of work and one or more security projects.

Governance, Risk Management, and Compliance

Governance, risk management, and compliance (GRC) is a term used to describe an integrated approach to these three practices and their associated activities. Some organizations implement GRC programs to enable a cohesive, holistic approach to organizational GRC, ensuring that the organization acts in accordance with its internal policies, external compliance requirements, and risk appetite through the alignment of strategy with organizational objectives. The benefit of GRC is the synchronization of information between these functions across the organization to ensure they are not siloed off from one another.

- **Governance**   Ensuring that strategic goals, rules, policies, and practices align with business objectives
- **Risk management**   Managing risk to acceptable levels by analyzing risk probability and impact and prioritizing control implementation
- **Compliance**   Monitoring and reporting on the organization's conformity with both internal requirements (policies and procedures) and applicable external requirements (laws and regulations)

GRC is often aided by technology through the implementation of a GRC system. A *GRC system* enables an organization to accomplish GRC-related initiatives using a centralized tool. Each GRC function produces and manages a variety of information, such as asset inventory, policies, standards, procedures, audit work papers, security incident information, risk management information, compliance information, control monitoring and reporting information, and so on. This information is often maintained in distributed documents, spreadsheets, and/or systems. Key benefits of a GRC system include the ability to consolidate data into a central location, automate business processes, and compile and report on centralized GRC data.

GRC systems provide a range of features, which may include some or all of the following:

- Managing policy and procedure development, management, and review workflows
- Documenting policy exceptions
- Documenting controls and managing control monitoring workflows
- Maintaining an inventory of assets
- Managing risk assessments for assets

(Continued)

- Documenting and managing control deficiencies
- Maintaining a risk register and risk documentation
- Tracking control testing
- Managing audit documentation, plans, and engagements
- Recording and tracking of incidents
- Dashboards and reporting

When deciding whether to implement a GRC system, an organization needs to consider many factors. As with any tool, realizing value requires up-front work. With a GRC system, this up-front work may be significant, particularly for smaller security teams, if the organization fails to identify use cases or lacks a robust governance, risk management, and compliance foundation. To realize the full value of a GRC system, the organization should consider the following:

- Does the organization have a complete inventory of assets, compliance obligations, and controls?
- Are asset owners and data owners identified?
- Is there a solid foundation of policies, procedures, standards, and such?
- Have use cases for the GRC system been identified?
- Is there a thorough understanding of manual process workflows to be automated?
- Are individuals involved in the workflows identified?
- Does the organization have staff and resources to implement, manage, and maintain the GRC system?
- What kind of customization will be required?
- What kind of reporting requirements are required from the GRC system?

Although it provides many benefits, a GRC system cannot fix a poorly defined GRC program. A GRC system provides good value when used to augment a well-defined GRC program.

Areas of focus include laws, regulations, standards, or policies that the organization must comply with. The process for addressing compliance (and therefore areas of focus) is described in Chapter 1 in the "Compliance" section. The CISO is responsible for ensuring that the areas of focus are correctly integrated into the security program.

Security Streams of Work

Activities that are ongoing and do not have a beginning, middle, and end fall into the category that some CISOs call *streams of work* and others call *subprograms* of the information security program. For the purpose of this discussion, we use the term streams of work. Due to their nature, these activities go on for the life of the security program. These ongoing security activities vary from organization to organization. Here is a list of some typical security streams of work:

- Security document maintenance (security charter, policies, procedures, standards, and guidelines)
- GRC
- Risk analysis and management
- User identity management and provisioning
- Asset management
- Threat intelligence
- Security monitoring and intrusion detection
- Intrusion prevention
- Security administration
- Configuration and patch management
- Application security
- Security training and awareness
- Security testing
- Physical security
- Business continuity
- Disaster recovery

Although these activities are ongoing, they still have a life cycle process that is somewhat similar to a project management life cycle. Streams of work can be accomplished following a process model such as the Plan, Do, Study, Act (PDCA) process model, previously discussed in Chapters 1 and 2. The often-quoted William Edwards Deming, who championed the PDCA model, once said: "It is not enough to do your best; you must know what to do and then do your best." Following Deming's advice, the PDCA cycle that is commonly used in many industries works well for performing streams of work because each stream should be

- Well planned
- Performed in accordance with a plan
- Measured against criteria for success
- Continuously improved to address any shortcomings and get better over time

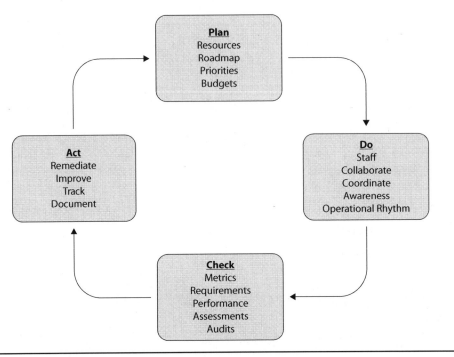

Figure 3-2 Stream of work process

Chapter 1 introduced the PDCA process as it applies to compliance management. However, the PDCA model (also called the Deming cycle or Shewhart cycle) works well for any stream of work, compliance or otherwise. Figure 3-2 illustrates how the PDCA model can be used for security streams of work, as described next.

Plan

Ongoing streams of work should be well planned, both individually and together, as a coordinated portfolio of activities. The CISO should build a roadmap for accomplishing these activities based on priorities established from performing the governance and risk analysis activities described in Chapter 1. The roadmap should be reflected in a document such as a security charter or security program plan. The roadmap reflects both short-term and long-term plans and should be updated on at least an annual basis.

Planning should reflect areas of emphasis based on the organization's business, stakeholder needs, or the results of security audits or assessments. For instance, if a vulnerability assessment indicates the organization has many unpatched systems, the organization may need to give its *patch management program* a higher priority in the short term. Plans should be updated frequently based on real needs of the organization.

Planning streams of work includes scoping the resources needed to accomplish the activities that comprise the security program. Resources may include the following:

- **Staffing** Discussed in greater detail later in this chapter in the section "Security Program Resource Management: Building the Security Team," staffing involves determining the right team to best accomplish the goals of the stream of work. Staffing planning also includes determining the organizational structure for the stream of work team and how the team structure fits within the structure of the information security department as a whole.

- **Supporting infrastructure and tools** Each stream of work has its own requirements for tools and IT infrastructure. Planning includes identifying which tools are needed and whether the organization should acquire each tool or build it in house (build versus buy). Tools also require maintenance. The needs and resources for maintaining the tools are part of the planning activity.

- **Financial resources** The money required for executing a stream of work may be expended over time. The stream of work activity may experience periods of greater spending, such as when equipment is purchased, staff is expanded, or a spike in activity occurs (for example, during an incident or compliance exercise). Budgets for spending are most often established on an annual basis.

- **"X as a Service"** Today, instead of using in-house resources or tools, many CISOs choose to outsource security functions using an "as a service" model. Such services can range from small segments of the security program such as antivirus to large segments such as complete security monitoring and intrusion detection of the enterprise. Virtually any aspect of the security program could be implemented using an as-a-service model.

The plans associated with a stream of work should include a clear definition of the objectives and goals. Without clear goals, the stream may not produce outcomes that benefit the organization. The plan should also address how the outcomes are measured and reported. Stream of work plan documents are stored in a document repository with *access controls* in place following need-to-know principles and *change control processes* in place to manage document baselines. The plans identify the assets to which the stream applies. The plans should also address the *security relationship*, including how the streams of work impact other departments, people within the organization, and external entities. The description of the security relationship should also identify the methods of communicating, coordinating, and collaborating with these stakeholders as well as the frequency of such communications.

Do

Based on the plans described in the previous section, the streams of work proceed with activities to meet the defined goals. All activities should follow the processes and procedures identified or defined in the plans. Each stream of work is staffed with a stream owner or stream manager, which may be the CISO or a designated manager or supervisor.

The security organization under the direction of the CISO should develop and refine an *operating* (or *operational*) *rhythm*, which refers to communications, usually reports and meetings, that occur on a regular basis but do not adversely impact the operational flow of the stream of work or other activity. Meetings are needed to enable team members to communicate and collaborate, resolve problems, report status, and discuss improvements. Reporting is needed to provide data and metrics to management and decision-makers. These communications must occur on a regular cadence and in a defined and repeatable manner. The security organizations that tend to perform the best are those that understand the value of an optimal operational rhythm and adjust their programs accordingly.

Stream activities should be accomplished with self-awareness. This means that everyone working on the stream should know not only what they are doing and how it fits with what everybody else is doing, but also how well the stream is performing against its goals. Streams that fail tend to be ones in which the only person that knows what is really going on is the boss. Successful streams are enabled when everyone has a stake in the outcome and knows how they can contribute to the stream's success.

The stream of work staff should document everything, including plans, procedures, guidelines, reports, and metrics. To create a living library of useful information, stream of work data should be stored in a document repository. These documents, while important to the organization, also contain information about the organization's security vulnerabilities and weaknesses. Therefore, access to stream of work documents and data should be available only to those people with a *need to know*.

Security Liaisons

To be successful, security activities, including streams of work, must be performed in close collaboration with the other groups and personnel in the organization. Therefore, the security team needs to build a *security relationship* with other organizations. Many security groups use *security liaisons*, members of the security team that conduct outreach to the rest of the organization. Security liaisons provide two-way communications, providing security *messaging, expertise, and advise* to spread the word about information security practices, including what the organization is doing to improve security, and act as the eyes and ears of the CISO to *listen to what employees think and feel about security policies, practices, and initiatives*. We all know that people are the weakest link in information security. Security liaisons can help to improve the security culture of the organization and, in turn, reduce security incidents.

Check

How does a CISO determine if the streams of work are working? They must be measured against criteria for success. Every stream of work should have a clear set of goals along with metrics to measure how well those goals are being met. Stream of work planning includes establishing how success is measured and reported. However, the PDCA check phase involves more than just performance metrics against the primary goals of the activity. It also includes ways to assess all aspects of the activity. This may include measuring things like accuracy, usefulness, suitability, resiliency, or adaptability. The CISO should always be looking for ways to measure and understand how well each aspect of the security program is performing.

Some indicators of performance are measured daily, such as monitoring logs and detecting alerts. Other indicators are measured as part of assessments or audit actions. As explained in Chapter 2, security auditing is usually accomplished as part of a larger auditing program, but these audits can be used as a tool to assess stream of work performance. However, there may also be other measures outside of the auditing program. Many organizations use a security dashboard to show the status of stream activity, such as statistics on tickets from the security monitoring function or patched/unpatched systems from the patch management stream.

Assessments should be part of the operational rhythm, which, as previously described, is a cadence of communication reporting that includes measures of how well streams are performing.

Act

The purpose of the act phase is to maintain the quality of the security functions (streams) and to seek ways to improve them. This is accomplished by reviewing and analyzing the results and data from the check phase. The results are compared with the defined goals and objectives of each stream of work. Shortcomings and gaps are then scoped for remediation.

Some organizations formalize the remediation process using a Plan of Actions & Milestones (POA&M) or a Corrective Action Plan (CAP). These terms are from FISMA and the various guides and publications that support FISMA; however, they are also used generically to describe methods for capturing, tracking, and communicating security remediation activities. POA&Ms and CAPs are created on a system-by-system basis to track resolution of issues uncovered during security testing as part of the Risk Management Framework (RMF) process, but they can also be used to support resolution of deficiencies or needed improvements in security streams of work. The POA&M is a plan that describes the course of treatment to resolve deficiencies. It contains a CAP that describes exactly what will be done (or has been done) to resolve the deficiencies.

Part of the act phase of the PDCA cycle includes looking at the aggregation of results across the streams of work to uncover trends and determine root causes.

The activities performed during the act phase include tracking the actions undertaken to address gaps, resolve root causes, and implement improvements. If the tracking data is stored in a database, the organization will have a repository and living record of how well the streams are performing and improving over time.

Asset Security Management

Chapter 1 discussed security categorization and risk mitigation of assets. Chapter 4 describes the core competency of asset security along with other core competencies. The security management of assets is discussed in this section and illustrated in Figure 3-3.

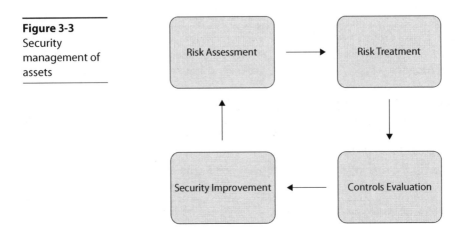

Figure 3-3
Security
management of
assets

Figure 3-3 is derived from ISO/IEC 27001 and shows the life cycle of how risk management is applied to a given asset. Each asset is assessed as part of the risk assessment and risk analysis process, which results in prioritization and categorization of the asset. Based on this, risk treatment is defined for the asset. The treatment is implemented, usually in the form of controls, and then evaluated. Any deficiencies or gaps uncovered during testing are then resolved. Security improvement results from monitoring the asset over time and undertaking subsequent risk analysis activities. This cycle continues for the life of the asset.

A critical aspect of an information security program is knowing what all the assets are, where they are, and what their security posture is. This situational awareness is a key function of security program management. Ideally, the security team maintains, or has access to, a single database containing this information. However, in practice, this information often is in disparate data repositories or the data is maintained by other groups such as the IT department.

Regardless of where the data is located, the security team should have access to or maintain data about each asset. Here is an example of the information that may be maintained for an asset:

- Asset name, make, model, serial number, and so on
- IP address and MAC address
- Asset type
- Name of asset owner and custodian
- Location
- Configuration information such as the security baseline, configuration settings, or standard build identification
- Licensing information and status
- Security categorization, classification, risk or impact level, or other information indicating the intended security characteristics of the asset

- Results of the most recent assessments, audit, or compliance reviews
- Current method of security monitoring of the asset
- Current operational status
- Current patch status or level
- Relationship to other systems or assets
- Security authorization status

Keeping control of the organization's assets and knowing they are properly secured is one of the biggest challenges for the CISO. Rogue devices can appear on the network either accidentally or intentionally. In addition, portable devices, including phones, tablets, and PCs, are part of the enterprise but are harder to keep track of. Many organizations use automated solutions to discover assets for the purpose of helping with asset situational awareness and to prevent unauthorized assets from connecting to the enterprise or causing disruptions.

Information assets, for the purpose of this discussion, are data. Data is quite literally the life blood of any organization and is most often the target of cyberattacks and the object of security incidents and subsequent recovery activities. Information assets, like the assets that support them (systems, hardware, and software), require management by the security team. Information asset management includes the following:

- **Information asset classification**   The security team ensures that all data is classified in accordance with the organization's data classification policy and associated guidelines. Classification schemes vary based on the nature of the business environment, but every organization has at least two types (or classifications) of data:
  - Private data that requires some degree of protection
  - Public data that does not require protection
- **Data handling**   The security program establishes policies, standards, and guidelines for how each classification of data should be handled while it is stored, processed, or transmitted. These rules define who, where, and how data is handled, including defining implementation methods such as encryption, access controls, labeling, and physical media.
- **Data inventory**   Like supporting assets (hardware and software), information assets are tracked using inventories and associated processes to maintain an understanding of where the organization's information assets are, how they are protected, and the organization's compliance with the policies and rules that apply to the asset.

Security Projects

Security projects are activities within the security program that have a beginning and an end. Whereas streams of work are continuous, security projects have an end in mind, and when the end is achieved, the project is over. The list of active security projects for an organization is ever changing. Each year new security projects are needed as older ones are completed. Example projects that may be part of a security program include the following:

- Acquiring and implementing a vulnerability scanning tool
- Performing a network security architecture review
- Developing a security tool
- Deploying an incident response capability
- Designing physical security controls for a datacenter
- Performing a risk assessment of a service provider
- Developing software development security standards
- Aligning security practices with an industry framework (for example, ISO/IEC 27001, NIST SP 800-53, and so on)

All of these examples result in some kind of project being created that must be properly managed to ensure success. Projects, like streams of work, require disciplined management to be successful. But the project management process differs somewhat from streams of work because projects have a defined end state and all the activities are geared toward achieving that end state. The process for project management is discussed in detail later in this chapter in "Project Management."

Security Program Budgets, Finance, and Cost Control

The extent to which the CISO is responsible for the security budget and spending varies by organization and usually aligns with the top-level organizational chart that shows who reports to whom. If the CISO reports to the CIO, the security budget is most likely part of the IT budget and the budgeting and spending process is managed through that chain. In situations where the CISO reports directly to the CEO, the CISO is usually afforded more autonomy in budgeting and spending.

When Security Functions Are Shared

In some organizations the CISO does not have responsibility for some parts of the information security budget. For instance, many security breaches are caused by unpatched systems, but in some organizations, *patch management* is not the responsibility of the CISO, instead falling within the purview of the IT group or maybe an IT service management group. Another example is *security awareness*. The CISO may be responsible for security awareness training, but the training budget may be administered by the human resources department. In situations where various security-related functions are not under the budget authority of the CISO, the CISO may be asked to provide input to the budget process for the responsible group. Such collaboration in the budget process is common.

Establishing the Budget

As discussed in the Chapter 1 section "Sizing," covering the sizing of the information security organization, some executives and CISOs like to compare their organization's security spending to the spending of similar organizations. While looking at comparative organizations can be a good data point, it should not be the primary method of determining an information security budget. The security budget should be that which is required to provide the right level of protection for the organization.

Unless the organization is a startup, in almost every case the information security budget is based on the organization's historical spending, as in, "What did we spend last year?" In fact, that isn't a bad place to start the budget process. Budgeting is all about predicting the future, and the more data the CISO has about the past, the better informed the CISO will be about what might happen down the road. This approach can be helpful especially after many years of operation, as prior learning and experience can inform the CISO as to what is working and what isn't. However, the security program is always changing, evolving, and facing new threats. As a result, there will always be changes to spending year to year. In general, what works best is a bottom-up approach built by first estimating the smallest pieces of the work, then integrating the pieces into a larger plan. The lowest-level elements should be estimated using a risk-based approach that is informed by prior experience.

Here is a list of some of the methods and factors that go into establishing the information security budget:

- **Start with a baseline**   Use the prior year's data as a starting point. The CISO should consider not just the past year's spending but also the past year's budget. How did the prior year's budget compare with what actually was spent, and what can be learned from that information?

- **Build a work breakdown structure (WBS)**   A WBS is a method of estimating the work required on a large effort by breaking down the work into smaller units that are easier to estimate and control. Using a WBS (which is explained in more detail in the "Project Management" section later in this chapter), the CISO can perform a bottom-up estimate of what each activity costs. The WBS aligns with the streams of work and all other activities of the security group and should align with the way the organization collects and reports costs. It wouldn't make sense to build a budget using one method but report spending using another. If the budget aligns with the way costs are reported, the CISO will be better able to manage spending and improve the budgeting process each year.

- **Look at risk assessment results**   If the spending for firewall administration was X but testing indicates the firewalls are frequently misconfigured, maybe the future spending for firewall administration should be more than X. Or, as discussed in Chapter 1, if the annualized loss expectancy (ALE) of a system is $10,000, the organization likely shouldn't be spending $100,000 per year to protect it. The results of risk assessment and analysis activities can and should inform the budget process.

- **Estimate costs of addressing gaps**   The CISO uses the results of assessments and audits to determine where spending should occur. Areas of noncompliance usually require spending to address them. In fact, the POA&M or CAP process should include estimating costs of the recommended actions, which in turn should be worked into the budget.

- **Address life cycle costs**   Many items of hardware and software have a defined life. Modern systems and technologies can become end of life (aka end of support), become obsolete, or require upgrades. The costs of technology refresh and maintenance agreements are included in the budget.

- **Conduct value engineering**   A good CISO is always considering if there is a less costly way to do something. Where efficiencies can be gained there may be a cost savings as well.

- **Determine what's new**   The CISO should estimate the costs of addressing new initiatives, making improvements, incorporating new technologies, or addressing new regulations. Organizations change as well. They buy or merge with other companies, introduce new products and services, enter new markets, and so forth. All the changes each year are considered and reflected in the budget if necessary.

- **Consider what could possibly go wrong**   Bad things can and will happen. The CISO should establish budgets for unexpected items such as significant security incidents, pandemics, disasters, labor strikes, or things that may pop up that can't be specifically predicted. The CISO should consider the cost and viability of purchasing security breach insurance for the organization.

- **Establish management reserves**   Few organizations allow the CISO to create a budget for undefined spending, but the CISO should allow some *wiggle room* in the budget (which is sometimes referred to as a *management reserve*). It is simply an extra amount added to the estimate "just in case." Sometimes, this is done by including in budget items extra amounts that can be tapped into if needed. The best CISOs are careful not to misrepresent costs, but they don't want to leave themselves short either.

- **Do a rolling forecast**   Information security program budgets are typically established annually, but many organizations create a forecast that extends beyond the next year. The CISO needs to look ahead and plan beyond the next year. It is common to create a three-year forecast that is updated on an annual basis along with the annual budget.

- **Determine what's in the budget**   The budget includes all the items that the CISO is responsible for. This includes hardware, software, employees, consultants, outsourced services, vendors, managed services, and any other items within the scope of the security program for which the CISO has been designated responsibility.

- **Establish not just what to spend but when**   The CISO should establish how much can be spent on each WBS element and when that spending will occur. This is usually estimated by allocating costs on a monthly basis. The finance and accounting department needs to know this information to estimate accruals and cashflow.

But the CISO needs to know this information to plan when activities will occur and track and approve spending. If a budgeted line item assumes costs that will be spread over the entire year, the budget should reflect the spending timeline. Allocating the budget by month allows the CISO to manage spending in accordance with a plan.

Capital Investment vs. Expenses

During a discussion with one CISO about *managed services*, he told us that he does not use such services, but the reason was not an obvious one. His decision was based on the financial preferences of his company. For accounting reasons, his company favors capital expenses (CAPEX) over operating expenses (OPEX), so he is encouraged to spend on infrastructure rather than pay for services. Therefore, he invests in building security capabilities in-house (considered CAPEX) instead of outsourcing the services (considered OPEX).

After estimating the budget, the CISO has to sell it to the next people up the approval chain. This process varies considerably from organization to organization, but in all cases the CISO must be able to justify the estimate. The budget should be supplemented with solid data. More importantly, the CISO must be able to speak the language of those up the chain and address their sensitivities and way of doing things. What type of data is more likely to hold water with the CEO? How has the organization *done it before*? Has the CISO thought of everything? Can *it* be done for less? The authors have seen budgets created with a great deal of effort and precision only to have them rejected or cut because the CISO couldn't convince management that all the expenditures were necessary.

CISOs use a variety of tactics to justify their budget requests. As previously mentioned, one useful tactic is to include comparisons to budgets of other organizations in the industry. Although the CISO would be ill advised to put too much emphasis on industry comparisons to *create* the budget, such comparisons can sometimes be helpful in *justifying* the budget to others. CEOs love to hear that the organization is spending less on something than the competition is spending. If industry comparisons show that is the case, the CISO can use that information to his or her advantage. Industry sources such as Gartner and Forrester and vendors such as RSA, Verizon, and IBM can be good sources of security spending data.

The two most common approaches to justifying the information security budget are to frame the discussion around risk and/or regulatory compliance:

- **Risk** The CISO has likely performed risk analysis to understand the organization's assets and their value to the business and has used this information to establish priorities and determine where and how much to spend on protecting those assets. This same information can be used to justify the spending. If the CEO or budget approver understands the relationship between the risk, impact to the business, and the cost of mitigating that risk, they are more likely to support the spending.

- **Compliance** Regulations are a common forceful driver to security spending. If the regulation says information must be protected and specifies fines for noncompliance, then the risk of those fines can justify spending.

Managing and Monitoring Spending

Once the budget is approved, it can be used as the benchmark for monitoring and controlling costs. The individual items that make up the budget, as defined in a WBS or other method, can be used to establish how costs are accounted for and tracked. For instance, if the WBS includes an element of cost for operating the security operations center (SOC), the accounting department can establish a cost account and charge numbers to be able to approve and record spending associated with the SOC. This alignment between the budget and actual spending allows the security finances to be controlled and monitored by comparing *budget versus actuals*. Comparing the actual spending to the budget on a periodic basis is key to managing security finances.

Cost accounts should be established for all items, or groups of items, in the budget. This requires close collaboration between the CISO and the finance or accounting team. Establishing the cost accounts includes defining who can approve spending and at what thresholds. Responsibility for cost accounts may lie with the CISO, or the CISO may delegate other managers to approve spending. In practice this is implemented by defining who can approve timesheets, create or approve purchase orders, or commit to contracts.

Actual spending for labor or expenses is reported to the CISO by the accounting team for each cost account. If the cost accounts align with the budget line items, as they should, the CISO can compare the planned spending as defined in the budget with the actual spending that is occurring. This shows spending underruns or overruns and allows the CISO to adjust future spending accordingly.

Security Program Resource Management: Building the Security Team

The security team is the most important resource the CISO has available to secure and protect the organization's information assets. The CISO "drives the bus" and is responsible for getting the *right* people on the bus—the *right* people are not necessarily the people with the best technical skills but rather the people that can best carry out the vision of the CISO. Therefore, the right people for the team may be those with the best mix of technical, communication, and interpersonal skills, coupled with personality traits like integrity, honesty, and humility.

Here are some of the factors that go into creating and maintaining a great security team:

- **Define the staffing strategy** Staffing the security team starts with defining a staffing strategy. The CISO should define what kind of team he or she wants and then define the path to achieving that team. Ideally, the CISO defines the goals for the team's culture, abilities, approach, methods of working, recruiting, and retention. This provides guidance for how the team is staffed. For instance, if the CISO wants a team that is highly collaborative but hires people who are introverted and communicate poorly, achieving the collaborative team that the CISO is seeking may not be possible. Likewise, if the CISO decides that technical security knowledge is paramount, then that should be part of the staffing strategy so that the CISO obtains the strong technical staff that he or she desires.

- **Conduct a job analysis**   A job analysis is a process to collect all available information about the type of work and job functions required, which enables the CISO to identify all job roles required for the team and create job descriptions for those roles. Information to be collected includes duties, responsibilities, outcomes, technologies, processes, regulatory drivers, standards, and related data. The more information collected, the easier the CISO's task is to define the roles.

- **Define job roles and create job descriptions**   Job roles and descriptions are used to help recruit staff and to set clear expectations for employees. Using data collected from the job analysis, the CISO can create functional job descriptions that define each role on the team. In some organizations this activity is the responsibility of HR, and in some cases the CISO does not have the authority to define job roles and instead must use the job roles defined or enforced by HR. This may limit the CISO's ability to create and use job roles and job descriptions as a tool to hire and build the staff. Or this situation may be an opportunity for the CISO to collaborate with HR to define the team. The goal is to have a set of job descriptions that can be used as a tool to build the staff and communicate expectations to employees.

- **Use the NICE Workforce Framework**   The US National Institute of Standards and Technology (NIST) has created a framework for cybersecurity job roles in which job descriptions and training requirements are available in a library for any employers to use. It is called the National Initiative for Cybersecurity Education (NICE) Cybersecurity Workforce Framework (NIST Special Publication 800-181). CISOs can take advantage of these predefined *work roles* to create the organization's security job descriptions. This not only saves the CISO time but provides an additional advantage of enabling the use of work roles that have been vetted by industry and updated over time.

- **Define career paths**   One tool used by many companies to attract, support, and retain employees is to define and use *career paths*. Career paths are defined sequences of job roles, training, and performance criteria that employees can follow to grow their careers while staying within the organization. In today's highly competitive recruiting landscape, employers look for ways to attract and retain employees. One thing employees want is an understanding of how they can advance their careers at a given company. Defining and documenting career paths that the organization and employees can follow helps keep employees satisfied and helps the organization to retain talent and enable employees to expand their skills and get better at their jobs.

- **Training**   Like many areas in business, the security landscape is ever changing and evolving. People need training almost continuously to keep their knowledge and skills current. It is essential that the CISO has a training plan and associated budget to keep the security team properly educated. Some CISOs establish relationships with training organizations or colleges and universities to provide unique learning opportunities for their employees. We know a CISO who brings in experts throughout the year, every year, to teach security certification classes so that the entire security staff is better able to obtain important industry certifications. CISOs know that they need to invest wisely in training to enable their staff to meet the goals of the security program.

- **Handling personnel and teamwork issues**   All CISOs should have a plan for handling personnel issues without disrupting operations. However, most CISOs address this by trying to prevent issues in the first place. One way to accomplish this, as mentioned earlier, is to include character and communication as part of the hiring criteria. Having the right people will go a long way in preventing issues involving relationships and teamwork. Other methods to prevent these types of issues include creating a portal to help teammates collaborate, having clearly defined roles and responsibilities, and holding regular interworking sessions to foster and facilitate better communication. If problems do occur, there should be documented procedures for bringing issues to the attention of HR, the CISO, or both and rules with disciplinary actions for causing problems that impact any aspect of the security program performance.

Is Finding Good IT Security People Really That Hard?

It is widely reported in the media and by industry groups that there is a huge shortage of people to staff IT security positions. We recently asked a CISO how he is dealing with this shortage of available talent. His reply: "What shortage?" This CISO of a multibillion-dollar company has a very large staff that has doubled in size over the past two years. He hasn't had any problem growing his staff. Why? He gets his people from within his company. Historically, most IT people did not want to do security work. But not anymore. His company's IT people are begging to work for him. His firm encourages people to move around within the company, and management encourages him to staff from within. The CISO has created a great culture within his group, resulting in people from the IT department seeking him out for roles on the security team. He chooses people based on personality rather than experience, because he knows he can provide training to give them the needed security knowledge and skills. As he put it, "You can train skills, but you can't train character."

Project Management

Project management is the lowest level in the management hierarchy (portfolio, program, and project). The goal of project management is to ensure that every project achieves the desired outcome on time and within budget. Project management includes identifying and controlling resources, measuring progress, and adjusting the plan as needed as progress is made. The CISO may directly serve as the project manager for some or all security projects, or the CISO may delegate others to serves as project managers. In either case, the CISO should be familiar with project management principles and techniques.

It is important to apply good project management practices to projects of all sizes. Some organizations focus project management efforts on large projects and tend to neglect small projects. These small projects can end up costing the organization significant time and resources if they are not properly managed. Project management may not be formalized for all projects. The extent of formalization may be governed by project size or importance; however, good project management principles should be applied to all projects. This includes, at a minimum, identifying the scope, developing criteria for measuring success, monitoring and controlling resources, and documenting these items in a plan. This section discusses some of the fundamental tenants of project management and provides a walkthrough of the project management process.

Project Management Fundamentals

Similar to the CIA triad (confidentiality, integrity, and availability) of information security, project management also has a triad, composed of the following elements:

- **Scope**   Boundary of work to be performed
- **Schedule**   Timeline to perform the work
- **Budget**   Cost and resources required to perform the work

If one of these components changes, the other two components usually are affected. For example, changes to the scope of a project will likely affect the project budget and schedule. The manner in which these elements are applied determines the quality of the project. This interdependency is illustrated in Figure 3-4.

Ultimately, project management as a practice is focused on managing and controlling these three fundamental components to achieve the goals of the project. There is always a trade-off in project management. Decisions around cost, schedule, and scope affect the quality of the project deliverables. Successful projects are completed on time (schedule), within cost expectations (budget), and achieve the technical and business objectives (scope).

 EXAM TIP   CCISO candidates should be familiar with the fundamental project management terms scope, schedule, and budget and understand how these components affect the project.

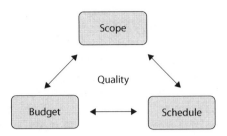

Figure 3-4
Project
management
fundamentals

Project Management Considerations

There is an old saying in project management and software/system development: "Good, fast, or cheap—pick two." This is a simplistic representation of the situation, but it is an important concept to illustrate. The idea is that while the goal is always to strike a balance between the three principles, sometimes two have to outweigh the other. On every project, some key decisions must be made about what principle is most important. Is the goal an end product that is of high quality (good), inexpensive to develop (cheap), or delivered quickly (fast)? There is always a trade-off to be made, as illustrated in Figure 3-5 and described here:

- Good + cheap = slow to deliver
- Cheap + fast = poor quality
- Fast + good = expensive
- Fast + good + cheap = sweet spot

The ultimate goal is usually to harmonize the three principles. It may not be possible, but it should be the goal.

Project Management Training and Certifications

There are several project management certification bodies; two well-known ones are the Project Management Institute and AXELOS. These organizations provide a range of benefits to the community, including publications, forums, conferences, networking opportunities, and best practice resources, and offer certifications and training for continuous learning.

NOTE This section does not present a comprehensive survey of project management training organizations. The organizations introduced here are simply a few of the prevalent ones in the industry, used to illustrate the range of project management training and certifications available.

Figure 3-5
Good, fast, or
cheap—pick two

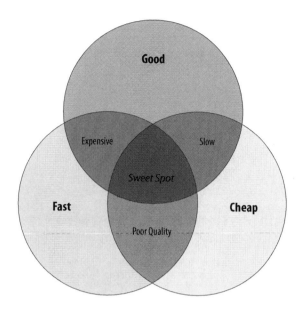

Project Management Institute

The *Project Management Institute (PMI)* is a global nonprofit organization focused on project management certification and education. PMI develops standards, conducts research, produces publications, hosts conferences, and facilitates networking and collaboration for project management professionals. PMI's flagship certification is the Project Management Professional (PMP), but it also provides training and certification for the following:

- Program Management Professional (PgMP)
- Portfolio Management Professional (PfMP)
- Certified Associate in Project Management (CAPM)
- PMI Professional in Business Analysis (PMI-PBA)
- PMI Agile Certified Practitioner (PMI-ACP)
- PMI Risk Management Professional (PMI-RMP)
- PMI Scheduling Professional (PMI-SP)

AXELOS

AXELOS is a global best practice organization that provides certification and training in a variety of subject areas, including project management, IT service management, and cybersecurity. The AXELOS certification tracks include the following:

- IT Service Management (ITIL)
- Cyber Resilience (RESILIA)

- PRojects IN Controlled Environments (PRINCE2)
- PRINCE2 Agile
- AgileSHIFT
- Managing Successful Programmes (MSP)
- Management of Risk (M_o_R)
- Portfolio, Programme and Project Offices (P3O)
- Portfolio Management (MoP)
- Management of Value (MoV)

Phases of Project Management

Good project management allows a project to move in the right direction by allocating appropriate resources, providing leadership, and planning for events that may cause the project to drift astray. Projects are made up of one or more phases which collectively represent the activities and tasks involved in a project. Project management should be put in place to ensure that each phase of the project is followed. This is accomplished by choosing and following a project management model. There are many project management models from which to choose. The model outlined in this book is based on the PMI Project Management Body of Knowledge (PMBOK) process groups, outlined in Figure 3-6, which include the following:

- **Initiating** Identify the business need and define the project.
- **Planning** Develop a plan to ensure the project meets the scope, time, and cost goals.
- **Executing** Coordinate resources to execute the project plans.
- **Monitoring and Controlling** Measure project performance, monitor deviations, and take corrective actions.
- **Closing** Formal acceptance and organized closing of the project.

While these phases are discussed sequentially, in practice they may be implemented sequentially, iteratively, or concurrently. In the model depicted in Figure 3-6, the monitoring and controlling process occurs throughout the project. In practice, the monitoring and controlling process occurs during the executing phase and to some degree

Figure 3-6
Phases of project
management

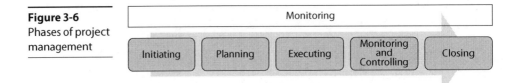

in the initiating, planning, and closing phases. In addition, the initiating and planning phases may happen simultaneously in some organizations. The project management process groups can be tailored and customized to fit the organization's needs. In this section we examine project management by breaking down each of these processes and discussing the components of each.

 NOTE Although the project management model discussed in this section is based on the PMI PMBOK process groups, this section is not intended to align completely with the way PMBOK approaches project management. This section is written based on the authors' experience observing how project management is applied in practice.

Initiating

Before a project can begin, up-front work must be completed in the initiating phase. First, a business need or problem must be identified, and a potential solution discussed. Depending on the feasibility of the solution, this may warrant the creation of a project. The key initiatives that take place in the initiating phase include the following:

- Collect requirements
- Define the project scope
- Identify and interview stakeholders
- Define assumptions and constraints
- Establish the general project budget and timeline
- Develop the project scope document

Collect Requirements

Every project must have a set of *requirements*, a collection of capabilities or items that are required in the final deliverable to meet the project objectives. The requirements provide the foundation for defining the project scope. The work required in collecting the requirements can vary. In some cases, the requirements are provided by the customer or defined prior to the beginning of the project. Other times the requirements are developed as part of the project. The requirements that are provided may vary in detail, and additional information gathering sessions may be required to create clear and complete requirements.

Define the Project Scope

As part of project initiating, it is important to put some kind of boundary on the work to be done. The *scope* of a project defines the boundary of the project. It is the work that is required to fulfill the customer requirements. The scope should outline what is and is not included in the project. The scope includes the project goals, requirements, stakeholders, schedule, and budget. A well-defined, documented, and monitored scope is an important factor in a project's success. A poorly defined project scope can result in one or more of the following:

- **Scope creep**   Uncontrolled growth in a project's scope due to the addition of requirements, desires, or targets
- **Cost overrun**   Unexpected costs incurred during the course of a project that are in excess of budgeted amounts
- **Schedule overrun**   Unexpected schedule delays incurred during the course of a project

Scope is defined in a *project scope document* or *scope statement*, which describes project deliverables and outcomes.

Identify and Interview Stakeholders

As part of project initiating, stakeholders should be identified and interviewed and their needs should be assessed. *Stakeholders* are people with a *vested interest or stake* in the project. This includes both internal and external stakeholders.

- **Internal stakeholders**   Individuals within the organization such as team members, business area managers, senior executives, and so on
- **External stakeholders**   Individuals external to the organization such as customers, vendors, users, contractors, suppliers, or investors

The stakeholders are identified and their details documented, including, at a minimum, their names, roles, contact information, and areas of interest. For example, some stakeholders may be performing the work, others may be affected by the work, and others may be the recipients, such as a customer, business owner, or investor. Stakeholder identification is typically accomplished through interviews, lessons learned, brainstorming sessions, or utilizing checklists. Stakeholders are sometimes classified based on their influence, interest, and power. Stakeholders with a high degree of influence and interest who can directly affect project output are sometimes referred to as *key stakeholders*.

The stakeholders are interviewed and assessed to determine their needs, expectations, and definition of success for the project. This information is documented to ensure their requirements are clearly understood.

Define Assumptions and Constraints

In the initiating phase, the possible assumptions and known constraints should be captured and documented. These form the basis for project planning.

- **Assumptions**   Beliefs or expectations in planning based on knowledge or experience that may not be certain, true, or real (for example, assume that resource *X* will be available for the duration of the project).

- **Constraints** Limitations or restrictions to the project's schedule, resources, quality, budget, scope, or risk that may impact the project during executing (for example, resource X can be tested only during the weekends). Constraints can be business oriented or technically oriented.

Assumptions and constraints are documented at a high level during the initiating phase and should be tracked during the project life cycle. Assumptions are beliefs that may turn out to be false, and constraints are restrictions or barriers to project execution. Both can add to project risk and effect project requirements, which is why it is critical to document, analyze, and monitor them throughout the project.

Establish the General Project Budget and Timeline

The initiating phase includes discussing and estimating the initial budget for the project. The budget may not be very detailed in the initiating phase; however, it is important to have an estimate of what the general budget for the project will be. The project timeline also needs to be discussed and estimated to predict when the results generally need to be delivered.

Develop the Project Scope Document

All the components described in the initiating phase should be captured and the information integrated into a project scope document. The *project scope document* captures all scope data and high-level decisions regarding the project and typically contains the following, at a minimum:

- Scope definitions
- Stakeholder inputs
- Assumptions and constraints
- Budget and time frame
- Initial schedule and resources

The project scope document may also be referred to as the *scope statement*. The purpose of the project scope document is to document the boundary of the project. This is used to ensure that there are not deviations in the project that lead to scope creep and that there are well-defined project objectives so that success is tangible.

Planning

The planning phase encompasses the following components:

- Determine the SDLC methodology
- Develop measurable goals
- Develop the work breakdown structure
- Develop the project schedule

- Assign project resources and budget
- Assess project risk
- Document the project plan

Determine the SDLC Methodology

An important step in the planning phase is to decide which methodology and techniques to use to manage the project. This decision may be governed by the organization's project management standards and preferred methodologies or it may be left up to the discretion of the project manager. This determination includes consideration of whether to follow a systems development life cycle.

As previously introduced, the project management model outlined in this chapter includes initiating, planning (the topic of this section), executing, monitoring and controlling, and closing processes. Within this model, if the project involves developing or managing a system, product, or service, the project manager may choose to incorporate a *systems development life cycle (SDLC)* to establish a methodology to follow during (typically) the planning and executing phases. The systems development lifecycles discussed in this section include the *waterfall* methodology, *incremental*, and *agile*.

 NOTE Not all projects use an SDLC within the project processes. For example, if a CISO is managing a project to map the company's security controls to NIST SP 800-53, the CISO may follow the project processes (initiating, planning, executing, monitoring and controlling, and closing) but most likely would not use an SDLC, because no system, product, or service is being developed. However, if the project includes developing and implementing new controls, such as security tools, systems, or applications, the CISO might choose to incorporate an SDLC within the project processes.

Traditional/Phased/Waterfall The phased life cycle is characterized by linear-sequential distinct steps, each of which must be completed before the subsequent step is started. This method is also commonly referred to as the *traditional* or *waterfall* approach. In this model, the project scope, schedule, and budget are determined in the beginning (planning phase) of the project. The scope is fixed going into the project, and changes to schedule and budget are carefully managed throughout. The key factor is that all the activities for each phase must be performed, documented, and completed before beginning the subsequent phase. This concept is illustrated in Figure 3-7. This model places a heavy emphasis on up-front planning and administration.

This model is useful for projects with controlled, predictive development and requirements that are clear and well documented in advance. The downside of this method is that it is an inflexible process, as it assumes the requirements can be defined in the beginning and will not change during the project. This may be beneficial for some projects, but it is detrimental for projects that have many variables that affect the project scope or projects for which the requirements are uncertain or incomplete. This method can result in the accrual of significant cost increases if changes are required later in the project.

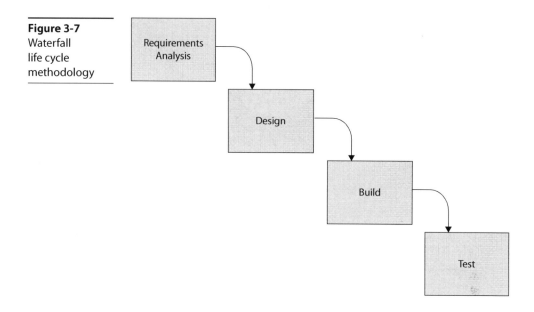

Figure 3-7 Waterfall life cycle methodology

Incremental   In an *incremental* life cycle model, multiple development life cycles are carried out. Each of the life cycles has a predetermined timeframe and produces a complete increment of a capability. Each capability is then integrated with that of the previous phase to produce the whole product. This concept is illustrated in Figure 3-8.

Agile   *Agile* is an overarching term for several development methodologies that utilize iterative and incremental development processes and encourage team-based collaboration. Instead of detailed requirements up front followed by rigid development,

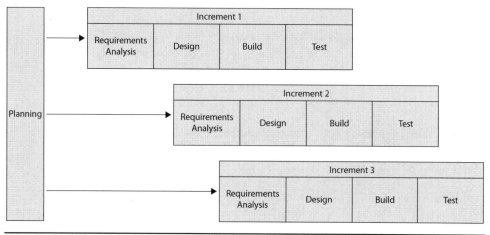

Figure 3-8   Incremental build model

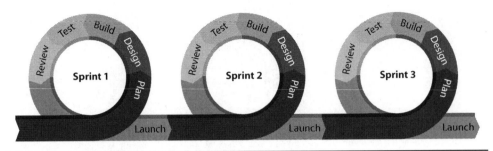

Figure 3-9   Agile methodology

the agile methodology incorporates iterative models along the way to enable speed and flexibility. In the agile methodology, the product development work is broken out into scheduled iterations known as *sprints*. This process is illustrated in Figure 3-9. The length of each sprint varies, but sprints tend to be two to four weeks long. The scope is defined before the start of an iteration.

 EXAM TIP   CCISO candidates should be familiar with the various development life cycle methodologies.

Develop Measurable Goals

A critical part of the planning phase is the development of measurable goals. These are used to develop metrics used in the monitoring and controlling phase throughout the project to measure success, identify deviations that require corrective action, and determine when the project is complete. A project can't be deemed a success if no one knows what success looks like. One of the methodologies for setting and measuring goals is S.M.A.R.T., introduced in Chapter 2.

Develop the Work Breakdown Structure

One of the first activities of project planning is breaking down the larger project into smaller, more manageable, bite-size chunks or efforts. These are defined as part of the previously introduced *work breakdown structure (WBS)*, which is a hierarchical decomposition of the work to be performed by the project team to accomplish and deliver against the project goals. The WBS is a project management tool used to break down the project into organized individual work elements (tasks, subtasks, and deliverables). Figure 3-10 illustrates a representation of a graphical WBS; however, a WBS can be something as simple as a task list.

The idea is that every element or task in the WBS is broken down and assigned its own budget, resources, scope, and schedule. This is one way to organize everything. The trick to creating a good WBS is including the right level of detail. If the WBS has too much detail, the project manager will have great control and a well-thought-out plan but

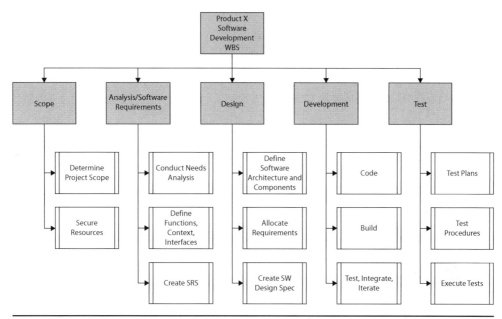

Figure 3-10 Work breakdown structure example

may get bogged down in management overhead and overload. If the WBS isn't detailed enough, the project manager will have less control and a fuzzier plan, which can lead to scope creep, budget overruns, and schedule delays.

Work breakdown structures can be *function oriented* or *task oriented*. For example, a function-oriented WBS would define tasks based on each of the project phases, such as:

- Analyze, Design, Build, Test
- Plan, Do, Check, Act
- Initiate, Plan, Execute, Monitor, Close

A task-oriented WBS would be organized by task, configuration items, or items that need to be built, such as:

- Select Scanning Tool, Implement Tool, Perform Scans, Adjust Profiles and Policies
- Asset Inventory, Hardware, Software, Network, Data
- User Interface, Communication Stack, Database, Middleware

Both function-oriented and task-oriented WBSs can be useful. The decision of which type to use ultimately comes down to the style or preference of the project manager and what makes sense for the project and the organization.

Develop the Project Schedule

Once the WBS has been developed, budgets and schedules are assigned to each element in the WBS. In developing the project schedule, it is important to factor in the following:

- **Resources and duration**   What resources are involved in each particular element? What duration is expected?

- **Dependencies**   What are the dependencies? What does each particular item/element require?

When going through this part of the planning phase, the project manager begins to see more clearly which activities are on the critical path. The *critical path* is the series of events or activities that, if changed, would change the overall end date of the project. If any one of the activities in the critical path is delayed, the end date of the overall project delivery is impacted. A project manager must always keep an eye on the items on the critical path.

One method for documenting and visualizing project dependencies is to use a *Gantt chart*, a type of chart that illustrates the project schedule and shows the dependencies of tasks. It provides a great way to visualize all the outputs of tasks that must be fed as input into other tasks. It shows which tasks must be completed for other tasks to commence. This helps the project manager to identify project dependencies and conceptualize and visualize items on the critical path. Microsoft Project is a popular project planning tool that uses Gantt charts to help plan and show project schedules. Figure 3-11 illustrates a high-level example of a Gantt chart in Microsoft Project.

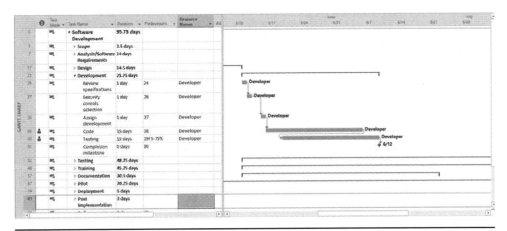

Figure 3-11   Gantt chart example (with critical path) in Microsoft Project

Assign Project Resources and Budget

Once the WBS and project schedule have been created, the resources and budget for each project element are assigned. This part of the planning phase is typically where decisions are made regarding whether to use in-house resources or external resources and whether to build, buy, or rent. The following are some of the considerations:

- **Internal resources**
  - Select and assign resources to each WBS element
  - Tailor the WBS to the resources that are available
  - May require new hires or new training of staff
  - May require acquisition of hardware and software
- **External resources**
  - Conduct competitive selection process if time/resources allow
  - Establish contracts and statements of work (SOWs)
  - Define deliverables, milestones, and obligations
  - Establish service-level agreements (SLAs)

Responsibility Matrix

A *responsibility matrix* can be used to demarcate responsibilities for each activity or task involved in meeting project deliverables. The responsibility matrix is often known as a *RACI chart*, with the acronym representing the following:

- **Responsible**   Individuals responsible for completing specific project tasks or activities
- **Accountable**   Typically implies management of an activity or task
- **Consulted**   Individuals whose opinions are consulted regarding specific activities or tasks, typically subject matter experts (SMEs)
- **Informed**   Individuals informed on progression of specific tasks or activities

Figure 3-12 shows an example of a high-level RACI chart.

Assess Project Risk

Every project has some degree of risk. In the context of project management, the risks are project risks rather than information security risks. *Project risks* are things that may occur during the project that may adversely impact the project's success. Project risks should be considered during the planning phase and managed throughout the project. An initial *project risk assessment* should be performed to understand and predict potential

Deliverable or Task	Roles			
	Project Sponsor	CISO	Project Manager	Project Team
Phase 1				
Deliverable/Task 1	CI	A	R	
Deliverable/Task 2	I	A	R	R
Phase 2				
Deliverable/Task 1	A	R	R	I
Deliverable/Task 2	I		RA	

Figure 3-12 RACI chart representation

project risks. The perceived project risks should be identified, analyzed, and ranked in a risk ranking. There are three general types of risk to consider:

- **Technical**   Risk of not meeting requirements for technical reasons
- **Schedule**   Risk of missing project deadlines due to internal or external factors, such as a vendor not delivering on time
- **Budget**   Risk of cost overruns due to poor budget estimation or scope creep

The initial project risk assessment is followed by a determination of which actions should be taken to reduce or mitigate the risks to the project.

Document the Project Plan

The last step in the planning phase is to document the project plan. The project plan serves as a roadmap of activities to be distributed to and followed by the project team and communicated to the stakeholders. The project plan should address, at a minimum, the following components:

- Scope management plan
- Schedule management plan

- Resource management plan
- Cost management plan
- Quality management plan
- Change management plan
- Configuration management plan
- Communication plan
- Risk management plan
- System security plan

Organizations may use something as simple as a Word document or Excel spreadsheet for the project plan, or may implement a more elaborate project planning tool such as an application with a back-end database that provides a web portal to manage tasks and store documents. The choice depends on the needs and sophistication level of the organization and the complexity of the project. The plan can be documented and managed in many ways. The key is that it should be documented.

Depending on the organization and its project management practices, the project plan developed in the planning phase and the project scope document developed in the initiating phase may be the same document. In any case, some type of plan must be developed and followed throughout the life cycle of the project. Sticking to the plan is important to prevent scope creep. If the scope continually expands in an uncontrolled manner, the project might never meet its goals, might run out of funds, or might run over schedule.

Executing

Once the planning has been completed, it is time to follow the plan in the project executing phase. This phase is where the deliverables are created and produced based on the scope of the project described in the statement of work. This phase includes the following activities:

- Follow the plan, execute project tasks, and manage project budget
- Implement changes and track project progress
- Communicate and report on progress to stakeholders and other vested parties
- Report status within the team and to management
- Hold staff and vendors accountable

It is important to remember to adjust the plan as needed. No project goes completely according to plan. Project management is really all about planning and making strategic adjustments when needed.

Monitoring and Controlling

The monitoring and controlling phase of the life cycle is focused on monitoring and controlling key project variables. Although this phase is being discussed sequentially after the executing phase, in practice this phase occurs throughout the life cycle of the project. Monitoring and controlling consists of the following activities:

- Monitor and manage scope creep
- Monitor and manage project budget
- Monitor, track, and report on key performance indicators (KPIs)
- Process change requests
- Track project variations
- Track and report on project metrics and performance
- Monitor and manage costs, scheduling, resource utilization, budget, and risk

This section discusses some of the key aspects of monitoring and controlling that must occur throughout the project life cycle, including configuration management, change management, and quality management.

Configuration and Change Management

It is important to incorporate configuration management and change management on every project. *Configuration management* consists of processes and tools to manage the requirements, specifications, and standard configurations of the product or deliverable. *Change management* consists of processes and tools for identifying, tracking, monitoring, and controlling changes to the project plan and baseline.

The *configuration management plan* defines the process for making changes to the configuration of the deliverable. It documents configurable items that require formal change control and describes the process for controlling those changes. The *change management plan* documents the process for managing changes to the project and describes how to perform monitoring and controlling of changes.

The processes used for configuration and change management are documented in their respective plans and incorporated into the project plan in the planning phase of the project life cycle. Configuration and change management processes are then monitored and controlled throughout the life of the project.

Quality Management

Project *quality management* is the practice of ensuring that all project activities meet a defined level of excellence. It involves defining quality standards and putting processes in place to ensure the standards are applied correctly on the project. A *quality management system (QMS)* is a collection of processes and activities intended to ensure desired levels of quality are met. The QMS incorporates quality assurance and quality control practices,

Figure 3-13
Quality
management
concepts

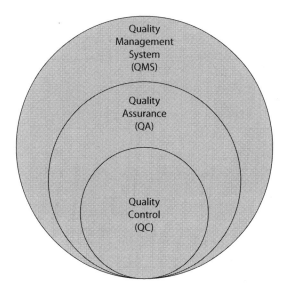

as illustrated in Figure 3-13. These terms are sometimes used interchangeably in discussions of quality management, but there are some key differences:

- **Quality assurance (QA)** Focused on proactive *prevention* of project defects by creating a system to measure and control quality throughout the *process*
- **Quality control (QC)** Focused on *detection* of defects in the *deliverable* based on quality assurance criteria

Decisions regarding how quality management will be handled during the project are documented in the quality management plan in the planning phase, incorporated into the project plan, and monitored and controlled throughout the project life cycle. This section discusses two common methodologies for quality management, Six Sigma and the ISO 9000 family of standards.

Six Sigma Six Sigma is a process improvement methodology focused on improving process quality by using statistical methods of measuring operational efficiency and reducing variation, defects, and waste. It was originally developed by Motorola with the goal of identifying and removing defects in the manufacturing process. The maturity of a process is described by a sigma rating, which indicates the percentage of defects that the process contains. Six Sigma projects use the DMAIC and DMADV project methodologies, which are based on Deming's Plan, Do, Check, Act (PDCA) cycle. DMAIC stands for "define, measure, analyze, improve, control" and DMADV stands for "define, measure, analyze, design, verify." Although the Six Sigma methodology was originally intended for manufacturing, it has evolved and is used by many industries and business functions. Some organizations use Six Sigma to improve security assurance by measuring the success factors of different security controls and processes.

ISO 9000   Chapters 1 and 2 discussed the ISO/IEC 27000 family of standards, which focuses on implementing an information security management system (ISMS). The ISO 9000 family of standards is focused on various aspects of quality management and implementing a QMS. The publications provide guidance and tools to help organizations meet customer requirements for deliverables while ensuring quality is managed and improved. The key publications in the ISO 9000 family are outlined here:

- **ISO 9000**   Quality management systems – Fundamentals and vocabulary
- **ISO 9001**   Quality management systems – Requirements
- **ISO 9004**   Quality management – Quality of an organization – Guidance to achieve sustained success
- **ISO 19011**   Guidelines for auditing management systems

In addition, there are industry-specific standards based on ISO 9001, which include the following (with abbreviated titles indicating their application):

- **ISO 13485**   Medical devices
- **ISO/TS 54001**   Electoral organizations at all levels of government
- **ISO 18091**   Local government
- **ISO/TS 22163**   Rail organizations
- **ISO/TS 29001**   Petroleum, petrochemical, and natural gas industries
- **ISO/IEC/IEEE 90003**   Software engineering

Closing

The last phase of the project is *project closing*. The closing phase includes the following activities:

- Review of project scope document to ensure requirements are met
- Ensure signoff of deliverables by stakeholders
- Close out contracts, process and pay invoices, and shut down project expenditures
- Update final project costs accounting
- Securely dispose of project materials, as some records may contain sensitive information
- Archive project records that must be maintained for future reference
- Conduct lessons learned, including any feedback from stakeholders
- Release and reassign resources

A proper closing phase allows for a final review and acceptance of the project, closeout of contracts and financial activities, and release of resources. While this particular project may be complete, there is most likely another project around the corner that may require some of the resources that have been tied up.

 EXAM TIP CCISO candidates should be familiar with the general phases of project management and corresponding project activities.

Project Management Oversight

The CISO typically is not responsible for actively managing every security project. The CISO is involved in project oversight but may enlist another resource such as a security project manager, deputy CISO, or other staff as the project manager. When reviewing security projects, the CISO should consider questions such as the following:

- Are projects following the organization's project management practices?
- Are the processes based on industry standards and best practices?
- Is the project plan being followed?
- Is the critical path well defined?
- Do team members and the project manager have a thorough understanding of activities in the critical path?
- How often are projects on time and on budget?
- Does the project have a defined communication plan?
- Are business objectives being achieved in a cost-effective manner?
- Is the project maintaining compliance with industry regulations and local laws?

Chapter Review

The CISO is responsible for managing the information security program of the organization. The key aspects of a security program include security areas of focus (internal and external drivers that impact how the streams of work and security projects are carried out, such as PCI DSS, HIPAA, and internal policies and requirements); security streams of work (subprograms such as the vulnerability management program, incident response program, and risk management program), often managed using the PDCA approach; security project management; asset and data security management; and security program budget and resource management. Managing these elements in a cohesive and coordinated manner is not simple and requires a thoughtful approach.

Project management is a critical skill for the CISO to master. Although the CISO typically is not the project manager for every security project, the CISO must oversee and be accountable for the projects being undertaken within the information security program. The triad for project management includes scope, schedule, and budget. If one of these components changes, the other two components usually are affected. Projects follow a project management model, which typically includes initiating, planning, executing, monitoring and controlling, and closing processes.

Quick Review

- Security program management is focused on overseeing and managing security areas of focus, security streams of work, security projects, asset and data security, and security program budget and resources.

- Security areas of focus are internal and external organizational drivers that impact how the streams of work and security projects are carried out, such as PCI DSS, HIPAA, and internal policies and requirements.

- Security streams of work (aka subprograms) of the information security program are activities that are ongoing and do not have a beginning, middle, and end, such as identity and access management, vulnerability management, and incident management.

- The triad for project management includes scope, schedule, and budget.

- The traditional project management model is made up of the following processes: initiating, planning, executing, monitoring and controlling, and closing.

- The scope of a project defines the boundary of the project. It is the work that is required to fulfill the customer requirements.

- Scope creep is uncontrolled growth in a project's scope due to the addition of requirements, desires, or targets.

- The systems development life cycle (SDLC) refers to the phases within the project that are associated with the development of a system, software, service, or product. The SDLC typically occurs within the planning and executing processes of the project management model.

- SDLC models include waterfall, iterative, incremental, and agile.

- A work breakdown structure (WBS) is a hierarchical decomposition of the work to be performed by the project team to accomplish and deliver against the project goals. It is a project management tool used to break down the project into organized individual work elements (tasks, subtasks, and deliverables).

- The critical path of a project is the series of events or activities that, if changed, would change the overall end date of the project.

- A Gantt chart illustrates a project schedule and shows the dependencies of tasks.

- A responsibility assignment matrix or RACI chart can be used to demarcate responsibilities for each activity or task involved in meeting project deliverables. RACI is an acronym for responsible, accountable, consulted, and informed.

- Configuration management focuses on the requirements, specifications, and standard configurations of the product or deliverable.
- Change management focuses on identifying, tracking, monitoring, and controlling changes to the project plan and baseline.
- Six Sigma is a process improvement methodology focused on improving process quality by using statistical methods of measuring operational efficiency and reducing variation, defects, and waste.
- The ISO 9000 family of standards is focused on various aspects of quality management and implementing quality management systems (QMSs).

Questions

1. Which of the following activities is an example of a subprogram or stream of work?

   A. Conduct network monitoring

   B. Deploy an intrusion detection system

   C. Build an identity management system

   D. Conduct a penetration test

2. When creating an information security budget, which of the following is the least important factor to consider?

   A. What your boss's perception is about security

   B. Ensuring the budget grows each year so the security department can continue to grow

   C. The costs of labor to staff all the streams of work

   D. How much the organization spent on security last year

3. Which of the following is not a good approach to use to build a strong security team?

   A. Provide career paths for employees

   B. Select people based on character, not just technical skills

   C. Limit employee training so that employees do not increase their skills and decide to leave the company

   D. Provide an environment that encourages communication and collaboration

4. What is essential to determining how well a security subprogram is performing?

   A. Use the "two-person rule" whenever possible

   B. Establish criteria for success and measure the activity against it

   C. Bring in outside experts to review the activity

   D. Interview the subprogram staff

5. Which of the following statements regarding project management is the most accurate?

   A. Project management is only important for small projects.

   B. Project management is important for large projects, while program management is important for ongoing projects.

   C. Project management is only important for large projects.

   D. Project management is important for projects of all sizes.

6. Which of the following terms describes the uncontrolled growth of a project's requirements?

   A. Stakeholder input

   B. Scope creep

   C. Definitions creep

   D. Organic growth

7. Which of the following best describes the critical path in project management?

   A. Activities that, if changed, will change the end date of the project

   B. Activities that will change the end date of the project

   C. Activities that are critical to the project

   D. Activities that are not critical to the project

8. A CISO reviewing current security projects determines that the security project manager for a network redesign did not use the approved WBS. What is this an example of?

   A. Scope creep

   B. Waterfall method

   C. Alternate WBS

   D. Not following the plan

9. Which of the following activities should occur during project closeout?

   A. Conduct lessons learned

   B. Outline the scope

   C. Requirements gathering

   D. Continue billing to the project

10. Which of the following is the main difference between a program and a project?

    A. There is no difference.

    B. A program consists of projects, and a project consists of activities.

    C. Unlike a program, a project has no end.

    D. A program may consist of many projects, while a project consists of only one project.

Answers

1. **A.** An information security program includes streams of work (aka subprograms) that continue throughout the life of the organization. Conducting network monitoring is an ongoing activity that continues for the life of the organization and security program. Building systems and deploying systems are most often projects rather than ongoing subprograms or streams of work. Penetration tests have a defined end to the activity.

2. **B.** It is a good idea to start the information security budget process by looking at what was spent the previous year, include all labor costs, and present the budget to management in terms they can understand. The desire to expand the security staff should not be a factor in defining the security budget.

3. **C.** The organization should not limit employee training for fear that employees may leave the company. That is always a risk, but if the employees aren't properly trained, the organization won't be able to build a strong team. Providing career paths, choosing people based on character, and encouraging communication are all good things to do.

4. **B.** Although interviewing the subprogram staff is always a good idea, the most essential way to determine how well a security subprogram is performing is to establish criteria for success and measure against that criteria.

5. **D.** Although a project may seem trivial, project management is critical for projects of all sizes, not only larger projects.

6. **B.** Scope creep describes the uncontrolled growth of a project's scope.

7. **A.** The critical path of a project is the series of events or activities that, if changed, would change the end date of the project. If any of the activities in the critical path is delayed, the end date of the overall project delivery is impacted.

8. **D.** The security project manager not using the approved work breakdown structure (WBS) is an example of an employee not following the approved plan. Scope creep is when the scope increases during the project, and waterfall is a type of software development methodology. Alternate WBS is an incorrect option intended as a distractor.

9. **A.** The lessons learned component of project closeout is often overlooked. This is a critical activity to learn from past mistakes and improve future projects.

10. **D.** A program may consist of multiple projects, while a project is self-contained.

Information Security Core Competencies

This chapter discusses the following topics:

- Malicious software and attacks
- Social engineering
- Asset security
- Data security
- Identity and access management
- Communication and network security
- Cryptography
- Cloud security
- Physical security
- Software development security
- Forensics, incident handling, and investigations
- Security assessment and testing
- Business continuity and disaster recovery

This chapter discusses core competencies that every CISO should have a solid understanding of. These topics vary in technical depth from competencies that are more administrative in nature, such as security assessment and testing, to very technical competencies, such as cryptography. The CISO doesn't necessarily need to be an expert in each of these areas, but it couldn't hurt to be. The greater the CISO's understanding of these IT, business, and security topics, the better equipped the CISO will be to make decisions and react to problems.

 NOTE Some of these core competencies may not fall under the CISO's area of responsibility in some organizations. For example, not all CISOs are responsible for physical security of the organization or for business continuity planning. These areas may be the responsibility of other leaders or may be shared with other departments.

Malicious Software and Attacks

Chapter 1 described the following steps that an attacker generally carries out during a typical cyberattack:

1. Reconnaissance

2. Enumeration

3. Exploitation

4. Action on objectives

During the exploitation step, the attacker exploits vulnerabilities to gain access to a system and ultimately move on to carrying out the attacker's offensive objectives. Many times this activity involves *weaponization*, which is the deployment of malware, scripts, or other means to exploit a system or systems. This section explores the following types of weaponization:

- Malware

- Scripting and vulnerability-specific attacks

The landscape of malware and cyberattacks is vast and ever-changing. This section is certainly not an exhaustive or thorough compendium of malware and related attacks. Instead, it describes the major types of weaponized attacks that are encountered by security professionals.

 EXAM TIP The CCISO exam may not contain questions about specific types of attacks. However, we included this section because every CISO should have a good understanding of how attacks are planned and executed in order to be able to appropriately defend against them.

Malware

Malware, a contraction for *malicious software*, is any software designed to infiltrate and gain unauthorized access to computer systems to cause damage or disruption. Attackers use malware to compromise systems and carry out objectives such as the following:

- Logging user's keystrokes to capture passwords and other sensitive information

- Using spyware to collect sensitive information for resale

- Carrying out phishing attacks

- Carrying out ransomware attacks to force users to pay a ransom to prevent their data from being lost or destroyed

- Conducting denial-of-service attacks to disrupt business operations

- Redirecting Internet traffic to unintended or malicious websites

This section describes the following types of malware:

- Viruses
- Trojans
- Worms
- Botnets
- Ransomware
- Rootkits

Viruses

A *virus* is a program or segment of code that infects a legitimate program to carry out its malicious job. Viruses use other programs as vehicles to deliver their payload or reproduce themselves. The *payload* is the portion of the virus that carries out the malicious activity, such as deleting, exfiltrating, or encrypting data, modifying files, or sending spam. Here are a few common types of viruses:

- **Macro virus**   Many applications have macro features that allow a user to create and use scripts that automate functions of the application. Microsoft Word and Excel are common applications that have macro capabilities. Each macro is a script that is executed to carry out a task, and it is possible to write macros that perform malicious tasks. Macros can also duplicate themselves and infect other files used by the application.

- **Compression virus**   This term is used to identify a virus that is embedded within a compressed file. When the user decompresses the file to access its contents, the virus executes and performs its malicious task.

- **Stealth virus**   A stealth virus hides both its presence and the bad things that it does to the infected file or system. Stealth viruses are, by design, hard to detect.

- **Polymorphic virus**   Similar to a stealth virus, a polymorphic virus hides itself to avoid detection. It does this by changing itself (actually changing the code) each time it is run. Therefore, antivirus programs designed to look for specific programs or files will not be able to find the virus because it never looks the same.

- **Boot sector virus**   This is malicious code inserted into the boot sector of the disk. Upon installation, the virus either moves data from the boot sector or overwrites it with new information. When the system is rebooted, the malicious code is executed.

- **Multipartite virus**   Viruses that infect both the boot sector and other files in the system are called *multipartite*.

Other types of viruses include the *transient virus*, which runs only when its host application is running, and the *resident virus*, which resides in memory and can remain active even when the host application is closed.

Trojans, Worms, and Botnets

Other types of malware are similar to a virus but have differing characteristics and functions. Here are a few of them:

- **Trojan**   A Trojan, or Trojan horse, is a malicious program that tricks the user into running it because it appears to be a legitimate program. Sometimes the Trojan includes the actual program that the user intends to run, so it appears the program is running correctly when it is in fact also running the malicious code.

- **Worm**   A worm is similar to a virus but, unlike a virus, is able to replicate itself. And unlike a virus, which requires a host program to infect, a worm can stand alone and does not require a host program to do its damage or replicate itself. Worms usually enter a system through a known vulnerability and, once there, can scan the network for other computers that have vulnerabilities and spread to them. Some worms do not attempt to make any changes to a system; their job is to simply spread to other systems and cause disruption by increasing network traffic.

- **Botnet**   A botnet is a group of infected systems that work together to perform an attack. A botnet most often is remotely controlled by cybercriminals to carry out denial-of-service (DoS) attacks or attacks aimed at stealing data or sending messages. Remote control is carried out by some form of command and control system that enables the attackers to control the botnets as a group. Sometimes bots are used to create networks of "zombie" computers that are remotely controlled to perform virtually any kind of operation.

Some Well-known and Common Computer Viruses and Attacks

Of the thousands of computer viruses, several have become well known because their impact was significant or newsworthy. Here are few such viruses as well as a few common ones that are still in the wild today:

- **Gameover ZeuS**   Discovered in 2011, this Trojan horse steals user's web login credentials by inserting malicious code into a web page that logs the user's keystrokes.

- **Code Red**   This virus exploited vulnerabilities in Microsoft IIS web servers and was discovered by two engineers at eEye Digital Security (who were drinking Code Red soda at the time, hence the name). The virus spread quickly and was used to launch denial-of-service attacks on well-known websites including the US White House. According to some estimates, Code Red may have caused up to $2B in lost productivity worldwide.

- **ILOVEYOU**   This virus was released in 2000 and combined social engineering with exploitation of flaws in Microsoft Windows. The victims received an e-mail with an attachment that supposedly contained a love note. Some people found the name of the attachment too enticing to resist, and when they opened the TXT file, it contained a Visual Basic script that overwrote the victim's files and sent itself via e-mail to everyone in the user's address book. ILOVEYOU is believed to have infected 10 percent of the computers in the world at the time.

- **PoisonIvy**   Originally released in 2005 (and believed to have originated in China), this virus allows an attacker to remotely control an infected system using a backdoor. The cybercriminal can move data, change settings, and even invoke the system's microphone and speaker. Even today PoisonIvy is used to carry out attacks on government and private systems throughout the world.

- **Mydoom**   Similar to ILOVEYOU, Mydoom is another backdoor Trojan spread via e-mail. It was written in 2004 and is reported to have caused over $30B in damage by causing denials of service. It is transmitted via e-mail with enticing subjects such as "Error" or "Mail Transaction Failed." When the user opens the attachment, a backdoor program is installed. Newer variants of Mydoom prevent the operation of some antivirus software and interferes with antivirus program updates.

- **W32.DisTrack**   Also known as Shamoon, this virus was released in 2012 and was targeted at Saudi government and commercial firms. It is transmitted by a macro embedded in a document file that, when executed, allows attackers to communicate with the infected system using Microsoft PowerShell. The macro enables the remote installation of the W32.DisTrack malware, which then wipes the hard drive of the computer.

- **Sapphire (or SQL Slammer)**   Originally released in 2003, Sapphire was another DoS worm. It spread incredibly fast and caused over $1B in damage, most notably knocking thousands of Bank of America ATM machines offline. Sapphire is transmitted from one SQL server to another, taking advantage of known vulnerabilities in Microsoft SQL Server software.

Ransomware

Ransomware is a particularly insidious type of malware that forces its victim to choose between paying a ransom or losing valuable assets. Ransomware is delivered through any of the usual mechanisms: phishing e-mails, social engineering tricks, or by exploiting known vulnerabilities in operating systems or other programs. Once the ransomware infects a system, it usually encrypts files and notifies the user that unless a ransom is paid, usually with bitcoins or other difficult-to-trace transaction methods, the data will remain encrypted and lost to the user and their organization.

Variants of a ransomware attack include threatening to reveal sensitive information or pornographic material (which may have been stored by the victim on their system or placed there by the attacker). But all ransomware presents the organization with a dilemma: pay the ransom or something bad will happen.

Paying a ransom doesn't always mean the user or organization will get their assets back. After all, they are dealing with criminals. However, sometimes when the ransom is paid, the cybercriminals follow through on their promise to provide decryption keys or otherwise help the victim recover from the attack. This is because the cybercriminals want to be able to continue their operation, and its success is more likely if future victims know that the criminals will do what they promised if the ransom is paid. In fact, some cybercriminal organizations have "call centers" that help their victims make payments and decrypt their data.

Ransomware puts the organization in a difficult position in which it must weigh the impacts of two very bad options: pay the ransom or lose the assets. The CISO is right in the middle of this decision. Like all responses to security breaches, the response to ransomware attacks should be well planned and practiced. The time to decide how to respond to such a crisis is not while it is happening, as the intensity of the situation can cloud the judgment of even the coolest leaders. The organization should plan ahead of time by understanding the value of various information assets and how much ransom the organization might be willing to pay in the event of an attack. Ransomware planning should also include when to involve law enforcement as part of the incident response. Ransomware planning also includes having a good BCP/DR plan and associated measures to be able to restore lost data and recover from an attack.

Ransomware Examples

- **SamSam** This is "ransomware-as-a-service" whereby an organization of cybercriminals exploits targets and sells the compromised targets to other cybercriminals that try to further exploit the victims for ransom. It is estimated that SamSam has been responsible for over $30M in losses by US firms.

- **Zeppelin** This ransomware avoids systems running in Russia, Kazakhstan, Ukraine, and Belarus. It has been deployed in many ways, including through exploited managed security service providers (MSSPs).

- **Ryuk** Ryuk was widely prevalent in 2018 and 2019 and was used in conjunction with relatively high demands for payment by the criminals. One feature of Ryuk is that it disables the Windows System Restore feature, thereby preventing the victim organization from going back to an earlier, noninfected point in time in an attempt to recover from the attack without paying a ransom.

- **PureLocker** This is malware that is installed by taking advantage of backdoors installed by other malware programs. It targets Windows or Linux systems that are high-value assets such as enterprise servers and, as a result, these attacks usually involve high ransom demands.

Rootkits

Rootkits are tools that enable and maintain privileged access to an operating system. Rootkits are not always malicious (they can have legitimate uses), but this discussion covers only rootkits that carry malicious code. Rootkits, like other malware, must be delivered to the target in some manner. Therefore, a rootkit is always combined with some other type of exploit in order to get the rootkit installed. Once installed, the rootkit can hide itself from detection. Rootkits can be difficult or impossible to detect, especially when they reside inside the kernel. Sometimes removal can be accomplished only by reinstalling the operating system or even replacing hardware in cases where the rootkit has impacted firmware or caused damage to electronics.

There are many kinds of rootkits, but most fall into either of two categories: kernel mode or user mode. These modes refer to the modes of an operating system, such as Windows.

Kernel-mode rootkits operate at the kernel level by adding code or replacing parts of the core operating system. The modification of the core OS is accomplished by using modified OS features, such as Windows device drivers or Linux loadable kernel modules (LKMs). Because these types of rootkits modify the core OS, they are difficult to write and can seriously damage system operation. Since these rootkits operate at the system's highest security level, they can subvert security controls and hide from detection.

User-mode rootkits modify or replace applications such as system libraries instead of modifying the low-level core like a kernel-mode rootkit. For instance, the rootkit may inject a dynamic link library (DLL) into a process that forces an application to invoke unauthorized functions that the attacker desires.

Rootkit Example: ZeroAccess

ZeroAccess is a kernel-mode rootkit that was discovered in 2011 and has infected over 2 million systems throughout the world. The rootkit, which is still active, installs well-hidden malware that makes the system part of a worldwide botnet. Attackers use ZeroAccess to invoke one of two unauthorized actions by an infected system. ZeroAccess causes an infected system to become part of either a bitcoin mining network or a *click fraud* network in which the system simulates clicks on sites for which ads are paid for on a pay-for-click basis. ZeroAccess is delivered via social engineering or exploit packs. An *exploit pack* is a set of scripts stored on a web server that is under the control of the attacker. When the victim's system tries to access the web server, the scripts attempt to exploit vulnerabilities on the system and install the payload consisting of rootkit software. Many systems are infected using exploit packs, and these packs may install many kinds of malware at once. Attackers also install ZeroAccess using social engineering methods to trick a user into running an executable program that installs it.

Scripting and Vulnerability-Specific Attacks

Cybercriminals use scripts to take advantage of vulnerabilities in operating systems and applications. These vulnerabilities are due to programming or configuration errors on the part of the manufacturers (in the case of commercial software) or developers (in the case of custom or in-house developed software). Manufacturers discover such vulnerabilities in their products quite often and regularly release bug fixes in the form of patches or software updates. For instance, Microsoft releases patches to fix security vulnerabilities in Windows monthly on the second Tuesday of each month (referred to colloquially as *Patch Tuesday*). For noncommercial software, vulnerabilities are most often discovered by in-house security staff, operations personnel, or third-party testers and auditors, either by accident or as the result of formal security testing.

Vulnerabilities can occur in any operating system or program but fall into several common types. Some of the most common security vulnerability types are discussed in their own sections that follow.

Buffer Overflows

When a program is expecting input, either from another program or from a user entering text into a field, it stores that data in a buffer, or area of memory. The program usually expects the data to be of a given size and therefore creates a buffer of the right size to accept the expected data. If the data received is greater in size than the size of the buffer, the extra data overflows into other buffers or areas of memory, which can cause erroneous operation. Cyberattackers craft attacks to take advantage of programs that do not perform proper checking of input data and are therefore vulnerable to buffer overflow attacks.

When a buffer overflow occurs, the data that exceeds the size of the buffer overflows into adjacent areas of memory. If that memory is another buffer, the data can corrupt the operation of the program that uses it. In some cases, the overflowed data is executed by the system as if it were a command or even an executable program. Buffer overflows can be used for denial-of-service attacks but more often are used to force a system to execute commands without the correct authorization. Often the attacker injects into the buffer malicious code that will be executed on the attacker's behalf but under the context of the program that is currently executing. This can lead to the attacker taking control of the system and escalating privileges, resulting in major security breaches.

Buffer overflows can be prevented during the development phase of software engineering by implementing proper input checking to ensure only the right type and size of data is accepted by the program. Buffer overflows can also be mitigated by preventing data to be written to certain areas of memory, thus minimizing the potential impact of an overflow. One common approach is to simply use programs that have automatic boundary checking such as Java.

Timing and Race Conditions

A *timing attack*, also called a *race condition attack*, takes place when the attacker takes advantage of the time between a sequence of events. One example is a time of check/time of use (TOC/TOU) attack. This occurs when the system checks to see if a specific file exists for a later operation, and the attacker replaces that file with a malicious one in between the time of the check and the time of use. There are countless variations of this type of attack. Any instance where a program implements a specific sequence of events that depends on other programs or external events might be vulnerable to a race condition or timing attack. Such attacks require great precision on the part of the attacker but they can and have been done.

Backdoors

A backdoor is not a specific type of attack but rather a *feature* of many different kinds of attacks. *Backdoor* is a broad term used to describe any method whereby an unauthorized user can bypass security controls to gain access to a system or program. Backdoors can be present when a system or program is not designed or coded correctly, or they can be created by a cybercriminal using malware. The backdoor facilitates communication between an infected or compromised system and an unauthorized system or user.

Cross-Site Scripting

Cross-site scripting (XSS) is a type of attack whereby the attacker injects a malicious script into a website that is trusted by the intended victim(s) of the attack. Then, when an unsuspecting victim visits the site, the script is executed by the victim's browser. Such scripts can access the victim's cookies, tokens, or other sensitive information. XSS attacks take advantage of a trust relationship between a web page and a browser. Generally, there are two types of XSS: persistent (or stored) and nonpersistent (or reflected).

A *persistent XSS* attack occurs when the malicious script is stored on the target server. Attackers typically use websites that allow them to enter information which is stored and then presented to other users who become the victims. Examples are message boards, forums, or other social media sites such as dating sites. The attacker may post legitimate information for the victim to see alongside a script that is hidden to the victim but is executed by the victim's browser to carry out the attack.

A *nonpersistent XSS* attack occurs when the malicious script is reflected back to the victim's browser. One example is where a user receives a malicious e-mail message that entices the victim to click a link. The e-mail not only contains the link to a web server but also contains the malicious script that is reflected by the server to the victim's browser. The browser then executes the script, carrying out the malicious activity.

HTTP Response Splitting

Another type of vulnerability that results from a software program that does not properly perform input checking and validation is called *HTTP response splitting*. In this type of attack, the attacker crafts data that contains malformed headers. This can be used to take over a user's browser, steal cookies, or redirect traffic to another website or server which can then be used to harvest a user's credentials. HTTP response splitting can also be used to "poison" the web cache with false data that can result in defacement of a website.

SQL Injection

Many times the data that a user enters into a form on a web page is sent by the web server to a database such as one that uses Structured Query Language (SQL). If the web server software does not properly check the data input by the user, it could allow an attacker to put SQL commands in the field, which are then executed by the SQL database. Such an attack may be used to take control of the database, escalate privileges, and modify or exfiltrate data from the database without the proper authorization.

NOTE The Open Source Foundation's Open Web Application Security Project (OWASP) publishes tools and resources to help developers create secure web applications. OWASP publishes a variety of excellent and proven guidance for secure coding practices that help protect against scripting attacks. These web security resources can be found at https://owasp.org.

Social Engineering

Today's cybercriminals know that people are the weakest link in information security and thus craft their attacks accordingly using social engineering. The term *social engineering* refers to the use of deception to trick someone into doing something that may not be in their best interest. Social engineering has been used by scam artists for years and now is an integral part of cyberattacks. The bad guys figured out long ago that it is easier to trick someone into revealing their password than it is to break into a system using technical means. To combat this requires a cyber defense program that focuses on defending against the things humans do that result in security breaches. This section covers the following topics:

- Types of social engineering attacks
- Why employees are susceptible to social engineering
- Social engineering defenses

Types of Social Engineering Attacks

Social engineering takes many forms but can be considered in three categories: pretexting, quid pro quo, and baiting.

Pretexting

Pretexting refers to using a fake scenario to deceive someone. Many people have heard of the Nigerian prince scam, where a criminal tells a victim that he is a Nigerian prince who is due a large sum of money but is unable to receive it unless he can use the victim's bank account to do so. The scammer convinces the victim to let the "prince" use the victim's bank account with the promise of paying the victim a fee. Of course, once the victim gives the scammer access to his bank account, the scammer steals his money. This is a non-cyber example of pretexting. Pretexting is now used in the cyberworld. Here are a few examples:

- A user receives a call from "Tech Support" telling them that their computer has a virus and that the technician needs remote access to their computer to "fix" the problem. The attacker convinces the victim to provide remote access or to share their login credentials. Of course, the caller is not from Tech Support.

- A company CFO gets an e-mail from the "CEO" telling him to transfer a large sum of money to a new vendor's bank account. The CFO follows the CEO's instructions, only to find out later that the e-mail came not from the CEO but from a cyberattacker, by which time the transfer to the foreign bank account has taken place. This attack happened recently to a large US manufacturer, resulting in the loss of millions of dollars.

- A user receives an e-mail from their bank telling them their password has expired and they should click a link to change it. The e-mail looks legitimate to the user, as does the web page used to change the password. But the e-mail and the web page are fake, and the bad guys used the web page to steal the user's login credentials. The attackers then use the credentials to access the user's bank account and steal their money.

Quid Pro Quo

A quid pro quo (QPQ) is an exchange of information or goods, such as a purchase. If a deal sounds too good to be true, it probably is. Here are some QPQ social engineering examples:

- A buyer for a company needed to buy 1,000 USB drives. Most online sites the buyer visited sell USB drives for $50 each but he found a company in China selling them for only $10 each. What a bargain! Too bad the cheaper drives contained malware and infected all of the company's computers.

- Many online sites sell versions of software products for a fraction of the cost of the real thing. But many of these are fraudulent versions of the product and, if they work at all, contain adware and/or malware that can cause serious security breaches.

Baiting

Baiting is simply luring someone into a trap. We've all heard the story of the famous Trojan horse sent by the Greeks as a gift to the city of Troy in the 12th century BC. When the Trojans brought the giant horse sculpture into the city, it contained Greek soldiers hidden inside, and the rest, as they say, is history. Here are a few cyber examples of baiting:

- An unsuspecting person finds a keychain on the floor and turns it in to the front desk receptionist. It has a USB drive attached to it. The receptionist decides to plug the drive into his computer to see who it might belong to. But it contains malware and infects the receptionist's system and then spreads to other systems on the network. Dropping USB drives onto the ground is a very common method of attack by hackers. It's the bait some people just can't resist.

- An employee receives an e-mail announcing that they are the lucky winner of a new computer game. But the e-mail lures the victim to a website which contains an exploit that runs from the user's browser. This is another successful attack using a combination of social engineering and cross-site scripting.

Why Employees Are Susceptible to Social Engineering

Many organizations invest heavily in training their employees about cyber and social engineering risks. Despite this, human error, including errors as a result of falling victim to social engineering attacks, is currently by far the greatest security risk to enterprises. Many of the controls, technologies, and processes described in this book, and being practiced by CISOs and security organizations today, can be rendered useless by simple social engineering tricks executed by a clever scammer.

How is this possible? How can employees fall victim to these tricks when they receive training about them? Here are some of the major reasons people are susceptible to social engineering attacks:

- **Job priority**   For most people, job performance is more important than information security. People are under pressure to do their jobs, and security is rarely considered when measuring job success. Maybe one reason is that employee performance appraisals nearly always rate a person's job performance but almost never rate a person's security practices. Therefore, being security-aware and following good security hygiene are not necessarily at the forefront of an employee's attention.

- **Workplace culture**   Workplace culture and climate contribute greatly to employee security awareness and social engineering defenses. In many industries, *workplace safety* is a big concern, especially when risk of injury and death is possible. In these environments the organization has policies, procedures, and a workplace culture that raise employee awareness of dangers and safety practices to great heights. In these safety-oriented workplaces, employees adapt their behavior and integrate safety into everything they do. However, security rarely gets attention similar to safety. Security is typically not ingrained into the workplace climate.

- **Human nature**   People are not necessarily on alert for potential social engineering tricks. There is a tendency for people to be trustful of others, which is the opposite of what is required for good social engineering defense.

When organizational leadership and culture are not aligned with security goals, they can contribute to a chain of events that leads to a security incident or data breach. Examples include leaders pressuring employees to get the job done (leading to security shortcuts) or praising those who get the job done more quickly (but without regard for security risks taken to get that result). This can lead to a deviation from security procedures or rules. This deviation is sometimes unintentional (people may not realize that they are deviating from rules), or deviations may be intentional (people may make a conscious decision to break a rule). In many cases people fall victim to social engineering because they fail to recognize the risk.

Social Engineering Defenses

Security training and awareness programs alone historically have not been effective in helping organizations defend against social engineering attacks. One reason is that training is simply an action. As compared to a tried-and-true life cycle of how to get things done, such as *Plan, Do, Check, Act (PDCA)*, training is just one piece (the *Do* piece). What is being done to *Check* to make sure the training is effective? And what is being done to take what is being measured to *Act* on it? Training by itself doesn't address the social engineering problem. What works better than mere training is a comprehensive social engineering countermeasures program that has the following components:

- Leadership
- Training and awareness
- Testing
- Practice and exercises
- Operational monitoring and remediation

Leadership

The degree to which security is important (or not important) to the organization's leadership will drive the number and extent of social engineering vulnerabilities and resulting security breaches. The security culture starts at the top of the organization. We know that if an employee's compliance with security policies is part of their annual performance evaluation, the employee is much more likely to follow the policies. However, making security part of the evaluation usually requires the approval or sponsorship of leadership. Buy-in at the top of the organization in large part drives the extent to which good information security practices are part of the organization's culture.

Training and Awareness

All employees should be made aware of the organization's security policies and processes as well as good security practices in general. Most organizations accomplish this by implementing an organization-wide security training and awareness program. Social engineering training should be a key component of the security training program.

Social engineering security awareness training should include the organization's entire user population. It should contain training delivered in a variety of forms, especially practices, drills, and exercises to provide users with reality-based experience dealing with cyberattacks. The best training programs take advantage of a combination of commercial off-the-shelf (COTS) training to teach general concepts and customized training to teach concepts that are unique and specific to the company or organization.

The training should cover each of the social engineering attack types introduced previously: pretexting, quid pro quo, and baiting. The training program should have the following features and characteristics:

- **Modularity**   A large library of short training modules works better than a small library of longer modules. Short training has been proven to be more effective because it facilitates learning and retention better. Also, it is easier to manage the delivery of short training courses to the user community because shorter courses can be more easily integrated into the employee's work schedule.

- **Relevance** The training should be relevant to the business environment. Many organizations attempt to save money by purchasing a COTS training product, hoping that it will apply to their business, only to find that it misses the mark. For instance, training that is oriented to a corporate office environment (as many COTS products are) may not ring true to workers on the manufacturing floor or those out in the field. Relevance brings the training closer to the users and helps them relate to the material better, which aids in learning retention and, more importantly, helps them apply the learned skills to their jobs.

- **Conformity** The training must conform to the organization's security policies and practices so that it reinforces them. One of the most common mistakes organizations make is choosing information security training that does not match, or conflicts with, the organization's security policies. If the training tells employees to take one action but a policy says to take a different action, it creates confusion and increases the likelihood of a security breach.

- **Skills oriented** Social engineering and information security training should not just teach knowledge; it should also teach *skills* that employees need to have to practice good security hygiene. An employee does not need to learn how passwords are stored on their computer in order to know they should not give their password to someone else. By focusing on skills, the employee can practice and learn what they should do in situations they may face in their job.

Training is often coupled with awareness programs to provide a continuous flow of information about security to employees. Many organizations publish frequent newsletters or blogs from the CISO or other security personnel that discuss security topics. Security awareness is often promoted by the use of information security web portals whereby employees can view security policies, standards, and guidelines, gain access to security testing tools, and learn more about security risks and practices. These resources can be an extremely effective way to expand on the information security training and promote a culture of security.

Testing

Social engineering tests are a subset of tests that should be performed as part of an ongoing vulnerability assessment and penetration testing program. The purpose of conducting these tests is to improve the security posture of the organization by revealing weaknesses and providing useful information that can guide security improvement. These tests progress the same way a real attacker works, by testing, probing, re-testing, and re-probing. Each success is an incremental step toward the goal of compromising sensitive information. Here is a list of some social engineering testing activities an organization should have in its toolbox.

- **USB drive drops** In this scenario the organization places USB drives in various locations throughout the facility. The drives contain COTS or custom-developed software that simulates malware by providing the testers with remote control of the system, similar to a real attack. However, the software is not real malware and is completely removed at the conclusion of the test.

- **Phishing e-mails** The testers send specially crafted e-mails to selected persons or groups in the organization enticing them to do something or click a link. These e-mails may appear to be from external third parties or from impersonated persons of authority.

- **Phishing text messages** Like phishing e-mails, these messages appear legitimate and entice the person to do something or reveal information.

- **Fake websites (fictitious and impersonated)** Usually used in conjunction with an e-mail or text message, these sites appear legitimate and entice the person into revealing sensitive information.

- **Phone calls to employees to conduct pretexting attacks** The testers use a variety of fake scenarios that use telephone calls as the attack vector. Each call seeks to establish trust and convince the victim to reveal sensitive information that can be used in an attack.

- **Tailgating** This is a physical intrusion in which test personnel follow employees through normally secured doors to gain unauthorized physical access. The employee uses their authorized access method, such as a badge, and then the tester sneaks through the already opened door without using a badge.

- **Physical impersonation** In this test, testing staff use a variety of techniques to appear as a legitimate visitor, in order to gain access to a physical area. Techniques include wearing uniforms and carrying tools to look like service personnel or using fake badges to pose as real employees.

- **Social media employee reviews** One key part of a cyberattack is reconnaissance or collecting information about the target. Social media is a key reconnaissance tool used by cyberattackers. During these tests, test personnel use a variety of means to learn about the organization based on corporate or personal social media posts. Cyberattackers also engage with employees via social media to get them to reveal information that can help with an attack. The test staff will test employee resilience against such techniques.

- **Inspection of trash (dumpster diving)** Test staff can use this tried-and-true method to conduct reconnaissance about the target organization or seek ways to gain access.

- **Inspection of disposed or donated equipment** Many organizations do not properly sanitize unneeded equipment or storage media prior to its disposal. The testing staff can use techniques of the cyberattacker to follow the trail of such items and look for sensitive data.

 NOTE Conducting social engineering tests is a highly sensitive and somewhat controversial activity. It is important to ensure that social engineering tests do not embarrass employees or cause workplace disruption. This is why such tests must be approved and endorsed by leadership and management and should be socialized throughout the organization to gain acceptance ahead of time. CISOs must work closely with HR, legal, and other departments to coordinate social engineering testing.

Practice and Exercises

Imagine you are being prepped for surgery and you meet the surgeon. You ask, "How many times have you performed this procedure? I'll bet you've practiced it a lot!" And he replies, "Practice? We don't have time to practice. But don't worry, I've attended training and watched a lot of videos about it." You wouldn't expect someone to be able to perform an important task without practice, so why would you expect a worker to be able to defend against social engineering without practice? Social engineering defense is an unusual and sometimes unnatural skill that requires practice to develop and sharpen skills. Training is important, but without practice, the information conveyed during training is quickly lost.

Every organization should have a set of activities available to employees that allow them to practice social engineering defense (and other security-related) skills. Many vendors are now offering social engineering testing software that presents employees with scenarios and tests their ability to respond to them. In fact, many of the tests discussed in the previous section can be used over and over again so that employees can develop and improve their defensive skills.

Group exercises are another way to practice social engineering defenses. Some organizations conduct role-playing exercises whereby one employee calls another posing as a hacker to conduct a social engineering attack, allowing the potential victim to practice recognizing the attack. As stated earlier, these practice exercises must be vetted through management and be well coordinated to avoid controversy and disruption. But a well-planned and executed social engineering practice program can be an extremely effective countermeasure against such attacks.

Operational Monitoring and Remediation

Organizations should be tracking, recording, and studying all security incidents and breaches that occur. This includes social engineering–related incidents. One purpose of this tracking is to learn the sequence of events that led to the incident and gain an understanding of the underlying or root cause of the incident. From this understanding, security remediation activities can take place.

Situational awareness refers to having an understanding of the security posture of the enterprise. This includes understanding the security posture of *each asset* in the enterprise. In social engineering defense, the concept of situational awareness expands to *each person* in the enterprise. As part of the security operations function, the organization should have situational awareness of each person's system and data access; operational behaviors; security training attendance; the results of social engineering practice, drills, and exercises; and a record of security-related activities. The point of all this is to build and maintain a picture of each person's potential vulnerabilities and exposures. This gives the organization data from which improvements can be made, measured, and tracked. Situational awareness is the practice of knowing what assets the organization has, where they are located, and what the security posture of each asset is.

User behavior analytics (UBA) is another subset of security operations that uses tools to monitor user network activity. UBA tools collect data and build a profile of each user's normal behavior over time. When the tool sees user behavior that is abnormal for that user, it could be an indication of a security vulnerability, exposure, or even an incident or breach. Years ago, security professionals monitored system activity only. But now organizations understand that humans are at the core of many cyber issues, so UBA tools are used to monitor people activity to detect security events based on human elements.

Asset Security

The domain of *asset security* is focused on the organization's understanding of its assets and the determination of the appropriate controls for each asset based on risk and classification. Essentially this entails knowing what the organization has and how each asset is being protected. The focus is often on assets that support information-related activities, such as storing or processing data. These assets may include hardware (laptops, desktops, mobile devices, servers, network equipment, and so on), software (databases, applications, and so on), and information (files, documents, and so on). The types of assets in the environment and the types of controls used for each are identified and addressed in the organization's policies, standards, and procedures.

Asset security controls are often implemented as part of an information security control life cycle framework, as described in Chapter 2. For example, the *categorization* step of the NIST Risk Management Framework is used to determine the baseline security controls for a system, which are influenced by the types of data stored on the system. An organization may perform a risk assessment to determine the risks associated with an information system, as well as the information the system stores, and select controls to mitigate identified risk. The risk assessment may be guided by previous risk assessments or by the organization's risk management process.

The formal *risk management* process (discussed in Chapter 1) is where the organization performs ongoing risk management of the enterprise to keep track of assets, assign values to them, evaluate risk, and decide how to handle the risk (avoidance, acceptance, transference, or mitigation). The outputs of the risk management process provide the organization with information that it can use to make decisions around asset security, such as:

- What assets does the organization have?
- What role do the assets play in critical organizational processes?
- How should the assets be protected?
- What priority does each asset have?
- What data is stored on the assets?

Implementing a solid asset security stream of work allows the organization to have a better understanding of the threats and risks, the value of the assets, and the necessary level of protection required for each asset. Assets should be inventoried, have the appropriate level of security controls applied to them, and monitored thereafter. This section discusses the following asset security topics:

- Asset inventory and configuration management
- Secure configuration baselines
- Vulnerability management
- Asset security techniques

Asset Inventory and Configuration Management

Assets should be tracked in an asset inventory to enable monitoring and management. One of the most important security challenges organizations of all sizes face is maintaining visibility and situational awareness of the assets in the organization's environment. As previously stated, *situational awareness* refers to having an understanding of the security posture of the enterprise. This includes knowing what assets the organization has, where they are located, and what the security posture of each asset is. Many organizations use asset discovery and inventory tools to identify devices and software on the organization's network and track them in an asset management system.

The organization must also manage the configuration and change control process for the asset in order to track the state of the asset and its relationship to other assets. (Configuration and change management were introduced in the "Project Management" section of Chapter 3.) To achieve these efforts, some organizations use a *configuration management database (CMDB)*, a repository of information about the assets and components in the environment. A CMDB can serve as a baseline tracking tool for configuration changes made to the assets. Some organizations use CMDB systems that include asset discovery functionality to automatically populate asset entries. Other organizations use a separate discovery tool or a separate asset management tool that may integrate with their CMDB. CMDBs provide a variety of features, including the following:

- Asset management and inventory
- Configuration management
- Change management
- Asset relationship mapping
- Asset discovery

The CMDB contains records commonly known as *configuration items (CIs)*. A CI is an element stored in the CMDB representing a configurable asset or component in the organization's environment, such as hardware, software, location, networks, documentation, and even people. This allows for tracking of these items as well as their relationship.

Secure Configuration Baselines

Assets should be configured to reduce their attack surface and eliminate potential attack vectors that an attacker can exploit. This is often accomplished by changing default passwords, removing unnecessary accounts, programs, and functions, and disabling unnecessary services and ports. The goal is to prevent attackers from exploiting potentially vulnerable programs and services. This is often referred to as *hardening* the asset. Assets are hardened by establishing, implementing, and managing secure configuration baselines. A *secure configuration baseline* is a set of configuration settings for a specific asset (such as an OS, database, and so on) that have been identified and selected as the standard set of configurations adopted by the organization. For example, an organization will often develop OS secure configuration baselines for each flavor of OS in the organization (for example, Windows Server 2019, Red Hat Enterprise Linux 8, and Oracle Linux 8 would each have a hardening standard). The configuration baseline standard is applied to each asset that is deployed. The Center for Internet Security (CIS) is a great resource for guidance on hardening assets (https://www.cisecurity.org/). CIS provides secure hardening benchmarks for a variety of systems including OSs, network devices, databases, mobile applications, cloud environments, printers, and more.

Vulnerability Management

Another core function of asset management is monitoring the assets in the environment for known vulnerabilities. This is done through a well-managed vulnerability management program. Vulnerability management is an ongoing process to identify, prioritize, remediate, and mitigate known vulnerabilities in the organization's environment. Known vulnerabilities are defects or configuration settings in products that can be exploited to cause a security compromise. Security organizations must check their assets continually to see if known vulnerabilities exist so they can be remediated. Here are some key components of a vulnerability management program:

- **Vulnerability scanner**   Scanners are programs that examine devices on the network for known weaknesses (vulnerabilities or other weaknesses such as configuration errors). Scanner manufacturers maintain libraries of products and their associated weaknesses. These libraries are used by the scanners to perform scans and are constantly being updated. The product vendors and scanner manufacturers share vulnerability information to enable organizations to detect and remediate vulnerabilities by patching systems or changing configuration settings. NIST maintains a national database of vulnerabilities (the National Vulnerability Database) that many vendors use for the latest vulnerability information. (Because unknown vulnerabilities have not been identified and documented by the community at large, vulnerability scanning tools can't scan for them.) Many scanners also serve as tracking tools that maintain a database of identified and remediated vulnerabilities.

- **Patch management**   Vulnerability scanning tools can assist with verifying that assets have been properly patched. Automated patch management tools should be utilized to ensure operating systems, third-party software, and other assets are running up-to-date software.

- **Configuration management**   Vulnerability scanners can also assist with configuration management by scanning assets against known configuration profiles to determine if they are hardened according to specifications.

- **Authenticated scanning**   Some vulnerabilities cannot be detected without authenticating (logging in as an approved user) to the device. This is because some vulnerabilities can be seen only by a privileged (or administrative level) user. Vulnerability scanning returns the most accurate results when authenticated scans are performed. This can be accomplished through an agent installed on the system or by providing the scanner with elevated rights on the system being scanned.

- **Regular review** Vulnerability scans should be performed regularly at an organization-defined interval. Scans should be reviewed and compared to past scans to ensure vulnerabilities have been remediated.

- **Risk-based prioritization** Vulnerability results should be ranked based on risk to determine the priority for remediation.

Vulnerability management incudes regularly reporting and tracking the state of the vulnerabilities in the environment. This includes reporting and tracking open vulnerabilities, new vulnerabilities, and closed vulnerabilities, as well as reporting and tracking remediation actions, such as who the remediation is assigned to and the status of the remediation.

Asset Security Techniques

This section discuses several techniques for protecting organization assets such as media, paper, fax machines, and other endpoint devices. The topics discussed include

- Endpoint security
- Media controls
- Paper records security
- Facsimile security
- Printer security
- Safes

NOTE The Center for Internet Security (CIS) is a great resource for guidance on hardening assets. CIS provides secure hardening benchmarks for a variety of systems, including operating systems, network devices, databases, mobile applications, cloud environments, printers, and more.

Endpoint Security

Every endpoint on the organization's network must be properly secured, hardened, and managed throughout its life cycle to ensure that it is patched and its vulnerabilities are remediated. Endpoints include servers, desktop computers, laptops, network infrastructure devices, and other assets on the organization's network. Here are some key endpoint security controls that should be considered when hardening assets:

- **Endpoint protection software** Servers, desktops, laptops, and mobile devices should be configured with endpoint protection software to protect them against viruses, malware, and other attacks. Traditionally this protection was accomplished with antivirus software, but modern endpoint protection software provides antivirus protection plus additional tools that give the organization insight into what is going on internally on the endpoint. This information can be used to facilitate investigations and provide visibility into security-related events on the endpoint device.

- **Remove unnecessary software and services**   Systems should be configured with the minimum amount of software and services enabled to perform their intended function. Unneeded software or services are potential attack vectors even if they are not used during normal operation. To be safe, all unneeded software should be removed or disabled and unneeded services should be turned off.

- **Encryption**   Ensure that data is encrypted at rest (for example, full disk encryption) and in transit (for example, SFTP, HTTPS, and so on).

- **Vulnerability management**   Regularly scan systems to identify and remediate known vulnerabilities.

- **Patch management**   Ensure systems are running up-to-date software and firmware to protect against known vulnerabilities.

- **Configuration baselines**   Maintain secure baseline configurations for devices for use in the provisioning process and follow configuration and change control practices.

- **Data and configuration backups**   Data should be regularly backed up to ensure its availability in the case of an emergency or system failure. This includes system images for servers, desktops, laptops, and so on, as well as device configuration files for network equipment.

- **Network access control (NAC)**   NAC is an integrated approach to endpoint management that allows for specific policies to be defined that govern the security requirements for network access as well as the access levels for specific roles. For example, a NAC policy may not allow devices to connect to the network unless they meet specific security requirements such as having antivirus installed and recent patches applied.

- **Access control**   Assets should be configured with properly authenticated access control such as passwords, smart card, biometrics, multifactor authentication, and so on.

Mobile devices can present unique challenges in terms of visibility and management. A large number of mobile devices (such as phones and laptops) are stolen every year. This presents a risk to the data stored on the devices as these devices often are used for e-mail, connecting to the organization's network, and storing organization data. These devices must be considered in the asset security strategy. In addition to the controls mentioned earlier, the following should be considered to ensure the security of data stored on mobile devices:

- **Mobile device management (MDM)**   Many organizations utilize enterprise MDM software that enables centralized management of mobile devices. MDM functionality often includes remote device tracking, device locking, device sanitization capability, as well as policy settings such as password length and complexity, encryption, VPN, applications management, and containerization. *Containerization* is a technology that allows organizations to establish separate encrypted containers on devices to separate personal information from organization data.

- **Bring your own device (BYOD)**   BYOD is a concept referring to the ability for employees to bring their own personal devices (laptops and/or smartphones), use them for business purposes, and potentially connect them to the organization's network. While BYOD can potentially increase productivity and reduce costs, it also has the potential to increase risk by adding insecure devices on the network. In addition, there are added concerns of how organizational data is protected and managed on personal devices. Organizations address these risks by implementing MDM and NAC software to better control the device as well as the policies for accessing the network.

Media Controls

Media controls include a variety of measures to provide physical protection and accountability for tapes, disks, USBs, and other physical media. Media controls include

- **Media marking**   Media should be clearly marked and labeled to indicate the data classification of the stored information.

- **Media access**   Access to organization media should be restricted to authorized individuals with a need to know.

- **Media storage**   Policies and procedures should be developed around media handling, including storage. These should include measures such as the use of cryptography to protect data at rest as well as physical access control protection through the use of locked cabinets, safes, and so on.

- **Media transport**   Media should be protected during transport using appropriate security measures defined by the organization, such as cryptographic measures or locked containers for transport.

- **Media sanitization**   When media is no longer needed, it should be securely disposed of according to the organization's media sanitization policies and procedures. This includes methods discussed later in the "Data Security" section of this chapter.

Data Remanence

When media is not properly sanitized, it can contain remanence of data. *Data remanence* is data that can be reconstructed after being erased. When data is erased or deleted, the data itself is typically still present on the medium. The pointer to the data has simply been removed and that storage space has been marked as free to be used. Even after erasure, sensitive data may still be available for retrieval with the right tools and expertise. Proper techniques to sanitize data include purging, overwriting/zeroization, degaussing, and physical destruction.

Paper Records Security

Although we live in the age of digital information, organizations still rely on physical resources to make things work, including paper records. It is important that documents are appropriately labeled based on their classification level and that employees are educated on the classification scheme and handling requirements. Documents containing sensitive information (such as health information, credit card numbers, or Social Security numbers) should be physically destroyed when no longer needed. Secure destruction methods include shredding and burning.

Facsimile Security

Fax machines may be used to transfer sensitive data and can present their own unique data security challenges. For example, if a sensitive document is faxed, the paper may end up sitting in the bin for anyone to see. Often times organizations put a classification mark on the document, but printing a classification banner or cover sheet may not provide enough protection. Here are some controls that may be implemented to secure faxed information:

- Implement a fax server rather than a fax machine to allow OS-level access controls
- Disable the print feature so that sensitive documents remain digital
- Harden the fax server using full disk encryption and access controls

While the controls previously covered are focused on protecting the data at rest, consideration must also be given to protecting the faxed data in transit. The best control for protecting data in transit is proper encryption. The following are some security controls to consider for fax transmission:

- **Traditional fax** For faxes transmitted over a traditional public switched telephone network (PSTN), implement a fax encryptor for bulk data-link encryption
- **Internet fax** Ensure faxes sent over the Internet, such as the use of a cloud fax service, are sent using modern versions of Transport Layer Security (TLS) 1.2 or greater
- **Auditing and logging** Ensure logging and auditing is enabled on fax servers or services

Printer Security

A printer is simply another computer on the network that is designed to print hard-copy representations of files. While printers may seem like unimportant assets on the surface, they are often troves of valuable sensitive information and often run their own web server. When a printer is retired, it becomes a serious security and privacy concern because of the potential sensitive information stored on the printer. Printers should be hardened like any other asset with the following controls being considered:

- Secure jobs with a unique pin requiring users to enter their pin at the printer to print
- Utilize an approved destruction process to properly sanitize and dispose of printers
- Utilize encryption for the transmission of data to and from the printer (such as HTTPS for print servers)
- Utilize a vulnerability scanner to scan printers for vulnerabilities
- Ensure the printer is running up-to-date software with the most recent security patches

Safes

Safes are commonly used for asset security for the physical protection of drives, disks, tapes, paper contracts, and other valuable media. In addition to being penetration resistant to prevent theft, safes should also provide fire protection to ensure the contents are protected from fire. Commonly used safes range from floor safes and wall safes to vaults that encompass an entire room and provide walk-in access. The following controls should be considered when using safes:

- Ensure only those with a "need to know" have access to the safe key or combination
- Ensure that if a combination is used that is it changed periodically
- Consider placing the safe in a badge access room or in view of a camera to provide an audit trail of access

Data Security

Data security controls are applied to information to protect it from unauthorized access, disclosure, and modification. These controls are applied as part of the data life cycle, discussed later in this section. Data security controls vary based on the state of the data. Data states include *data at rest*, *data in transit*, and *data in use*. This is a conceptual model used by security professionals as a way to describe where and how data must be protected in various states. Data security controls are implemented by properly configuring and hardening assets that store and process the information, such as servers, network equipment, applications, and so on. This section discusses the following topics:

- Data at rest
- Data in transit
- Data in use
- Data life cycle

Data at Rest

The term *data at rest* refers to data residing on persistent storage devices such as hard drives, flash drives, optical disks, magnetic tape, or other storage media. Many organizations today have policies that require certain data to be encrypted whenever it is stored in an information system. Data at rest security controls include the following:

- Whole disk encryption
- Database encryption
- Specific data structure encryption (file, record, or field encryption)

Data in Transit

The term *data in transit* (also known as *data in motion*) refers to data that is moving between computing nodes on a network or between networks. This includes data flowing over public untrusted networks as well as data flowing over private enterprise networks, such as a local area network (LAN). Data-in-transit security controls are focused on utilizing encrypted network connection protocols, including the following:

- Transport Layer Security (TLS)
- IPSec (IP Security)
- Virtual private network (VPN) encryption

Data in Use

The term *data in use* refers to data currently being processed or used by the system or applications. This primarily refers to data residing in system memory that is being accessed for processing. This includes data residing in primary storage such as volatile memory (RAM), CPU registers, and memory caches that are being processed. The challenging part about protecting data in use is that even if proper encryption is utilized for storage and transmission, the data typically must be unencrypted to be used and processed. Protecting data in use includes implementing good access controls, using antivirus software that specifically looks for, alerts on, or prevents improper writing to and reading from memory, and designing applications to prevent unauthorized or improper access of application data (such as preventing cut and paste functions or screen captures of certain applications).

Data Life Cycle

The data life cycle (briefly introduced in Chapter 1) refers to how data is acquired or created, how it is protected and used, and how it is eventually disposed of. The life cycle generally includes the following phases, illustrated in Figure 4-1:

- Acquisition
- Data classification and marking

Figure 4-1
Data life cycle

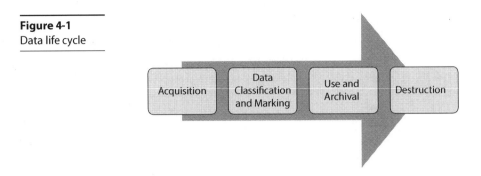

- Use and archival
- Destruction

This section describes each phase of the life cycle and its corresponding activities.

Acquisition

The first phase concerns the origin of the data. Data is generally obtained by one of two methods:

- **Acquisition**   Acquired from an external source such as a vendor, customer, or other stakeholder
- **Creation**   Created or developed from scratch within the organization

The next step in the life cycle is to classify the data so that appropriate security controls may be applied (such as encryption, access control, and so on).

Permissions: Access Control Matrix

One tool used for data security to define access control permissions is an *access control matrix*, a table that lists subjects (users) and their corresponding permission level for specific data elements or data sets. Here is an example of what an access control matrix might look like for a specific data element or data set:

Subject	Read	Write	Print	Data Owner
Mike	X	X	X	X
Steve	X		X	
Michelle		X		
Jordan			X	

Alternatively, the matrix may be structured with the data elements or objects as the column headers (for example, file 1, file 2, and so on) and the X's replaced with the permissions the subjects have over each object (read, write, print, data owner, and so on).

Table 4-1	Private Sector Classification Levels	Government Classification Levels

Example Classification Levels	Confidential
	Private
	Sensitive
	For internal use only
	Public
		• Classified
		  • Top secret
		  • Secret
		  • Confidential
		• Unclassified
		  • Controlled unclassified
		    information
		  • Public

Data Classification and Marking

After data has been acquired or created but before it is used, it should be protected through the use of security controls. However, to protect the data (at rest, in transit, and in use), some kind of framework or process needs to be used to determine what level of protection is required. This is where data classification comes into play. *Data classification* is essentially assigning sensitivity values to data to determine the level of protection (security controls such as encryption, access control, and secure destruction) required based on the organization's classification policies, procedures, and guidelines. Table 4-1 illustrates some examples of commonly used classification schemes in the private sector and public sector (military and federal government) from highest classification level to lowest classification level.

In practice, classification levels vary from organization to organization. Some organizations may have two levels and others may have four or five. Each organization must decide which classification levels to use and identify what those levels mean. To develop the classification levels, the organization should do the following:

1. Define the classification levels and specify the criteria to determine how data is classified.

2. Identify responsible parties such as the *data owner* (responsible for classifying data) and the *data custodian* (responsible for maintaining the data and implementing security controls).

3. Determine the security controls required for each classification level.

Data Owner Requirements

The data or system owner is responsible for the classification of the data. To properly classify the data, the owner must

- Be intimately familiar with the data being classified as a process owner
- Understand the organization's classification scheme and criteria
- Be familiar with the organization's legal and regulatory requirements
- Carry out the classification processes in a consistent, repeatable manner
- Carry out declassification procedures when necessary

As with most things in information security, developing the classification levels is a balancing act. Too many classification levels become impractical and confusing and too few classification levels may provide little value or practical use. When classification levels are defined, there should be no overlap between the levels so that the data owner can easily identify which classification level particular information belongs to. When developing the data classification criteria, the following should be considered:

- Usefulness and value of the information
- Impact to the organization if the information were disclosed, modified, or corrupted
- Laws, regulations, and liability responsibilities pertaining to the information
- Roles and responsibilities around data ownership, custodianship, and use

All classified material should be clearly marked and labeled and have distinct handling requirements for each level based on the format (for example, paper, digital, media, facsimile, and so on). It is critical to ensure that the organization is consistent in following the security policies, procedures, and controls for respective classification levels to ensure consistent application in the environment.

Data Classification Policy, Procedures, and Guidelines

Organizations should create policies, procedures, and guidelines surrounding data classification. The data classification policy should outline

- The classification scheme
- Definitions for each classification level
- Criteria for each classification
- Roles and responsibilities for classification

The data classification procedures and guidelines should answer the following questions:

- What is the process for data classification?
- How is information classified?
- How is a classification level changed if needed?
- How should classification changes be communicated to IT?
- How should material be declassified and destroyed?

Use and Archival

During this phase of the data life cycle, the information is utilized (read, modified, and potentially shared externally) by a variety of users and parties with different access levels. This phase presents several challenges in regard to data confidentiality, integrity, and availability (CIA). Data must be available, but only to those with proper authorization based on their organizational role (for example, some users may only be authorized to read certain data elements). Each classification level should have specific handling requirements and procedures for how data is accessed, used, handled, shared, and ultimately destroyed based on its classification level.

As part of the data life cycle, data may need to be archived in accordance with the organization's data retention policy and requirements. *Archival* is when data is taken out of production use and retained for future use or reference. This is often to assist with managing storage space and to ensure long-term retention requirements are met. Retention requirements are influenced by the organization's internal requirements (such as the potential need to access or restore the data in the future) as well as external requirements (such as laws, regulations, or other compliance drivers). Archival and retention may apply to both digital/electronic information and physical documents.

Destruction

When data has passed its useful lifetime and retention requirements, it must be securely destroyed. As security professionals well know, when data is erased by pressing the DELETE key on a computer, that data storage location on the drive is essentially being marked as free for use by the operating system. This tells the OS that that sector of the drive, cluster, or block (depending on what filesystem is being used) is now free to be re-consumed. However, all the "deleted" data is still on the drive. This method is known as *erasure*. Since all the data is still on the media, erasure is not a secure method of data disposal. When media is securely cleared of its contents, it is said to be *sanitized*. This means erasing information so that it is not readily retrievable using routine OS commands or commercially available forensic/data recovery software. Media can be sanitized in several ways: purging, overwriting/zeroization, degaussing, and physical destruction. These methods are used to securely sanitize data in assets such as hard drives and other storage media. Each of these methods is defined and discussed here:

- *Purging* means making information unrecoverable even with extraordinary effort such as physical forensics in a laboratory. Purging is required when media either will be removed from the physical confines where the information on the media was allowed to be accessed or will be repurposed to a different compartment.

- *Overwriting/zeroization* deals with some sort of data overwrite. Several common methods are used:
  - **Single pass** Data is overwritten with *one* pass of 1's or 0's.
  - **US Department of Defense (DoD) method** Data area is overwritten with *three* passes; once with all 0's, then with all 1's, and finally once with pseudo-random data.

- **US National Security Agency (NSA) erasure algorithm**   Data is overwritten *seven* times, first with all 0's, then with all 1's, and so on.

- **Gutman method**   Data area is overwritten 35 times.

- *Degaussing* is a process that demagnetizes magnetic media so that a very low residue of magnetic induction is left on the media. This entails exposing the media to an extremely powerful magnetic field. Degaussing sanitizes legacy magnetic media sufficiently for it to be reused; however, degassing modern media such as disks and tape with chipsets will render them inoperable (essentially destruction).

- *Physical destruction* is the process of destroying the media so that it cannot be reused and the data cannot be accessed. This is the most secure method of data destruction. This includes shredding, crushing, burning, disintegration, and dissolving in chemical compounds. Physical destruction is also the method that is used for physical documents, as you cannot purge, zeroize, or degauss paper documents.

Weak Link: The Dumpster!

After their useful life is over, old computers along with their hard drives and other magnetic storage media are replaced and thrown away. To mitigate the risk that residual data is on these assets, several methods for data sanitization are used, including purging, zeroization, degaussing, and physical destruction of media. However, digital data is not the only type of information that must be protected. Other forms of information, such as paper, also require secure disposal to protect against dumpster diving. *Dumpster diving* is the act of searching through trash (dumpsters, office trashcans, recycling bins, and so on) to locate valuable information that was discarded without proper sanitization (such as sensitive paper documents or non-sanitized physical media). The best method for the disposal of sensitive documents is physical destruction such as shredding or burning. This will protect against the dumpster diver.

Identity and Access Management

Identity and access management (IAM) refers to systems and processes put into place to manage and control access to enterprise resources. IAM involves the management and implementation of *who* is accessing *what* and what they can *do* with it. This suggests three key terms:

- **Subject**   The entity that actively accesses an object
- **Object**   The entity that is accessed by a subject
- **Access**   The actions that subjects can perform or impose on an object

A *subject* is an active entity such as an individual, system, process, or device that accesses an object. The management and verification of the subject's identity is where identity management comes into play. *Identity management* is focused on identifying who the subject is and verifying (authenticating) they are who they say they are. An *object* is an entity such as a network, computer, file, device, record, table, process, domain, database, or program containing information that is accessed by a subject. An object is typically a resource that stores, processes, or sends/receives data. *Access* is the action that a subject imposes on an object such as read, modify, delete, create, or execute. This is where access management comes into play. *Access management* systems manage which objects subjects can access and what they can do with them.

Hardcopy Example

The concept of access can be illustrated by considering how it might apply not just to digital data but also to hardcopy data. For example, if an organization stores sensitive documents in a safe, the organization must limit who has access to the safe through the use of a combination lock only provided to authorized employees (access management). In order for someone to be provided with the combination, the organization must know who the person is and verify their identity to ensure they are who they say they are (identity management). In this example the authorized employee with access to open the safe using the combination is the *subject* and the safe is the *object*.

This section discusses the following topics:

- Identity and access management fundamentals
- Identity management technologies
- Authentication factors and mechanisms
- Access control principles
- Access control models
- Access control administration
- Identify and access management life cycle

Identity and Access Management Fundamentals

Identity management is focused on identifying and verifying the subject's identity, whereas access management is focused on managing the subject's access to objects, defining the actions that can be performed, and tracking of these actions. These are enabled through identification, authentication, authorization, and accountability/auditing as defined next:

- **Identification**   The identification function identifies who the subject is. In many systems the subjects supply information to identify themselves, such as a username, account number, or user ID.

- **Authentication**   The authentication function verifies the subject is who they say they are. Verification of an identity is typically performed though the use of a password, passphrase, token device, smart card, cryptographic key, or biometric. These are methods of authentication.

- **Authorization**   The authorization function grants access to an object based on predefined access management rules that establish which operations subjects are allowed to carry out on objects.

- **Accountability/auditing**   The accountability/auditing function enables tracking of activity through audit logs and monitoring. This holds subjects accountable for their actions and can only be accomplished if subjects are uniquely identified through identity management.

Protocols that implement authentication, authorization, and accounting/auditing are known as AAA ("triple A") protocols. Examples are protocols such as RADIUS, TACACS+, and Diameter.

Identity Management Technologies

Identity management technologies include a range of products, applications, and solutions that identify, authenticate, and authorize subjects for access. Here are some key technologies that support identity management:

- **Directories**   Most organizations utilize directories that contain information about the organization's users, resources, and network. A directory stores and centrally manages resource information, policies, and user credentials. The most common example is Microsoft's Active Directory (AD) used for managing Windows domain networks.

- **Password managers**   Password managers are commonly used by smaller organizations and home users that may not have the infrastructure or resources to stand up a directory service. Password managers provide a centralized encrypted database for password storage and management. The offerings vary from cloud-based solutions to desktop applications.

- **Single sign-on (SSO)**   Single sign-on allows users to authenticate one time with one credential set in order to access a range of resources (versus having a separate password for each system). SSO can help reduce administration because it reduces the number of passwords to manage and it can help encourage the use of stronger passwords because users have fewer passwords they need to remember. However, SSO can also be a security concern, as a compromised account can be used to access a variety of resources.

- **Federated identity management (FIM)**   Federated identity management is a variant of single sign-on that allows organizations to establish arrangements to utilize the same identification and authentication data to authenticate users across multiple organizations. Whereas SSO only allows a user to authentication to systems within a single organization, FIM allows a user to authentication to systems across any organization involved in the arrangement. The Security Assertion Markup Language (SAML) is an Extensible Markup Language (XML) standard that enables the exchange of identity information between organizations.

- **Identity as a Service (IDaaS)**   IDaaS is another cloud-based "as a service" model. Cloud-based identity management provides identity and access management functions that include the ability to provision and revoke identities as well as to monitor, including logging and reporting. IDaaS often includes the ability to configure other technologies such as directory synchronization, single sign-on, and federated identity.

Authentication Factors and Mechanisms

The three main factors of authentication include

- **Type 1, something you *know*** (such as a password, passphrase, or PIN)
- **Type 2, something you *have*** (such as a token device, smart card, or USB drive)
- **Type 3, something you *are*** (biometrics such as voice, fingerprint, or palm scan)

The use of only one of these factors is known as *single-factor authentication*. The use of two authentication factors is known as *dual-factor authentication* (such as a smart card and PIN, password and biometric, or password and physical token). *Multifactor authentication* is the use of two or more factors.

 TIP   In terms of "best bang for your buck," the implementation of multifactor authentication has been shown time and time again to significantly increase security posture and reduce the risk of compromise. This is due to the fact that each factor increases the amount of work required for the cybercriminal to implement an attack. For instance, even if a user is tricked into giving up their password, the attacker still needs the additional authentication factor in order to gain access.

Access Control Principles

Access controls are security controls that regulate and control how objects (systems, buildings, and data) are interacted with by subjects to ensure approved access. The goal is to prevent unauthorized subjects from accessing objects such as systems, files, and data. Here are some fundamental access controls that the CISO should be aware of:

- **Access control policy and procedure**   Like any information security stream of work or subprogram, organizational access control strategies and approaches must be documented in access control policies and procedures.

- **Least privilege**   Access permissions should be granted using the *principle of least privilege* model where users receive only the necessary level of permissions to accomplish their job and corresponding tasks.

- **Need to know**   Users should have a valid need to know for information they have access to. The *need to know principle*, similar to least privilege, means that the user has a legitimate reason for accessing specific information.

- **Separation of duties**   Ensuring that one individual cannot complete a critical process, activity, or task singularly prevents fraud and other nefarious activities from taking place. Separation of duties for audit functions is particularly important to ensure that individuals completing the tasks are not auditing themselves.

- **System use notification**   Organizations often utilize warning banners that provide a system use notification or message prior to granting access to a system. These banners provide privacy, security, and acceptable use notices that inform users of monitoring practices and communicate expected behavior.

Access Control Models

Access control models are sets of rules used to regulate the interaction between subjects and objects. These models are implemented by vendors in the design of products such as operating systems and applications. They are also used by organizations to design how access controls are implemented in the enterprise. The following are the primary types of access control models:

- **Mandatory access control (MAC)**   MAC models use a central authority that regulates access based on the *clearance* of subjects and *classification* of objects. A subject's clearance must be greater than or equal to the object's clearance. MAC models are typically utilized in specialized government and military systems or specialized OS distributions such as Security-Enhanced Linux (SELinux) developed by the NSA and Red Hat.

- **Discretionary access control (DAC)**   DAC models provide the owner, usually the creator, full control of the object (resource) to determine which subjects (users and groups) can access and share that object. DAC is an identify-based model. Examples of DAC systems include most flavors of Unix and Linux as well as all Windows and macOS systems. DACs are integrated into the kernel of the operating system and can be applied to individual files as well as entire directories using access control lists (ACLs).

- **Attribute-based access control (ABAC)**   ABAC, also called policy-based access control (PBAC) or claims-based access control (CBAC), grants access rights based on technical policies that combine various attributes such as who is making the request (subject), what resource is being requested (object), environmental conditions such as time of day or location (environmental context), and what action is being requested. Access can be granted based on a variety and combination of attributes such as date, time, IP address, and so on.

- **Role-based access control (RBAC)**   RBAC, also called nondiscretionary access control, enforces access based on a subject's role within the organization. Each role is assigned certain permissions, and users are assigned to a role based on their function. For example, User, IT Administrator, HR, and Developer roles may be built with permission sets and users assigned to those roles based on their job responsibilities. This type of model simplifies administration and provides better support for organizational structures. RBAC can be (and often is) used in conjunction with DAC and MAC.

 NOTE   Modern operating systems like Windows, Linux, and macOS have DAC and MAC used together. They have different names in each OS; however, what were considered traditionally DAC-based systems have MAC functionality sprinkled in under the hood, often times to mitigate the risk of malware being executed by an admin user. For example, Windows employs User Account Control (UAC), which is a MAC enforcement that isolates processes with different privilege levels.

Access control models are applied at the enterprise level using a combination of operating system/application design features and organizational implementation. For example, Microsoft Active Directory provides tools for an organization to implement RBAC. Using AD, the organization can define organizational roles that have certain privileges assigned to each role and then provision each user by assigning a role to them.

While systems like AD handle the implementation of RBAC, the job of figuring out what roles are needed by the organization and what privileges are associated with each role is a challenge. In fact, many organizations find implementing RBAC to be difficult because it requires a large collaborative effort across the organization to define the roles and privileges. To overcome this, some organizations implement RBAC in phases, first defining roles coarsely and then adding more granularity over a period of time.

Access Control Administration

Access control is typically managed using a centralized, decentralized, or hybrid approach as illustrated in Figure 4-2. Each of these administration types is defined and discussed here:

- **Centralized**   Most organizations utilize a centralized access control administration model where one department or entity is responsible for governing, managing, and configuring technologies to enforce access decisions (typically IT). All requests and changes to access go through that department and accounts are centrally monitored. This method provides greater process consistency; however, changes may not be as quick compared to a decentralized model.

- **Decentralized**   In a decentralized access control administration model, access administration is typically managed by the owner of the asset or resource. This means changes may be processed quicker since there is not one entity managing all access requests; however, it can lead to inconsistencies in how the access control and identity management life cycle is applied. For example, terminated employees

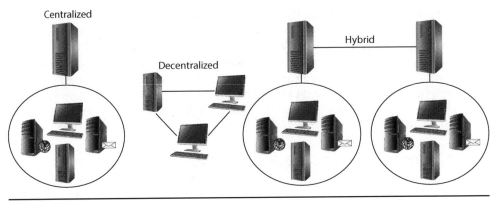

Figure 4-2 Access control administration

may not have all access rights properly removed, leading to inconsistencies and security holes across the organization. In addition, this model can lead to conflicts of interest as there may be insufficient separation of duties.

- **Hybrid** The hybrid access control administration model utilizes a combination of centralized and decentralized access control administration technologies. For example, an IT department for an organization may manage access control for critical resources such as Active Directory (centralized administration), while systems belonging to individual departments, such as the sales team CRM, may be managed by individual departments (decentralized administration).

Identity and Access Management Life Cycle

The operation of identity and access management follows a general life cycle, illustrated in Figure 4-3 and described here:

- **Provisioning** The first step in the life cycle is the provisioning of the account, which typically occurs as part of an onboarding process. Provisioning is the process of creating, changing, disabling, and deleting user accounts as well as giving and revoking account permissions during the account life cycle. The organization should have documented procedures that include management approval for account requests. In addition, care must be exercised to ensure that permissions and access levels are the minimum required for the job that needs to be performed (least privilege) and that the user has a legitimate business need for access (need to know).

Figure 4-3
Access control
and identity
management life
cycle

- **Review**   Accounts must be regularly reviewed and monitored to ensure that there is still a need for access over time. This is particularly important for administrator accounts and other privileged accounts with elevated access levels. When employees are transferred to new roles within the organization, their accounts and permissions should be reviewed to ensure the level of access is appropriate for the role (least privilege and need to know). *Privilege creep* is a term used to describe when a user gradually accrues more access rights beyond what is required for their role. This can occur particularly in small IT shops when accounts are not carefully managed. Privileged employees who act as IT generalists may move from helpdesk to systems administration, database administration, security administration, or another privileged role and end up with dangerous permission levels. Account reviews should be performed regularly, and this is often a requirement for many legal and regulatory compliance drivers.

- **Revocation**   The last step of the life cycle consists of removing access after an employee has separated from the organization or when the employee no longer has a need for the account or access in question. An error that is often made during this step is to revoke some but not all accounts of the employee. This can be particularly problematic if an employee with heightened permission levels is fired and decides to retaliate against the organization. Procedures must be established and followed for the revocation process to ensure that all accounts in question are revoked.

Communication and Network Security

The network can be thought of as the circulatory system of the organization, giving life to the servers and endpoints that perform essential functions. This section describes how modern local and wide area networks are designed and implemented, how these networks are best defended, and how they are viewed from a security perspective. Specifically, this section covers the following topics:

- WANs and LANs
- IP addressing
- Network address translation
- Network protocols and communications
- Wireless
- Network technologies and defenses

WANs and LANs

Contemporary data communication takes place over local and wide area networks. A local area network (LAN) enables communication of computing devices and equipment within a facility, home, office building, or group of buildings (such as a campus). A wide area network enables communication between and among LANs. Sometimes the term metropolitan area network (MAN) is used to refer to a campus network that connects several LANs. A MAN can be viewed as a WAN that covers a smaller geographic area.

WANs use telecommunication circuits suitable for communication over long distances (tens or thousands of miles). Up until the last decade, these technologies included circuit- or packet-switched networks that use transport protocols including Asynchronous Transfer Mode (ATM), SONET, Frame Relay, and X.25. However, in recent years these technologies have been largely replaced by IP-based technologies including *metro Ethernet (MetroE)* and *virtual private LAN service (VPLS)*. LANs use communication equipment and devices suitable for shorter distances. However, both LANs and WANs use networking protocols including Transmission Control Protocol/Internet Protocol (TCP/IP) to manage the delivery of information from a source, across the networks, to the intended destination.

One major difference between WANs and LANs is that WANs are usually provided by a third-party WAN service provider or carrier, whereas LANs are usually operated and maintained in-house by the organization.

WAN Topologies

The service provider provides the WAN infrastructure using a choice of topologies, including

- **Point-to-point**   A point-to-point topology consists of a single path or circuit between two endpoints. In this case the organization connects to the service provider's network that provides a single path through the network to the other side, which may be a peer facility or another LAN.

- **Hub and spoke**   A hub and spoke arrangement is used when the organization's facility requires connections to multiple locations. In this case, while using multiple point-to-point connections is an option, hub and spoke provides a lower-cost alternative. The organization connects to a hub that maintains connections with multiple sites. This topology is also called *single homed*, which refers to the use of a single hub. A *dual-homed* arrangement uses two hubs at the organization's facility, each of which maintains its own spoke of connections to the other locations for redundancy and improved performance.

- **Full mesh**   A full-mesh network is also used to provide connectivity between multiple locations. It is implemented when each location (node) has circuits connecting it to every other location. This arrangement provides the greatest redundancy and flexibility.

The choice of which topology to select depends on the nature of the business, performance considerations, and costs. Point-to-point is the simplest and lowest cost option but has limited flexibility to adjust for capacity and offers no redundancy. Mesh can be the most expensive but provides better redundancy and control for load balancing and performance optimization.

WAN Technologies

The portion of the WAN link that interfaces with (or terminates at) the organization's LAN perimeter is called the *local loop* and is sometimes referred to as the "last mile" of the connection. Figure 4-4 provides an illustration.

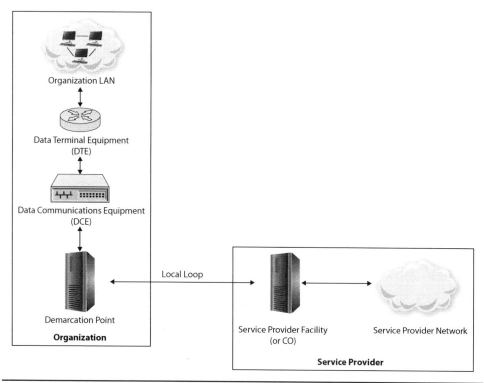

Figure 4-4 WAN last-mile components

The local loop terminates at the organization's demarcation point, which can be as simple as a junction block used to connect the local loop to the facility. The *data communications equipment (DCE)* is a device that interfaces the local loop with the *data terminal equipment (DTE)*, which can be a computer or router that sits at the perimeter of the LAN. The characteristics of the local loop connection are dependent on the type of communication link and the service provider network used.

Service provider networks can implement any of the topologies discussed previously. They also can use a variety of connection technologies as follows:

- **Leased lines** These are physical point-to-point communication lines connecting two locations. Dedicated lines are expensive but are still widely used. These lines are leased from providers. The T1 links carry data at 1.544 Mbps and T3 links (also called Digital Signal 3 or DS3) are 44.736 Mbps. T3 links carry 28 multiplexed T1 channels.

- **Circuit-switched networks** These networks provide a dedicated circuit path between the two ends of a call. A common circuit-switching technology is the Integrated Services Digital Network (ISDN), which is a switched telephone network that supports data and voice communications. ISDN was widely used in the early

2000s but has largely been replaced by much faster services like cable, fiber, or DSL. Another example of circuit-switched communications is the public switched telephone network (PSTN) used primarily for voice and low-speed data communications.

- **Packet-switched networks** Packet switching uses a shared network instead of dedicated circuits provided by leased lines or circuit switching. Since the network is shared between many service provider customers, data is placed into *packets*, which are *routed* to their proper destinations. Packet-switched networks can also be used to provide virtual circuits, which are logical connection paths between two network devices. Examples of packet switching connections include X.25, Frame Relay, ATM, and Metro Ethernet. The former technologies are still in use but are diminishing in favor of Metro Ethernet and other Ethernet-based technologies.

Other WAN communication technologies include DSL, cable and FTTP, satellite, and wireless:

- **DSL** *Digital subscriber lines* provide data communication over telephone lines. Although many such circuits have been supplanted in recent years by cable or fiber services, DSL is still widely used and available in many areas. Asymmetrical DSL (ADSL) refers to DSL with asynchronous speeds whereby data travels downstream faster than upstream. ADSL is usually used by residential users. With symmetrical DSL (SDSL) data travels upstream and downstream at the same rate. Higher-speed versions of DSL are high data rate DSL (HDSL) and very high data rate DSL (VDSL). Speeds can reach up to 1000 Mbps and beyond as DSL technology continues to evolve. SDSL is usually used by businesses.

- **Cable and FTTP** The term *cable* or *cable Internet* refers to broadband Internet access provided by cable television providers. Such providers also act as the *Internet service provider (ISP)*. Cable uses either broadband electrical or fiber to the premises (FTTP) technology as the medium of the last-mile link to the user's (organization or residence) facility. Communication rates are usually asynchronous and can reach up to 1 Gbps per link.

- **Satellite** Business use of satellites for Internet and business-to-business connectivity is growing despite some technical limitations. Modern satellite links can provide downlink speeds of up to 1000 Gbps and uplink speeds of up to 1000 Mbps. Satellite communication performance can be hindered by weather, which can impact the line of sight necessary for communication. And satellite communication suffers from latency due to the long distances and hops between the satellites, ground stations, and premise equipment. New technologies such as low-Earth orbit (LEO)–based services may result in better performance and may lower costs in the near future.

- **Wireless** Wireless WANs differ from the more ubiquitous wireless LANs in that they use cellular technologies enabling communication over longer distances. Wireless LANs use cellular technologies such as 2G, 3G, 4G LTE, and 5G. Since wireless WANs are not subject to the physical protections of wired technologies, they typically use authentication and encryption to protect communications from interception or eavesdropping.

LAN Infrastructure

A typical LAN consists of one or more external connections enabled by border equipment and an internal network that is usually segmented to achieve performance and/or security objectives. The internal network may be a wired network, almost always Ethernet nowadays, or wireless, or a combination of wired and wireless. Figure 4-5 depicts a typical network. Some of the components shown in the diagram are introduced here while others are discussed later in this section.

External users and customers access the organization's network via the Internet, with the "last mile" being terminated at the organization's premises by an Internet router that routes and controls traffic to and from the organization's LAN. The way the various devices are physically arranged is called the network *topology*. Figure 4-5 does not show

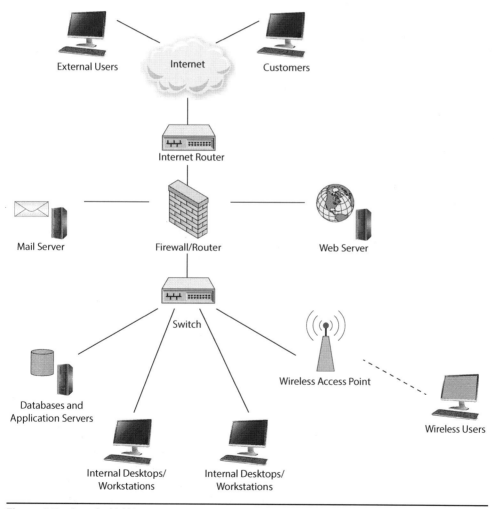

Figure 4-5 A typical LAN

a specific topology. There are many possible networking topologies, including bus, ring, tree, star, mesh, and hybrid. Most modern LANs use star topologies.

Every device on the network has an Internet Protocol (IP) address. Data is routed between devices using these IP addresses. Routers are devices that connect similar or different networks together and "route" traffic using IP addresses.

All data communication within and between LANs use standard message formats which are defined by *protocols*. The message contains all of the information that each device and application needs in order to process the message in accordance with the protocol. Each message consists of a *packet*, which contains the following information:

- Identification of the source or originator of the message

- Identification of the destination of the message

- Control information, which may include sequence numbers, flags, pointers, length, checksums, and so on

- Data (but not always—some messages just contain control information with no data)

Based on information in the packet, the various devices on the network route and/or act on the data. Here is a brief summary of some of the most common network devices:

- **Internet router**   This is the device at the perimeter of the LAN that provides the interface to the WAN link.

- **Router**   Sometimes the Internet router is combined with the border router and can even perform as an external firewall, filtering traffic depending on the organization's security policy. The router performs routing of data between network segments and may perform other functions such as network address translation (NAT), discussed in an upcoming section.

- **Firewall**   Firewalls are specialized equipment used to enforce a security policy such as allowing or denying certain types of traffic. Discussed in more detail later in the section, firewalls play an important role in securing the organization's network. In Figure 4-5 a firewall is used to control traffic at the border of the LAN and specifically filter traffic going to/from the organization's mail server, externally facing website, and internally segmented network.

- **Switch**   Switches operate at OSI Layer 2 (more on the OSI model later) and allow the network to be configured in segments, which makes better use of the available bandwidth and can be used to create security zones.

IP Addressing

Addresses enable how data is sent and received throughout Ethernet networks. Much like the address of a house enables mail to be delivered to the intended recipient, IP addressing enables data to be sent to the right place on a network. And just like houses are addressed using multiple elements (such as city name, street name, house number), components on the network are addressed using two elements: *network* and *node* (or *host*). In fact, every IP address contains two parts: the network identifier and the node identifier.

In IPv4 the IP address is composed of 32 bits consisting of four octets. There are public and private IP addresses; public IP addresses are routed throughout the Internet and private IP addresses are used within corporations, organizations, and government entities (private IP addresses cannot be routed on the Internet). Public IP addresses are assigned by the Internet Assigned Numbers Authority (IANA), which is the organization responsible for managing IP addresses worldwide. Private IP addresses are freely assigned by any company, organization, or individual for their own use. The following are the ranges of private IP addresses that are nonroutable on the Internet:

- 10.0.0.0–10.255.255.255
- 172.16.0.0–172.31.255.255
- 192.168.0.0–192.168.255.255

IP addresses are used in combination with a *subnet mask*, which identifies which portion of the IP address specifies the network and which portion specifies the node (or host). The mask, like the IP address, is 32 bits long. Each bit is turned on (1) or off (0) and reads left to right. Bits turned on indicate which parts of the address specify the network; bits turned off specify the node. The subnet mask is defined as part of the address using Classless Inter-Domain Routing (CIDR) notation as follows:

- The IP address followed by a slash (/)
- Decimal number (from 0 to 32) indicating the number of bits of the IP address that constitute the network ID

For example, the address 192.168.0.10/24 indicates that the first 24 bits of the address (starting at the left) is the network address and the remaining bits is the address of the node or host.

Network Address Translation

Internet routers are not configured to route private IP addresses across the Internet. So, how is data routed across the Internet to devices within a network if the private address is not used? For this, IPv4 uses network address translation (NAT).

Using NAT, routers at the border of the private organization are configured to map external (public) IP addresses to internal (private) IP addresses. There are many types of NAT, the most basic of which provides a one-to-one mapping of external addresses to internal addresses. We don't cover all the various types of NAT in this book, but they each provide a way to traverse public and private networks in a manner that is transparent to the source and destination hosts.

The Move to IPv6

IPv4 uses 32-bit addressing, which enables over 3.7 billion addresses. That would seem to be enough, but considering there are about 6 billion people on earth (and who knows how many elsewhere), it would seem that someday we will run out of addresses. To solve this, IPv6 was developed and released in 2012. IPv6 uses 128 bits, which supports 2 to the 128th power (or 340,282,366,920,938,463,463, 374,607,431,768,211,456) addresses. That should be enough. However, adoption of IPv6 has been slow even though adopting it now would simplify some things, such as eliminating the need for NAT. Currently IPv6 has been adopted by about 30 percent of the world. Reasons for the slow adoption vary, but in many cases IPv4 represents a huge investment that has already been made in equipment that cannot be easily upgraded to IPv6. Also, many people and organizations in the industry have mastered and tamed IPv4 and are reluctant to make such a change. IPv4 will not be shut down anytime soon, but eventually the industry will catch up and 128-bit addressing will be the norm.

Network Protocols and Communications

Communication between devices on a modern network can occur only if there is a common model that they all follow. The industry most commonly uses the Open Systems Interconnection (OSI) model (or a variant called the TCP/IP model) as a way of establishing and describing how every device on the network will communicate with each other. The OSI model has the following features:

- Explains how networking takes place and is used to architect network services and protocols
- Allows for interoperability between vendor products by defining interface standards
- Provides a modular approach so that one piece can be changed out without affecting others

The OSI reference model, as defined in the ISO Standard 7498, segments the networking tasks, protocols, and services into layers (or a networking stack) as follows:

- **Application (Layer 7)** Primarily responsible for interfacing with the user. This is the application interface that the user experiences.
- **Presentation (Layer 6)** Primarily responsible for translating the data from something the user expects to something the network expects.
- **Session (Layer 5)** Primarily responsible for dialog control between systems and applications.

OSI Layer	Protocol
Application	DNS, FTP, TFTP, BOOTP, SNMP, TELNET, HTTP, HTTPS, SQL, SSL
Presentation	ASCII, TIFF, GIF, JPEG, MPEG, MIDI, MIME
Session	NetBIOS, NFS, RPC
Transport	TCP, UDP, SPX, SCTP
Network	IP, ICMP, RIP, IGMP, IPX
Data Link	SLIP, PPP, L2F, L2TP
Physical	HSSI, X.21, EIA/TIA-232, EIA/TIA-449

Table 4-2 Common Protocols

- **Transport (Layer 4)**   Primarily responsible for handling end-to-end data transport services.

- **Network (Layer 3)**   Primarily responsible for logical addressing (such as IP addresses) and includes specifications for routing, among other things.

- **Data Link (Layer 2)**   Primarily responsible for physical addressing (such as MAC addresses).

- **Physical (Layer 1)**   Primarily responsible for physical delivery and specifications such as voltage changes and durations.

Protocols are sets of rules and standards for communicating data. Protocols define the process and message format used to exchange data between systems, devices, or applications. Many protocols include methods of authentication, quality of service, or error correction. Table 4-2 shows commonly used protocols and the layer of the OSI model at which they operate.

Application Layer

Application layer protocols handle file transfers, perform network management functions, and fulfill networking requests from applications. The following are some common application layer protocols:

- **Domain Name System (DNS)**   DNS is like the address book of the Internet. It allows us to use domain names (such as google.com) instead of having to remember IP addresses of specific servers. The DNS protocol enables applications to exchange and fulfill DNS requests.

- **File Transfer Protocol (FTP)**   This protocol is used to transfer entire files between systems.

- **Simple Network Management Protocol (SNMP)**   This protocol was first released in 1998 as a way to manage devices on a network. It uses a client-server architecture whereby the clients use *agents* running on the network devices to be managed. The agents collect information about the device and report it back to the *manager* at the server. The early versions of SNMP provided a good way to control and obtain status from devices on the network but had significant security flaws. SNMP used a system of passwords, called *community strings*, for authentication and, in practice, they often were sent across the network or stored in cleartext, making it easy for an attacker to obtain information about how network devices were configured and how the network could be compromised. SNMP version 3 added encryption and better authentication. Older versions of SNMP should not be used.

- **Hypertext Transfer Protocol (HTTP)**   This protocol is a method of transmitting and formatting messages between clients and servers. It is the primary way that browsers obtain information for display and communicate with servers on the world wide web. When a user enters // in the browser as part of the Uniform Resource Locator (URL), that tells the browser to use HTTP as the protocol.

- **HTTP Secure (HTTPS)**   This protocol is HTTP with encryption added for security. HTTPS formerly used the now downgraded SSL protocol but now uses TLS as the encryption method. HTTPS ensures that once an HTTPS session is established, all traffic, including passwords and authentication information, is protected using encryption. This protects HTTP sessions from eavesdropping, man-in-the-middle, and spoofing attacks.

- **Secure Sockets Layer (SSL)/Transport Layer Security (TLS)**   SSL and TLS are frequently lumped together, as SSL was the predecessor to TLS. Both are protocols that use *public key encryption* (discussed later in this chapter) to protect communications. Earlier versions of TLS had security issues. Organizations should be sure they are using TLS version 1.2 or greater to ensure proper implementation.

Presentation Layer

Presentation services are those that handle the translation of data into standard formats for transmission. These services usually perform compression, decompression, encryption, and decryption. These functions are really services rather than protocols. The following lists a few of the most common presentation layer standards:

- **ASCII**   The American Standard Code for Information Interchange is a character encoding standard. Every time a user types on a keyboard, an ASCII code is the representation of the key. It is primarily used to transmit alphabetic and numeric information.

- **TIFF, GIF, JPEG**   These are formats used for compressing images for easier storage and transmission.

- **MIME**   Multipurpose Internet Mail Extensions (MIME) establishes formats for mail message content other than ASCII.

Session Layer

Session layer protocols are used to set up connections between applications. They set up and tear down connections and do housekeeping to help communications operate smoothly. The following are some common session layer protocols:

- **Network File System (NFS)**   This is a method of sharing files using a client/server relationship.

- **Network Basic Input/Output System (NetBIOS)**   NetBIOS provides services that allow applications on separate computers to communicate over a LAN. NetBIOS runs over TCP/IP but has its own method of identifying applications that use it using NetBIOS names. It has three distinct services: naming service, datagram distribution service, and session service.

- **Remote Procedure Call (RPC)**   This is a protocol that an application can use to request a service from another program located on another system.

Transport Layer

Transport layer protocols handle end-to-end transmission and segmentation of data. The following protocols, among others, operate at this layer:

- **Transmission Control Protocol (TCP)**   TCP is a connection-oriented protocol that uses a three-way handshake to establish a connection between two systems. The establishment of a connection ensures reliability, and the protocol periodically checks the connection to make sure it is still established.

- **User Datagram Protocol (UDP)**   In contrast to TCP, UDP is not connection-oriented. As such, it is used in situations in which it is not important for the sender to know if the message was actually delivered or not. While not as reliable, UDP requires less overhead than TCP.

TCP Three-Way Handshake and Associated Attacks

TCP uses a "three-way handshake" to establish communication, as illustrated in Figure 4-6. In the first step, the client sends a synchronize (SYN) message, which tells the server that it wants to begin communication. The server responds with the sequence number plus an acknowledgement (SYN+ACK). Then the client responds with its own acknowledgement (ACK) and the transmission can proceed.

Attackers have historically taken advantage of this sequence to perform denial-of-service attacks. In a SYN attack, the cybercriminal sends many SYNs, which overwhelms the server. Or a variant of this attack is a SYN-ACK attack, whereby the cybercriminal crafts the SYN message so that it appears it is coming from another client. The server then responds with SYN-ACKs to the spoofed client instead of the attacker's system. This might be OK except TCP is a resilient protocol and will keep sending SYN-ACKs until it gets a response. These SYN-ACKs can overwhelm the spoofed client system.

Figure 4-6
TCP three-way
handshake

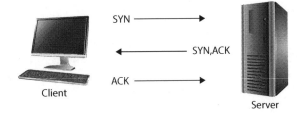

Network Layer

The network layer protocols are primarily involved in routing and other networking and internetworking services. The following are commonly used network layer protocols:

- **Internet Protocol (IP)** IP is responsible for the delivery of packets, also called datagrams, from a source to a destination based on an IP address. Routers maintain tables that keep track of IP addresses and corresponding systems and follow IP rules and other protocols to route traffic throughout the network.

- **Internet Group Management Protocol (IGMP)** IGMP is used to manage multicast groups. When a system wants to participate in multicast traffic, it becomes a member of a multicast group. IGMP is used to inform the routers the system is part of a group. Once membership is established, the Protocol Independent Multicast (PIM) service is used to direct the multicast traffic to the member systems.

Data Link Layer

The *data link* layer is composed of sublayers: Logical Link Control (LLC) and Media Access Control (MAC). Protocols at the data link layer transform data into frames for transmission.

- **Address Resolution Protocol (ARP)** ARP maps IP addresses to MAC addresses. The MAC address is a 48-bit address that is hard-wired into a network device or computer system. Computers on the network use ARP to learn which MAC address corresponds to which IP address and then use that information for future communication. *ARP poisoning* is a type of attack whereby the attacker tricks a switch into saving the wrong information in its cache, causing data to be misrouted on the network.

- **Point-to-Point Protocol (PPP)** PPP is used to provide communication between two entities. It provides services including authentication, encryption, and compression. It is frequently used for dial-up access and serial communication links.

- **Ethernet** Ethernet has replaced older local area networking technologies and is now the de facto standard for LAN communications. Ethernet divides the communication into pieces called frames, with each frame containing the source and destination MAC addresses and error checking data used to enhance transmission reliability.

Layer	OSI Name	TCP/IP Name	Description	Data Name	Protocols/Services	Device
7	Application	Application	Handles file transfers and fulfilling networks requests of applications	Data	DNS, FTP, TFTP, BOOTP, SNMP, TELNET, HTTP, HTTPS, SQL, SSL	Computer/Gateway
6	Presentation		These services handle translation into standard formats, data compression, encryption		ACSII, EBCDIC, TIFF, JPEG, MPEG, MIDI, MIME, GIF	
5	Session		Sets up and tears down connection between applications		NFS, NetBIOS, RPC	
4	Transport	Host-to-Host	End-to-end transmission and segmentation of data streams	Segment	TCP, UDP, SPX, SCTP	
3	Network	Internet	Internetworking, addressing, routing	Packet	IP, ICMP, IGMP, RIP, IPX	Router
2	Data Link	Network Access	Puts data into frames for transmission, defines how computers access the network	Frame	SLIP, PPP, L2F, L2TP	Switch/Bridge
1	Physical		Implements specific hardware media	Bit	HSSI, X.21, EIA/TIA-232, EIA/TIA-449	Hub/Repeater

Figure 4-7 Network summary

Physical Layer

The physical layer doesn't really have protocols, but instead has standards that define the physical aspects of transmission. These standards include EIA-232, 422, 423, 449, and so on for serial transmission, Ethernet physical layers (10BASE-T, 10BASE2, 10BASE5, others), Optical Transport Network (OTN), and other physical technologies capable of carrying OSI-compliant protocols.

Networking Protocols and Devices Summary

The prior discussion about the OSI model and associated protocols is summarized in Figure 4-7. Note that the figure also shows the alternative TCP/IP model (also known as the DoD model), which combines some of the OSI layers.

Wireless

Wireless technologies allow computers and other devices to connect to LANs using radio frequency (RF) communications. This provides great flexibility in the physical layout and location of the computers. Today's wireless LANs follow the IEEE 802.11 LAN protocol and most operate in two RF frequency bands: 2.4 GHz and 5 GHz. Wireless is implemented on LANs using two components:

- Wireless router (access point)
- Wireless network adapter, implemented as either an add-on or built into computers, cellphones, and other devices

Wireless networks use a service set identifier (SSID) as the name of a network. The SSID allows all devices to connect to and be part of the same wireless network. All devices connected to a wireless network are called *stations*.

There are two basic forms of 802.11 networks: *infrastructure* and *ad hoc* (also called *mesh*). In infrastructure networks, all stations communicate through an access point or wireless router. The access point serves as a bridge to other networks, most commonly a wired LAN or an Internet connection. Ad hoc mode enables stations to communicate in a peer-to-peer fashion without the need for an access point.

The lack of physical controls of a wireless network presents special security challenges. Any passerby can access the 802.11 signals emanating from a station. In the early days of wireless, authentication mechanisms either didn't exist or were poorly implemented, making wireless an easy way for cybercriminals to carry out cyberattacks. However, better security features have been added to wireless through the years. The old method, called Wired Equivalent Privacy (WEP), had ineffective security and has been replaced with evolving versions of Wi-Fi Protected Access (WPA, WPA2, and WPA3).

Network Technologies and Defenses

This section discusses some of the risks associated with LANs and organization networks and common ways to mitigate those risks.

Firewalls

Figure 4-5 in the earlier "LAN Infrastructure" section shows a network with a single point of egress for data protected by a firewall. Firewalls are a versatile and widely used technology used to control access between two networks or two segments of a network. There are three general types of firewalls: packet filter, proxy, and stateful/dynamic packet filter. Sometimes these types are referred to as generations 1, 2, and 3, respectively.

Packet Filter   Packet filters are the most basic and least expensive firewall. A packet filter is a router that screens traffic based on an internal access control list (ACL). The router screens all traffic and makes decisions as to whether to allow or deny traffic to pass from one of its interfaces to another based on the network and transport layer header information of each message. The firewall can make access decisions based on criteria including

- Source and destination IP addresses
- Source and destination port numbers
- Protocol
- Direction of traffic

For instance, an ACL may contain a rule that says web traffic using the HTTP protocol can enter the LAN only if it contains the destination IP address of the organization's web server. By limiting what type of traffic can enter and leave the network and for what specific purpose, the risk of malicious or erroneous activity can be reduced. Firewalls can be used at the perimeter of the LAN or internally to create special security zones to further control the security of the enterprise.

Proxy   Proxy firewalls are placed between a trusted network and an untrusted network, serving as a guard. In plain English, a *proxy* is someone who does something on behalf of someone else. The proxy acts as a middleman. Using a proxy firewall, no direct communication takes place between the networks, as the proxy impersonates the system at the other end of the connection and hides the IP address of the devices within the network it is protecting. The proxy intercepts and repackages all traffic, applies a security policy, and prevents direct connections between the two networks. This makes it harder for cybercriminals to discover information about what is on the other side of the proxy.

Stateful/Dynamic Packet Filter   A stateful/dynamic packet filter is like a nosy neighbor listening in on people's conversations and inserting itself into their business. These firewalls don't just examine messages to make decisions, they keep track of what they previously learned about a conversation so they can make smarter decisions about what type of traffic to deny or allow. They make access decisions based on the following information:

- IP address
- Protocols and commands
- Historical comparisons with previous packets
- The content of packets

A stateful firewall monitors the state of network conversations and allows packets to flow through the firewall only if they are part of existing authorized conversations. When an authorized host creates a new conversation, the "state" of that conversation is tracked so that the return traffic (coming from the other party) will be allowed through. When the conversation is complete, the firewall notices the end of the conversation, since it is monitoring the state of the conversation, and closes the hole for the return traffic. Then, even if the same host (the other party) who was previously in the conversation, and whose traffic was previously allowed, tries to communicate through the firewall, its traffic will be blocked.

 EXAM TIP   CCISO candidates should be familiar with the different types of firewalls and their functions.

Network Segmentation and DMZs

Networks are often divided into *segments* to implement security controls that limit access to or from portions of the network. Segmentation limits the flow of traffic to parts of the network based on policies. For example, an organization may use segmentation to limit access to a portion of its network used for their financial systems. Only authorized users can access that portion of the network. Segmentation creates more barriers for an attacker to go through to reach sensitive systems, increasing the *work factor* of an attack.

Segmentation can be accomplished *physically* by separating a network into smaller networks. Or segmentation can be accomplished *logically* by creating logically separate

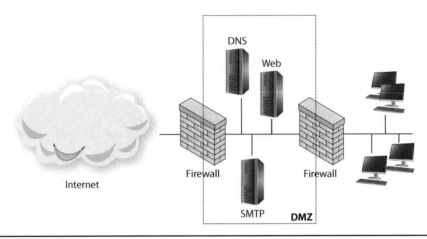

Figure 4-8 Demilitarized zone

networks (virtual networks or VLANs) using the same physical network hardware. VLANs are implemented by configuring network switches and routers to associate specific nodes on the network with logical segments and restricting communication between segments based on security policy.

A demilitarized zone (DMZ) is a network segment that is in between the protected internal network and the external network, as shown in Figure 4-8.

A DMZ creates a buffer zone. Two levels of firewalls form the DMZ border and protect the internal network assets. Companies usually place their e-mail, web, and DNS servers in the DMZ. Although these servers are "Internet facing" they are still behind one firewall. But servers in the DMZ are still vulnerable and should be carefully hardened since they are first in line to external attacks.

Virtual Private Networks

A VPN is a secure private connection to an organization's protected network that travels through a public untrusted network. Using VPN technology, an organization can extend, virtually, its private network outside the network's normal perimeter. It does this by using tunneling technology that provides an encrypted channel through untrusted networks, such as the Internet, into the organization's protected enterprise. Therefore, remote users such as employees working at home offices can access resources on the internal corporate network almost as if they had a direct connection.

VPNs use tunneling protocols that encapsulate the frame/packet so it can be transmitted through a network. They preserve the original protocol headers so the message can be "unwrapped" at its destination but they allow the encapsulated frame to be routed as normal traffic. These are the most commonly used VPN protocols:

- **Point-to-Point Tunneling Protocol (PPTP)**   PPTP was for many years the de facto VPN standard. However, there are newer VPN technologies that are better and in wider use such as IPSec.

- **Layer 2 Tunneling Protocol (L2TP)**   L2TP was developed by Cisco as a solution to the limitations of PPTP. However, L2TP does not provide encryption, so it is commonly used in combination with other methods such as IPSec.

- **IP Security (IPSec)**   IPSec is a suite of protocols that, in combination, provides data integrity, authentication, and confidentiality. It is now the de facto standard for VPNs.

IDS/IPS

Intrusion detection systems (IDSs) and intrusion prevention systems (IPSs) are companion technologies involving specialized tools to detect (IDS) and prevent (IPS) malicious activity. Both deploy sensors throughout the network that communicate with a control or reporting system that allows the security staff to view indicators of malicious activity and take measures to prevent security breaches.

A *network-based IDS (NIDS)* uses sensors deployed throughout the network in the form of computers or specialized appliances. A *host-based IDS (HIDS)* uses agents installed on host computers that monitor for, and detect, malicious activity on the host. HIDS agents look for host- or OS-specific activities such as running processes, registry changes, file alteration, and so on. Whether network or host based, there are several detection methods employed by IDSs. Modern IDS products usually take advantage of more than one of these methods:

- *Signature-based IDSs* look for specific patterns in traffic, specific messages, or specific files on systems. These specific patterns are called *signatures*. Usually signatures are maintained in a library. Very often IDS product vendors provide access to a subscription service whereby a third-party vendor conducts threat intelligence activities to continually learn about new attacks and what kinds of signatures would be indicative of their presence. Those signatures are downloaded to the IDS products so that they are continuously monitoring for and able to detect the latest attacks. Signature-based IDSs are good at detecting already known attacks and malware but not as good at detecting new kinds of attacks.

- *Anomaly-based IDSs* are better for detecting unknown attacks. If a signature-based IDS is good at knowing "what bad looks like," an anomaly-based IDS is good at knowing "what good looks like." An anomaly-based IDS uses specialized methods such as artificial intelligence and machine learning to build a picture of what normal activity looks like on the network or system. Then if the IDS sees activity that deviates from the norm, it passes an alert to indicate the activity should be investigated. Anomaly-based IDSs are good at detecting previously unknown attacks for which signatures may not exist.

IDS and IPS products use essentially the same technology and methods to detect potentially malicious activity. The difference lies in what each one does about that activity. An IDS simply reports the activity to a console where the security staff can see the alert and perform an investigation to determine if the alert represents actual malicious activity or a breach and then determine the correct course of action. An IPS goes beyond mere detection and reporting by taking action to try to stop the attack or minimize its impact. Candidate actions may include blocking traffic from a particular IP address, turning off a port on a firewall, resetting a device such as a router, or even changing data in packets or hosts to remove or replace malicious messages or files. While it sounds tempting to deploy an IPS that can automatically stop an attack in its tracks, many organizations, especially government/military/defense organizations, are reluctant to use IPS functions due to the risk of automatically making changes to the environment without first testing the impact.

The key to using IDS/IPS solutions wisely comes down to *tuning*. Tuning involves choosing the sensitivity level of the detection, reporting, alerting, and prevention functions. If security operations staff set the threshold level very low, they can detect all potentially malicious events; if they set it very high, they may miss some events but will be sure to catch the most important ones. However, setting the level too low may result in the organization and the security operations staff being overwhelmed by too many messages and alerts that do not indicate intrusive activity (false positives). Likewise, setting the threshold too high could allow serious security breaches to go undetected (false negatives). The challenge for every security organization and the CISO is settling on the right level of IDS/IPS operation.

So, how should the CISO decide what the right level is? Like all security decisions, it comes down to risk management. How valuable are the assets being monitored? And what is the cost of detection? Setting the levels low and capturing more events than are necessary increases operation costs. It may be unwise to spend $2M per year to operate an IDS capability to monitor a $1M network. The CISO and the security organization should create models to predict the equipment and operational level of effort required to deploy and maintain an IDS/IPS at various detection thresholds as compared with the organization's appetite for risk.

An IDS/IPS is essentially just another security control and its implementation should be considered alongside the other candidate controls based on risk.

Cryptography

Cryptography is one of the most fundamental information security practices, and possibly the oldest. Modern *cryptography* is the practice of using mathematics to secure information by rendering it unintelligible to unauthorized parties. This section presents the following cryptographic topics and concepts:

- Cryptographic definitions
- Cryptographic services
- Symmetric, asymmetric, and hybrid cryptosystems
- Hash algorithms
- Method authentication codes
- Digital signatures
- Public key infrastructure

Steganography

Steganography is a technique used to hide secret information in plain sight, typically in innocuous looking digital files. This is accomplished through the use of special software that embeds messages inside images, videos, audio, text, or other files.

Steganography and cryptography are two sides of the same coin. Although both are used to communicate secret information, the method for doing so varies. Steganography hides the fact that the communication has even taken place, as an unintended recipient of a file is unaware that the file contains a hidden message. Cryptography does not hide the communication but hides the data itself through encryption. If an unintended recipient receives an encrypted message, they know the message is there but they cannot read it. Steganography does not encrypt the message; it simply hides the message in another file.

Cryptographic Definitions

Some fundamental definitions must be established to facilitate the discussion of cryptography. The foundational components of cryptography include the following:

- **Cryptographic key**   A string of values used in conjunction with cryptographic algorithms for operations such as encryption and decryption. In general, the longer the key size the more security that is provided; however, this also depends on the algorithm and the implementation used.

- **Cryptographic algorithm**   A mathematical equation that can be used for encryption, decryption, or hashing.

- **Plaintext**   Information in a readable format that has not been encrypted or has been decrypted.

- **Ciphertext**   Information in an unreadable format that has been encrypted.

- **Encryption**   The process of transforming plaintext to ciphertext using cryptographic keys and algorithms.

- **Decryption**   The process of transforming ciphertext to plaintext using cryptographic keys and algorithms.

- **Hashing**   A one-way function that uses algorithms to transform information to a string of data, often used for integrity checking.

- **Cryptosystem**   Includes all the necessary system components for encryption and decryption such as software, protocols, algorithms, keys, key management, and so on.

Figure 4-9
Cryptographic
operations

Plaintext   Encrypt   → Ciphertext   → Decrypt → Plaintext

The cryptographic key values are used by the cryptographic algorithms to indicate which equations to use, in what order, and with what values. Together, keys and algorithms allow for encryption and decryption operations to take place to transfer plaintext to ciphertext and vice versa. The encryption and decryption operations are illustrated in Figure 4-9.

Cryptographic Services

One of the beautiful aspects of cryptography is the range of security services that can be provided, including

- **Confidentiality**   Ensures data is only accessible to authorized parties and remains unintelligible to unauthorized entities (for example, encryption)
- **Integrity**   Ensures data has not been altered by unauthorized parties (for example, digital signatures or message authentication codes)
- **Authentication**   Verifies the identity of a system or user that created a resource
- **Nonrepudiation**   Prevents a sender from legitimately denying that they sent a message (for example, digital signatures)

These services are discussed throughout this section as we explore various algorithms and cryptographic implementations.

Symmetric, Asymmetric, and Hybrid Cryptosystems

The two types of cryptographic algorithms in use today for encryption and decryption are symmetric and asymmetric. In addition, there are hybrid approaches that utilize the strengths of both.

EXAM TIP   CCISO candidates should be aware of the differences between symmetric and asymmetric cryptography.

Symmetric Encryption

Symmetric encryption, also known as symmetric key cryptography, is characterized by the use of a single key for encryption and decryption. This means that the sender and receiver of an encrypted message must both have a copy of the same key. Because anyone with access to the key will be able to decrypt the message, the key must be kept private. This is why it is referred to as a *private key*. For example, in Figure 4-10, Alice and Bob want to exchange confidential information. To send the message to Bob, Alice encrypts

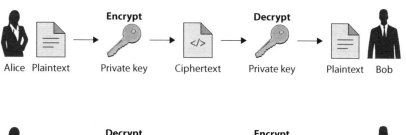

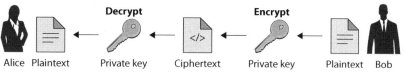

Figure 4-10 Symmetric encryption example

the message with the shared private key to convert the message from plaintext to cipher-text. Bob in turn must have a copy of the same private key to decrypt the message from ciphertext to plaintext. Likewise, if Bob wants to send a message to Alice, he encrypts the message with the shared private key and Alice decrypts the message with the same private key.

Examples of symmetric algorithms include the following:

- **Data Encryption Standard (DES)** The algorithm uses a 56-bit key and is considered insecure due to the short key length, which is susceptible to brute-force attacks. Consequently, DES was replaced with 3DES and AES.

- **Triple-DES (3DES)** 3DES was released as an interim replacement for DES while AES was still being created. 3DES applies DES three times to each block of data during the encryption process. Modern implementations of 3DES provide 168 bits of security.

- **Advanced Encryption Standard (AES)** AES was built as a replacement for DES. AES comes in key sizes of 128, 192, and 256 bits. AES is a mature, internationally used standard for symmetric encryption.

Symmetric encryption's strength lies in its speed. Symmetric key encryption is much faster and less computationally intensive than asymmetric encryption. The downsides to symmetric encryption are that it requires a secure method to transfer the private key out of band and it does not scale well because each pair of users must have a unique key. As the number of users increases, so does the number of keys, which can make key management difficult. The formula to calculate the number of keys needed for symmetric encryption based on users (denoted as N) is as follows:

$$\frac{N(N-1)}{2} = \text{number of unique keys needed}$$

For example, if Alice, Bob, and Carole wanted to communicate with each other separately so as to not have anyone else read their messages, they would need three keys (one for Alice and Bob, one for Alice and Carole, and one for Bob and Carole). However, if the number of users grows, for example, to 100, that would require 4,950 keys as shown:

$$\frac{100(100-1)}{2} = 4,950$$

Symmetric encryption provides confidentiality through encryption but does not provide authenticity or nonrepudiation. Asymmetric cryptography is needed to provide those services.

Asymmetric Encryption

Asymmetric encryption, also known as public key cryptography, is characterized by the use of two mathematically related keys: a public key and a private key. The public key may be provided to anyone that the owner is interested in securely communicating with, but the private key must be known only to the owner. For example, in Figure 4-11, Alice and Bob want to exchange confidential information. To send the message to Bob, Alice encrypts the plaintext message with Bob's public key, which has been shared with her. Bob in turn must decrypt the message from ciphertext to plaintext using his private key known only to him. Likewise, if Bob wants to send a message to Alice, he encrypts the message with Alice's public key and Alice decrypts the message with her private key. In terms of security services, asymmetric cryptography provides confidentiality through encryption and provides authenticity and nonrepudiation by utilizing digital signatures (discussed later in this section).

Common asymmetric algorithm implementations include the following:

- **Diffie-Hellman** Key agreement protocol that allows two entities to generate and agree upon a symmetric key (session key) value that is then used by a separate symmetric algorithm to perform encryption and decryption. It provides key agreement functionality but not encryption or digital signature functionality.

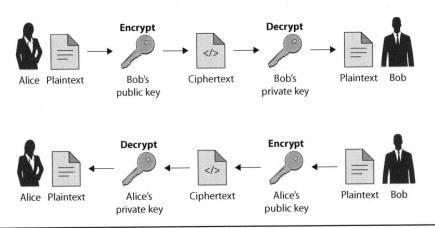

Figure 4-11 Asymmetric encryption example

- **Rivest-Shamir-Adleman (RSA)**   RSA was developed by Ron Rivest, Adi Shamir, and Leonard Adleman. The algorithm provides digital signature, key distribution, and encryption services. The public and private keys are mathematically related and the algorithm is based on the mathematics involved in the difficulty of factoring the product of large prime numbers.

- **Elliptic curve cryptography (ECC)**   ECC is another asymmetric implementation that provides digital signature, key distribution, and encryption services when combined with other encryption schemes. The differing factor is its efficiency and how keys are created. ECC is much more efficient than other asymmetric algorithms, allowing for faster encryption/decryption and smaller key sizes while maintaining the same security level. In addition, keys are generated based on properties of elliptic curves instead of factoring the product of large prime numbers.

The main benefits of asymmetric cryptography are scalability and key distribution. Asymmetric cryptography is easier to scale as each user needs only two keys (one public and one private). The formula to calculate the number of keys needed for asymmetric encryption based on users (denoted as N) is shown here:

$2 \times N$ = number of unique keys needed

In addition, since the public keys can be freely shared, key distribution is made easier; the public key does not require protection since it is shared with everyone. The downside to asymmetric encryption is that it is slower and more computationally intensive than symmetric encryption. Symmetric key encryption is much faster and less computationally intensive than asymmetric encryption. This is why symmetric encryption is often used for encrypting data (content) in conjunction with asymmetric encryption for exchanging cryptographic keys. This is why symmetric encryption is often used for encrypting data (content) whereas asymmetric encryption is most often used for encrypting keys.

Hybrid

As discussed, symmetric and asymmetric cryptography have their own strengths and weaknesses. Modern cryptosystems typically utilize a hybrid model that makes use of both. The use of these two techniques is often referred to as *hybrid cryptography* or as a *digital envelope*. Figure 4-12 provides an illustration for how common hybrid cryptosystems operate. The steps are as follows:

1. Alice shares her public key with Bob.
2. Bob generates a session key and encrypts it with Alice's public key to create a digital envelope.
3. Bob sends the digital envelope to Alice.
4. Alice decrypts the digital envelope with her private key to access the session key.
5. Alice and Bob both have access to the session key (symmetric key) and can use this to encrypt and decrypt messages from one another.

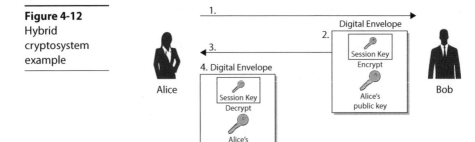

Figure 4-12 Hybrid cryptosystem example

The hybrid approach provides the best of both worlds as it allows for the message data to be encrypted quickly with symmetric encryption and for ease of key exchange of the symmetric key using asymmetric encryption. Protocols that utilize a hybrid approach include

- SSL/TLS
- SSH
- OpenPGP

For simplicity, this example uses two users, Alice and Bob. However, in practice, this is often a user communicating with a web server to share files (for example, SFTP or FTPS) or to access a site securely (for example, HTTPS).

Cryptosystems Summary

Table 4-3 provides a summary and comparison of the fundamental differences between symmetric and asymmetric cryptographic functionality.

Functionality	Symmetric Cryptography	Asymmetric Cryptography
Keys	One shared private key that must be distributed securely between two or more entities	One public key available to anyone and one private key kept secret by the owner, for each party
Algorithm speed	Less computationally intensive and faster	More computationally intensive and slower
Primary use case	Bulk encryption of content (files, packets, e-mails, hard drives, database content, and so on)	Key distribution and digital signatures
Services provided	Confidentiality	Confidentiality, authentication, and nonrepudiation

Table 4-3 Comparison of Symmetric and Asymmetric Cryptography

Figure 4-13
MD5 hash
example

```
[bash-3.2$ echo my-secret | md5
aefd9a754b19e3c6ff33e65f499f4cf3


[bash-3.2$ echo My-secret | md5
b560e5de5641d91446d8c9cdda00d326
```

Hash Algorithms

Hashing was briefly introduced in the "Cryptographic Definition" section. To recap, a hash algorithm is a one-way function that maps information to a fixed-length string of data, referred to as a hash value, fingerprint, or message digest. It is referred to as a one-way function because the original message cannot be reproduced from the hash value, unlike encryption where the ciphertext can be converted back to plaintext using the decryption operation. In addition, there is no key involved when using hash algorithms. For example, consider the MD5 hash values for the text strings "my-secret" and "My-secret" illustrated in Figure 4-13.

If one single bit of the message changes (such as a capital M instead of a lowercase m), the hash value dramatically changes, as shown in the output of Figure 4-13. The hash value can be used for integrity checking to ensure that a message has not been modified. Common hash algorithms include the following:

- **MD5** Message-digest algorithm version 5, produces a 128-bit hash value
- **SHA-1** Secure Hash Algorithm 1, produces a 160-bit hash value
- **SHA-2** Secure Hash Algorithm 2, includes a family of hash functions that produce 224, 256, 384, or 512-bit hash values: SHA-224, SHA-256, SHA-384, SHA-512, SHA-512/224, SHA-512/256
- **SHA-3** Secure Hash Algorithm 3, includes a family of hash functions: SHA3-224, SHA3-256, SHA3-384, SHA3-512, SHAKE128, and SHAKE256

Utilizing another Alice and Bob example, suppose Alice wants to send Bob a message but Bob wants to be sure the message has not been altered. Hashing can help with this. The general steps for utilizing hashing in this example are illustrated in Figure 4-14 and outlined here:

1. Alice puts the message through a hashing function to generate a message digest (MD).

2. The MD is appended to the message and sent to Bob.

3. Bob puts the message through the same hashing function to generate his own separate MD.

4. Bob then compares the two MD values. If they are the same, the message has not been altered.

Figure 4-14
Hashing example

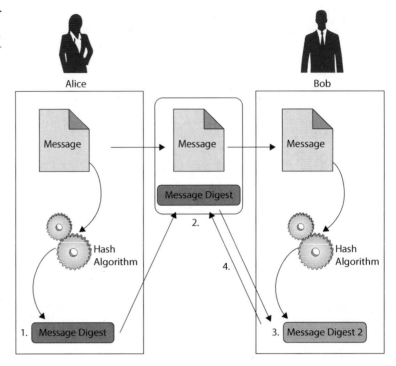

Collisions

If a hash algorithm creates the same hash output for two different messages, this is known as a *collision*. To reduce the risk of collisions occurring, a hash algorithm with a larger message digest output (in bits) should be used. This means that a hash algorithm that produces a 256-bit hash value is typically more resilient to collisions than a hash algorithm of 128 bits.

Collisions can cause security problems depending on how a hash is used. MD5 has been shown to be susceptible to collisions. Does this mean that MD5 should not be used? The answer is, *it depends*. A hash value can be used for a variety of purposes. It can be used for performing an integrity check of a file or for hashing a password before it is stored in a database. For a simple file integrity check, MD5 may be suitable, but for hashing passwords in an application, a more secure algorithm such as SHA-256 may be a better choice.

Password Hashing

Plaintext passwords should not be stored in a system. If an attacker compromises such a system or password database, they would have access to the plaintext passwords. In modern-day operating systems, password hashes are stored instead of storing the plaintext password. This reduces the risk of an attacker accessing the plaintext password if the system is compromised and also prevents system administrators from knowing the passwords that are stored (as only the hashes are stored). In Windows, users and password hashes are stored in the Security Account Manager (SAM) database or Active Directory. On Unix/Linux systems, user account information and password hashes are stored in the /etc/passwd and /etc/shadow files.

Password Attacks

There are a few different methods that attackers use to attack passwords:

- **Dictionary attack**   An attacker utilizes a tool that has a dictionary list of words and terms to try as password attempts into a system. For this reason, it is important to discourage or prevent the use of dictionary words as passwords. Some systems can perform checks on passwords to prevent dictionary words from being used.

- **Brute-force attack**   An attacker tries all possible combinations of characters, one at a time, as password attempts to break into a system. This is why password complexity is important. The longer and more complex the password (a combination of uppercase and lowercase letters, numbers, special characters, and so on), the greater the work factor in performing a successful brute-force attack.

- **Rainbow table attack**   An attacker uses a precomputed table of plaintext input and corresponding hashed values for cracking password hashes. For example, if an attacker has stolen or compromised a system's hashed password database, they can compare the hashes to the values in the rainbow table to determine the plaintext password. This risk is often mitigated through the use of cryptographic salts.

Cryptographic Salts and Salting

A *salt* is additional random, or pseudorandom, data that is appended to the message (content) that is going to be hashed. Salts are used to add resiliency against dictionary and rainbow table attacks. A different salt is used for each hashing operation; thus, if the same content (such as a password) is hashed twice using two different salts, the resulting hash value will be different. This means that two users who happen to have the same password will have different hash values stored in the password database. This is illustrated in Figure 4-15.

Message Authentication Codes

Hash algorithms provide integrity that a message has not been modified, but they do not provide authenticity of the message. A *message authentication code (MAC)* is a type of cryptographic function that provides both integrity and authenticity using a key that is shared between the sender and recipient. MACs can be created using hash algorithms

Figure 4-15
Cryptographic
salt example

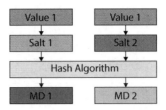

and symmetric encryption algorithms in certain modes. Examples of MAC algorithms include

- **Hash-based Message Authentication Code (HMAC)**   HMAC, also referred to as a *keyed hash*, uses a hash algorithm and a shared key to produce a MAC.
- **Cipher Block Chaining Message Authentication Code (CBC-MAC)**   Cipher block chaining is one of many modes for symmetric block encryption algorithms. Though these algorithms are predominantly used for encrypting data, CBC-MAC is a method for providing authenticity and integrity using symmetric algorithms, such as AES, to produce a MAC. *Cipher-based Message Authentication Code (CMAC)* is a more recent implementation of CBC-MAC with a slight tweak that adds an additional operation to enhance security.

Digital Signatures

A *digital signature* is a hash value that is encrypted with the sender's private key. Digital signatures provide integrity, authenticity, and nonrepudiation. This provides assurance that the message has not been modified (integrity), provides assurance that the message came from the sender (authenticity), and prevents the sender from denying that they sent it since only the sender should have access to their private key to perform the encryption (nonrepudiation). The general steps involved in this process, based on the hashing steps discussed earlier, are as follows:

1. Alice puts the message through a hashing function to generate a message digest.
2. The message digest is encrypted with Alice's private key and appended to the message sent to Bob.
3. Bob decrypts the message digest with Alice's public key and runs the message through the same hashing function to generate his own separate message digest.
4. Bob then compares the two message digest values (the one he received from Alice and the one he created). If they are the same, the message has not been altered (integrity), it must have come from Alice (authenticity), and she can't deny sending it (nonrepudiation).

Public Key Infrastructure

Key management is a critical part of any cryptosystem. Given the use of a strong algorithm, the keys are the weakest link in the cryptosystem. If a private key is compromised, so is the security of the cryptosystem. Keys require secure creation, distribution, storage, recovery, and destruction. In addition, one of the issues with public key cryptography is that anyone can generate their own key pairs. With everyone generating their own key pairs, how do you know the public key you receive is actually from the individual you think it's from? For example, Bob could create a key pair and send his public key to Alice and claim that it is Tim's public key. Alice needs some way to verify who the owner of the key is. This is where public key infrastructures come in. *Public key infrastructure (PKI)* is defined by NIST as "a set of policies, processes, server platforms, software and workstations used for the purpose of administering certificates and public-private key pairs, including the ability to issue, maintain, and revoke public key certificates."

A *public key certificate*, also known as a *digital certificate*, is an electronic certificate that contains data that identifies an entity as the owner (referred to as the *subject*) of a public key. These certificates are issued and digitally signed by a trusted third party (referred to as the *issuer* or the *certificate authority*) that has verified the identity of the public key owner. The certificate authority validates the subject's identity and creates a certificate containing the name of the subject and their public key and then signs the certificate with a digital signature using the certificate authority's private key. Figure 4-16 is a screenshot from a Chrome browser running on a Mac viewing a certificate for a website using an HTTPS connection.

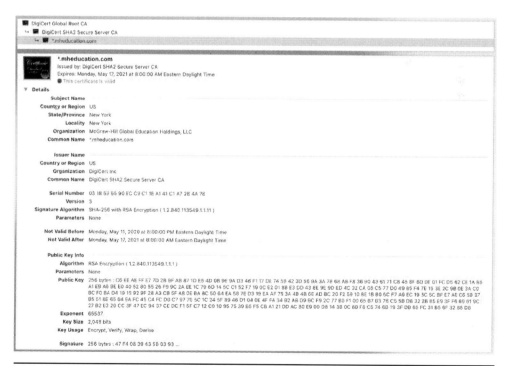

Figure 4-16   Digital certificate example

The main components that typically make up a PKI include

- **Registration authority (RA)**   The registration authority performs the duty of accepting registration requests from users, validating their identity, and passing the request to the certificate authority. The RA cannot create certificates; it simply acts as a verifier and sends the request to the certificate authority.

- **Certificate authority (CA)**   The certificate authority creates, issues, and manages revocation of digital certificates signed with the CA private key.

- **Digital certificates**   Each person participating in a PKI must be issued a digital certificate by a trusted party. Each individual must have their own public/private key pair. This is either generated locally on their machine or issued by the CA. In either case the public key must be provided to the CA. The CA binds the individual's identity to the public key and embeds that in the digital certificate. This acts as a credential for that individual binding their identity to the public key. The digital certificate is signed by the CA's private key, which proves that the certificate was issued by the CA and that the CA has validated that the public key belongs to the subject in question. This provides assurance to recipients of this key.

- **Certificate directory**   The certificate directory serves as a repository to store the digital certificates.

- **Certificate revocation**   The CA is responsible for handling certificate revocation. Certificates may be revoked if the user loses their private key or leaves the organization. Revoking the certificate tells others not to trust the public key of that individual. Revoked certificates are stored on the certificate revocation list (CRL).

A PKI is used for implementing a hybrid cryptosystem approach (symmetric and asymmetric cryptography) with the added benefit of key management and public key assurance. A PKI provides confidentiality through encryption as well as integrity, non-repudiation, and authentication through signing and digital certificates. In practice the communication flow would look like the following:

1. Alice wants to communicate with Bob.

2. Alice sends Bob her digital certificate that she received from the CA.

3. Bob validates the certificate by ensuring that it was created by a CA that he trusts, is not expired, matches Alice's information, and has the CA's valid digital signature.

4. After Bob is assured of the certificate's validity, he extracts Alice's public key with assurance that it came from Alice.

5. Bob sends his certificate to Alice and Alice goes through the same steps as Bob.

6. Bob sends Alice a message by encrypting it with a session key (symmetric key) and encrypts the session key with Alice's public key.

7. Now that both parties have each other's public keys as well as the session key, they can share messages back and forth.

Cloud Security

NIST Special Publication 800-145, *The NIST Definition of Cloud Computing*, defines *cloud computing* as "a model for enabling ubiquitous, convenient, on-demand network access to a shared pool of configurable computing resources (e.g., networks, servers, storage, applications, and services) that can be rapidly provisioned and released with minimal management effort or service provider interaction." One of the biggest concerns that organizations have when utilizing cloud services is the lack of control. For example, the cloud service provider (CSP) typically manages the datacenter, the hardware, and other functions depending on the service, but the organization is still accountable for security and must ensure that the CSP is implementing appropriate security practices. This section discusses the following fundamentals of cloud computing:

- Cloud computing characteristics
- Cloud deployment models
- Cloud service models
- Cloud security risks and assurance levels
- Cloud security resources

Cloud Computing Characteristics

The following are the essential characteristics of cloud computing per NIST SP 800-145:

- **On-demand and elastic**   Organizations that use cloud computing can configure what they need when they need it, allowing them to tailor their resources to their needs with agility.

- **Resource pooling**   Computer resources are shared across multiple tenants in a manner that is transparent to the organizations and their users.

- **Measured service**   The amount of resources used can be metered and measured, allowing the organization to understand its usage and acquire more or less capability as needed.

- **Broad network access**   Access is enabled over the network and supported by thin or thick client platforms that run on a wide variety of endpoint devices.

ISO/IEC 17788, *Information technology — Cloud computing — Overview and vocabulary*, also provides a definition for cloud computing. It lists characteristics, including those mentioned previously, with the addition of multitenancy. *Multitenancy* describes the allocation of physical or virtual resources in a way that multiple tenants can utilize a pool of resources while computing and data is isolated from other tenants.

Cloud Deployment Models

The following four types of cloud deployment models are available, each of which is characterized by the location of the infrastructure:

- **Public** In public cloud deployment models, cloud resources are operated by a third-party cloud service provider for use by the general public typically through a subscription or on-demand pricing models. Examples of public CSPs include Microsoft Azure, Amazon Web Services, and Oracle Cloud Infrastructure.

- **Private** A private cloud deployment model consists of computing infrastructure and resources that are dedicated for use by a single organization. The resources are owned and operated by the organization, a third party, or a combination of both and are used exclusively by one organization and not shared among many like they are in a public cloud model. Some companies operate a private cloud in their datacenter or pay a third party to host the private cloud.

- **Community** A community cloud deployment model consists of infrastructure that is shared between many organizations for a specific purpose such as collaboration, a specific mission, or for security and compliance reasons. Ownership is by one or more of the organizations involved, or by a third party.

- **Hybrid** A hybrid cloud deployment model is a mix of the other models. For example, an organization may operate a private cloud in its environment and utilize a public cloud service for "cloud bursting." This is where loads are load balanced between the environment. An application or resource may run on the private cloud and, if there is a spike in demand, switch over processing to the public cloud to enable the use of additional compute processing resources.

Cloud Service Models

To understand the implications of using a cloud service, it is best to start with the service model to understand each party's responsibility. The following are the three primary cloud service models:

- **Infrastructure as a Service (IaaS)** Provides customers with access to a pool of infrastructure resources such as network, server, and storage resources that can be virtually provisioned. The CSP manages the underlying physical infrastructure. The customer manages the platforms and software such as OS, development tools, and applications.

- **Platform as a Service (PaaS)** Provides customers with development or application platforms the customer can use to deploy applications. This is essentially a place to develop, test, and run code for applications developed in various programming languages, allowing for a simplified deployment process. In this model the CSP manages the underlying infrastructure (network, servers, and storage) and the OS.

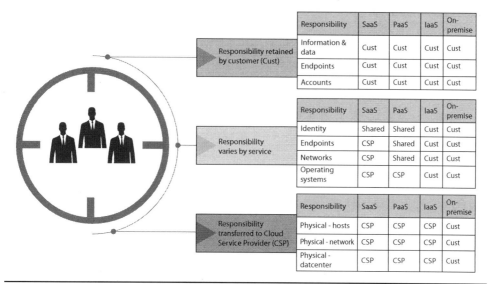

Responsibility	SaaS	PaaS	IaaS	On-premise
Information & data	Cust	Cust	Cust	Cust
Endpoints	Cust	Cust	Cust	Cust
Accounts	Cust	Cust	Cust	Cust

Responsibility	SaaS	PaaS	IaaS	On-premise
Identity	Shared	Shared	Cust	Cust
Endpoints	CSP	Shared	Cust	Cust
Networks	CSP	Shared	Cust	Cust
Operating systems	CSP	CSP	Cust	Cust

Responsibility	SaaS	PaaS	IaaS	On-premise
Physical - hosts	CSP	CSP	CSP	Cust
Physical - network	CSP	CSP	CSP	Cust
Physical - datcenter	CSP	CSP	CSP	Cust

Figure 4-17 Cloud shared responsibility model

- **Software as a Service (SaaS)**   Provides customers with access to an application hosted by the CSP. The CSP manages the underlying infrastructure and platform while the customer typically only manages user-specific application configurations. Examples of SaaS include web-based e-mail or other web-based applications such as a customer relationship management (CRM) system.

Ensuring that security exists within a cloud environment begins with a thorough understanding of the cloud service models and how they contribute to shared responsibility. Figure 4-17 provides an overview of the respective responsibilities of the customer and the cloud service provider.

As Figure 4-17 illustrates, the responsibility for specific functions lies with the CSP for IaaS, PaaS, and SaaS. However, even with the CSP taking on these responsibilities, the organization is still liable for ensuring protection of the organization's data and must ensure proper security practices are being implemented. For example, the CSP may be providing a security function (such as physical security for systems hosted in a public cloud), but the organization must perform due diligence to ensure that the CSP is implementing appropriate controls and countermeasures.

Cloud Security Risks and Assurance Levels

One of the risks associated with using a cloud service provider is the loss of control the organization has over certain functions while still being accountable for security. Here are some various cloud-relevant security assurance levels commonly provided by CSPs to customers to assist with the organization's due diligence:

- **Service level agreements (SLAs)**   SLAs are helpful in understanding what service levels the CSP agrees to provide and can assist the organization in determining if a service meets its operational and security requirements.

- **SOC 2/SOC 3**   The organization can request a CSP to show SOC 2 or SOC 3 reports, which report on the assessment of System and Organization Controls related to trust service (Security, Availability, Processing Integrity, Confidentiality, and Privacy).

- **ISO 27001**   Some CSPs may have their information security management system (ISMS) ISO 27001 certified as a way to demonstrate compliance with industry best practices in information security management.

- **FedRAMP**   The Federal Risk and Authorization Management Program (FedRAMP) is a US federal government program that provides a standard approach for assessing, authorizing, and continuously monitoring cloud-based products and services. In order for a CSP to sell services to the US federal government, the CSP must be FedRAMP authorized (essentially FISMA for cloud services). If a CSP is FedRAMP authorized, then its controls have been assessed by an accredited Third-Party Assessment Organization (3PAO). Cloud service products that have been authorized are listed on the FedRAMP website at https://www.fedramp.gov.

- **CSA STAR**   The Cloud Security Alliance (CSA) Security Trust Assurance and Risk (STAR) program is a multilevel assurance program that enables CSPs to document the security controls provided with various cloud services. The program ranges from self-assessment options to certifications issued after assessments have been conducted by approved third-party assessment firms.

As Ronald Reagan said, "Trust, but verify." The CISO is still accountable for the security of the organization's information and assets and must ensure that there is proper governance and risk management around cloud programs and that all CSPs the organization uses are implementing sound security practices.

Cloud Security Resources

Here are some key resources for cloud security best practices:

- **Cloud Security Alliance**   A nonprofit firm focused on promoting cloud computing best practices and security. CSA provides tools, research, frameworks, certification programs (STAR, for example), and other documents such as the Consensus Assessments Initiative Questionnaire (CAIQ) and Cloud Controls Matrix (CCM) discussed in Chapter 2.

- **Center for Internet Security**   A nonprofit organization that provides security tools and best practice information such as OS hardening standards and benchmarks.

Physical Security

Physical security is often the first line of defense for an organization's personnel and assets. The responsibility for physical security varies from organization to organization and may not fall under the CISO's purview. Some organizations have a separate chief security officer (CSO) or other individual responsible for physical and/or personnel security. Therefore, information security functional responsibilities may overlap or be integrated with physical security. Regardless of the implementation and organizational structure, the CISO should be aware of physical security and its relationship with information security. This section discusses the following topics:

- Physical security threats
- Physical security program planning
- Physical security resources
- Physical security controls
- Physical security auditing and measurement
- Personnel security

Physical Security Threats

Physical security threats come in many forms such as storms, power outages, or human error. Understanding the types of threats the organization faces is critical for the design of appropriate controls. Threats can generally be categorized into the following:

- **Natural/environmental**   Threats that come from natural or environmental risk factors, such as earthquakes, floods, tornadoes, fires, or extreme temperatures.
- **Supply system**   Threats against supply systems, such as power outages, network and communication interruptions, HVAC disruption, or interruptions to other utilities such as gas or water.
- **Manmade**   Threats from people, such as disgruntled employees, human error, vandalism, fraud, theft, or unauthorized access.
- **Political**   Threats that are politically motivated, such as terrorism, civil disobedience, riots, or strikes.

Each of these categories of threats represents potential risks. The organization should include them in the risk analysis introduced in Chapter 1. To review:

- First, a business impact analysis is performed:
  - A list of potential physical threats is created.
  - Each threat is assessed to determine its likelihood of occurrence and the assets to which it applies.
  - Based on the threats and associated assets, the impact of the loss to the business is assessed.
- Then risk mitigation actions and controls are selected that are appropriate to each asset based on the risk.

The key is to balance the impact of a threat against the cost of the countermeasures against it.

> ### Safety Is the Key
> When it comes to physical security, the most important thing is protecting the safety of employees and people within the work environment. Safety even trumps security. For instance, in the event of a disaster, the best security may be achieved by automatically locking all the doors to the facility, referred to as *fail-secure*. However, this may trap people inside, so the safer and better practice is to automatically unlock the doors in an emergency, referred to as *fail-safe*. Organizations should ensure that fail-safe mechanisms are in place, as the safety of personnel is always paramount.

Physical Security Program Planning

The organization should have a physical security plan that defines the goals for the security program. Here is a list of the topics commonly addressed in the physical security plan:

- Plans for physical controls, including deterrence, delaying mechanisms, and detection controls
- Plans for assessing the physical controls on a periodic or aperiodic basis
- Plans for responding to physical incidents to ensure personnel safety, assess the level of impact, and ensure the restoration of normal business functions
- Plans for identifying, acquiring, and supporting resources required to carry out the plan

Like all security functions, physical security must be supported by policies and procedures to ensure consistent, reliable, and measurable physical security activities are performed.

Physical Security Resources

When it comes to staffing for physical security, resources are either hired directly as in-house employees or outsourced from a third party or service provider.

- **Insourcing**   Organizations may elect to hire physical security resources to manage the physical security program. This may include the following roles:
  - A facilities manager to oversee buildings and facilities operations
  - A safety officer to oversee personnel safety
  - Security guards to patrol key areas, manage entry points, and monitor surveillance systems
  - IT resources to manage technical components (badge readers, card access systems, and other technical physical access controls)

- **Outsourcing**   Some organizations choose to contract with a third-party physical security company that may provide a range of services, from guards to entire alarm, monitoring, and video surveillance systems. In today's world of cloud services, physical security is provided by the cloud service provider. If an organization uses a CSP to host its infrastructure, the physical security of the CSP's datacenter is certainly a concern. When the systems that host an organization's informational assets and sensitive data are hosted in a CSP's datacenter, the organization must have some assurance that the CSP has proper physical security controls alongside its information security controls. Physical security should be addressed in the CSP's contract or service level agreement, and there should be some independent or third-party evaluation of the CSP's facilities and practices that the CSP can provide as proof.

Physical Security Controls

Physical security controls can be considered in categories as follows:

- *Deterrent controls* are for prevention of physical intrusions by communicating to potential intruders that they may want to reconsider their actions. Deterrent controls include fences, security guards, guard dogs, warning signs, lighting, and other measures to cause the intruder to think twice about whether or not to proceed. Of course, criminal laws and their associated punishments are also good deterrent controls.

- *Delaying controls* are what most people think of when they think of physical controls. They are usually implemented in layers that slow down the attack or intrusion (or increase the *work factor*) at each step as each layer presents another defensive obstacle the intruder must overcome. Delaying controls include doors, locks, walls, fences, and barriers.

- *Detective controls* communicate to the organization or the public that something disruptive has happened. These controls include smoke detectors and fire alarms, burglar alarms, sensors on doors and windows, security cameras, and closed-circuit TV (CCTV) systems.

Facility Security and Controls

Physical security should be addressed as part of the *environmental design and construction* of the facility and the selection of the site and location. Environmental design involves three factors that impact security:

- **Natural access control**   The design of the facility exterior involves creating pathways for people to travel around the building(s) to gain access. These natural pathways are the first layer of access control as they guide people where the organization wants them and prevents people from going where the organization does not want them to go. These natural access controls include sidewalks, bollards, trees and shrubs, fences, and lighting.

- **Natural surveillance**   The same features that contribute to natural access control can also provide natural surveillance. The use and placement of physical environmental features, personnel walkways, lighting, and so on, all contribute to the ability to see people who are near the entrances and exits of the building.

- **Territorial reinforcement**   Territorial enforcement refers to the physical design of the building exterior to provide visual cues that cause people to distinguish private areas from public ones. For instance, the design and appearance of a loading dock should tell people to stay away from that area if they aren't loading or unloading something. Likewise, the more welcoming design and appearance of the front entrance should make it obvious to people that's where they should go.

While the environmental design of a facility uses natural and manmade means to control access, support surveillance, and provide territorial reinforcement, the *physical design and construction* provides the first level of hardening. Hardening involves the physical construction and materials composition of the exterior and interior components of the building to provide the right level of protection. It would not make sense to build the local bank branch with the same type of hardening as Fort Knox, as each facility is protecting assets of differing values. The key is to choose the right type of construction and hardening for the situation, *based on risk*.

Security Zones

Internally, buildings may be built to provide *security zones*. Much like networks can be segmented with access controls to support the concept of least privilege, buildings can be designed in a similar fashion. In this case the building is divided into zones with different security levels depending on who needs to be in each zone and the associated risk.

Doors and walls are the widely used methods of controlling access between security zones, rooms, or other areas of segmentation in the building. Construction and materials of doors, walls, flooring, and ceilings are chosen based on the predicted threat and the assets under protection. The least amount of protection is provided by hollow walls and doors; the strongest are built of solid materials reinforced with stronger materials such as concrete or steel.

The key is to balance the impact of a threat against the cost of the countermeasures against it.

Prevent or Detect?

Sometimes it may not be important to keep the bad guys out as long as you know that they were there. Many buildings use drop ceilings that have easily removed tiles that can be used to gain access to the area above the ceiling. Walls may be built just high enough to stop at the drop ceiling, allowing someone to climb into the ceiling area, over the wall, and into the adjacent room, bypassing doors and locks. But this may be okay if *ceiling clips* are used. These clips ensure that if someone removes a ceiling tile, the tile is destroyed, leaving a hole in the ceiling and a trail of debris on the floor. In this case there is no way an intruder can access the room in the described manner without someone knowing it occurred. Depending on what the room is used for, this level of security may be good enough.

Locks and Access Control

Doors control ingress to and egress from a building or room. However, doors don't provide *authentication* unless they have a lock. Locks limit *who* can open a door and are the physical equivalent of identity management because only certain people, or groups of people, have the key, combination, or other method to open the door. Therefore, locks can be used to enforce the principal of least privilege for a physical facility. Locks have been around for centuries and there are many types from which to choose to provide different levels of protection and usability features. Here are a few:

- Conventional locks that use physical keys or combinations.
- Smart locks that use electronic keys (card keys, fobs, and such) or keypads.
- Biometric locks that read a person's physical attributes to identify the individual and grant access based on who they are. Biometric readers include fingerprint, iris, hand, and facial recognition systems.

Smart locks and biometric readers are usually used as part of a *physical access control system*. Such a system makes managing who has access to an area much easier than having to manage and distribute physical keys or having to manually change lock combinations. Access control systems enable the following functions:

- Electronic inventory of who has access to what buildings, areas, and rooms
- User account creation, editing of access rights, and deactivation when users no longer need access or are terminated
- Automated record of who accessed what area and when they did it

Physical access control systems can also provide a physical implementation of single-factor, dual-factor, or multifactor authentication, as described in the "Identity and Access Management" section of this chapter. For instance dual-factor authentication could be implemented using a system that requires a visitor to use a card key (something you have) and enter a PIN (something you know) into a keypad as the mechanism to open a door. Similarly, a system may require both a PIN (something you know) and a scan from a fingerprint reader (something you are) for authentication.

Mantraps

Another commonly used building or room access control mechanism is a *mantrap* (sometimes called a person-trap), which is a small area or vestibule with two doors built so the first door must be closed before the second door can be opened. Mantraps require the visitor to go through two doors and open two locks in order to gain access to a secure area and are used in situations that require a higher degree of security. Datacenters often use mantraps.

Fences

Fencing provides a physical barrier and access control to the area around a building or group of buildings. Similar to the construction of walls and doors, the strength of materials, thickness and size, and construction methods determine the level of protection provided by the fence. The type of fence that is suitable for a given situation is based on risk. For instance, a three-foot-high fence may deter casual trespassers but can easily be climbed, but an eight-foot-high fence with barbed wire at the top is a challenge for most people. Most critical areas have fences at least eight feet high.

Lighting

Lighting is used for security in critical areas, parking lots, and near doors, windows, and building perimeters. Lighting provides several important security functions; it discourages intruders since they don't usually want to be seen, it provides safety for personnel, and, most importantly, it provides a way for security guards, employees, and security cameras to see and record people and activities. Lighting features and types include the following:

- **Glare protection**   Light is directed toward areas where potential intruders are most likely to be but not toward guards or cameras that may be impaired by glare.
- **Continuous lighting**   An array of lights provides an even amount of light across an area such as a parking lot or field.
- **Controlled lighting**   Lighting does not bleed over property lines, so only the organization's area is lit and not their neighbor's area.
- **Standby lighting**   Different lights turn on and off automatically, so it appears that people are in the building when they may not be.
- **Responsive area illumination**   Lights turn on automatically in response to detection of a possible intruder.

Security Guards

Security guards are an expensive tool to use in security but they have special value in that they can perform all three of the core physical access control functions at the same time:

- **Deterrence**   The mere presence of a guard can deter an intruder.
- **Delay**   Guards can physically challenge an intruder and provide an obstacle the intruder must overcome to carry out their exploit.
- **Detection**   Guards have eyes and ears and can use them to detect an intrusion and then sound an alarm to alert others.

Similar to human security guards, guard dogs can also perform all three physical access control functions and can be a valuable tool.

Detective Controls

Detective controls most often are deployed as a monitoring or alarm system. Similar to a network IDS, a physical monitoring system uses sensors that report to a central point to provide information to the organization that an event has occurred. Depending on the event details, it can be further investigated.

Physical intrusion sensors include motion detectors that detect a possible intruder and security cameras that record a possible intrusion and store video for later inspection. Various other types of sensors include ones that can detect when doors or windows are opened or broken, detect sounds above the ambient noise levels, and detect heat given off by bodies.

Like logging and monitoring systems discussed elsewhere in this chapter, physical security monitoring systems must be *tuned* to provide the right level of detection and information to the organization.

Datacenters

Datacenters often hold the crown jewels of an organization's information assets. In addition, datacenters concentrate many of an organization's high-value assets in an enclosed space, which increases the vulnerability associated with a single threat event. Therefore, the impact of a serious physical security incident or environmental disaster is potentially massive.

Datacenter security controls should be highly resilient and redundant to provide maximum protection. The following are some aspects of datacenters that require special consideration:

- **Location** Datacenters should be located to provide maximum protection against exterior threats. Locating datacenters on the top floors or in the basement of a building may be unwise. Likewise, datacenters with windows to the outside may not be a good idea. Depending on the region of the world the datacenter is in, hurricanes, tornadoes, floods, and earthquakes may be some of the threats that drive building construction and datacenter placement.

- **Separation** Datacenter electrical facilities and HVAC systems should be located separately from the rest of the facility. This allows the organization to control and adjust temperature and humidity in the datacenter as conditions require and to provide alternate facilities redundancy. Datacenter backup power, using batteries or external power generators, also may be separate from the rest of the facility.

- **Environmental** Due to the special nature of computer equipment, environmental controls in the datacenter are unique and are highly important in order to meet equipment requirements for power, temperature, and humidity. And fire suppression is a special concern for datacenters and requires tailored solutions.

Fire Suppression

Fires start for a variety of reasons, including electrical failures or ignition of combustible materials due to carelessness and even arson. To ignite and burn, fire requires four things:

- Heat
- Fuel
- Oxygen
- Chemical reaction

Remove any of these four things and the fire stops. Modern fire suppression systems perform two functions: detect the fire and deploy an agent. The agent works by accomplishing one of the following:

- Reducing the temperature
- Removing the fuel or the oxygen
- Disrupting the chemical reaction

Fire detectors operate by detecting smoke (smoke activated), heat (temperature activated), or flames (infrared-flame activated). Upon detection of a fire, the system sends an alert to a central console or directly to the fire stations and deploys an agent (liquid or chemical) to put out the fire. There are generally three types of fire suppression systems in use today:

- **Wet pipe** Wet pipe systems are simple arrangements of pipes mounted on or above the ceiling that are filled with water and are ready to be released onto whatever is below them. Putting out a fire in this manner is quite destructive, especially to electronic equipment.

- **Pre-action** Pre-action systems are much like wet pipe systems except the pipes do not contain water until a fire is detected and then the pipes are quickly filled and the water is deployed. Dry pipes are considered safer than wet pipes because there is less chance of an accidental leak and dry pipes may be less likely to drip moisture due to condensation.

- **Gaseous** Gaseous systems deploy gas agents to remove oxygen and heat. Since these agents are gaseous, no water is used and therefore gaseous systems are much more friendly to electronic and office equipment. Most modern gaseous systems use agents such as FM-200 or similar agents.

For datacenters, gaseous systems are preferable because they are the least destructive; however, they are also the most expensive of the three types. To reduce costs, some organizations choose pre-action systems for datacenters.

Physical Security Auditing and Measurement

Physical security can be audited and measured using access logs as well as ongoing review and assessments of physical security measures.

- **Access logs** Organizations should audit physical access logs. These may range from sign-in sheets to software with auditing features that produces an audit trail of all individuals who attempted to access a room or facility. Regardless of the type of access logs that are used, they are an important detective control that can be utilized to understand the events leading up to an unauthorized access or intrusion. For the logs to be useful, the following must be recorded, at a minimum:

  - The date and time of the access
  - The identity of the person who accessed the location (such as name and some form of identification number)

- **Physical vulnerability assessment**   Physical vulnerability assessments, also known as physical security audits or reviews, are performed to identify weaknesses in physical security controls and strategies. An assessment typically includes a review of the following protection categories:

  - Facility and perimeter protection

  - Interior protection

  - Protection from manmade, natural, or technical threats

> **NOTE**   Physical vulnerability assessments are discussed in greater detail in the "Vulnerability Assessments" section later in this chapter.

Personnel Security

A physical security program should take into account personnel safety and security. As stated earlier in the chapter, personnel safety should be a top priority for the organization. Personnel security is a broad topic that includes implementing general safety practices, employment procedures, and vendor, consultant, and contractor procedures.

General Safety Practices

The most important part of personnel security is keeping people safe. Here are some key practices that should be implemented to enable a safe environment for personnel:

- **Physical security incident response**   Policies and procedures should detail how the organization responds to personnel safety threats. A key component of this is ensuring that employees receive training on the procedures.

- **Drills and training**   It is important that employees receive training and practice on how to respond to various physical security threats. This includes training and practice drills for active shooters, fires, storms, pandemics, and so on.

- **Succession planning**   Plans must be in place to ensure that there is a succession plan that outlines who should take the helm if executives, managers, or supervisors are not available or are incapacitated.

- **Travel**   Employees or executives traveling to certain parts of the world may need special training or third-party security services such as bodyguards or escorts. In addition, special practices might be required; for instance, an organization may decide that certain senior executives should not travel on the same transportation medium (such as the same flight) to reduce the risk of losing multiple key leaders if there were to be an accident or disaster.

- **Operational security**   Also called OPSEC, operational security refers to the fact that an attacker can glean sensitive information from collecting seemingly benign information and piecing it together. Personnel should practice good OPSEC by limiting who they share information with, when, and for what purpose. Security incidents have occurred as the result of people not being careful about what they post on social media, what they say to someone in a restaurant, and even what information they share with a coworker.

Employment Procedures

Part of personnel security includes managing the life cycle of the employment process, which includes the following:

- **Employment screening procedures**   These are procedures that are followed as part of the hiring process to determine employee suitability. These may include
  - Background checks
  - Drug screenings
  - Security clearance requirements
  - Credit checks
- **Employment agreements and policies**   These are documents such as the following that employees sign that communicate expected behavior:
  - Nondisclosure agreement (NDA)
  - Code of conduct policy
  - Ethics agreement
  - Conflict of interest policy
- **Employment termination procedures**   These procedures are followed when an employee/employer relationship is terminated. These include procedures such as
  - Completing an exit interview
  - Reviewing the nondisclosure agreement
  - Revoking ID badges, keys, and company assets
  - Disabling the user's accounts
  - Changing passwords, combinations, or pin numbers that the user had access to
  - Escorting the individual out of the office/facility

Vendor, Consultant, and Contractor Procedures

Physical security must also take into account third-party security for situations in which vendors, consultants, or contractors visit the organization's facilities. Common procedures include the following:

- Escorting third parties while they are on site
- Ensuring proper access control mechanisms are in place to verify identity:
  - Verify license or other form of identification
  - Require completion of sign-in sheet
  - Require name badge

- Ensuring appropriate agreements are in place:
  - NDAs
  - SLAs
- Ensuring appropriate screening for vendors, consultants, and contractors

Software Development Security

Many organizations, especially medium and large ones, build their own software applications to perform business functions. For those organizations that choose to go down the path of software development, addressing information security during development is sometimes taken lightheartedly, which can lead to bad consequences. Organizations that fail to address security early and correctly during the software development process end up introducing vulnerabilities into their enterprise. It's one thing for an attacker to introduce risk into the environment but it's yet another for the organization to introduce risk by its own doing. As the guardian of the organization, it is the CISO's job to make sure this doesn't happen. Building in security is better than adding it later on. Addressing security during the development effort rather than afterward is cheaper, easier, and, in most cases, more secure.

Even in today's environment in which cybercriminals are active and cyberattacks are prevalent and widely reported, some engineering organizations fail to include security requirements in the planning phases of a software development project. Here are a few of the reasons why security is frequently not addressed during the SDLC:

- **Oversight**   In some situations, failure to address security is simply an oversight. Somebody isn't paying attention to something they should be paying attention to. The root cause of oversight is lack of security awareness on the part of the people planning and scoping development efforts.

- **Ignorance**   We have frequently seen leaders dismiss security because they fail to understand its significance due to a lack of knowledge. This lack of understanding can lead to a failure of the organization to address security in many areas of the enterprise, including during development of business applications.

- **Resources**   Does addressing security during development increase the time, effort, and cost? Many people think so. After all, adding even one requirement can impact the effort required to build something. Therefore, adding security requirements certainly causes more effort than would otherwise be spent if the security requirements were ignored. But any such savings in effort or costs are temporary at best. Ignoring security requirements simply delays the inevitable costs of addressing security vulnerabilities and shortcomings down the road. The increased risk will require additional costs and level of effort down the road, either due to actual damage from a security breach or due to the cost of having to add security features or fixes later.

- **Developer knowledge** Many developers do not have foundational knowledge of information security and do not know how to address it during development.

Adding security after the fact usually includes adding *compensating controls* to the software or environment to make up for the fact that security wasn't built in. Compensating controls are correctly used to satisfy security requirements that are deemed to be too difficult or costly to implement. However, compensating controls are also used to add security into an environment to make up for a security shortcoming of a product, system, or software. For instance, if an application intended to be used by the finance staff was not built with effective access control functions, some other means may need to be put in place to accomplish access control. In this case a compensating control might be to deploy the system behind a firewall that limits access to only the computers that belong to the finance staff. Such a control may not be as good as a true identity management/access control solution but, depending on the risk of the system, may be an adequate compensating control.

The remaining parts of this section explore the following topics:

- Integrating security into the SDLC
- Security SDLC roles and responsibilities
- Software vulnerabilities
- Secure coding practices
- Software vulnerability analysis and assessments

Build vs. Buy

Organizations either buy commercial off-the-shelf (COTS) software or develop their own. The build versus buy decision has information security impacts. If an organization is considering buying a COTS product, its security team should evaluate whether the product meets the organization's security requirements. Such requirements should be defined for any product that is a candidate to become part of the enterprise. Requirements for products are defined as part of the project or stream of work process, discussed in Chapter 3, and are part of the system categorization and controls selection process, discussed in Chapter 2. COTS products are evaluated for compliance with security requirements by analysis or testing (or sometimes both). Analysis includes a review of the manufacturer-provided data about its product, which may include the results of third-party testing of the product. It is up to the organization to determine whether, and to what extent, COTS software meets security requirements. Likewise, custom software developed by, or for, the organization must meet security requirements as well. The creation of security requirements should be one of the first steps in the product development planning process.

Integrating Security into the SDLC

Several types of development life cycles are used for software projects (waterfall, incremental, agile, and such) and are discussed in Chapter 3. Regardless of the type of SDLC, security must be built into the process so that it is adequately addressed during each phase. The goals of integrating security into the SDLC are to ensure the following:

- Security requirements for the software are defined
- Security functions are designed, coded, tested, and verified against security requirements
- Secure coding practices are followed and the software contains no security vulnerabilities

Figure 4-18 depicts generic but typical SDLC phases and shows how security can be addressed during each phase. Different organizations may choose different SDLC approaches but the goals for security are ubiquitous: integrate security throughout the SDLC so security is built into the software.

Each phase is discussed here:

- **Plan project**   During the project initiation or planning phase, the initial goals of the project are scoped, taking into account security drivers. Drivers include laws and regulations that pertain to the business; stakeholders such as customers, shareholders, or other parties that have information security or privacy concerns; or factors that stem from the organization's business environment. The project planning phase may also include risk analysis such as that explained in the "Risk Management" section in Chapter 1. Risk analysis provides the initial view of the software product's value to the business, relationship to other components of the enterprise, threats, potential vulnerabilities, and the nature and value of the data that it will process, store, or transmit. All this information is documented and is sometimes captured in a security plan.

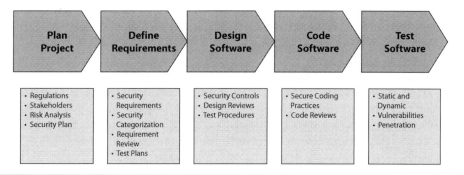

Figure 4-18   Security in the SDLC

- **Define requirements**   During the requirements definition phase, security requirements are defined alongside the functional, operational, interface, or other requirements of the software. This phase may include the security categorization of the system such as that required by the NIST Risk Management Framework (RMF) process. Security requirements are modeled and expressed in a database, requirements list, or software requirements specification and may be reviewed during formal requirements reviews. Test plans that address security requirements may also be developed during this phase.

- **Design software**   During the design phase the implementation of the security controls is reflected in the software design. Security requirements are allocated to applicable portions of the software architecture and the specific components that will be coded in the coding phase. Design solutions may be derived from industry best practices such as those from OWASP.

- **Code software**   The coding phase is when the components of the software are built and tested to implement the security requirements. The developers should follow secure coding practices as defined by internal standards or published by industry entities such as OWASP.

- **Test software**   To be sure the security requirements are met, the software undergoes thorough testing using static and dynamic techniques. Dynamic testing should include thorough vulnerability testing as well as penetration testing to manually probe for potential attack vectors.

Security SDLC Roles and Responsibilities

To develop secure software, the development team should include members that have specific security-related roles. These roles may be filled by team members that have other roles on the project or they may be filled by dedicated security personnel. The assignment of roles is usually driven by the size and complexity of the project. The following are some of the key security roles that may be present on a software development project (the names may differ depending on the organization, but the activities should always be performed):

- **Information security manager or officer**   This role ensures that security is addressed by publishing security doctrine, including policies, standards, and guidelines, and ensuring they are properly applied on a software development project.

- **Information security engineer/subject matter expert**   Security engineers and subject matter experts work with the developers to design and code solutions that meet the security requirements. The security engineers are also involved in evaluating and testing the software to validate it against requirements and to ensure there are no vulnerabilities introduced into the environment.

As stated earlier, the information security roles may be combined with other roles on the project as determined by the management and the needs of the project. The roles may also be combined with each other.

Software Vulnerabilities

The "Malicious Software and Attacks" section at the beginning of this chapter describes scripting and vulnerability-specific attacks that take advantage of vulnerabilities in software. Many of these attacks take advantage of vulnerabilities resulting from system design or coding errors. The following sections provide a brief summary of some of the most common software vulnerabilities from the most recent OWASP Top Ten application vulnerabilities list (https://owasp.org/www-project-top-ten/).

Injection

Injection is a software vulnerability that allows an attacker to send untrusted data to an interpreter. The data can be crafted to cause the interpreter to execute unintended commands without authorization. There are various types of injection flaws depending on the back-end system being exploited, which include SQL, NoSQL, OS commands, LDAP, and others. Developers can prevent injection vulnerabilities by applying the following practices:

- Use a safe API instead of an interpreter
- Filter input fields by only allowing certain strings or characters
- Include controls in the commands to back-end systems to limit available functions to only those that are allowed (such as the SQL LIMIT control)

Broken Authentication

Broken authentication is a family of problems all related to identity management, authentication, and session management being implemented incorrectly. Attackers use these weaknesses to compromise passwords, keys, and tokens and take advantage of other flaws to assume user's identities. Applications are vulnerable if they contain any of the following weaknesses:

- Permit automated authentication attacks that allow an attacker to attempt logins with many usernames and passwords
- Permit the use of simple or easily guessable passwords
- Use weak password recovery features
- Do not store or transmit passwords in a secure manner
- Have poorly implemented authentication, including multifactor
- Expose, do not rotate, or invalidate session IDs

Developers can prevent broken authentication by applying the following practices:

- Implement multifactor authentication whenever possible
- Limit failed login attempts
- Implement weak-password checks

- Use secure session management techniques such as secure random session IDs
- Follow NIST 800-63B guidelines for memorized secrets
- Avoid the use of default credentials that could be obtained by an attacker

Sensitive Data Exposure

Sensitive data exposure is a family of problems all related to the failure to properly protect sensitive data. Even if the application uses encryption, the sensitive data may be susceptible to attacks before it is encrypted or after it is decrypted. Sensitive data can be any data deemed sensitive by the organization but is most commonly personal information such as health care data, credit card data, credentials, and proprietary information. Applications are vulnerable if they contain any of the following weaknesses:

- Sensitive data has not been properly identified and classified to enable the corresponding level of protection to be applied
- Sensitive data transmitted in cleartext
- Use of weak or outdated encryption algorithms or methods
- Use of poor cryptographic key management such as using weak keys, regenerating keys, or not rotating keys
- Not enforcing the use of encryption
- Not validating certificates

Developers can prevent sensitive data exposure by applying the following practices:

- Classify data correctly and apply controls based on classification as defined by the organization's security policies
- Store sensitive data only as needed and only for as long as it is needed; do not retain or cache sensitive data unnecessarily
- Store passwords using strong hashing functions
- Encrypt sensitive data at rest
- Use current and up-to-date cryptographic algorithms and protocols
- Protect sensitive data during transit using up-to-date secure protocols

XML External Entities

XML documents can contain *external entities* (storage units) that access local or remote content. Each entity uses a Universal Resource Identifier (URI) to reference the content source. The XML processor (or parser) reads the URI and replaces the reference with the intended data. However, not all XML processors do this correctly and can be modified or compromised to process external entities to use unintended data as the content. An attacker can exploit this vulnerability by using XML files to retrieve sensitive data. Applications and XML-based services are vulnerable if they contain the following weaknesses:

- Accept XML data from untrusted sources
- Insert untrusted data into XML documents
- Use XML processors that have document type definitions (DTDs) enabled
- Use SAML for identity processing
- Use Simple Object Access Protocol (SOAP) versions prior to version 1.2

Developers can prevent exploitation due to XML external entities by applying the following practices:

- Use SOAP 1.2 or higher
- Disable DTD and XML external entity processing on all XML parsers
- Ensure XML parsers are patched with the latest upgrades
- Use XML validation

Broken Access Control

Applications should enforce what operations authenticated users are permitted to do, but many applications do not. This can lead to attackers being able to access users' accounts, access sensitive data, or perform unauthorized functions. Applications are vulnerable if they contain any of the following weaknesses:

- Bypass the access control checks of other software
- Permit the elevation of privileges
- Permit cross-account access
- Permit manipulation of metadata, such as modifying tokens, cookies, or hidden fields
- Permit cross-origin resource sharing (CORS), which allows restricted web resources to be used from another domain

Developers can avoid broken access controls by applying the following practices:

- Deny by default
- Enforce access controls in accordance with the organization's policies
- Avoid using CORS
- Disable web server directory listing

Security Misconfiguration

Misconfigured software and operating systems are certainly the most commonly encountered vulnerabilities. Operating systems and software are often incorrectly configured due to the use of default settings, incorrect security settings, unneeded features, and even being out of date or unpatched. Applications are vulnerable if they contain any of the following weaknesses:

- Out-of-date or unpatched software
- Default accounts enabled
- Unneeded functions enabled
- Security features not enabled
- Security settings or values incorrectly set
- Overly verbose error messages (reveal more information than necessary)

Developers can prevent vulnerabilities due to misconfiguration by applying the following practices:

- Keep all software up to date with the latest versions and security patches
- Harden all software following configuration guidelines such as US DoD Defense Information Systems Agency (DISA) Security Technical Implementation Guides (STIGs) or Center for Internet Security (CIS) Benchmarks
- Enable only those features and settings that are absolutely necessary
- Review and apply security settings recommended by the product developer

Cross-Site Scripting

Cross-site scripting (XSS) is a flaw that allows attackers to embed untrusted data in a web page. The data contains scripts that are executed by a victim's browser, which can compromise systems and data. Victims are lured or redirected to the infected or malicious web page using social engineering techniques. Applications are vulnerable if they contain any of the following weaknesses:

- Lack of filtering of website input data (for example, allowing any content to be posted on a blog or social media site without checking it for malicious code)
- Applications or APIs that dynamically include attacker-controlled data

Developers can prevent XSS by applying the following practices:

- Use frameworks specifically designed to prevent XSS (such as Ruby on Rails or React JS)
- Educate users to not select links to untrusted web pages
- Disallow untrusted HTTP requests
- Apply content-sensitive filtering to browser APIs

Insecure Deserialization

Serialization is the process of converting an object to bytes of data; deserialization is the reverse. If an attacker enters specially crafted data into a web page field of a vulnerable application, when the object is deserialized it can cause any number of exploits, including remote code execution, SQL injection, or other malicious unauthorized functions. Applications are vulnerable if they accept serialized objects from untrusted sources.

Developers can prevent insecure deserialization vulnerabilities by applying the following practices:

- Do not accept serialized objects from untrusted sources
- Perform integrity checking of serialized objects
- Run deserialization functions on separate isolated systems
- Restrict network traffic from systems that deserialize
- Monitor deserialization operation

Using Components with Known Vulnerabilities

Components libraries used by applications can contain vulnerabilities and should be validated or sanitized before use, just like any software deployed to the environment. Applications are vulnerable if they contain any of the following weaknesses:

- Components of unknown origin
- Unknown versions of components
- Out-of-date or unsupported components
- Untested components

Developers can prevent exposure by applying the following practices:

- Implement an ongoing program to inventory, upgrade, and patch all component libraries
- Use components libraries only from trusted sources
- Obtain components from trusted sites and over secure links

Insufficient Logging and Monitoring

Without sufficient logging, monitoring incidents may go undetected and be difficult to investigate and resolve. This can make a bad situation worse by delaying or complicating response and remediation actions. Applications are vulnerable if they contain any of the following weaknesses:

- No logging of errors and warning messages
- No logging of audit-worthy events such as failed logins
- Data is logged in format unsuitable for supporting investigation and understanding

- Local-only storage of audit logs
- Logging thresholds set too low or too high
- Incident detection thresholds not well-defined or aligned with logging

Developers can prevent logging shortcomings by applying the following practices:

- Tune logging thresholds based on the organization's appetite and goals for risk
- Ensure data is logged in usable formats
- Log high-value transactions
- Implement a well-defined and well-rehearsed incident response capability

Secure Coding Practices

Every organization that develops software should have a program in place to integrate information security into its SDLC. The program, whether formal or informal, should include *secure coding practices*, which are specific methods for developing software that does not contain security vulnerabilities. OWASP publishes guidance for developers, and the authors have found OWASP to be the most widely used industry guidance for this topic. OWASP provides secure coding guidance for developers to follow in the following categories:

- Input validation
- Output encoding
- Authentication and password management
- Session management
- Access control
- Cryptographic practices
- Error handling and logging
- Data protection
- System configuration
- Database security
- File management
- Memory management
- General coding practices

Many organizations follow OWASP guidelines or augment them with their own adaptation or specific implementation of coding practices based on their own environment and experiences. Secure coding practices should be documented so the organization has a consistent approach that can be applied, measured, and improved over time.

Secure coding practices are best implemented as part of an overall program that includes the following:

- Incorporating security coding into SDLC, as discussed previously.
- Incorporating security into the supply chain to ensure software products acquired from COTS vendors or third-party developers do not contain security vulnerabilities.
- Establishing coding and development standards and libraries of reusable code.
- Continuously training developers

Training is probably the most important and overlooked aspect of secure software development. Surprisingly, secure coding is not taught in many computer science programs, although some schools now offer specialty degrees in secure software development. Therefore, it is up to companies and organizations that employ developers to provide the training that is essential to their software development workforce. Organizations typically bring in consultants or use third-party training organizations to fill this need. This approach can be highly effective, depending on the quality of the instructor and curriculum.

Software Vulnerability Analysis and Assessments

All developed software should undergo testing and assessment to ensure that it meets security requirements and is free of vulnerabilities. To accomplish this, organizations use a combination of automated and manual techniques. Automated tools are used to examine source code for programming errors or conduct automatic vulnerability scans of programs deployed in test or production environments. Manual testing includes review of the software architecture, manual inspection of source code, and manual penetration testing of operational systems, as discussed here:

- **Security architecture assessment**   The goal of a security architecture assessment is to determine and evaluate the key security design characteristics of the application. One method to accomplish this is to break down the application into components whereby each component is evaluated as to its confidentiality, integrity, and availability characteristics. Another model is to assess each component with respect to its ability to control access between actors (users or systems) and assets (data). Regardless of the model used, an architecture assessment should include definition of the review criteria, collection of evaluation evidence, evaluation of the evidence against the criteria, and reporting of results.

- **Source code review (static analysis)**   Static analysis of source code identifies flaws and weaknesses that can lead to security vulnerabilities. Tools in this class include source code analyzers that examine uncompiled code, software composition analysis tools that trace the origin of components and libraries, and specialized tools such as mobile application analyzers. (Also see SAST in the "Vulnerability Assessments" section later in this chapter.)

- **Vulnerability testing (dynamic analysis)**   Dynamic analysis is performed by tools against applications that are compiled and deployed, either in test environments or in live production. These tools test interfaces, transactions, session management, access controls, and other functions for security flaws. (Also see DAST in the "Vulnerability Assessments" section later in this chapter.)

- **Penetration testing**   Manual application penetration testing usually starts with the results from source code reviews and vulnerability scans. Utilizing the artifacts and having an understanding of the system, the assessment team performs targeted tests of the implementation to uncover and identify weaknesses and demonstrate how weaknesses can be exploited from the perspective of an attacker.

The philosophy of application security testing is to find functionality that isn't supposed to be there. Testing is used to uncover behavior that may not have been deliberately designed and may be unexpected. Testing is also used to find backdoors or ways of circumventing designed access controls. Testing should be performed both in test environments before live deployment and again after the software is deployed to the production environment. Reporting of security testing results usually uses some kind of ranking systems as a way to understand the relative risk and impact of each *finding*, vulnerability, or shortcoming discovered. For instance, an assessment team may score each finding (high, medium, low) with respect to the *business impact* and *likelihood of occurrence*. That information is then presented in a graph to provide a visual representation of the application's risk profile.

Software security testing can be very comprehensive and expensive, quick and inexpensive, or increments in between. The more extensive the testing, the greater the likelihood of producing meaningful results. This scaling is illustrated in Figure 4-19.

Organizations must choose the right extent of testing an application to meet their needs. Usually, the extent of testing is based on risk. For instance, a military system containing top secret data would justify undergoing extensive testing at a large cost, whereas a system with no sensitive data would undergo a less extensive review at lower cost.

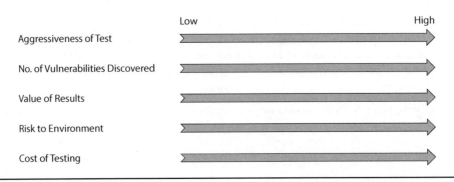

Figure 4-19   Software security testing scaling

Forensics, Incident Handling, and Investigations

Bad things happen and, when they do, the organization must have the processes and technologies in place to understand what happened and respond appropriately. This section discusses how organizations detect security events, conduct investigations, respond, and recover. It also covers laws that pertain to security breaches and forensics concepts that the CISO should understand. This section covers the following topics:

- Relevant law
- Logging and monitoring
- Incident response and investigations
- Forensics and digital evidence

The important concept about detecting and responding to events is *preparation*. The time to decide what to do about an event is not when it occurs. During the heat of the battle there is value in being able to fall back on established processes and procedures that have been carefully developed, practiced, and refined over time. When the CISO and the security team are well prepared to respond to security events, the impact of those events to the business can be minimized.

Relevant Law

Although the CCISO is an international certification, this discussion about relevant security laws has an admittedly US orientation.

EXAM TIP   The CCISO exam may not contain questions about specific laws, but CISOs should be well aware of the laws that apply to their organizations in the jurisdictions in which they operate.

In understanding laws that pertain to computer crime, the following common fallacies should be understood and dispelled:

- *Writing computer viruses is free speech and is protected by law.* Not really: writing a virus is not illegal but in most countries spreading a virus is.
- *Information should be available to all; therefore acquiring it isn't illegal.* Wrong: information belongs to its owner, which is usually the person or entity that created it. Nobody has the right to steal or modify someone else's information.
- *If cybercriminals do not profit from their hacking activity, it isn't illegal.* Wrong: laws such as the US Computer Fraud and Abuse Act do not require the perpetrator to profit from the illegal act.
- *Systems should be protected, and if they aren't locked down, it's the victim's fault, not the hacker's.* Wrong: if you forget to lock your front door it's still illegal for a criminal to walk into your home and steal your TV. The same principle applies to cybercrime.

While the details of computer crime laws vary tremendously, it's safe to say that most computer crime laws contain provisions to protect the public against the following:

- Unauthorized access
- Insertion of malicious code
- Unauthorized modification or destruction of data
- Unauthorized disclosure of information

Computer crime can be difficult to fight, for a few reasons. First and foremost is that determining the identity of the cybercriminal responsible for an attack may be very difficult. Investigative capabilities are getting better all the time, but so are the methods cybercriminals use to avoid detection. Second, cybercrime leaves behind electronic evidence but usually no physical evidence. Electronic evidence can be difficult to find and interpret, which contributes to the obscurity of the crime and the difficulty in finding the culprit.

Laws related to cybercrime can be grouped into the following categories:

- **Integrity laws**   There are laws in place that seek to protect the integrity of information used by the public. For instance, the *US Sarbanes-Oxley Act* (also called the Public Company Accounting Reform and Investor Protection Act of 2002) was created in the aftermath of several corporate scandals involving acts of fraud committed by publicly traded companies. The law contains provisions that help to ensure the accuracy of company financial information and associated security practices.

- **Privacy laws**   Privacy laws seek to protect personal information of individuals from unauthorized disclosure. In the United States these laws include the *Health Insurance Portability and Accountability Act (HIPAA)*, which contains provisions to protect the unauthorized disclosure of individuals' protected health information (PHI), and the *Gramm-Leach-Bliley Act (GLBA)*, which includes the protection of individuals' financial information. Similarly, the European Union's *General Data Protection Regulation (GDPR)* contains provisions to protect individuals' personal information.

- **Fraud and abuse**   In the United States, laws including the *Computer Fraud and Abuse Act (CFAA)*, *Identity Theft Enforcement and Restitution Act*, and state laws define illegals acts and associated punishment for intentional unauthorized access to computers including such acts that cause damage or loss.

Other laws that pertain to computer security and forensics are cyberbullying laws (these laws vary by locale), child pornography and sexting laws (US federal and state laws such as Section 2256 of Title 18 US Code, dealing with the storage or dissemination of prohibited material), and a variety of laws to specifically protect governments against hacking, espionage, cyberterrorism, and cyberwarfare.

Logging and Monitoring

There are two sides to the information security coin: protection against an attack and recovery afterward. Most of this section covers recovery, the first step of which is detection. The most basic tools available to the CISO to detect that a security event has occurred are logging and monitoring, each of which are expanded in the following sections.

Tuning Logging and Monitoring

Both logging (the recording of events) and monitoring (the examination of events) capture and report large amounts of data. One can literally log every event that occurs throughout the enterprise and spend large amounts of resources (automated and manual) monitoring them. But there is a price to pay in storage, processing, and interpretation of all of this data. Every security department has a practical limit of how much information it can reasonably log and monitor. The trick (as discussed in the "IDS/IPS" section earlier in this chapter) is *tuning* to log and monitor the right data. How much is the right amount of data? The answer is to tune the logging and monitoring based on risk and the capacity of the organization. After a comprehensive risk analysis, the CISO will know the most critical systems, threats, and the value of assets to the business, enabling the CISO to determine what information is important to collect and process and how much can sensibly be spent on logging and monitoring the environment.

Logging

Logging is the capturing and storing of activities for later analysis. Logging is used to support auditing, troubleshooting, functional/operational analysis of systems, and of course security. Logs can capture events that occur throughout the enterprise and include the following types:

- **System and event logs** Servers, workstations, databases, and even some network devices have the capability to configure and perform logging to capture events and store them for later retrieval and analysis.

- **OS, application, IDS/IPS, and firewall logs** These logs are useful to identify anomalies or to help reconstruct past security events. Anomalies include changes to configuration settings or important files, which may be indications of malicious activity.

The events typically captured to support security investigations include

- Input/output failures
- Authentication/authorization events
- OS and application errors
- System startup and shutdown events

- Security indicators such as adding/deleting users, changing privileges, and adding/deleting tokens
- Actions performed by administrators or privileges users

The information typically captured about events include

- When the event happened
- Where the event happened (system, application, service, geolocation, component, web page)
- Who performed the action (username, IP address)
- What happened (type, severity, priority, description)

Log management refers to all activities undertaken to maintain logs so that they are useful to the organization. Logs are not only highly valuable to the organization but also highly sensitive and should be protected from modification/deletion and should be accessible only by authorized users. Logs must be considered during storage capacity planning to ensure that logs will not fill up the available storage and run out of room, resulting in the failure to log important data.

Monitoring

Once events are captured as part of the logging process, they can be examined to detect security-related events, such as breaches, and to support investigation of those events. Most organizations employ some kind of security information and event management (SIEM) system that aggregates and correlates event logs from a variety of sources into a central repository. SIEM systems facilitate event analysis and provide a big-picture view of the enterprise. SIEM functions include

- **Log aggregation**   The monitoring solution collects event data from a variety of sources, including systems and servers, network devices, databases, and applications.
- **Secure storage**   The SIEM central repository must be in a secure location, such as a properly secured database, as the logged information is sensitive. In fact, the SIEM database often is more secure than the original source of the logs.
- **Correlation and analysis**   The biggest value and possibility the biggest discriminator when comparing different SIEM solutions is how well it helps the security staff to draw conclusions from the event data. The SIEM software analyzes the data to build trends and establish relationships to be able to detect anomalies activities. The better SIEMs continuously build trend data to provide an evolving capability that improves over time.
- **Alerts**   SIEMs have the capability to sift through the noise and send or display an alert when something happens that requires the operator's attention. Most SIEMs allow the organization to tune the thresholds to provide alerts for the organization's most critical events.

- **Compliance**   One selling point of SIEMs touted by vendors is their ability to help an organization determine and report compliance with regulatory drivers. Usually this feature is enabled with templates or plug-ins to help build reports that are specific to the regulations important to the organization.

 EXAM TIP   CCISO candidates should be familiar with the purpose and functions of SIEM systems as well as IDSs and IPSs.

Incident Response and Investigations

Security incident handling begins with an indicator of a potential security incident and ends with resolution and closing. There are many steps along the way, and each step must be well planned, guided by policies, and performed following well-crafted and rehearsed procedures. As with all aspects of security, the *extent to which* the organization plans, rehearses, and documents incident handling procedures is based on the nature of the business and its tolerance for risk.

Involving Law Enforcement

During the course of an investigation, the organization may identify suspect actors. These actors may be external individuals or internal employees of the organization. In either case, if there is a suspicion that a crime may have been committed, law enforcement should be called in. However, the decision of when and how law enforcement is contacted should not be taken lightly as there may be implications for the organization. There should be procedures in place to provide guidance regarding when law enforcement agencies should be contacted (the reporting threshold), who should be involved in the decision, and how such contact should be carried out and by whom.

The organization should involve legal counsel in the formulation of incident handling procedures, especially those procedures that address suspected criminal activity and interacting with law enforcement.

When law enforcement is contacted, the organization relinquishes control of the investigation to the law enforcement agency. As a consequence, the law enforcement agency may take control of, or possession of, the organization's asset(s) to conduct their investigation. This may cause a disruption of the organization's business operations and is one, sometimes overlooked, reason to have good BCP/DR processes in place so that the organization can restore business operations using backup or alternate systems and data.

Certain information must immediately be reported to law enforcement agencies as required by law, such as if certain kinds of contraband is discovered on a company computer. However, some incidents are reported at the organization's discretion, such as employee violations of access control policies which technically may violate the law but are often unreported if no sensitive data (such as HIPAA PHI) is illegally accessed.

Employee Policy Violations

Security policies are no different than HR policies in that employees must be held accountable for compliance. The obligation of the organization is to ensure policies are enforced consistently. If an organization does not enforce policies consistently, it leaves itself open to employees filing claims against it. Rules for good security policy enforcement include the following:

- Publish policies and ensure all employees are made aware of them.

- Define and document processes for reporting security violations, investigating them, and carrying out enforcement. Enforcement may include disciplinary actions up to and including employee termination.

- Provide training to managers and supervisors not only in the policies themselves but in reporting and enforcement.

- Include security policy coverage in new hire orientations and periodic refresher briefings.

Every organization should have a mechanism in place for employees to report suspected violations of security policies. Employees should be made to feel safe from any repercussions of reporting what they see. Some organizations accomplish this by having an anonymous reporting option, a whistleblower program, or a designated ombudsman that serves as a proxy between the person reporting the violation and the organization.

Incident Handling Process

As introduced in Chapter 1, incident handling is commonly implemented using a process similar to that depicted in Figure 4-20.

The figure shows the current industry practice for handling incidents. Although the exact names and number of steps vary from organization to organization (NIST defines a four-step process), the underlying concepts are universal: prepare for incidents ahead of time, investigate and resolve them, restore the organization to normal operations, and

Figure 4-20
Six steps of
incident handling

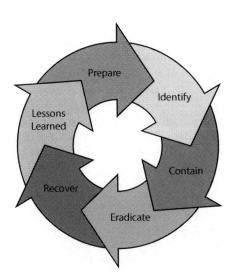

then see what can be learned from what happened so incidents like it can be prevented or handled better in the future. Each step from the diagram is discussed in the following sections.

Prepare   The preparation phase involves addressing the following prerequisites for a good incident handling program:

- Provide oversight of incident handling activities, to ensure that each business unit or group within the organization conducts appropriate incident handling processes.

- Produce, publish, and maintain an incident handling plan, with supporting policies, guidelines, and procedures, that covers the entire organization and enterprise.

- Put a training program in place to ensure that personnel are adequately trained in incident handling methods.

- Define roles and responsibilities for all personnel involved in incident handling and ensure that the roles and responsibilities align with the incident handling plan, policies, and procedures.

- Acquire and deploy adequate tools to support incident handling activities.

- Prepare specific procedures to handle specific types of incidents.

Identify   Once an incident occurs, the security team must identify what is happening. This starts when a team member sees evidence of an incident. They may begin to see alerts from an IDS or SIEM, indications of anomalous activity in log files, unusual network activity, reports from employees, and so on. At some point the evidence (or accumulation of evidence) reveals that a security incident may have occurred (or is in the process of occurring) and it is time to begin containment.

Contain   Once an incident is identified, the team must contain it so that it can be further assessed while preventing it from spreading or causing additional damage. Containment strategies should be defined in advance so (ideally) a specific strategy can be invoked for a given type of incident. Containment strategies may include

- **Perimeter containment**   Actions to prevent the spread beyond the network perimeter, such as inbound/outbound traffic blocking, updating perimeter firewall policies, and switching to alternate communication links

- **Internal containment**   Actions to prevent the spread beyond a portion of the network, such as isolating segments or VLANs and updating router, firewall, and switch settings to block specific IP addresses or ports

- **Endpoint containment**   Actions to prevent the spread beyond a device, server, workstation or laptop, such as disconnecting network access for specific endpoints

Eradicate   This step could also be called "fix it." The security team removes from the affected system(s) the malware, program, settings, or accounts causing the issue. Ideally, the team takes care to minimize the loss of data, but this is not always possible.

Eradication is often combined with the recover phase, such as re-imaging the disk, which wipes out the bad content and replaces it with good content all in one step.

Recover   Recovery involves bringing the system(s) back to an operational state. Recovery may include re-imaging the disk, installing new operating systems and applications, updating the STIGs, or hardening settings and installing patches. Recovery brings the system to a new clean and fully functional operating state.

Lessons Learned   Once everything is back to normal, the security team can review everything that happened. First, they document the incident events, actions, and handling activities to provide a record of what occurred, by whom, and when. The security team captures and stores logs, alerts, e-mail messages, and all relevant data and develops and publishes an incident report for management. Management will review the report and identify lessons that could lead to changes in architectures, policies, systems, and procedures or whatever is required to improve the organization's security posture as a result of the incident.

Incident Response Team

The incident handling process is implemented by a team consisting of managers and analysts that interact and coordinate with stakeholders within or outside of the organization. Depending on the size of the organization, the incident response team may be quite large, with people that specialize in specific aspects of the process or have expertise in unique technologies. At a minimum, most incident response teams consist of at least three roles:

- **Manager or Lead**   Coordinates the activities of the team and manages communication with the rest of the organization.
- **Level I Analyst**   Monitors logs and alerts from monitoring devices, performs triage, and serves as the first level of investigation and response.
- **Level II Analyst**   Serves as the second level of investigation, which may involve forensic activities.

This minimal team may be supported by internal or external specialists in areas including incident investigation, law enforcement, and recovery, or in technical areas such as communications, server technology, or specialized applications.

The incident response team usually has formal interactions with people or groups within the organization to establish monitoring and incident handling policies, processes, and procedures. Such interaction may be part of an integrated incident response committee. Roles with which the team interacts may include the following: the organization's CFO or finance team, general counsel or legal team, upper management and department heads, human resources, and the CIO or information technology group.

For some incidents, additional individuals or their associated departments may be involved in actual incident response activities. For instance, the legal counsel or legal department would certainly be involved in the decision to contact law enforcement agencies. Likewise, the human resources group would be contacted if the incident investigation indicates employee misbehavior or violations of policy.

Forensics and Digital Evidence

During the course of investigating a security incident, it is important to preserve the *admissibility of evidence*. The admissibility of evidence is determined by the judge when it is submitted to the court as part of a criminal or civil trial. To be admissible, evidence must be relevant and reliable, defined as follows:

- **Relevant**   To be relevant, evidence must have a reasonable relationship to what happened. Joe's browsing history may be relevant to the fact that copyrighted material not owned by him was found on his hard drive. A judge makes the determination of relevance, but the incident response or investigation team should assume everything is potentially relevant during an investigation.

- **Reliable**   The evidence must be accurate. It must be established that the evidence was obtained and handled in such a way that it was not, or could not have been, altered so that its reliability can reasonably be assured.

Probably of most interest to the incident response or investigation team is that evidence must be legally permissible, which means it was obtained legally and chain of custody was followed. *Chain of custody* is a paper trail that proves how evidence was obtained, stored, and handled during its entire life cycle. *Proper chain of custody* is a practice that should be followed to ensure that the chain-of-custody record shows the evidence was handled properly such that it is *reliable and admissible*. As an example, if the content of a notebook is deemed relevant to an investigation, there should be a record maintained of how the notebook is stored, transported, and preserved from the moment it is obtained by the investigators right up until it is presented to the court. The intent is to be able to prove the evidence was not altered since it was first obtained.

Handling Digital Evidence

Proper chain of custody requires the incident response or investigation team to follow written procedures for how evidence is handled and stored. This includes procedures for capturing the evidence, tagging it, packaging, storing, and transporting it, and maintaining its integrity while it is being analyzed.

Chain of custody presents several challenges when it comes to digital evidence. Digital evidence must be read by electronic means, and the normal process of booting up systems and reading data may alter the evidence. As a result, digital evidence must first be copied following specific standards to ensure the quality and reliability of the copy while maintaining the integrity of the original. The original should then be packaged, sealed, and labeled with tracking information that is stored in a database. The database is used to record where the evidence is and is updated to reflect each time the evidence is transported throughout its life. The database itself should be properly protected with access controls to ensure only personnel with proper authorization can access it.

Digital Evidence Analysis

Not all organizations have the financial resources to perform their own analysis of digital evidence. Those that do may have a forensics lab in which they can maintain chain of custody, duplicate media from its original source, and perform forensic analysis on duplicate media. Many organizations choose not to perform forensics in-house and instead use outside firms that specialize in digital forensic investigations. Whether in-house or outsourced, a forensics lab should have the following basic capabilities:

- Physical facilities for securely storing, packaging, labeling, and transporting equipment and media that are the subject of an investigation.

- Copying capability to be able to safely and securely make exact digital copies of media. The lab should be capable of examining and accessing digital media from servers, workstations, laptops, cell phones, tablets, printers, and network devices.

- Analysis tools to be able to examine media containing duplicates of the device under investigation. Due to the way data is stored on a disk, data often must be reconstructed from various parts of the disk or media.

 NOTE Digital evidence can be *persistent*, meaning it is stored on media such that it remains available even after a system is restarted or rebooted. Or digital evidence can be *volatile*, meaning the data is only present as long as the system remains running. Persistent data can still be modified or overwritten while on disk, so the forensics team must use great care to ensure the data is preserved. Volatile data must be collected using live forensic methods. Recovery of volatile data starts with the most volatile evidence first (such as CPU, cache, and register content) and progresses following an *order of volatility*.

Digital evidence analysis supporting security investigations seeks to reveal the story behind a security breach. The examination team is provided a list of what type of incident occurred and what kind of information they are looking for during the investigation. The forensic examination team generally follows the following process:

1. Develop a *Search Lead* list, which is a list of items the team is looking for in the data. For instance, if the incident under investigation is that an employee may have downloaded bootleg music or movie files, the team adds such files to the Search Lead list.

2. During the course of the investigation, the team may add new items to the Search Lead list as it learns more about what is on the media.

3. If during the course of the investigation the team finds incriminating data, the team may stop immediately and report the findings to management for reporting to law enforcement.

4. When the team finds what it is looking for from the Search Lead list or makes another significant finding, the team adds that item to another list called the *Relevant Data* list, documents it, and extracts it.

5. The team analyzes relevant data to piece together a story of activity showing, if possible, what happened, who did it, how it occurred, when it took place, and what other data or events are associated with the activity. This is recorded in a *Analysis Results* list.

All of these lists and events are recorded in an *Analysis Results Report*, which describes the results of the investigation and is provided to management.

Anti-Forensic Techniques

Cybercriminals are aware of the forensic methods investigators use to discover digital evidence. In response, cybercriminals use techniques to try to cover their tracks. Here are a few anti-forensic tricks the bad guys use that the CISO should be aware of:

- **Overwriting data**   One way cybercriminals cover their tracks is to overwrite data or metadata with patterns or randomized data. If they do it right, it is hard or impossible for the forensic analysts to know this has been done. However, the challenge for the attackers is to know what data to erase in order to cover their tracks. If they aren't thorough, they may miss something and leave evidence behind.

- **Hiding data**   Data can be hidden inside of file system structures such as in unused portions of file tables, inside of directories, or in slack space of disks. Cybercriminals can also hide data using steganography or encryption. Encrypting data can render it unreadable, but if the associated metadata, such as file headers, is not encrypted, the existence of the encrypted data can be revealed, which may indicate to the investigator that something has happened. Steganography, on the other hand, hides the data inside of a container that is normally used for another purpose, such as an image file. In this case the very existence of the data may be hard to detect.

- **Hiding behaviors**   Operating systems and applications create metadata that indicates when files are created, modified, or accessed. Cybercriminals use a variety of methods to cover up their activities by obfuscating metadata that could normally be used to indicate behaviors.

Security Assessment and Testing

Security programs are ultimately made up of people, processes, and technology. Each of these aspects of the security program must operate effectively to facilitate a wholistic security program. To understand how these components are operating, it is important to test their effectiveness. This is accomplished through security assessments and tests to measure and validate the effectiveness of program components. This section provides an overview of some of the ways to assess and test the security program:

- Vulnerability assessments
- Penetration testing
- Regulatory compliance assessments
- Security program assessments

Each type of assessment provides a distinct way of examining different aspects of the organization's security posture. Each type of security assessment follows a general life cycle that includes

- Identifying requirements and goals of the assessment
- Assessing the current landscape of the environment
- Identifying and reporting on the gaps from the desired state

 EXAM TIP CCISO candidates should be familiar with the different types of security assessments and be able to select which type of security assessment may be appropriate given a scenario.

Cautions and Considerations

Security assessments can provide the organization with valuable insight into weaknesses in its security posture, but before an assessment is undertaken, there are a few important considerations. Two of the main considerations are ensuring that proper authorization for testing has been received and that any potential disruptions to the organization's business operations are understood, communicated, and managed.

- **Authorization** With any of the security assessments mentioned in this section, the assessor must have the organization's permission and sign-off for the engagement, regardless of whether it is an internal assessment or an external assessment. A clear scope that outlines the systems that may be tested and the types of assessments that are approved must be defined and agreed upon. This is particularly important for invasive tests such as penetration tests, since breaking into a system without the proper documented permission in place can violate laws. Such documentation is sometimes referred to as the "get out of jail free card."

- **Managing business disruption** Security assessment and testing can be disruptive or, in the worst case, destructive to the organization. Testing can cause servers or applications to shut down or resources to be overtaxed. Therefore, testing must be coordinated throughout the organization by involving the necessary stakeholders and departments. Consideration should be given as to how the test will be performed without disrupting the organization's business operations. For example, there may be some mission-critical systems that cannot be directly tested as the risk may be deemed too high. In cases like this, some organizations may opt to perform tests in a test environment instead of in live "production" systems. The test environment allows the organization to test and identify vulnerabilities without the risk of directly disrupting production systems.

Vulnerability Assessments

Vulnerability assessments are tests that are focused on finding and identifying vulnerabilities in a defined environment. These assessments vary in scope and technical depth. For example, a physical vulnerability assessment may simply consist of a checklist of physical security controls, whereas a network or system vulnerability assessment may consist of using a vulnerability scanning tool to identify technical vulnerabilities in an environment. Testing may be done from inside the organization (internal testing) or external to the organization (external testing). Vulnerability assessment engagements may include one or all of the vulnerability assessment testing types:

- Network and system vulnerability assessment
- Application vulnerability assessment
- Physical vulnerability assessment
- Human-based vulnerability assessment

During a vulnerability assessment, the assessment team identifies assets (systems, applications, buildings, or people), enumerates them, and identifies vulnerabilities. This section walks through each of the preceding types of vulnerability assessments.

Network and System Vulnerability Assessment

Network and system vulnerability assessments are among the most common types of assessments. They are typically accomplished by utilizing automated scanning tools to identify vulnerabilities such as the following:

- **Vulnerable software**   End of life, unpatched, or deprecated software
- **Open ports**   Ports and services that are available, unintentionally increasing exposure
- **Vulnerable protocols**   Deprecated versions of TLS/SSL, use of cleartext protocols such as FTP or Telnet, and so on
- **Misconfigurations**   Configurations that may allow information to be gleaned by an attacker or may provide a foothold into a system

·A variety of tools can be used for network and system vulnerability scanning, including open source tools, commercially available tools, and proprietary testing tools. Network and system vulnerability scanning is an important part of a healthy vulnerability management program and should be done on a regularly scheduled basis (for example, weekly or monthly) based on the needs and requirements of the organization.

A network and system architecture assessment is a manual examination of the design and implementation of the organization's enterprise architecture. This typically involves examining and evaluating the following:

- Network architecture, including network diagrams and supporting documentation
- Services and protocols that are enabled on ports, to verify that only necessary services are enabled
- Access controls that are implemented on ports and features
- Password strength for any connections and features that require credentials
- Devices providing security controls at the network boundary (firewalls, border routers, and so on)
- Other network devices (telecom, wireless devices, and so on)
- The firewall rule set, border routers, wireless implementation, and intrusion detection system

A network architecture assessment can be complex, time consuming, and costly, so typically it is not performed often. It may be performed when major changes are made to the environment or when dictated by a risk assessment.

Application Vulnerability Assessment

An application vulnerability assessment assesses the security characteristics of applications through the use of manual and automated means. This testing applies not just to custom application software developed in-house, but to COTS applications or systems of integrated applications. These tests are utilized to identify application-level vulnerabilities such as the following:

- Cross-site scripting (XSS)
- SQL injection
- Security misconfigurations
- Directory traversal
- Vulnerable components
- Sensitive data exposure

 NOTE Application vulnerabilities and corresponding protection measures are discussed in greater depth in the "Malicious Software and Attacks" and "Software Development Security" sections earlier in this chapter.

Application vulnerability assessments vary in scope from simply using automated vulnerability scanning tools to performing application architecture and design assessments, code review, manual penetration testing, automated source code analysis, and utilizing runtime scanning technologies. Here are several different types of application security testing methods:

- **Static application security testing (SAST)**   Application source code is scanned and analyzed before it is compiled or executed to detect vulnerabilities at the source code level. SAST is an example of a *white box test* as the assessor is given information about the application such as source code access, architecture diagrams, and so on.

- **Dynamic application security testing (DAST)**   Applications are tested during execution to detect vulnerabilities in the application's running state. This is the type of test typically performed as part of a basic application vulnerability assessment scan. DAST tools perform a variety of tests, including *fuzzing* (or *fuzz testing*), where invalid or unexpected data is sent to the application as input to the application, often in large volume, to see how the application responds.

- **Application Security Testing as a Service (ASTaaS)**   Another "as a service" type model where an organization pays someone else to perform application security testing. The type of testing varies based on the service offering but may include SAST, DAST, application penetration testing, or more.

As part of the engagement, the assessors may assist the organization in adopting and implementing application security best practices to ensure that current and future applications are developed and deployed in a manner that protects data and assets.

Physical Vulnerability Assessment

Physical vulnerability assessments, also known as physical security assessments, are focused on identifying, assessing, and potentially remediating physical security controls in the environment (office, datacenter, and so on). Physical vulnerability assessments typically consist of a review of the following:

- **Facility and perimeter protection**   This may include fences, locked doors, cameras, and so on

- **Interior protection**   Controls for protecting server rooms, wiring closets, and sensitive systems and assets

- **Protection from manmade, natural, or technical threats**   Dumpster diving prevention, fire suppression, and so on

Human-based Vulnerability Assessment

Humans are assets too. Just like hardware and software they should be enumerated and assessed. Human-based vulnerabilities must first be identified before they can be remediated. Human-based vulnerabilities can be uncovered through testing, interviews, observation, and interactive exercises with identified personnel. Some human-based assessment methods include

- **Interactive training**   Security awareness training products often include assessments that test an employee's knowledge of security concepts and measure their skills in putting that knowledge to work to protect and defend the organization's assets.

- **Proficiency questions**   Organizations use proficiency tests to evaluate employees' understanding of organization security policies as well as general security best practices.

- **Social engineering tests**   Organizations test employees' resilience against social engineering attacks. This includes phishing security testing, which consists of sending employees simulated phishing e-mails to test if they click links or attachments. Whereas real phishing e-mails contain harmful links and attachments, simulated phishing e-mails contain safe links and attachments that are used to track if employees click them.

The topic of human-based vulnerability assessments is covered in greater detail in the "Social Engineering" section earlier in this chapter.

Penetration Testing

While vulnerability assessments provide a comprehensive view of an organization's vulnerabilities (identify the vulnerabilities), penetration testing shows how specific vulnerabilities can be exploited to compromise data or otherwise adversely impact the organization (demonstrates impact of compromise). Penetration testing is a targeted test focused on providing real examples of how an attacker can exploit vulnerabilities to gain access, escalate privileges, and ultimately compromise customer or other organization data. Penetration testing personnel take advantage of configuration errors, missing patches, and overly accessible services to try to gain remote access to internal systems. They also evaluate how deep within the internal network they can penetrate by taking advantage of additional discovered vulnerabilities on internal systems, which can allow external attackers to leap-frog their way from system to system to gain access to more sensitive systems or data. Penetration testing methods vary but typically follow the methodology outlined here:

1. **Reconnaissance/discovery**   Assessors attempt to gain information about the organization and its systems. In this step reconnaissance is typically passive. *Passive reconnaissance* focuses on being as covert as possible, collecting information through web searches and other methods so as to not directly alert the organization.

2. **Enumeration**   Assessors attempt to gain more information about systems using active reconnaissance. *Active reconnaissance* involves actively scanning and probing systems to gain information.

3. **Vulnerability analysis**   Vulnerabilities are identified and analyzed.

4. **Execution/exploitation**   Vulnerabilities are exploited to gain a foothold into the system.

5. **Documentation of findings**   Findings are documented and reported to management as part of the final report.

Penetration testing utilizes other vulnerability assessment tools as part of the assessment in order to identify vulnerabilities to exploit. Penetration tests may also include human-based vulnerability assessments through the use of social engineering tactics to gain initial foothold into the network. There are different types of penetration test methodologies, which include

- **Black box testing**   Also known as *zero-knowledge testing* or *blind testing*, the assessors have no prior knowledge about the target of the assessment. *Double blind testing* is when the operational staff, such as the IT or security team, is not aware of the test and it can be used to test their response to a potential intrusion.

- **Gray box testing**   Also known as *partial knowledge testing*, the assessors have some knowledge of the target being evaluated

- **White box testing**   Also known as *full knowledge testing*, the assessors have full knowledge of the target such as a network map, inventory, system names, IP addresses, and so on.

NOTE   These testing methodologies apply to other types of security assessments as well. For example, a vulnerability assessment can be conducted as a black box, gray box, or white box assessment.

Penetration testing provides demonstrable proof of security deficiencies and allows for specifically targeted risk remediation activities.

Regulatory Compliance Assessments

Regulatory compliance assessments focus on assessing the extent to which organizations are compliant with legal and regulatory requirements as well as other compliance requirements related to the organization. These engagements address regulatory requirements such as the following:

- Health Insurance Portability and Accountability Act (HIPAA)
- Payment Card Industry Data Security Standard (PCI DSS)
- Gramm-Leach-Bliley Act (GLBA)
- ISO/IEC 27001
- Service Organization Controls Audits (SOC 1, SOC 2, and/or SOC 3)
- General Data Protection Regulation (GDPR)
- Federal Risk and Authorization Management Program (FedRAMP)

Often these assessments are performed as part of an internal or external audit. The engagement typically begins with an assessment of the organization's compliance requirements (this may already be known for framework-specific audits and assessments such as PCI DSS or ISO/IEC 27001), an evaluation of organizational current practices, and identification and documentation of the gaps. The result is typically a *gap analysis* report that outlines the gaps that have been identified. Depending on the nature and scope of the engagement, it may include remediation assistance, or the report may provide guidance for remediating the gaps identified.

Security Program Assessments

Security program assessments evaluate the organization's information security program or a specific component or *process* of the security program. This may include a review of organizational infrastructure, security policies and procedures, staffing, workforce, and workplace to determine how the security program addresses the risks and threats to the organization and its particular industry and sector. Security program assessments may focus on the governance of specific security streams of work or subprograms. However, a security program review may include technical components if combined with one of the other security assessment types discussed in this section. A security program assessment may include any or all of the following security program components:

- Security organization review
- Risk management review
- Regulatory compliance review
- Security policy, standards, and procedures review
- Security operations review
- Software development security review
- Physical security review
- Incident handling and response review
- Business continuity and disaster recovery review
- Security awareness and training review
- Data security review

Business Continuity and Disaster Recovery

Business continuity management (BCM) is the overarching management process that encompasses both business continuity planning (BCP) and disaster recovery planning (DRP). The goal of business continuity management is to provide answers to the following questions:

- Is the organization able to tolerate the impacts of disasters?
- Have controls been implemented to recover from disasters?

- Are personnel prepared for disasters?

- Are continuity plans documented and approved?

- Is staff properly trained on recovery procedures?

- Are continuity plans current and regularly tested?

- Do the continuity plans ensure timely resumption of critical business functions?

BCM includes disaster recovery planning and business continuity planning. *Business continuity planning* is focused on continuity of critical business functions. The goal is to ensure the business can continue to operate in the event of a disaster. This is long-term planning compared to disaster recovery planning and is documented in the business continuity plan (BCP). *Disaster recover planning* is typically very IT focused and is concentrated on returning resources to an operational state after a disaster occurs. Disaster recovery activities are documented in a disaster recovery plan (DRP), which contains short-term recovery procedures as compared to the BCP.

If a building were destroyed by a hurricane, the DRP would explain how the organization should restore IT functions, such as getting servers up and running again in an alternate location, possibly by firing up a cold site, and restoring data from backups. The DRP focuses on getting the critical systems in a state where they can service requests and organizational processes can resume. The BCP is more focused on business operations, such as explaining the procedures necessary to relocate personnel and get reconstruction underway with the goal of restoring critical business functions. The DRP keeps the business running through and immediately after the disaster. The BCP outlines how the business functions in an injured state and gets back to business as usual in the long term.

Different industry organizations, standards, and guidelines outline different processes for continuity planning; however, they all contain generally the same concepts. The process outlined and discussed in this chapter is illustrated in Figure 4-21. This process is

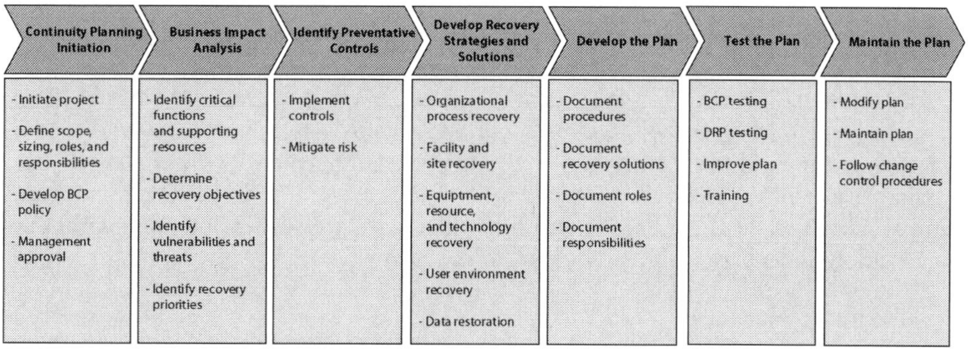

Figure 4-21   Business continuity management process

based on the steps outlined in NIST SP 800-34, *Continuity Planning Guidelines*. This section discusses each of the phases in the business continuity management process:

- Continuity planning initiation
- Business impact analysis
- Identify preventive controls
- Develop recovery strategies and solutions
- Develop the plan
- Test the plan
- Maintain the plan

Continuity Planning Initiation

As with any project, it is helpful for continuity planning to follow a project management methodology (as discussed in Chapter 3). The project is initiated and a project plan is developed that is approved by the organization's leadership. Once this has been completed, a business continuity policy, also known as a business continuity plan statement, should be developed. The initiation process for developing a business continuity plan may include the following steps:

1. Review the current BCP if one exists.
2. Outline the goals of the BCP specific to the organization.
3. Create a BCP policy statement.
4. Develop a preliminary BCP development budget.
5. Develop procedures for plan approval.
6. Appoint a BCP coordinator, project manager, and BCP project team.
7. Develop reporting procedures and frequency for reporting on BCP progress.
8. Identify required documentation and information gathering techniques.

As part of the process, the BCP team must be developed, a critical component of which is the *business continuity planning coordinator*, who oversees the business continuity management process from initiation to testing and maintenance. The BCP coordinator provides leadership to the BCP team and directs work as needed. The BCP development team should be made up of representatives familiar with key areas of operation within the organization, including representatives from the following:

- Senior management
- IT department
- Security department
- Risk management department

- Facilities management
- Organizational leaders and executives
- Public relations and communications department
- Legal department

NOTE It is important that the team be made up of people from all key areas of the organization. In addition, the people responsible for *carrying out* the BCP must be involved in the *development* of the BCP. All these stakeholders should have input and discuss what is needed from their perspectives. Together they can work to come up with a plan that addresses the organization's critical business needs.

BCP Policy Outline

The BCP policy provides the foundation for the BCP effort. It documents the purpose of the BCP, and helps communicate the importance of the initiative, and serves as a formal document signed off by management. The business continuity planning policy should outline the following:

- Scope of the policy
- Roles and responsibilities
- Risk assessment method requirements (qualitative, quantitative, impact analysis, functional analysis, metrics, and so on)
- Requirements for organizing and managing plan development
- Testing and training requirements
- Requirements to ensure plan currency

Business Impact Analysis

An essential component of the continuity planning process is the *business impact analysis (BIA)*, which is a functional risk analysis for continuity planning to determine organizational and system requirements, interdependencies, contingency requirements, and priorities in the event of a significant interruption. The BIA is essentially the risk analysis for business continuity management. The goal is to identify the organization's most critical business functions, assets, resources, and operations. The steps involved in the BIA are outlined here:

1. Identify critical functions and supporting resources.
2. Determine recovery objectives.

3. Identify vulnerabilities and threats.

4. Identify recovery priorities.

This section walks through each step of the BIA process and discusses the activities that take place in each phase.

 EXAM TIP Although CCISO candidates may not be tested on these exact BIA steps, they should be familiar with BIA terminology, the purpose of conducting a BIA, and how the BIA is used for business continuity management.

Identify Critical Functions and Supporting Resources

The first step in the BIA process is to identify the organization's critical functions. This is typically accomplished through the collection and gathering of information from key stakeholders. The team may carry out the following tasks to obtain the best data:

- Select stakeholders to interview
- Determine data gathering techniques (for example, workshops, surveys, interviews, and so on)
- Develop questionnaires to obtain operational and economic data
- Collect data through data gathering and documentary sources
- Document organizational functions, activities, and transactions
- Develop a hierarchy of organizational functions
- Apply a classification scheme to indicate each individual organizational unit function's criticality level

When determining critical functions, the team considers the business impact if a given function is not up and running. The team considers questions such as the following related to the function's unavailability:

- How much will it affect the revenue stream?
- How will it affect the production environment?
- How much will it increase operational expenses?
- How will it affect the company's reputation and public confidence?
- Could the company possibly lose competitive advantages?
- How will it result in violations of contract agreements or regulations?
- What delayed costs could be endured?
- What hidden costs are not accounted for?

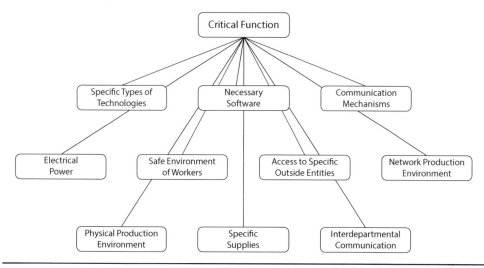

Figure 4-22 Supporting resources for a critical function

In addition to identifying the critical functions, supporting resources must also be identified and documented. These are resources that the organization's critical functions rely on for these processes to take place. Supporting resources may include information systems, personnel, procedures, supplies, tasks, external support from vendors or contractors, or other resources illustrated in Figure 4-22. The result of this step is a well-vetted list of functions categorized utilizing a ranking system such as critical, essential, necessary, and desirable.

Determine Recovery Objectives

The next step in the BIA process is for the team to analyze the functions and resources and determine the recovery objectives for each through discussions with key stakeholders. The focus here is determining the acceptable downtime for the functions and resources. The acceptable level of downtime can be expressed using the following values:

- **Maximum tolerable downtime (MTD)**   The amount of downtime management is willing to accept for a given process, function, or resource due to an outage or disruption. The MTD assists in decision making around restoration prioritization, RTO development, and recovery strategies and solutions.

- **Recovery time objective (RTO)**   The maximum amount of time that a resource can be unavailable before affecting critical functions, processes, or the MTD. The RTO is typically shorter than the MTD to ensure the MTD is met.

- **Recovery point objective (RPO)**   The point in time that data can be recovered to prior to the outage or disruption. This is a determination of how much data loss an organization function or process can tolerate when recovering from an outage.

This information is critical for determining recovery solutions and strategies later on and helps the team decide the order in which systems and resources must be brought back online to recover critical functions. For example, during discussions with stakeholders, it may be learned that if a critical server in the manufacturing facility is down for more than three hours, the entire production line will need to be restarted and that will take an entire day. Based on this information, the organization may decide that the MTD for the server should be no more than three hours.

Identify Vulnerabilities and Threats

The next step in the BIA process is for the team to identify the vulnerabilities and threats that may occur to ensure that the consequences to continuity are understood. There are a range of threats to consider:

- Natural (hurricanes, earthquakes, floods, viruses, and so on)
- Technical (system, network, and communication outages)
- Supply systems (electrical power, HVAC, and so on)
- Human-made (terrorism, disgruntled employees, riots, vandalism, and so on)

The aim is not to think of every type of threat event that could occur, nor is that possible, and those types of brainstorming sessions can run amuck (for example, alien invasion). The goal is to properly prepare for any threat event that may damage or disrupt critical organizational functions or processes and to ensure that the organization has plans to ensure the continuity of the critical functions. Certain threats may have a greater impact on the business than others and may therefore drive decisions about recovery priorities. For instance, if the organization's manufacturing capability is greatly impacted by an event that has a high likelihood of occurrence, such as a storm, the organization may decide to spend accordingly on corresponding recovery resources.

Identify Recovery Priorities

The last step in the BIA process is to examine the various types of harmful events and their corresponding impact to the organization to identify recovery priorities. These may be identified through an informal meeting or discussion or through a more formalized risk assessment (quantitative or qualitative). Recovery priorities can be established by estimating, measuring, and analyzing the following factors:

- Allowable interruption (MTD, RTO, RPO)
- Business process criticality
- Financial, productivity, and operational effect
- Regulatory compliance requirements
- Organizational reputation considerations

The BIA results are documented and presented to management for approval. They will then be used to create recovery and backup solutions for functions and resources based on tolerable outage times. The results from the BIA contain the following:

- Identified critical functions and supporting resources
- MTD, RTO, and RPO for each function and resource
- Identified threats and vulnerabilities
- Impact risk the organization would realize with each threat

Identify Preventive Controls

Once the BIA is completed, the organization has a better understanding of the business impact that would be caused if an asset were not available. The next step is to determine if any preventive controls can be implemented to mitigate these risks. In some cases, the impacts identified in the BIA may be reduced or eliminated. The results of the BIA may indicate the need for preventive controls. Here are some examples to consider:

- Fire detection and suppression systems
- Purchase of uninterruptible power supplies (UPS)
- Purchase of generators
- Offsite backup media storage location (tapes, hard drives, documentation, and so on)
- Communication link redundancy
- Server redundancy
- Purchase of insurance

Preventive controls can, in some cases, be more cost effective and preferable to relying on recovery systems after a disruption. Preventive controls do not negate the need for recovery systems or planning, but they do provide a means to reduce the probability of the outage occurring.

Develop Recovery Strategies and Solutions

The next step in the business continuity management process is to develop recovery strategies and solutions for critical functions, resources, and departments based on tolerable outage times. This section walks through considerations for the following recovery strategy and solution areas:

- Organizational process recovery
- Facility and site recovery
- Equipment, resource, and technology recovery
- User environment recovery
- Data restoration

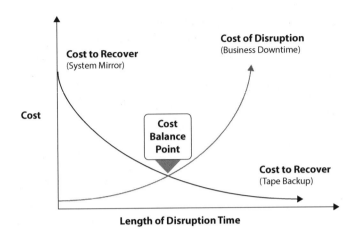

Figure 4-23
Recovery cost
considerations
(Source: NIST)

Cost

Cost to Recover
(System Mirror)

Cost of Disruption
(Business Downtime)

Cost Balance Point

Cost to Recover
(Tape Backup)

Length of Disruption Time

Deciding on recovery strategies and solutions is a balancing act. The organization must balance the cost of recovery against the cost of disruption. If the organization wants a short RTO, the cost of recovery will be very high to implement the required recovery technologies and solutions. However, a longer RTO may result in increased costs to the organization due to the disruption of critical functions and operations. This concept is illustrated in Figure 4-23.

Organizational Process Recovery

The business continuity planning team considers the critical business processes and determines the proper resources and strategies to restore them to normal operations. In this effort, the team must understand the following aspects of critical organizational processes:

- Roles involved in the processes
- Resource requirements
- Process workflow steps
- Interface and interdependencies with other processes

This information is often presented as a workflow documenting the process steps, roles, resources, and interconnections with other processes. This information assists the team in identifying controls and contingency strategies to mitigate process interruption from threats.

Facility and Site Recovery

A key consideration for any organization's disaster recovery planning is how data processing facility disasters will be handled. An organization may choose to purchase a dedicated alternate site, lease a facility, or enter into a reciprocal agreement. A *reciprocal agreement* is an agreement entered into with another organization to share building and/or resources in the event of a disaster. This could be sharing an alternate datacenter, office space, or other resources. Regardless of the type of alternate site arrangement that is selected, there are various facility and site recovery options to choose from:

- **Hot site**   A site that contains all the necessary processing systems, software, and devices that is ready for processing in a few hours or less. All that is needed are people and data backups. This is the *most expensive* option with the *quickest recovery time.*

- **Warm site**   A site that contains basic infrastructure (electrical wiring, air conditioning, plumbing, and so on) and is partially equipped with some system hardware, software, and peripheral devices. The site still requires additional computers, software, devices, people, and data backups and can be ready in a day or more. This is a middle-ground option as a warm site is a *cheaper option than a hot site* and provides *quicker recovery than a cold site.*

- **Cold site**   A site that contains only basic infrastructure (electrical wiring, air conditioning, plumbing, and so on) and no systems. This is the *least expensive* option; however, it has the *slowest recovery time* (approximately two weeks).

NOTE   The backup site location should be far enough away from the primary site that it is not affected by the same disaster, but not too far that moving costs are extreme. Like everything, the proper distance is a balancing act based on organizational objectives and priorities.

The following are a few variations of the facility and site recovery options:

- **Disaster Recovery as a Service (DRaaS)**   A cloud computing service used for recovery in the event of a disaster (also known as *Recovery as a Service*). The service can range from simply backing up data to a cloud environment to backing up all data and applications and serving as alternate processing infrastructure while the primary site is undergoing repair.

- **Redundant site**   A datacenter equipped and configured exactly like the primary datacenter (also known as a *mirrored site*). This is the most expensive option and is used when high availability is a requirement.

- **Rolling hot site**   A mobile site that is equipped with data processing equipment; essentially a mobile datacenter. Also referred to as a *mobile site.*

- **Tertiary site**   An alternate backup facility for use if the primary backup site is unavailable.

EXAM TIP   CCISO candidates should be familiar with the various facility and site recovery options and be able to select options based on recovery objectives or cost considerations.

Equipment, Resource, and Technology Recovery

There are other aspects of organization recovery that must also be considered, including, but not limited to, the following:

- **People**   Ensuring safety of human life, adequate staffing during a disaster, and proper succession plans are in place
- **Documentation**   Ensuring that critical documentation (policies, procedures, plans, and so on) is available
- **Hardware**   Consideration of network and computer equipment, replacement time requirements, SLAs from suppliers, as well as dangers of legacy and/or proprietary devices
- **Software**   Necessary applications, utilities, and operating systems for production
- **Communication**   Plans for communication to various stakeholders (customers, suppliers, media, and shareholders)
- **Infrastructure**   Requirements for voice and data communication, electric, and HVAC
- **Supplies**   Requirements for paper, cabling, physical storage, and so on
- **Other risks**   Potential for looting, vandalism, or other fraudulent activity after a disaster

Executive Succession Planning

The temporary or permanent loss of an organization's senior leadership can cause significant harm to the organization's operations. It is critical that organizations have an executive succession plan in place to protect the continuity of operations and leadership when a loss of executive staff is experienced. For example, the succession plan for the CISO may specify that the deputy CISO, information security officer (ISO), or information security manager (ISM) takes the helm. Succession planning is all about being ready to deal with these circumstances, so that a company can be skillfully guided through this critical period following extreme circumstances.

User Environment Recovery

Recovery of the end-user environment is critical to resuming organizational operations. This includes decisions around notification to employees, ensuring critical employee resources are available, and ensuring safe working conditions for employees. To facilitate the recovery of the employee environment, the BCP team must do at least the following:

- Develop a calling tree to inform employees of the disaster and to keep people updated
- Identify the critical users required to keep critical functions running
- Identify how current automated tasks can be carried out manually

- Identify user resource and supply requirements
- Develop transportation procedures for users to the new facility if required

Data Restoration

The traditional approach to restoration of data lost due to a disaster is to use a data backup solution. With this approach, data is backed up to centralized storage such as cloud storage, network attached storage (NAS), or storage area networks (SANs). Backup procedures should be documented, with regular backups taking place on a daily, weekly, and/or monthly basis. The three main types of data backups are as follows:

- **Full**   Backs up *all* files on the system. Provides the fastest restoration but takes the longest to perform the backup.

- **Incremental**   Backs up all files that have *changed since the last backup of any type*. Backups can be performed more quickly but restoration takes longer because the full backup must be restored as well as each incremental backup performed thereafter.

- **Differential**   Backs up all files that have changed since the last *full backup*. For restoration, the full backup is restored and then the most recent differential is restored.

 EXAM TIP   CCISO candidates should be familiar with the different types of backups.

In a perfect world, backed-up data is restored to the exact state it was in just prior to the disaster; in practice, the backup/restore process may result in a loss of some data due to the time between the last backup and the disaster event. To eliminate the potential for the loss of data using backups, organizations can use other methods to ensure *data resiliency*. One such solution is *disk mirroring*, which provides redundancy by writing the same data to more than one disk. If either storage medium is lost, the other is available for operations. Modern mirroring solutions can provide fast and seamless recovery from disasters, although there are implementation factors to consider. If the redundant disks are in the same location, they may be subject to the same disaster, such as a flood or fire, which makes such an implementation unsuitable for recovery from such an event. Also, the same event that caused data to be lost, such as a server going down and causing write errors, may produce the same errors on both disks, rendering the data unrecoverable. Therefore, many organizations mirror a partial solution for data recovery but still rely on backups.

Data can be stored on a variety of mediums, including tape and disks. Redundancy can be implemented at the tape or disk level using RAID (for disks) or RAIT (for tapes). *Redundant array of independent disks (RAID)* is a technology used for redundancy across disks. RAID essentially allows data to be written across multiple disks to allow for faster read/write operations as well as redundancy. The level of redundancy is dependent on the level of RAID that is used. *Redundant array of independent tapes (RAIT)* is similar to RAID but uses tapes instead of disks.

NOTE For some organizations utilizing cloud services, the cloud service provider may provide automated backup and recovery functionality as part of the subscription. This may be included in the offering or available as an add-on. In either case, it is important to ensure that data in the cloud is backed up and can be restored just as reliably as data stored locally.

Singe Point of Failure

Any system or network that uses only one component to do a job creates a *single point of failure*. If that single component fails, there is no alternate one to take its place. Examples of controls to mitigate the risk of single points of failure include

- Redundant LAN routes
- On-demand backup WAN connections
- Redundant and fault-tolerant technologies
- Documented procedures on how to deal with failures
- Properly trained personnel

Develop the Plan

After the BCP team has developed the BCP policy, performed the BIA, implemented preventive controls, and developed recovery strategies and solutions, the next step is to develop the plan. The general structure of a business continuity plan is illustrated in Figure 4-24.

Figure 4-24
BCP structure
(Source: NIST)

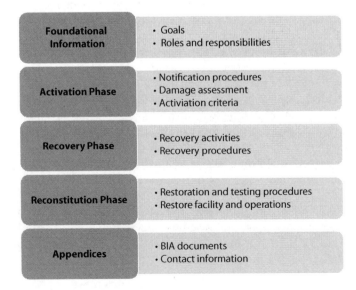

Foundational Information	• Goals • Roles and responsibilities
Activation Phase	• Notification procedures • Damage assessment • Activiation criteria
Recovery Phase	• Recovery activities • Recovery procedures
Reconstitution Phase	• Restoration and testing procedures • Restore facility and operations
Appendices	• BIA documents • Contact information

BCP Confidentiality

Most organizations have two versions of their business continuity plan, an internal version and a sanitized version to share with customers and other critical partners. Customers in particular may be interested to know that the organization has a BCP, and some may require receiving a version of it to satisfy their own compliance requirements. However, the BCP by its very nature is a sensitive document that could cause harm to the organization if released. It details the recovery technologies, solutions, and strategies utilized by the organization in the event of a disaster. This information could be very valuable to an attacker. This is why a sanitized "public" version is developed. The sanitized BCP should not contain

- Contact lists
- Business recovery procedures
- Process flows
- Risk mitigation methods
- BIA results

The sanitized version should be specific enough for customers to satisfy their security and compliance requirements but general enough as to not reveal sensitive information.

Test the Plan

A critical method of ensuring the effectiveness of the plan is testing to verify that the activities in the plan can be carried out effectively. An organization should not wait until a disaster occurs to test its business continuity and disaster recovery plans. Organizations should perform tests at least once a year and develop specific test objectives, scenarios, and criteria for success. These may include ensuring

- Response is within an acceptable timeframe
- Operations at alternate locations are adequate
- Backups can be successfully restored
- Key personnel can be reached within an acceptable timeframe
- Team members are aware of the specifics of the current plan
- Team members are able to perform their specific duties
- The plan is current and relevant

The following are some of the many different types of tests to choose from:

- **Checklist test**   Copies of the *BCP* are distributed to functional managers who review the parts of the plan that address their department or business area.

- **Structured walk-through test**   A meeting is held where functional managers come together to "walk-through" the *BCP*. This is also known as a *tabletop walkthrough* or *tabletop exercise*.

- **Simulation test**   A disaster scenario is carried out exercising the *BCP* up until the actual relocation to an offsite facility. The scope of the test can vary from a specific department or the entire organization.

- **Parallel test**   The *DRP* is tested using systems transported to the offsite facility for parallel processing to ensure specific systems can perform sufficiently at the alternate facility. This test helps ensure alternate systems are performing the same as systems at the primary site.

- **Full interruption test**   This is the most intrusive but most comprehensive type of *DRP* test. The original processing site is shut down and all processing is moved to the offsite alternate facility.

 EXAM TIP   CCISO candidates should be familiar with the different types of business continuity and disaster recovery plan tests.

After a test is completed, the team should conduct and document a lessons learned session. The lessons learned should indicate any deficiencies identified or other significant findings that need to be remediated. This information should be reviewed, reported to management, and added to the plan to improve its effectiveness where applicable. As part of plan testing, it is crucial to ensure that recovery personnel are trained on their roles and responsibilities regarding plan execution. Training frequency will vary from organization to organization based on the needs of the organization and risks identified. However, training should occur upon hire and typically annually, at a minimum. Recovery personnel should be trained on the following plan elements, at a minimum:

- Purpose of the plan
- Communication and coordination process
- Reporting process
- Security requirements
- Individual responsibilities as well as team-specific responsibilities and processes
- Responsibilities in each phase of the plan (initiation, activation, recovery, reconstitution)

Preparation and Testing Is Key

During the outbreak of the coronavirus disease (COVID-19), many organizations came to the realization that they had not sufficiently prepared for this type of disaster. In terms of business continuity, the conversation often focuses on disruption of IT services. In the wake of the coronavirus outbreak, one of the most prevalent issues was the lack of ability of some organizations to operate with a remote "work from home" workforce. Some organizations were technically limited due to insufficient technological and infrastructure capabilities to scale to allow remote work, while others were culturally limited due to a narrow mindset of how business operations could be conducted and managed remotely. Prior to the outbreak, organizations should have considered the following as part of business continuity and disaster recovery preparedness:

- Plan for continuity of service delivery with limited staff
- Ensure critical partners and suppliers have a continuity plan
- Ensure organizational technical ability to allow work from home (VPN licenses, network bandwidth, capability to scale, and so on)
- Ensure organizational cultural ability to work from home (change in management style, use of video conferencing, modified work schedules, and so on)

This is why it is crucial, when thinking about continuity of operations scenarios, to consider the range of events that could lead to a disruption of operations.

Maintain the Plan

The various continuity and contingency plans and components covered in this section must be kept up to date and represent how continuity situations should be handled. Business continuity plans can quickly become outdated due to personnel turnover or changes to organizational structure, processes, technology, or software that are not accurately reflected in the plan. Here are some strategies to consider to help ensure that plans are kept up to date:

- Assign an individual or team as responsible for updating the plans
- Include plan maintenance responsibilities as part of job descriptions and evaluations
- Integrate business continuity and disaster recovery reviews into organizational audits
- Implement a change control process that takes the BCP into consideration

- Regularly test the plan
- Ensure appropriate staff are trained on the process
- Incorporate lessons learned from tests as well as actual incidents

As part of maintenance of the plan, best practices around change control should be followed. Changes to the plan should be approved, tested, and documented. Strict version control should be implemented and enforced to monitor and control changes. With any new change, consideration should be given as to whether new training is required to ensure appropriate staff are knowledgeable and prepared to execute on the plan.

Chapter Review

The CISO should have a solid understanding of the core competencies of information security. The core competencies can be considered in three groups:

- Threats from cyberattacks
- Technical security domains
- Management and procedural security domains

Threats from Cyberattacks

Malware, scripting, and social engineering are the primary methods cybercriminals use to carry out cyberattacks. *Weaponization* is the deployment of malware, scripts, or other means to exploit a systems or systems. Malware includes Trojans, viruses, worms, and botnets. Scripting attacks are carried out by cybercriminals who use scripts to take advantage of vulnerabilities in operating systems and applications. The term *social engineering* refers to the use of deception to trick someone into doing something that may not be in their best interest. Social engineering has been used by scam artists for years and now is an integral part of cyberattacks.

Technical Security Domains

All organizations should have a good understanding of what assets they have and what controls need to be in place for each asset based on risk and classification. *Data security controls* vary based on the state of the data, whether the data is at rest, in transit, or in use. Data security controls are often applied as part of the data life cycle. Controls are implemented by properly configuring and hardening assets that store and process the information, such as servers, network equipment, applications, and so on. *Identity and access management* refers to systems and processes put into place to manage and control the access to enterprise resources and involves the management and implementation of *who* is accessing *what* and what they can *do* with it. This is enabled through identification, authentication, authorization, and accountability/auditing.

LANs and *WANs* provide the communication infrastructure for the enterprise. Modern networks are built following the OSI model, which defines layers for understanding and designing effective protocols, devices, and security. Firewalls, network segmentation, and encryption are some of the principle tools used in network security. *Cryptography* is the practice of using mathematics to secure information by rendering it unintelligible to unauthorized parties. Cryptography is used to support confidentiality, integrity, authentication, and nonrepudiation.

Cloud computing gives the organization access to a shared pool of configurable computing resources that can be provisioned and released with minimal effort. The three primary cloud service models include IaaS, PaaS, and SaaS. One of the risks associated with using a cloud service provider is the loss of control the organization has over certain functions while still being accountable for security. The organization must perform due diligence to ensure that the CSP is implementing appropriate controls and countermeasures.

Physical security is often the first line of defense for an organization's personnel and assets. Responsibility for physical security varies from organization to organization and may not fall under the purview of the CISO. However, the CISO should be aware of physical security and its relationship with the information security program.

Management and Procedural Security Domains

All software developed in-house or by third-party developers should be developed using an SDLC process in which security is integrated into the product at the earliest stages and addressed throughout the project life cycle. Integrating security into the development process minimizes vulnerabilities and reduces security incidents.

In responding to security incidents, preparation is the key. The time to decide what to do about a security incident is not when it occurs. The CISO and the security team should be well prepared to respond to security events with defined policies and procedures that have been practiced and refined.

Security programs are ultimately made up of people, processes, and technology. Each of these aspects of the security program must operate effectively in order to facilitate a wholistic security program. To understand how these components are operating, it is important to test their effectiveness. This is accomplished through security assessments and penetration tests to measure and validate the effectiveness of program components.

Business continuity planning is long-term planning focused on continuity of critical business functions. The goal is to ensure the business can continue to operate in the event of a disaster. *Disaster recover planning* is typically very IT focused, concentrated on returning resources to an operational state after a disaster occurs to ensure the continuity of an organizational process.

Quick Review

- Ransomware is a type of malware that forces its victim to choose between paying a ransom or losing valuable assets.

- Social engineering is more effective and used more successfully by cybercriminals than purely technical attacks.

- Organizations can best defend against social engineering attacks with a comprehensive program consisting of employee training, testing, practicing, and monitoring.

- Asset security controls are often implemented as part of an information security control life cycle framework, as described in Chapter 2.
- The term data at rest refers to data residing on persistent storage devices such as hard drives, flash drives, optical disks, magnetic tape, or other storage devices.
- The term data in transit (also known as data in motion) refers to data that is moving between computing nodes on a network.
- The term data in use refers to data currently being processed or used by the system or applications.
- The three main types of authentication include something you know (such as a password, passphrase, or PIN), something you have (such as a token device, smart card, or USB drive), and something you are (biometrics such as voice, fingerprint, or palm scan).
- The use of only one of these factors is known as single-factor authentication. The use of two authentication factors is known as dual-factor authentication (such as a smart card and PIN, password and biometric, or password and physical token). Multifactor authentication is the use of two or more factors.
- The primary access control models include mandatory, discretionary, attribute-based, and role-based access control.
- Identity and access management follows a general life cycle that includes provisioning the identity and accounts, reviewing the identity and accounts, and revoking the accounts.
- Key security features of networks include network segmentation, firewalls, DMZs, VPNs, and IDS/IPS.
- Symmetric encryption, also known as symmetric key cryptography, is characterized by the use of a single key for encryption and decryption.
- Asymmetric encryption, also known as public key cryptography, is characterized by the use of two keys, a public key and a private key that are mathematically related.
- The three primary cloud service models include Infrastructure as a Service (IaaS), Platform as a Service (PaaS), and Software as a Service (SaaS).
- There are four types of cloud deployment models: public, private, hybrid, and community.
- When it comes to physical security, the most important thing is protecting the safety of employees and other people within the work environment.
- Software developers should receive specialized training in how to create applications that do not contain security vulnerabilities.
- Most computer crime laws contain provisions to protect the public against the following:
  - Unauthorized access
  - Insertion of malicious code

- Unauthorized modification or destruction of data
- Unauthorized disclosure of information
- Security assessments include vulnerability assessments, penetration testing, regulatory compliance assessments, and security program assessments.
- Business continuity planning is long-term planning focused on continuity of critical business functions. The goal is to ensure the business can continue to operate in the event of a disaster.
- Disaster recover planning is typically very IT focused and concentrated on returning resources to an operational state after a disaster occurs to ensure the continuity of an organizational process.
- The business impact analysis (BIA) is a functional risk analysis for continuity planning to determine organizational and system requirements, interdependencies, contingency requirements, and priorities in the event of a significant interruption. It is essentially the risk analysis for business continuity management.

Questions

1. An organization's security team discovers a computer virus that is replicating itself and spreading from one computer to the next on the network. This is an example of what type of malware?

   A. Worm

   B. Trojan

   C. Botnet

   D. Ransomware

2. Of the methods listed, what is the best countermeasure against social engineering attacks?

   A. Training

   B. Practice and drills

   C. Observation

   D. Reading

3. Which of the following is an integrated approach to endpoint management that allows for specific policies to govern the security requirements for assets connecting to the organization's network?

   A. Antivirus

   B. Mobile device management

   C. Network access control

   D. Configuration baselining

4. The CISO of an organization wants to ensure that sensitive data is not recoverable from media before a system is disposed of. Which of the following is not an appropriate data sanitization technique to accomplish this goal?

   A. Physical destruction

   B. Zeroization

   C. Purging

   D. Erasure

5. A CISO is reviewing the organization's access control policies and procedures. The organization implements access control based on who the requestor is, what resource is being requested, and the time of access. What type of access control model is this?

   A. Centralized

   B. Mandatory

   C. Attribute-based

   D. Role-based

6. The security operations staff has adjusted the thresholds of the IDS because staff members were unable to keep up with all the nonintrusive activities being reported. This is an example of what practice?

   A. Packet filtering

   B. IDS scaling

   C. IDS tuning

   D. IDS resource adjustment

7. Which of the following is a disadvantage of symmetric cryptography compared to asymmetric cryptography?

   A. It encrypts data quickly.

   B. It can encrypt only small amounts of data.

   C. It uses weak encryption.

   D. It does not scale well with large numbers of users.

8. The CISO is working with the CIO to evaluate a new cloud-based hosted e-mail service provider. Which of the following cloud service models best represents this offering?

   A. IDaaS

   B. PaaS

   C. SaaS

   D. IaaS

9. What is the best way to determine whether a web application developed in-house is vulnerable to scripting attacks?

   A. Conduct static testing of the deployed software

   B. Conduct dynamic testing of the deployed software

   C. Both A and B

   D. Neither A nor B

10. A disgruntled employee breaks into the organization and steals critical data after finding out he will be laid off due to downsizing. This is an example of what type of physical security threat?

    A. Manmade threat

    B. Natural threat

    C. Environmental threat

    D. Supply system threat

11. The CISO decides a laptop should be forensically investigated to see if plaintext customer data is stored on it. Which of the following best describes how to analyze the data?

    A. To preserve the evidence on the laptop's hard drive, make a digital copy of it and analyze the copied data

    B. Reboot the system to clear out any scripts or malware

    C. Analyze the data directly on the laptop's hard drive, as copying the data may alter it

    D. Follow chain of custody by labeling the laptop and hard drive

12. A CISO of a health care organization is reviewing the organization's policies and procedures to ensure they comply with HIPAA. What type of security assessment is this an example of?

    A. Regulatory compliance assessment

    B. Application security assessment

    C. Vulnerability assessment

    D. Penetration testing

13. The CISO is working with the BCP coordinator to perform a business impact analysis for the organization. They must determine the maximum amount of time that a resource can be unavailable before affecting critical functions or processes. Which of the following terms best represents this?

    A. Maximum tolerable downtime (MTD)

    B. Recovery point objective (RPO)

    C. Recovery delimiter objective (RDO)

    D. Business impact analysis (BIA)

Answers

1. **A.** A computer virus that makes copies of itself and sends them to other computers is called a worm. The other types of malware listed in the question have other characteristics: a Trojan disguises itself as another program, a botnet is a network of infected systems under the control of cybercriminals, and ransomware is a type of attack in which cybercriminals attempt to collect a ransom from the victim.

2. **B.** Training, observation, and reading can all be helpful, but practice and drills provide reinforcing knowledge that helps people prepare for how to act in a particular situation.

3. **C.** Network access control (NAC) is an integrated approach that allows for specific policies to be defined that govern the requirements for network access. For example, a NAC policy may disallow devices on the network that do not meet specific security requirements such as having antivirus installed.

4. **D.** Erasure is not a secure method of data disposal. When an erasure command is issued, the data storage location on the drive is marked as free for use but the data is still on the media until it is overwritten by a subsequent operation.

5. **C.** Attribute-based access control (ABAC) is based on defined policies specifying which subjects can access certain objects and how they can access them, based on the specific objects being accessed and other environmental conditions, like time and location. Centralized access control is a type of access control administration, not an access control model. Mandatory access control (MAC) decisions are based on the clearance of the subject and the classification of the object. In role-based access control (RBAC), the user's access is based on their role in the organization.

6. **C.** Intrusion detection system (IDS) tuning is performed to achieve the optimum level of detection and reporting.

7. **D.** One disadvantage of symmetric cryptography is that it does not scale well with large numbers of users. This is one of the main reasons that hybrid cryptosystems are utilized, which use symmetric keys for encryption and are shared using asymmetric cryptography.

8. **C.** Software as a Service (SaaS) offerings provide the customer the finished product as a service, such as a cloud-based e-mail service. All the maintenance of the infrastructure, OS, databases, storage, and such is handled by the SaaS provider. Identity as a Service (IDaaS) is a cloud-based service that provides a set of identity and access management functions and is not one of the primary service models. Platform as a Service (PaaS) is a form of cloud computing that allows customers to manage applications without managing the infrastructure in-house. Infrastructure as a Service (IaaS) is a form of cloud-based computing that provides virtualized computing resources.

9. **C.** All developed applications should undergo both static and dynamic testing prior to deployment in the enterprise.

10. A. A disgruntled employee breaking into an organization to steal critical data is an example of a manmade threat.

11. A. Make a digital copy of the data and analyze it. Do not reboot suspected equipment, as rebooting will alter data on the storage media in some fashion. Never perform analysis directly on the suspect media. While labeling the laptop and hard drive is a good idea, it is not the best answer to the question of how to analyze the data.

12. A. Reviewing an organization's policies and procedures to ensure compliance against a regulatory driver such as the Health Insurance Portability and Accountability Act (HIPAA) is an example of a regulatory compliance assessment.

13. A. The maximum tolerable downtime (MTD) is the maximum amount of time that a resource can be unavailable before affecting critical functions or processes.

Strategic Planning, Finance, Procurement, and Vendor Management

This chapter discusses the following topics:

- Strategic planning
- Making security decisions
- Financial management
- Procurement and vendor management

This chapter discusses important aspects of managing the information security program. The first two sections, "Strategic Planning" and "Making Security Decisions," explore how the CISO goes about planning and prioritizing security activities based on business drivers. The third section, "Financial Management," provides essential information about accounting and financial management that every CISO should know. The final section, "Procurement and Vendor Management," describes fundamental concepts about procurement and presents a model for how the CISO can address the risks to the organization posed by third-party vendors that provide products or services.

Strategic Planning

The previous chapters discussed the myriad of activities that can be conducted as part of an organization's information security program. These activities include streams of work (or subprograms), security projects, and core competencies addressing threats, external and internal drivers, and compliance requirements. But how does an organization know what to do, when to do it, the amount of resources to apply, and what takes priority? Some of these decisions can be aided by the risk analysis portion of the risk management activities discussed in Chapter 1. But risk analysis is only part of the solution because it only addresses specific assets and does not address the organization's business strategy. To determine how to execute the security program, prioritize security activities, and establish a roadmap for accomplishing security goals, *strategic planning* is a useful tool.

Strategic planning helps an organization understand what is most important and therefore determine what to do when and what resources to apply. You can't *boil the ocean*, so you have to prioritize. The organization's culture and workplace climate should be shaped into what leadership wants them to be; they can't be left up to chance. These things are addressed through a well-conceived and well-implemented strategic plan.

Strategic planning for the entire organization is performed by the organization's leadership. The CISO may very well be part of the team that creates the organization's strategic plan. *Security strategic planning* is a subset of the organization's strategic planning.

This section discusses the following topics:

- Organizational strategic planning
- Organizational strategic planning teams
- Strategic planning process
- Security strategic plan example

Organizational Strategic Planning

An organizational strategic plan is a plan that describes *what the strategy is* and lays out a plan for *how it will be implemented*. The strategy is usually expressed by defining goals to be achieved during a specific timeframe. The implementation is usually expressed by listing the actions the organization will undertake to achieve each of them. Of course, this is only one type of strategic plan, but it is the most common and is the approach we discuss in this book.

Strategic planning first involves defining the organization's strategy. Frequently, organizations define the strategy at a very high level using vision and/or mission statements that describe what the organization hopes to be, along with strategic goals and sometimes an identification of the core values the organization wishes to convey. Then, for each goal, the organization lays out a plan for how the goal will be met, sometimes defining how it will be funded, when the work will be done, and how success is measured and determined. Figure 5-1 illustrates a strategic planning template showing the various elements that go into the plan.

For an organization following the method shown in Figure 5-1, strategic planning is conducted in the following manner:

1. Create a vision statement.

2. Create a mission statement.

3. Define core values.

4. Create measurable goals and objectives.

5. Create actions to achieve each goal.

6. Implement the actions and measure progress.

7. Maintain and update the plan.

Vision:	A visionary statement that communicates the aspirations of the organization.				S T R A T E G Y
Mission:	A statement that communicates what the organization does, for who, and how they do it.				
Values:	A list of the core values of the organization, their people, and the culture.				
Goals:	Goal #1	Goal #2	Goal #3	Goal #4	
Objectives:	List of objectives to achieve Goal #1	List of objectives to achieve Goal #2	List of objectives to achieve Goal #3	List of objectives to achieve Goal #4	I M P L E M E N T A T I O N
Actions:	List of Actions to achieve each Objective	List of Actions to achieve each Objective	List of Actions to achieve each Objective	List of Actions to achieve each Objective	
Measures:	Lists of measurable outcomes for each Objective or Action	Lists of measurable outcomes for each Objective or Action	Lists of measurable outcomes for each Objective or Action	Lists of measurable outcomes for each Objective or Action	
Resources:	Resources or funding required to achieve each Objective or Action	Resources or funding required to achieve each Objective or Action	Resources or funding required to achieve each Objective or Action	Resources or funding required to achieve each Objective or Action	
Timeframe:	Planned timeframe to complete each Objective or Action	Planned timeframe to complete each Objective or Action	Planned timeframe to complete each Objective or Action	Planned timeframe to complete each Objective or Action	

Figure 5-1   Typical strategic plan template

Create a Vision Statement

An organization creates a vision statement to convey to others how the organization views itself and how it wants the world to perceive it. Vision statements can be visionary, aspirational, sometimes utopian, and even romantic. Here are a few example vision statements:

- Telecom company: "A phone on every desk and in every pocket."
- Art supply company: "To inspire and enable artists everywhere."
- Online retailer: "To be the most visited and most profitable online shopping site."
- Cooking school: "Our vision is to provide the best culinary education experience in the Americas."

Some people use vision statements to describe the future state of an organization, whereas they use mission statements to describe the current state. Both statements describe the purpose of the organization, which is an important first step in communicating the strategy of the organization to employees, customers, and other stakeholders (such as shareholders or investors).

Create a Mission Statement

Whereas the vision statement is an inspirational message, a mission statement defines what the organization is, why the organization is important, and what problem it solves and for whom. The mission statement lays the groundwork for specific goals the organization wishes to accomplish. The imaginary companies listed in the previous section may have the following mission statements:

- Telecom company: "To connect people and businesses by providing innovative communication products and services."

- Art supply company: "We supply artists and craftspeople with the tools they need to create works that endure."

- Online retailer: "Promote, support, and innovate online retailing using electronic currency."

- Cooking school: "Provide collaborative learning products that allow restaurant personnel to experience culinary success by working with others."

An examination of these mission statements and corresponding vision statements shows how the mission statements begin to reveal each organization's strategy. The telecom company sees itself as product and service innovators. The art supply company makes tools not just for artists but also for craftspeople, and the tools specifically support creating works of art that last a long time. The online retailer is focused on using cryptocurrency and related technologies. The cooking school offers learning products that allow students to work collaboratively with other students.

As illustrated, the vision and mission statements convey what the organization will do and how the organization will do it from a high-level or strategic perspective. Many organizations combine the vision and mission statements, but just as many define and express them separately.

Define Core Values

Core values are the characteristics of the employees that the organization wishes to foster and promote. What kind of people does the organization want to have? Leaders or followers? Innovators or imitators? Extroverts or introverts? Is personal integrity important? An organization can create and shape its culture and workplace by defining the core values it wants and then implementing plans to recruit, hire, and foster those kinds of people and behaviors. Conversely, if an organization does not specifically define and communicate its core values, then the kinds of people the organization has, and the resultant workplace culture, is left to chance.

Here is a list of the core values one might find for a software engineering company:

- Drive
- Creativity
- Curiosity
- Integrity
- Adaptability
- Humility
- Accountability

In some strategic plans the core values are further defined with detailed descriptions of each. The core values are then used throughout the organization to drive things like HR policies, hiring decisions, career ladders, job descriptions, performance appraisals, workplace culture, employee reward programs, and even the nature of employee get-togethers and social events.

Create Measurable Goals and Objectives

Strategic plans are usually created to cover a specific period of time. Most strategic plans cover a three- to five-year period. Time periods shorter than three years tend to be not forward-thinking enough, whereas time periods of more than five years may be unrealistic, as things (political environment, technologies, laws, and so on) change. For the period in question, the strategic plan specifies goals. It is these goals that define the direction of the organization by expressing what is most important. Usually the organization defines a handful of goals. Too few goals may lack enough clarity to define the direction; too many goals may dilute what is most important.

For example, the hypothetical telecom products company introduced in the previous sections might define its three-year goals as follows:

- Goal #1: Develop product line of smartphones
- Goal #2: Create ability to manufacture 1M phones per year
- Goal #3: Become the recognized world leader in smartphone biometrics
- Goal #4: Implement 100 percent user self-service

It's fairly clear what this company wants to do and what it feels is important. It has defined goals for what it wants to design (#1), its manufacturing capability (#2), innovation and market exploitation (#3), and how it will deliver support to its customers (#4). Sometimes what is not listed as a goal is just as important as what is. Note there are no goals for efficiency or cost savings. Apparently, the leadership has decided that efficiency and saving costs aren't that important during this time period in the company's life cycle.

It is important for each goal to be necessary, attainable, and verifiable:

- **Necessary**   If a goal is not necessary for the organization, it shouldn't be defined as a goal. Goals should be the things that are important for the organization to be successful.
- **Attainable**   The organization should have a reasonable expectation that the goal can be achieved, although many times goals are aspirational in that there is a belief the organization has the capability to achieve the goal even though the exact means to do so have not yet been established. Goals can be highly ambitious and still can be considered attainable.
- **Verifiable**   The goals should be defined so that there is a way to measure whether or not each goal has been achieved and what progress is being made.

Create Actions to Achieve Each Goal

Usually goals are further defined by subgoals or objectives. For example, to achieve the telecom company's *Goal #1, Develop product line of smartphones*, the team would define the objectives that need to be met, such as the following:

- Conduct market analysis
- Develop requirements
- Create minimum viable products
- Create and release commercial products

Each objective can then be planned, defining

- What needs to be done
- What resources are required
- How much money is to be spent
- What the expected outcomes are
- How progress can be monitored
- How success of the objective can be measured

After completing this step for each goal, the organization has defined its vision, mission, and values, defined goals to achieve them, and created a plan to accomplish each activity needed to meet each goal. The next step is to put the plan into action.

Implement the Actions and Measure Progress

The objectives are essentially marching orders for the various groups and departments to do their part. Ideally, the strategic plan was developed by a team consisting of the leaders of all the major parts of the organization. For instance, if there are manufacturing objectives defined in the strategic plan, they should have been defined with participation by the head of manufacturing. Participation by the key leaders helps to ensure the attainability and viability of the various parts of the plan and of the plan as a whole.

The implementation of the strategic plan is managed by the organization's leadership, usually by the CEO, COO, general manager, or president. The plan is implemented following the general principles for program and project management that were discussed in Chapter 3.

Maintain and Update the Plan

After an organization creates its strategic plan, it should update the plan on a periodic schedule, but the plan may also need to be updated or changed due to external or internal events.

Most commonly the strategic plan is created when the organization is formed and then periodically updated. If the strategic plan covers a five-year period, the organization should have another plan ready to implement at the end of the five years. However, most organizations do not wait until the end of the five-year period to update the plan. More often, organizations revisit the plan each year and make modifications to it based on actual events and changes the business is experiencing. Agile organizations are able to stick to the themes of their plans but adapt to real-world factors as they go.

Occasionally, or even often for some organizations, the strategic plan needs to be updated due to external or internal events. External factors that may drive a major rewrite of the strategic plan include new laws or regulations that impact the business, emergence of competitor innovations or products, new developments in technology or manufacturing, and even social, economic, or political changes (such as a pandemic). Internal factors that may prompt an organization to alter its plan include such things as cost or schedule overruns of key projects, acquisitions and mergers, internal reorganizations, and internal development of new technologies and methods.

And of course, the emergence of new threats may also cause organizations to change their strategic plans, either to protect the business against the threats or to offer services or products to mitigate them.

Organizational Strategic Planning Teams

The development of the organizational strategic plan is most often performed by a team led by the CEO. Work is performed over the course of weeks or months during a series of collaborative brainstorming sessions involving the entire team or groups that break off to work on portions of the plan. The makeup of the team is of considerable importance. Having the right people on the team is critical to creating a plan that is a true reflection of the collective strategy and contains goals that are necessary, attainable, and verifiable. The best teams are composed of representatives across the entire organization and include the following members:

- **CEO** The best strategic plans are created when the CEO is the leader of the planning team because, by definition, the CEO is ultimately responsible for the organization's success. However, many times the effort is led by, or delegated to, a *strategic planning manager* that assists the CEO with coordination and tactical activities that help move the process along and ensure its successful completion.

- **Other C-level leaders**   All C-level officers of the organization should be involved because each has areas of responsibility reflected in the plan and each contributes to the execution of actions against the objectives. For instance, because all activities have a financial component, the CFO should be involved in the creation of the plan.

- **Key managers, supervisors, and employees**   Every organization has go-to employees that are not C-level executives but should be included in the strategic planning initiative because of their experience, insight, and talents.

- **Experts and stakeholders**   Outside consultants, subject matter experts, advisors, or board members often are involved in strategic planning because they have special insights, experience, or expertise to offer.

- **External facilitators**   Quite often organizations bring in consultants or firms that specialize in strategic planning to guide them through the process. These firms can provide value, but like any consultant, they should be chosen based on strong references and recommendations. As security consultants, we have seen organizations waste time and effort and end up with a disappointing strategic plan due to poor external facilitators.

As a C-level executive, the CISO may play a role in the organization's strategic planning alongside the other leaders. The CISO should approach this role from several perspectives:

- **Vision and mission statements**   The vision and mission statements are not just for the CEO, CMO, and CTO to define. Is there a security perspective that should be part of the top-level view of the organization? For the telecom company example discussed previously, isn't it important for customers to know their communications are private and secure? The CISO should bring security, privacy, and assurance into the discussion of what is the right vision and mission for the organization.

- **Core values**   Since the core values shape the workplace culture and the character of the employees, the CISO should certainly have a say in their definition. What are the core values the CISO wants to see in the security team? And maybe even more importantly, what are the core values that may make the entire workforce more security-aware, better able to defend against social engineering, and better able to collaborate with the rest of the organization on security initiatives?

- **Goals, objectives, and action plans**   There may be specific organizational goals that directly impact security. For instance, many organizations define compliance with regulations such as HIPAA, SOX, or PCI DSS as one of their major organizational goals if compliance is essential to the success of the business. The CISO helps to shape this definition. But even if security is not one of the major goals, it may be connected to some of the objectives and action plans. Just as security should be built into the system/software engineering process, as described in Chapter 4, security must also be built into all operations of the organization. Therefore, establishing the goals, objectives, and action plans are the first steps in defining the security strategic plan, which is described later in this section.

Strategic Planning Process

The process of creating the strategic plan is very much a brainstorming exercise. Most organization have their own way of conducting brainstorming activities. The methods introduced in Chapter 1 for brainstorming around risk analysis (SWIFT, Delphi, bowtie, decision tree) can be applied to strategic planning. In addition, we have seen organizations use the IDEO (www.ideo.com) Design Thinking method for strategic planning with great success. We do not prescribe or endorse any particular process, but we suggest the process should include the following essential items:

- **Get the right people in the room**   Does the organization have someone who is the company complainer? It might be a good idea to include them as a participant so they can be part of the solution instead of just complaining. The reality is that the quality of the strategic plan is totally dependent on the people that create it. Get all of the right people in the room. There should not only be key managers but key employees that provide real insight into the business.

- **Select an established model and facilitator**   The strategic planning team should not have to waste time figuring out the planning process while they are working on the plan. This is why it can be beneficial to use a facilitator that has a tried and true process to follow. Facilitators often have supporting templates that have been proven to work. Outside facilitators can be great—just check their references.

- **Set a schedule and stick to it**   The strategic planning process is very time consuming and can be a bit of a chore. We have seen teams lose their momentum and focus due to the amount of time required, which can interfere with team members' regular job duties. The planning process must be managed with discipline. Define a schedule and stick with it. Teams that have a sloppy schedule will usually produce a sloppy plan.

Security Strategic Plan Example

Strategic planning is a great way to define the direction of a complex organization. Individual groups within the larger organization can also benefit from such a plan. The CISO not only may be a participant in the organization's strategic plan, but may also create a strategic plan for information security. Many security organizations or departments have their own information security strategic plan. All of the features and activities discussed previously for organizational strategic planning apply to information security strategic planning:

1. Create a vision statement.
2. Create a mission statement.
3. Define core values.
4. Create measurable goals and objectives.
5. Create actions to achieve each goal.

6. Implement the actions and measure progress.

7. Maintain and update the plan.

To illustrate, suppose the hypothetical telecom company defines an information security strategic plan for a three-year period. The following is an example set of goals, objectives, and plans of action for the three-year period:

1. Identity: Incorporate biometrics into smartphone products
   - Choose core technology
     - Conduct research
     - Build evaluation lab
     - Conduct tradeoffs
   - Develop capability
     - Build and evaluate minimum viable product
     - Transition to product
     - Ongoing support
   - Conduct usability testing
     - Choose usability partner/vendor
     - Perform testing and incorporate results into product
2. Staffing: Ensure security team has adequate knowledge, skills, and abilities
   - Develop and implement staffing approach
     - Hire security staffing manager
     - Develop staffing process and procedures
   - Develop and implement career ladder
     - Hire career ladder consulting firm
     - Form career ladder team
   - Provide security training for staff
     - Develop in-house security basics and security operations courses
     - Deploy learning management system
     - Ongoing staff training, testing, and improvement
3. Influence leadership: Strengthen ability of leadership to make security decisions
   - Share threat information with corporate leaders
     - Select threat sources
     - Build and deploy threat feeds for leadership

- Collaborate with corporate leaders
  - Establish in-house Center for Security Leadership
  - Provide ongoing mentoring
  - Support programs to promote security awareness

For each action, the CISO and the security team can define measurable goals to be used to monitor and track performance and success. In addition, each action can be scoped to determine the resources required. Resource estimates include staffing, hardware, software, and outside services to be procured. Then, cost estimates can be prepared to establish the budgets to support these activities. In practice, one of the key uses for a strategic plan is to establish budgets for the security organization. By linking the security budget to the strategic plan, spending can be allocated to activities the organization feels are the most important and spending priorities can be established.

Making Security Decisions

Strategic planning enables the CISO to make security decisions based on business goals. However, other features of the security program may not be driven by the organization's strategic goals (for instance, aspects of the organization's manufacturing process may be important to security but not reflected in the strategic plan). To make informed decisions, the CISO must follow a process to make the connection between the organization's business goals and security decisions. The connection is often accomplished by interpreting *security business drivers*.

Understanding, interpreting, and translating *security business drivers* allows the CISO to make important decisions regarding aspects of the security program, including

- Security goals, objectives, and plans
- Security policies, standards, procedures, and guidelines
- Security architecture (including people, processes, and technology)
- Security controls

Security business drivers are features of the business that have an impact on security. The process the CISO uses to translate security business drivers to security program implementation depends on the organization. The wide array of methods range from informal approaches that are more conversational or instinct-based to formal approaches utilizing a framework or process.

Some organizations use an *informal approach* based on informal assessments or their "gut feel." These exercises may only be casual conversations or informational meetings and may not produce specific artifacts that show how decisions came to be. Decisions could also manifest as mandates or directives from senior management on what to prioritize or focus on. The CISO may also perform informal assessment of the organization, considering different organizational viewpoints such as compliance or financial.

Other organizations follow a *structured approach* using formal processes, industry frameworks or models, risk management exercises, or enterprise architecture models. These rigorous processes often produce artifacts that are used to justify key decisions, such as risk assessment documentation, spreadsheets, architectural diagrams, and other documents. These artifacts can be used to demonstrate due diligence on the part of the CISO.

Enterprise Architecture

One method used to translate security business drivers to security decisions is to follow a framework to produce an enterprise information security architecture (EISA). *Enterprise architecture (EA)* is the practice of diagramming and documenting the architecture of the enterprise to assist decision makers with aligning the organization's strategy around the business's people, processes, and technologies. EISA is simply applying an EA approach to the security program. The CISO can use an EA model to break down and document the information security program architecture and how it relates to the enterprise from a high-level *business architecture* perspective (such as an organizational chart) all the way down to low-level *technical architecture* processes (such as data flow diagrams or network architecture diagrams). The goal is to ensure that these components (such as security software, hardware, solutions, technologies, projects, processes, and operations) align and integrate with the organization's enterprise architecture, strategy, and business drivers. This allows for proactive decision making around solutions and technologies to enable efficiency and alignment.

An organization's enterprise architecture can generally be split into sub-architectures, such as business, information, application, and technical architecture, with information security components and implications throughout these layers, as illustrated in Figure 5-2. EA is essentially a conceptual framework for architecture analysis that includes a documenting and diagramming exercise that occurs at different layers of the enterprise.

- **Business architecture** Business strategy, goals, governance, and objectives for the organization that drives the information architecture.

- **Information architecture** Also known as data architecture, describes the structure, processes, and storage architecture of the organization's information assets. The requirements at this layer prescribe the application architecture.

- **Application architecture** Also known as the information systems architecture, provides the design of the business applications and services. These are supported by the technical architecture.

- **Technical architecture** IT infrastructure such as hardware, software, and network that supports the business applications and services.

There are many approaches to EA, and organizations may make use of standard frameworks such as the Zachman Framework, Federal Enterprise Architecture Framework (FEAF), Sherwood Applied Business Security Architecture (SABSA), and The Open Group Architecture Framework (TOGAF).

Figure 5-2
General
enterprise
architecture
layers

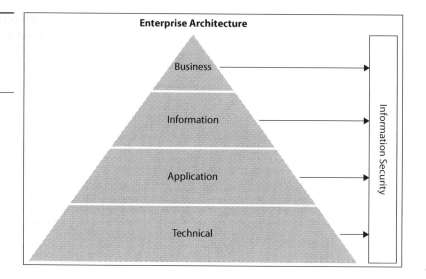

Zachman

The Zachman Framework is a model for the development of enterprise architectures that was developed by John Zachman. It is not a methodology as it does not prescribe a specific process to be used. Rather, it provides a schema that can be used to define and document the enterprise architecture of the organization around specific functions, elements, and processes by creating specific artifacts (such as inventory lists, design documents, process lists, data flow diagrams, and other documentation).

The model consists of a matrix of classification names (What, How, Where, Who, When, and Why) intersected with audience perspectives (Executive, Business Management, Architect, Engineer, Technician, and Enterprise). This allows for the documentation and integration of differing enterprise viewpoints and perspectives of the organization by answering the questions outlined in the classification names. For example, the executive team (business context) will have a different view of the enterprise from that of the technicians (business component implementers). Documenting these perspectives helps to achieve an integrated and holistic approach to enterprise architecture. A simplified instance of the framework is illustrated in Table 5-1. Remember that an EA is essentially an exercise in documenting and diagramming the architecture of the enterprise. The Zachman schema in Table 5-1 is essentially a list of all the artifacts that should be documented or diagramed and how they relate to the various perspectives of the enterprise architecture.

While the Zachman Framework was not built specifically for information security, most of these questions have an underlying security implication. In addition, it is a generic model that can be applied and customized to many types of enterprise architectures, including EISA.

	What	How	Where	Who	When	Why
Executive Perspective (Business Context Planners)	Critical asset and data inventory	Business process list	Business locations list	Organization stakeholders list (employees, clients, partners, and so on)	Event list	Business strategy
Business Management Perspective (Business Concept Owners)	Conceptual data/object model	Business process model	Business logistics system	Workflow model	Master schedule	Business plan
Architect Perspective (Business Logic Designers)	Logical data model	System architecture model	Distributed systems architecture	Human interface architecture	Processing structure	Business rule model
Engineer Perspective (Business Physics Builders)	Physical data/class model	Technology design model	Technology architecture	Presentation architecture	Control structure	Rule design
Technician Perspective (Business Component Implementers)	Data definition	Program	Network architecture	Security architecture	Time definition	Rule specification
Enterprise Perspective	Usable data	Working function	Usable network	Functioning organization	Implementation schedule	Working strategy

Table 5-1 Zachman Framework Example

FEAF

The *Federal Enterprise Architecture Framework (FEAF)* is an enterprise architecture framework developed by the Federal CIO Council in response to requirements outlined in the Clinger-Cohen act of 1996 requiring branches of the US government to develop and maintain an enterprise architecture framework. The goal was to help federal agencies utilize a common language to analyze their enterprise architecture investments and identify what "good" looks like. The framework consists of six reference models, illustrated in the FEAF Version 2 Consolidated Reference Model (CRM) in Figure 5-3, describing these architecture domains:

- Performance
- Business
- Data
- Application

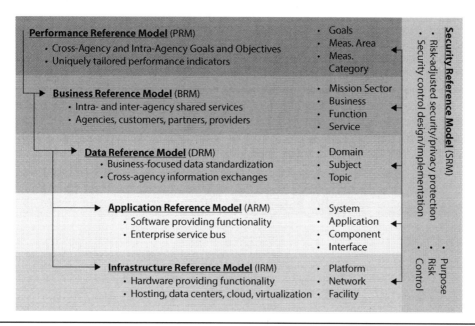

Figure 5-3 Federal Enterprise Architecture Framework Version 2 Consolidated Reference Model (Source: https://obamawhitehouse.archives.gov/sites/default/files/omb/assets/egov_docs/fea_v2.pdf)

- Infrastructure
- Security

Similar to the architecture layers discussed earlier in this section (business, information, application, and technical), each layer in FEAF drives and prescribes requirements to the next layer with security implications throughout (indicated with the security reference model).

SABSA

The *Sherwood Applied Business Security Architecture (SABSA)* framework is a model and methodology for developing an enterprise information security architecture. It is similar to the Zachman Framework in terms of the structure of the framework model (as shown in Table 5-1), but SABSA is also a methodology, meaning it includes process and life cycle guidance for building and maintaining the EISA. The SABSA framework breaks down concepts and requirements from the high-level perspective (Contextual) down to the low-level technologies and applications (Component) with an overlay of the Management architecture. The goal is to remove abstraction, increase granular definition, and build upon the concepts of other architecture levels.

TOGAF

The Open Group Architecture Framework (TOGAF) is an enterprise architecture framework based on the US DoD Technical Architecture Framework for Information Management (TAFIM). TOGAF provides a process life cycle methodology for designing, implementing, and governing an enterprise architecture using the TOGAF Architecture Development Method (ADM). Figure 5-4 provides an illustration of an architecture development cycle based on TOGAF ADM. The process is an iterative one with a focus on requirements and objectives. This is evident in the fact that each phase of the life cycle includes requirements and objectives checks.

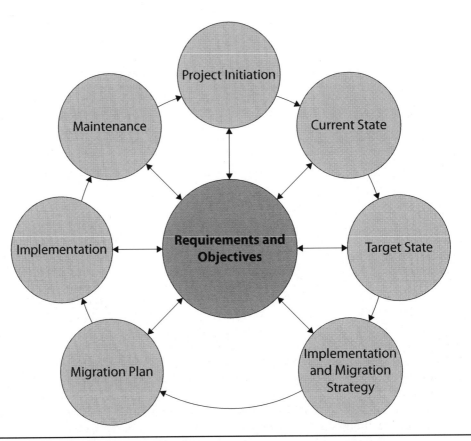

Figure 5-4   Example architecture development cycle

Architecture Maturity Models: Capability Maturity Model Integration

Capability Maturity Model Integration (CMMI) is a process improvement concept from the engineering world that consists of a collection of techniques used as a framework to allow for controlled, incremental improvement to organizational processes and practices. CMMI was developed by the Carnegie Mellon Software Engineering Institute (SEI) and is an upgraded version of Capability Maturity Model (CMM). CMMI was originally intended for maturing software development processes but has been leveraged for many different purposes including measuring and maturing enterprise architecture, systems engineering, security programs, controls, risk management (as discussed in Chapter 1), and other organizational process development practices.

CMMI lays out five maturity levels (Initial, Managed/Repeatable, Defined, Quantitatively Managed, and Optimizing), which represent the different evolutionary stages of process performance. The categorization of these levels depends upon the maturity of the organization's processes and its quality assurance practices. An organization can use CMCMI to develop structured steps on how to evolve from one maturity level to the next by continually improving its processes. This is illustrated in Figure 5-5.

The processes in the *Initial* level (CMM Level 1) are reactive, unorganized, and chaotic. At this level, processes are expected to thrive only through the extraordinary performance of individuals. This makes the environment of the processes more unstable. Success is not likely to be repeated at this level.

At the *Managed* level (CMMI Level 2), also known as *Repeatable*, the processes are executed according to a plan so that the success is repeatable. However, formal process models are not defined.

The basis of the *Defined* level (CMMI Level 3) is that the organizations are capable of producing or adopting standards and processes. This standardization is possible only after focusing on the definition of the process.

At the *Quantitatively Managed* level (CMMI Level 4), organizations are able to monitor and control their own processes. This level allows management to point out ways to adjust the processes in such a way that there is no considerable quality loss or diversion from specifications. This is accomplished through data-driven process management and improvement.

At the *Optimizing* level (CMMI Level 5), organizations focus on continually improving process performance through optimization. Process improvements are measured and evaluated. Continuous process improvement is the key objective of this level, allowing for agility and innovation.

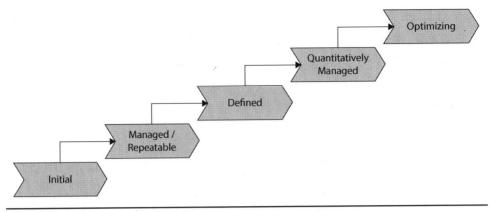

Figure 5-5 CMMI

Financial Management

CISOs are business leaders and the scorecard for the success of any business is money. This is why the CISO not only should possess good leadership and technical skills but should also have a strong grasp of business accounting and finance fundamentals. The CISO needs to be able to speak the language of finance with all of the other leaders of the organization. Every CISO should know how to read a balance sheet and income statement and grasp key concepts such as capital expenses and operating expenses. In addition, the CISO must be able to manage the finances of the security department, which may have an annual budget of tens of millions of dollars or more. This section presents an overview of financial management concepts and terminology that are relevant to the CISO:

- Accounting and finance basics:
  - The accounting system
  - Key concepts and terms
  - Income statement
  - Balance sheet
  - Capital expenses and operating expenses
  - The accounting cycle
- Information security annual budget

Accounting and Finance Basics

The security function of an organization is a financial investment. Every dollar spent on security should be justifiable by the CISO to the rest of the organization. The CISO must be able to contribute to the financial success of the organization along with the other C-level leaders. Just as the CIO must be able to show that IT expenses bring value to the organization, so must the CISO be able to show the value of security investments. This section explores the concepts of accounting systems, transactions, and financial reporting, all of which lay the foundation for the financial understanding of the CISO.

The Accounting System

An accounting system is a set of resources and business processes used by an organization to collect, store, and process financial information. Organization accounting systems usually include a data processing system used in conjunction with accounting policies and procedures following Generally Accepted Accounting Principles (GAAP). GAAP was developed by the Financial Accounting Standards Board (FASB) and establishes standards for accounting practices. Internationally, the International Financial Reporting Standards (IFRS) has been in place since 2001. IFRS is in wide use in over 110 countries throughout the world. However, the focus of this discussion is GAAP as it is applied in the United States.

US GAAP contains ten core principles:

1. **Principle of Regularity** This is the concept that the accountant should regularly adhere to GAAP and treat it as a standard.

2. **Principle of Consistency** This principle is that the same standards are applied consistently throughout the report process. This ensures reporting is consistent from one period to the next.

3. **Principle of Sincerity** This principle requires the accountant to aim for accuracy and impartiality.

4. **Principle of Permanence of Methods** Similar to the principle of consistency, this principle is intended to ensure procedures are used consistently throughout the process.

5. **Principle of Non-Compensation** Finances should be reported accurately without regard to compensation. In other words, the accountant should not expect to be paid more to provide more accurate reporting. Apparently in the accounting business, the concept of "you get what you pay for" isn't supposed to come into play.

6. **Principle of Prudence** This is the concept that reporting should be conservative. For instance, revenues should be based on facts, not speculation. Income should not be overstated and expenses should not be understated.

7. **Principle of Continuity** This is the concept that the business will continue to operate. This is important when considering the value of assets. If the business won't continue, that may imply certain assets will have no value, and if they have no value in the future, they should not have a value now. Therefore, there should be an assumption of continuity of the business in all reporting.

8. **Principle of Periodicity** This is the concept that entries should be allocated or distributed to the appropriate period of time. For instance, if a sale occurred in June, the revenue should be recorded as occurring in June, not July.

9. **Principle of Materiality**   Accountants should strive for accuracy and presentation of *relevant* financial information.

10. **Principle of Utmost Good Faith**   Derived from the Latin phrase "Uberrimae Fidei," this means the business should be honest in all transactions.

Key Concepts and Terms

There are a few key accounting terms and concepts every CISO should know. The first is the concept of *accounts*. An account is a record used to sort and store transaction data. Every business has a *chart of accounts*, which is a list of the accounts used to store assets, liabilities, income, expenses, and equity. Money is debited and credited to accounts using *transactions*, which are recorded in the accounting system's *general ledger*.

Another key concept is *reporting*. Reporting is the communication aspect of accounting. It involves conveying information about the business to interested parties. The following are the two primary forms of reporting found in an organization's financial statements:

- **Income statement**   An income statement (also called a profit and loss, or P&L, statement) is a summary of the organization's *financial activity* during a period of time. It lists all transactions, including revenue and expenses and any profit or loss during the reporting period.

- **Balance sheet**   A balance sheet is a snapshot of the organization's *financial position* at a specific point in time. It lists the value of the organization's assets (what it has), the value of its liabilities (what it owes), and what it is worth (the difference between the assets and liabilities).

Income Statement

The income statement generally has two sections:

- **Income**   Revenues and amounts billed to customers for sales in return for goods or services

- **Expenses**   The cost incurred by the organization for an asset or service

Figure 5-6 shows an example of a simple income statement.

In the example in Figure 5-6, the organization had revenues of $43M during Month #1 consisting primarily of product sales, services, and royalties. The organization also had uncategorized income, which is income that does not fall into the other categories (or the category has not yet been determined) but can still be recognized.

Cost of goods (or *cost of goods sold*) refers to the costs of labor, materials, or other items that are directly associated with the sale of goods (or the production of revenue). For instance, if the company makes and sells widgets, the income from the sale of the widgets is classified as income and the costs of making the widget are classified under cost of goods. Subtracting the cost of goods from the income shows the *gross margin* (or *gross profit*) from the sales of the organization. This is how much money the company made from the sale of the widgets, before accounting for the costs of operating the company.

Company X

Profit and Loss

Month #1

Accrual basis

All amounts in thousands

	Total
Income	
Product Sales	12,928
Royalties	3,156
Professional Services Income	27,228
Uncategorized Income	236
Total Income	43,547
Cost of Goods Sold	
Direct Labor Products	8,022
Direct Materials Products	8,978
Direct Labor Services	11,345
Total Cost of Goods Sold	28,345
Gross Margin	15,202
Expenses	
Manufacturing	5,233
Facilities	4,122
General & Administrative	1,284
Accounting	1,000
Legal	100
Uncategorized Expense	826
Total Expenses	12,565
Net Income	2,637

Figure 5-6 Example income statement

In the example, the gross margin for this organization in Month #1 was 35 percent (calculated by dividing the gross margin by the income), which is in the ballpark of how a typical company might operate.

Expenses shown on the example income statement are costs incurred to operate the organization other than costs of goods. Expenses may include rents, wages paid to the overhead staff (management, administrative, accounting, and executive staff), legal fees, and so on. Subtracting the expenses from the gross margin yields the net income or net profit of the organization.

Balance Sheet

The balance sheet generally has three sections that report the organization's financial state as of a certain date, most often at the end of an accounting period:

- **Assets** Assets are things of value held by the organization. Examples of assets are cash, *accounts receivable*, equipment, and furniture.

- **Liabilities** Liabilities are what the organization owes to other businesses or individuals. Examples are accounts payable, payroll taxes payable, and loans payable.

- **Equity** The net worth of the business. Also called *owner's equity* or *capital*, equity consists of cash put into the organization by investors, plus net profits of the business that have not been paid out to the owners (called *retained earnings*).

Figure 5-7 shows an example of a simple balance sheet.

The balance sheet shows the net worth of the organization at the end of an accounting period. In this example, for the period ending the last day of Month #1, the organization has chosen to categorize assets by *current assets* and *long-term assets* (the value of what the organization has) and has done the same for *liabilities* (what the company owes to others). In addition to assets, the organization's value is also determined by *equity*, which is the amount of money invested in the organization. Equity consists of *paid in capital*, which is the amounts invested in the organization by stockholders, partners, or other investors, and *retained earnings*, which is the accumulation of net profits that have not yet been distributed to the investors.

Cash vs. Accrual Accounting

There are two approaches to recording transactions based on the timing of when sales or expenses occur. *Cash accounting* recognizes sales or expenses when cash changes hands, whereas *accrual accounting* recognizes sales and expenses when they are earned or incurred.

In accrual accounting, revenue is considered earned when the work is performed or when an invoice is generated (regardless of when the money is actually received from the customer). Similarly, expenses are considered incurred when the organization makes a commitment to spend the money, usually when an order is placed or an invoice is received from a vendor.

The attractive feature of accrual accounting is that it provides a true representation of the financial performance of the organization as compared to cash accounting. This is because cash payments often lag behind the events that take place that cause them. If a reseller buys inventory and sells it in March, accrual accounting allows the firm to recognize both the sale and the expense in March. If the organization uses cash accounting, the sale and/or the expense may not be recognized until the cash changes hands, which may be months down the road. Therefore, accrual accounting provides a better picture of what actually happened in March in terms of financial performance. US publicly traded companies are required to use accrual accounting by the Securities and Exchange Commission (SEC) and most businesses, public and private, do so. In general, only smaller businesses uses cash accounting.

Figure 5-7
Example balance
sheet

Company X Balance Sheet As of the last day of Month #1	
Accrual basis	
All amounts in thousands	
	Total
Assets	
Current Assets:	
Cash	85,550
Accounts receivable	4,700
Inventory	3,850
Prepaid items	1,500
Total	**95,600**
Long-Term Assets:	
Furniture/Fixtures	2,000
Equipment and Tooling	3,400
Total	**5,400**
Total Assets	**101,000**
Liabilities	
Current Liabilities:	
Accounts Payable	1,600
Taxes	3,000
Wages	2,000
Interest	4,400
Total	**11,000**
Long-Term Liabilities:	
Loan #1	3,000
Loan #2	2,000
Total	**5,000**
Total Liabilities	**16,000**
Equity	
Paid in Capital	50,000
Retained Earnings	35,000
Total Equity	**85,000**
Total Liabilities and Equity	**101,000**

Capital Expenses and Operating Expenses

Expenses are funds spent by the organization and can fall into two categories: *capital expenses* and *operational expenses*. Expenses used for the day-to-day operation of the business are operating expenses (OPEX). Expenses used for a future, or long-term, benefit are capital expenses (CAPEX). Each category is treated differently from an accounting standpoint. Operating expenses are recognized when they occur, whereas capital expenses are recognized over a period of time using a process called *depreciation*.

Operating expenses are incurred during the course of ordinary business. Examples of operating expenses are software license fees, office supplies, rent, insurance, incidental equipment, repairs and maintenance, and legal services. Expenses are recognized on the date the expense is incurred using either accrual accounting (the transaction is recorded when the item it purchased or the service is performed) or cash accounting (the transaction is recorded on the date cash changes hands).

Capital expenses (or expenditures) are an investment by the organization in something that has a future benefit. Examples of capital expenses are equipment, facilities, construction, vehicles, intellectual property, and other assets. In contrast to operating expenses, which are recognized all at once at the time of acquisition, capital expenses are recognized over a period of time corresponding to the useful life of the item. For example, a piece of machinery may have a useful life of ten years; therefore, the cost of that item can be spread out over that ten-year period.

The recognition of the value of an asset over time, such as the piece of machinery in the previous paragraph, is called *depreciation*. The purpose of depreciation is to align the cost of an asset to the revenue that it produces. This is called the *matching principle of accounting*. For instance, the piece of machinery may be used by the company to produce goods for a period of ten years. Each year, the machinery produces revenue, so it would not make sense to recognize all the acquisition cost of the machinery when it was purchased. Instead, the cost is spread out over the life of the machinery. Every organization has a set of thresholds for how to depreciate different types of assets. The CISO should work with the CFO to ensure security assets are properly categorized and the proper useful life of the asset is used based on the nature of the asset and any applicable regulatory guidelines (such as US Internal Revenue Service rules).

There are various methods for calculating and allocating deprecation, including

- **Straight-line** The value of the asset is divided by the number of periods (years or months) and the same amount is allocated each period.
- **Sum of years** Since some assets have a greater value in the early years of their use, this method allows for a greater expense during the early years than later on. For instance, if an asset has a useful life of five years, the "sum of years" is 5+4+3+2+1=15. Then, each year the depreciation amount is
  - Year 1 = 5/15 of the value of the asset
  - Year 2 = 4/15 of the value of the asset
  - Year 3 = 3/15 of the value of the asset
  - Year 4 = 2/15 of the value of the asset
  - Year 5 = 1/15 of the value of the asset

- **Units of production**   This method allows the organization to scale the depreciation based on how the asset is actually used; for instance, based on the number of hours the asset is used or the units of production it produces. For instance, assume that a piece of machinery with a value of $10M can produce 1 million gadgets over its useful life. That works out to $10 per gadget ($10M \div 1M = 10$). If in Year 1 the machinery is used to produce 50,000 gadgets, the Year 1 depreciation amount would be $50,000 \times \$10 = \$500,000$.

Understanding and helping to manage OPEX and CAPEX is an important part of the CISO's job. The CISO should work with the CFO to ensure that an appropriate depreciation schedule and method is used for a given asset. For instance, if a new GRC system costs $100,000, has an expected useful life of ten years, and has no residual value at the end of its life, the CISO should make sure the depreciation schedule implemented by the CFO is appropriate and the budget established by the CISO takes into account the correct depreciation of the asset.

The Accounting Cycle

The *accounting cycle* is a workflow followed by the finance/accounting staff to implement financial management. The cycle implements the process of creating, organizing, and recording the financial transactions of the organization. The accounting cycle is implemented across an accounting period. The term *accounting period* refers to any period of time covered by the organization's financial statements. Usually an organization sets up an annual accounting period, which usually corresponds to the organization's fiscal year, divided into smaller accounting periods for each accounting month. Here are some examples of accounting periods used by businesses and other organizations:

- Calendar year of January 1 through December 31
- Company fiscal year such as October 1 through September 31 (this approach may be common for US federal government agencies or federal contracting firms)
- A contiguous 52- or 53-week period
- Calendar months, aligning with the organization's accounting year
- Fiscal months using a 4-4-5 week rotating schedule of months (every month starts and ends on the same day of the week and lasts either four weeks or five weeks)

 NOTE   Using a 4-4-5 week accounting calendar results in a few days left over at the end of the year. These days are usually just added to the last week of the fiscal year.

The accounting cycle for each month, whether the organization uses calendar or fiscal months, consists of the same set of activities each month. Figure 5-8 is an illustration of the accounting cycle.

Figure 5-8
The accounting
cycle

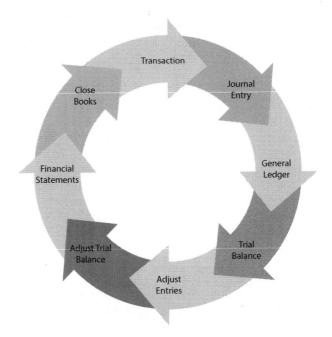

Here is a step-by-step description of a typical monthly accounting cycle:

1. **Transaction**   Financial transactions are any activity that involves an influx or outflux of money to or from the organization or between accounts within the organization's accounting system. Transactions include purchases, expenses, rent, revenues, royalties—any money moving from one account to another.

2. **Journal entries**   Transactions are initially recorded as *journal entries*. Every organization has a *journal* (sometimes called the *book of original entry*), which is a chronological list of all transactions starting at the beginning of the fiscal year or accounting period.

3. **General ledger**   Transactions are then posted to the general ledger, indicating the account to which they apply. Accounts are maintained in the general ledger, which is also called the *book of final entry*.

4. **Trial balance**   A trial balance is a check of all debits and credits to make sure they balance out. It is an accuracy check to make sure the journal and general ledger entries are correct.

5. **Adjust entries**   Usually the accountant uses a worksheet to make adjustments and test them before making corrections in the ledgers.

6. **Adjust trial balance**   After verifying adjustments from the worksheet, final adjustments are made to the ledgers and a final trial balance is created that demonstrates the debits and credits are in balance.

7. **Financial statements** Financial statements are reports showing a summary of recent accounting activity and the current state of the organization's finances. Financial statements come in the form of an income statement (also called *profit and loss* or *P&L* statement), balance sheet, and statement of cashflows.

8. **Close books** The final step in the accounting cycle is to *close the books* on the accounting period. Once the period is closed, no other entries that apply to that period can be made. Any adjustments or corrections must be made in subsequent periods.

There are many variations to the accounting cycle as described, but they always have the same general sequence: make entries to record transactions, check them and make adjustments, create financial statements, and close the books. This cycle is repeated every month.

Information Security Annual Budget

Each year the CISO puts together a plan for how much the organization will spend on the security initiatives the CISO is responsible for. Then the CISO follows that plan. This process is outlined in Chapter 3. Here we review some of the strategies for developing and managing the security budget:

1. *Start with the strategic plan.* Creating the annual information security budget usually starts with the strategic plan. The plan sets forth objectives and action plans that are then estimated and budgeted so funds can be approved for the activities to proceed. The strategic plan helps to prioritize activities from a standpoint of value to the business, which in turn can help determine the budgets for each activity.

2. *Create and approve financial plan (budget).* The information security budget is nearly always created, implemented, and managed on an annual basis, although the budget usually includes longer-term projections as well. The near-term, or current year's, budget should contain sufficient detail that each activity or line item can be reasonably managed to stay within the budgeted goal. Out-year budgets are less detailed but help leadership keep an eye on spending that is coming down the road. There are many methods for estimating the security budget, a few of which are described here:

   - **Zero-based budgeting** Also called *bottom-up budgeting*, zero-based budgeting starts each year's budget with a clean slate. The estimator starts at zero and works up from there, estimating the cost of each activity following a work breakdown structure (WBS, as introduced in Chapter 3). Starting at zero enables the estimator to take a fresh look at spending each year. Instead of just saying, "we spent X dollars last year so this year we should spend X plus Y," the CISO examines each line item and estimates what it should actually cost. The advantage of zero-based budgeting is that it forces the CISO to examine and then reexamine costs each year, even for the same item.

- **Baselining** Baselining is an approach that uses the prior year's spending as the starting point for the next year's budget. It is certainly reasonable that if a CISO spent X last year, she should expect to spend X plus or minus Y the following year (especially since a comparison to the prior year's spending may be the first thing the CEO asks to see when evaluating the budget request). Many CISOs use a combination of zero-based budgeting for estimating new activities and baselining for estimating ongoing ones.

- **Value-based (or ROI) budgeting** This approach seeks to determine what the value of an activity is to the business as a guide for how much to spend. This approach can be done on a project-by-project basis and also holistically by looking at the entire portfolio of security projects. Activities are examined, estimated, and justified based on business value and the return on the organization's investment in the activity. For example, a new identity management system may be justified because it mitigates the risk of identity theft attacks on a given asset with a known value. The value of the asset shows what should reasonably be spent to protect it. However, if it can also be shown that the new identity management system reduces the cost of identity provisioning, as compared to what was spent using the old system, the CISO can show a return on investment that can help justify the cost.

NOTE Many CISOs use a combination of zero-based budgeting, baselining, and value-based methods to create and justify the information security budget.

3. *Approve and monitor spending.* Once the information security budget is approved, the CISO monitors spending to ensure that it is in concert with the budget. The process of monitoring spending on the security program and projects is covered in Chapter 3. Organizations usually have some form of approval process whereby purchases or time charges are approved in advance. The CISO should ensure that spending against the financial accounts for which they are responsible require their approval. Spending is tracked either by the accounting and financial staff or personnel within the security team. The CISO or designated security managers compare actual spending against the budget to detect overruns and make adjustments as necessary.

4. *Create rolling forecast.* The budget is an estimate of spending for a fixed time period. Alongside the budget, a forecast should be produced and continually updated. The forecast is a prediction of future spending. In contrast to the budget, which once approved does not change, the forecast looks ahead and predicts costs based on what is actually happening on the project, stream of work, or subproject. Initially (for example, during the first month of the year), the budget equals the forecast. But after the first month, the prediction of spending may start to deviate from the budget. Since the budget does not change, the predicted shift in spending is reflected in the forecast.

5. *Reporting.* Each month, the CISO or designated manager compares the actual spending against the budget and updates the forecast so that they will know the planned spending for the next month and be able to convey to leadership and stakeholders how spending is progressing as compared to the budget and the previous month's forecast.

Finance Tips for the CISO

One reason why CISOs in many organizations do not report to the CEO is that they lack financial acumen. If the CISO does not participate in business discussions with leadership in the same way as other managers, the CISO may not receive the same respect. This can lead to security commanding less attention than other facets of the business. In a busy and high-pressure business environment, security can easily lose its voice if the credibility of the CISO is not established and maintained. Here are few things the CISO can do to participate as a financial leader in the organization:

- **Meet financial goals** The quickest way for the CISO to lose credibility with the other C-level executives is to overrun the security budget. Managing the finances of any team to stay within its budget is a basic and fundamental aspect of being a top-level manager. The budget should be carefully crafted and managed with great attention to head off any problems before they have an adverse impact. CISOs must show they are capable of staying within their budget and managing funds competently.

- **Use correct terminology** The CISO should use correct financial terminology when discussing financial topics. For instance, when speaking with the CFO about equity reporting, the CISO should not refer to the income statement (which doesn't show equity). Similarly, the CISO shouldn't mix up terms such as *budget* and *forecast* as they aren't the same. The CISO should become familiar with the terms the organization uses and speak the same financial language as the rest of the management team.

- **Learn the financial mechanics** Every organization operates differently. The CISO must learn the wheels and levers of the organization's financial and accounting machinery so he or she understands how the business makes money, what systems and processes it uses, and how the security function fits into the organization's chart of accounts and other aspects of the organization's financial model.

- **Build and use good models** Every CISO uses models and tools to help them manage their teams and finances. The CISO should refine their models and discuss them with the other leaders to improve their financial understanding and performance. The CISO should be able to show where all of their numbers came from and how they were determined to ensure and demonstrate to others that they are on top of their organization's financial performance.

- **Contribute to value**   Many CISOs view their role as helping the organization deal with risk. That is a good perspective, but what about helping the organization increase value for the investors or other financial stakeholders? This is something the other C-level executives do, so why not the CISO? The CISO can contribute by understanding the organization's financial drivers and taking actions to contribute to the organization's financial performance and success.

- **Build a financially aware culture within the security organization** Each member of the security team should be on the lookout for ways to work more efficiently, save costs, and contribute to value. The CISO should promote cost savings and encourage security team participation in security financial planning and execution decisions. The security team's financial awareness can be improved over time with training, communication, and engagement.

Procurement and Vendor Management

This section addresses the CISO's role in the procurement of goods and services from vendors. CISOs should be experts in their organization's process for procurement and vendor management for two reasons. First, the CISO uses the procurement process to obtain goods and services that apply to the security program. For instance, the acquisition of a new intrusion detection system or threat feed service by the security department follows a process for procurement. Second, all items procured by the organization may have a security implication, as they may introduce vulnerabilities into the enterprise or perform a function that has a security impact. Therefore, the security department should be involved in all acquisitions made by the organization, much like the quality assurance, accounting, or legal departments are usually involved to some extent in the procurement process. This section addresses the following topics:

- Procurement core principles and processes
- Types of contracts
- Scope agreements
- Third-party vendor risk management

Procurement Core Principles and Processes

Procurement is the process of acquiring goods and services. This includes finding sources (vendors), selecting a winner based on a competitive process, agreeing to terms, and conducting the business transaction. In managing procurement, procurement professionals often follow foundational concepts or pillars as follows:

- **Competition**   The source of the acquired product or service is selected through a competitive process whereby vendors submit bids and the organization chooses the winner that best fits its needs.

- **Ethics and fairness**   The process of conducting the competition and selecting the vendor should be transparent and fair. All potential sources should have an equal opportunity to provide the product or service without bias and using a level playing field.

- **Value**   The process should be optimized to ensure that the procuring organization obtains the best value. Product and service offerings are evaluated with respect to scope, price, and total cost of ownership. Vendor selection is made using competitive methods to facilitate acquisition at the lowest possible cost.

- **Accountability and reporting**   The process should be open so it can be monitored and measured and reported upon to convey its state to any and all stakeholders.

Figure 5-9 shows the foundational pillars of procurement along with the basic procurement process.

The basic steps of the procurement process are initiate, solicit, award, and acquire, although there is no industry standard or consensus on the number of steps or their names. Every organization implements procurement differently, as no widely used framework for procurement exists. While the implementations vary, the core features of each step that we see commonly used in most organization are discussed in the following subsections.

Initiate

The procurement process begins with the identification of a requirement or set of requirements for a new item, group of items, or service. The requirement may be as simple as "we need a Phillips screwdriver" or may be complex enough to require an entire specification. During the initiate step, it is not uncommon for the *requestor* (the person or team that needs the item) to engage with potential vendors to further develop the requirement(s) and/or develop cost estimates for the item.

Once the requirement is identified, the requestor performs an estimate of the approximate cost for the purpose of obtaining approval to proceed with the procurement.

Figure 5-9
Procurement
process

Cost estimates may be developed in-house, may be based on historical data, or may come from vendors. Each organization has its own requirements for how cost estimates are prepared and how they are to be presented to the people in the approval cycle.

In addition to requirements and cost estimates, justification for the purchase of the item may be required, depending on the rules of the organization. The justification for the item states the reason for the request and may include backup material or attachments if the organization requires supporting documentation.

Once the requestor prepares the required information describing the requirement, justification, and cost estimate, the request is routed to the proper people for review and approval according to the organization's approval rules. Once approval is obtained, the purchase can move on to the next step.

Solicit

Once the procurement is approved, the organization's procurement group can release or publish the requirement to industry and obtain bids. To do this, the procurement group needs a list of potential suppliers. Some organizations, such as US federal agencies, may publish a *Request for Information (RFI)* or a *Sources Sought* request, asking for parties who may be interested in bidding to identify themselves. Sometimes these requests contain a requirement whereby potential bidders are asked to submit their qualifications and capabilities, or respond to a questionnaire, in order to get on a bidders list. The organization should do as much outreach as possible to line up potential bidders that can provide the products or services that meet the organization's standards.

The requestor prepares the solicitation documents to be provided to bidders. This may be as simple as a line of text such as "screwdriver, Phillips #2" or an entire solicitation package that includes a specification, statement of work (SOW), and list of deliverables. For procurement of a system or service, here is a list of items that may be included in the solicitation package sent to potential bidders:

- **Statement of work**   Included in the solicitation package will be some form of document that defines the scope of the effort that will be the subject of the contract between the buyer and the seller. This may be in the form of a *statement of work*, but some organizations use *performance work statements* or other documents. The SOW defines the scope of the services or a description of the product to be provided, along with supporting information such as schedules, lists of items to be delivered, assumptions, and constraints.

- **Specification**   For more complex needs a specification or list of requirements may be developed. The specification contains a description of the requirements of the product or system. Specifications are most helpful when the need is for an item (hardware or software) to be developed, although specifications can also be helpful for procuring off-the-shelf items.

- **Contract or terms and conditions**   The solicitation package should contain a draft of the proposed contractual agreement the organization intends to use. The contract will be the legal agreement between the buyer and seller that sets forth the terms, conditions, and obligations of each party for the fulfillment of the requirements by the seller and the payments by the buyer.

- **Evaluation and award criteria** Sometimes the organization publishes a description of how it will go about choosing the winner of the competitive procurement. Such a description is helpful to bidders as it can guide them to propose a solution that is tuned to the organization's needs. There are several types of evaluation methods, but these are the most common:

  - **Lowest price technically acceptable (LPTA)** LPTA simply means the bidder with the lowest price wins. All of the bidders that offer a solution (product or service) that meets the requirement qualify, and whichever bidder has the lowest price is awarded the purchase. Note, however, that the criteria is simply "technically acceptable." With LPTA there is no concept of comparing proposals to determine if one bidder's solution is better or worse than another's. For that kind of comparison, *best value* is used.

  - **Best value** A best value evaluation takes into account *how well* an offeror's proposal meets the requirement or evaluation factor. It allows for a comparison of the *extent to which* the requirement, or each of the requirements, is met and permits an award to the bidder that provides the best solution even if the bidder did not propose the lowest price. Many procurements for development projects or for the acquisition of complex products or systems use best value criteria.

- **Proposal submission instructions** The solicitation package should contain instructions for how the bidders should prepare and submit proposals. The purpose of this is twofold. First, it ensures that each bidder provides the essential information needed by the organization to choose a winner. Second, it enables an easier comparison of the bids because they will all look similar and contain similar information about each bidder's offering. Providing clear proposal preparation instructions is one way to ensure a level playing field and a fair competition.

  The solicitation package is provided to all potential bidders and includes a specific due date and time. This ensures all bidders have the same amount of time to prepare their bid and is another way to ensure fairness.

Award

The organization evaluates all proposals in accordance with the predetermined evaluation criteria. It is important to follow such criteria and to ensure that it is applied consistently to all proposals. If during the evaluation the organization discovers that it needs additional information from some or all of the bidders, it can make requests for additional information or revised proposals. In such a circumstance, the organization may decide to release an updated SOW or other corrected information, as it is not uncommon for the organization to discover errors or shortcomings in the solicitation package.

During the period when information is being exchanged with offerors regarding their proposals, the organization should adhere to the following ethics rules:

- *Exchange information in writing.* The organization should avoid verbal instructions to offerors and always provide them in writing.

- *Provide the same information to all offerors except when doing so would reveal proprietary information about one offeror's bid to another.* For instance, if there is a shortcoming in one offeror's bid that requires an update, that request should not be revealed to another bidder (although it should be documented so it can be reviewed later if necessary).

- *Provide the same opportunity to all offerors.* For instance, if the due date for a proposal is extended for one bidder, it should be extended for all.

Once all information is obtained from offerors, the organization can complete the evaluation. The results of the evaluation of each proposal should be documented or captured in a repository such as a database. This enables future review of how an award decision was made and may be important if an offeror objects to an award or files a protest using legal recourse.

Evaluation of proposals for simple items using LPTA, such as the screwdriver example, is fairly straightforward: determine which offers meet the criteria, compare the prices of those that do, and pick the lowest one. However, for more complex requirements or ones that use best value, the evaluation process may be more rigorous. Such a procurement evaluation may require the following actions:

- List each requirement or evaluation factor
- Evaluate each requirement based on predetermined evaluation factors
- Assign a rating or measure to each requirement
- Process the results of all of the individual requirement ratings
- Compare and contrast the proposals

Rating systems may use a numerical value to assess the extent to which the requirement or evaluation factor is satisfied. For instance, one rating system may be

- 0 – No data
- 1 – Unsatisfactory
- 2 – Satisfactory
- 3 – Good
- 4 – Excellent

By assessing each requirement and evaluation factor, the organization can create a picture of the offer that can be compared with other offers to reveal the best choice. This information is combined with the price to enable determination of which offer provides the best value to the organization.

NOTE A proposal may be evaluated against a set of requirements or evaluation factors or both. A requirement is something that is needed or a mandatory condition, such as "The rope shall be ten feet long." An evaluation factor is a topic that is considered, such as "Offeror's experience in performing computer forensics." Both methods enable the buying organization to obtain information about the offer and assess its merits.

Once the organization chooses a winner, it notifies all parties. Some organizations, most notably, US federal, state, and local governments, have procedures in place to handle complaints from offerors that feel they were not treated fairly.

In some situations, the organization may perform additional steps to negotiate contract terms with the winning offeror prior to executing the purchase order or contract. For instance, some offerors may propose special payment terms or discounts that need to be discussed with the organization for inclusion in the contract.

Acquire

Once the purchase order or contract is signed, the offeror is obligated to deliver the product or service in accordance with the terms and conditions. Usually the quality assurance function within the organization is involved in assessing the item or items that are delivered to ensure that they are in compliance with the requirements of the contract. Testing may be a part of the quality assurance process to ensure that the delivered item or items meet requirements. Security testing to validate any security requirements may also occur.

Types of Contracts

Products and services subject to the procurement process can be acquired using any number of contract vehicles. The term *contract vehicle* refers to the legal mechanism that establishes the business relationship between the buyer and the seller. This section introduces common kinds of contract vehicles available to the organization and the CISO. These contracts can be used to acquire any product or service, including security products and services procured by the CISO.

Contract delivery terms can take one of two forms:

- **Completion** A completion contract is one in which the work (meaning the product or service) must be delivered or completed before payment is due. For instance, if the contract is for the acquisition of an IDS solution, payment may be due upon delivery of the IDS. This is completion terms.

- **Level of effort (LOE)** An LOE contract is one in which payments are made over a stated period of time. Usually used for services contracts, an LOE contract allows the seller to receive payments during the term of the work instead of having to wait until all the work is completed. LOE payments may be based on a variety of methods, including hours worked, incremental deliveries of capabilities, the achievement of milestones, or simply a percentage of the total effort.

Contract payment terms can take several forms, most commonly those listed here:

- **Firm fixed price (FFP)**   FFP means the work is performed or the product is delivered for a fixed price that is established in the contract. The contract contains a list of items, each having its own firm fixed price. The price is due upon meeting the conditions of the item's acceptance criteria. FFP contracts can be used to acquire services in the form of hourly labor. In this case the hourly rate is a FFP charged for each hour of work performed.

- **Time and materials (T&M)**   A T&M contract is one in which the seller is reimbursed by the buyer for labor and materials. Usually the labor is reimbursed using an hourly rate that is calculated to cover the seller's actual costs of employee salaries plus any overhead costs and profit. Similarly, the seller is reimbursed for the costs of materials such as hardware or software plus overhead and profit.

- **Cost plus**   A cost plus contract is similar to a T&M contract except the profit is broken out separately. The profit (the "plus" part) may be based on a percentage of the costs or may even be based on performance measures in which the seller can be paid a higher profit if certain conditions are met.

Contract delivery and payment terms are usually used in combination. For instance, an FFP-Completion contract means the work is done for a fixed price that is paid upon completion of the work. In contrast, an FFP-LOE contract means the work is done for fixed hourly rates that are billed and paid for across the period of time during which the hours are worked.

Scope Agreements

Contracts have some method of defining the scope of work or description of services to be performed. The most common method for defining the scope of the work is to use one of the following document types:

- **Statement of work (SOW)**   An SOW is a description of the work to be performed. It describes what work is required and how it is to be done. Therefore, the SOW is very prescriptive in that it tells the seller not only what should be done but how to do it.

- **Performance work statement (PWS)**   In contrast to an SOW, a PWS does not describe how the work is to be done. Instead, the PWS lays out the work in terms of the outcomes or results that are to be produced. The PWS also defines measurable performance standards and identifies how the buyer will measure the outcomes. Since the outcomes are clearly defined, it is entirely up to the seller to decide how they will accomplish the work and meet the outcomes.

- **Statement of objectives (SOO)**   An SOO is used when the organization (buyer) does not want to define how the work is to be accomplished (as in an SOW) and does not have enough information to be able to define measurable performance outcomes (as in a PWS). Instead, the buyer outlines general objectives for the seller to achieve, and it is up to the seller to create the SOW or PWS (or both).

- **Service-level agreement (SLA)** An SLA is used to define the services a contractor will perform for the buyer. It is especially helpful for *x-as-a-service* contracts in which the seller provides a service that is traditionally performed by the organization in-house. Similar to a PWS, the SLA lays out the provider's performance obligations in measurable terms. However, the SLA contains additional features that provide remedies for the seller's failure to achieve objectives, such as fee reductions, service credits, or termination provisions.

Third-Party Vendor Risk Management

One does not need to look any further than the well-known security breach of retail giant Target in 2013 to realize the importance of vendor security. In that security breach, the cybercriminal used a phishing e-mail to install a malware program called Citadel on a computer owned by a Target refrigeration contractor. The contractor would have been able to detect Citadel if it had been using up-to-date anti-malware software, but it wasn't and Citadel went undetected. The attacker then used the access enabled by Citadel to obtain the contractor's login credentials to Target's network. The result of this attack was the compromise of millions of customer payment card accounts. Although Target's network had weaknesses that contributed to the breach, the security shortcomings of the refrigeration contractor were a major weakness that the cybercriminal was able to exploit.

Target, which interestingly did not have a CISO at the time of the security breach, could have tried to place blame with the contractor, but the security of the customer payment records was ultimately Target's responsibility. If an organization allows a third-party vendor access to its network, the organization must use due diligence to ensure the vendor does not enable a compromise. If Target had a good *vendor security program* in place, it could have taken measures to ensure that the vendor was correctly using anti-malware software and had protections against phishing attacks in place.

CISOs should ensure that the use of third parties does not introduce vulnerabilities into the environment by implementing a third-party risk management program. A third-party vendor risk management program can be implemented as a stream of work or subprogram and can be managed following the process described in Chapter 3. The following section describes the features of a third-party risk management program.

Third-Party Risk Management Program

The third-party risk management program should address the variety of third-party products and services an organization may acquire. Here are a few examples:

- **Products and systems** Any product (hardware and software) can have security vulnerabilities in it. Once installed on the organization's network, the product vulnerabilities become vulnerabilities of the enterprise and can be exploited. This category includes both COTS products and open source products, as both can contain vulnerabilities.

- **Developed applications**   Organizations may acquire from third-party vendors custom-developed applications that contain vulnerabilities and introduce risk into the enterprise.

- **Consultants and service providers**   Organizations commonly use third-party vendors to provide services ranging from legal services to IT consulting to HVAC contractors. Any vendor that connects to the organization's network can introduce risk.

- **Cloud services**   X-as-a-service vendors are unique in that they provide assets that connect directly to the organizations network and/or provide enterprise services turnkey.

Although third-party risk management programs can be implemented in many ways, the approach discussed here is to adapt the NIST Risk Management Framework (RMF). RMF is usually thought of as a model used to apply information security controls to systems, but it can be tailored to provide a framework for applying security controls to vendor relationships. Figure 5-10 shows the typical RMF phases. The application of each phase to third-party security is discussed next.

Prepare   The Prepare phase involves the creation of the artifacts and tools used to support each of the other phases as well as obtain feedback during each of those phases to facilitate improvements. During this phase the CISO prepares the following:

- **Third-party risk management policy**   The policy reflects all requirements that guide the third-party program. Topics within the policy may include the following:
  - Third-party roles and responsibilities and organizational structure
  - Requirements pertaining to contract employees (since they are not employees of the organization and therefore HR policies do not apply to them)
  - Sections covering requirements for physical, asset, communications, and operations security

Figure 5-10
NIST Risk
Management
Framework

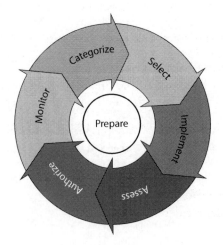

- Product development, including security during the SDLC
- Configuration, patch, and change management
- Incident management
- Business continuity
- Monitoring and auditing
- Legal and compliance
- Documentation and recordkeeping

- **Tailoring of other policies**   Some organizations prefer to keep the third-party policy lean and write it to contain reference to other policies. In this case those policies may require a review and tailoring to ensure they address third-party requirements correctly.

- **Supporting standards, guidelines, and processes**   In addition to policies, the organization may develop standards, guidelines, and processes to be used as guidance for third parties or for individuals within the organization tasked with supervising or working with third parties.

- **Acquire assessment tools**   The organization may acquire tools to be used to assess the security performance of third-party vendors. For instance, if a cloud service provider agrees to let the organization conduct vulnerability scans, the organization may identify and acquire scanning tools for this purpose.

- **Prepare questionnaires**   Information about the vendor may also be gathered in the form of a vendor security questionnaire that asks specific security program questions. The answers are often used to make procurement decisions. The Vendor Security Alliance (https://www.vendorsecurityalliance.org/) provides guidance for preparing vendor questionnaires for this purpose.

- **Line up assessors**   The organization may choose to use external assessors to conduct scans or perform other evaluations of a third party's security capabilities.

- **Contract terms and artifacts**   The CISO may prepare in advance contract terms and other language that will be used in third-party agreements.

The remaining phases are applied to each candidate third-party vendor, product, or service. At each phase, feedback is obtained and fed back into the Prepare activities to improve the preparation for the next time the process is used or for the next vendor.

Categorize   During the Categorize phase, the vendor, product, or service is categorized. Categories should be established in advance, with corresponding controls established for each. To illustrate, an organization may define three categories of third-party relationships as follows:

- Product
- Service provider
- Custom software developer

During the next phase, security controls are selected for each. Some organizations use a highly structured approach whereby they predefine controls for given categories, allowing for faster identification of controls for a new vendor.

Select During the Select phase, specific controls are chosen. Using the categories illustrated previously, here is a further illustration showing controls.

- **Global controls** These controls are artifacts that apply to all categories. These artifacts are tools used to establish the security posture of the vendor:
  - **Reputation of the security product or vendor** When establishing trust in a product, sometimes the reputation of the vendor is a valuable consideration. A vendor that has historically failed to deliver patches in a timely manner may not compare well against one that has delivered promptly.
  - **Independent assurance** Evidence that the product or vendor has been independently audited by a credible security assurance entity may be required. For instance, audits and third-party attestations can be performed following standards including SOC 1, SOC 2, ISO/IEC 27001, or FedRAMP.
  - **Legal agreement** A legal agreement may be used to establish a commitment from the vendor to the organization, for instance, to assume liability for a security breach.
  - **Security review** The organization may conduct a security review of the product or service to determine its security posture and suitability for use by the organization.
- **Product controls** Controls that may apply to the acquisition of a hardware or software product or system may include (in addition to the global controls listed previously) verification of the following:
  - The vendor has a program for timely reporting of vulnerabilities.
  - The vendor has a program for the timely release of security patches.

  Product controls may apply to COTS or open source products.
- **Service provider controls** Important controls may include verification that the vendor has and can provide evidence of the following:
  - An established information security program
  - Security policies, standards, and procedures
  - Security procedures for *fourth parties* (third-party vendors of the vendor)
  - Willingness to submit to security testing
  - Validation by an independent testing or auditing entity (such as a SOC 2 audit)
- **Custom software developer controls** In addition to all of the controls listed for the categories, software development organizations should be evaluated to determine the quality of their secure coding program and their SDLC.

Implement   Once the security controls for the product or service vendor are chosen, they are implemented. Contracts are written, negotiated, and executed. Audits and testing take place. Assurance vendors are engaged. The organization reviews vendor-provided documentation such as security policies and procedures. The Implement phase puts into action all of the controls identified from the Select phase.

Assess   In the Assess phase, all of the artifacts collected during the Implement phase are collected and the totality of the information is reviewed to make a determination regarding the use of the product or service. If there are control shortcomings, they are assessed for their risk impact to the business. As introduced in Chapter 1, there are four choices for how risk can be handled:

- *Mitigate* or reduce the risk by putting an additional control in place
- *Transfer* the risk (usually by using an insurance policy)
- *Accept* the risk when the organization can "live with" the risk
- *Avoid* the risk entirely by stopping the activity or changing a feature of the product or service or how it is used

Authorize   Ultimately it is the CISO who makes the final security recommendation as to whether the organization can proceed with deployment of the product, service, or vendor. Depending on the organization, the CISO's decision may be final or they may be overruled by others in leadership. If overruled, the CISO should make sure the decision maker knows they are choosing to accept the residual risk and document it for future reference if needed.

Monitor   Ongoing monitoring should be performed once the product is deployed or the service is initiated. Monitoring should be performed to ensure contractual obligations are being fulfilled, the controls are in place, and the vendor is doing what it is supposed to be doing. Shortcomings are assessed to determine their risk exposure and potential impact to the business so appropriate action can be taken.

Smaller Vendors May Pose the Biggest Risk

Some organizations suffer consequences when they pay attention to the wrong things. Many times, it isn't the large vendor to which all of the major IT functions are outsourced that causes problems leading to a security breach, but instead it is the small mom and pop operation (such as the refrigeration contractor). Sometimes the security requirements are relaxed for the smaller vendors due to their limited role in the enterprise. But even the smaller vendors can cause big problems, as evidenced by the Target breach. All vendors, large and small, should be part of the third-party risk management program.

Chapter Review

Strategic planning helps an organization understand what is most important and use that information to make decisions. Strategic planning for the entire organization is performed by the organization's leadership. The CISO may very well be part of the team that creates the organization's strategic plan. *Security strategic planning* is a subset of the organization's strategic planning.

Understanding, interpreting, and translating security business drivers allows the CISO to make important decisions regarding aspects of the security program (such as security goals, objectives, policies, procedures, architecture, and controls). To accomplish this decision-making process, some organizations use informal approaches (such as casual conversations, meetings, or informal assessments) while others use more rigorous structured approaches (such as a formal process, framework, risk assessment, or enterprise architecture model).

The CISO should have a strong grasp of business accounting and finance fundamentals. The CISO needs to be able to speak the language of finance, know how to read a balance sheet and an income statement, and grasp key concepts such as capital expenses and operating expenses. In addition, the CISO must be able to manage and justify the finances of the security department.

The security department should be involved in all acquisitions of products and services by the organization in order to ensure vulnerabilities are not introduced into the environment. The basic steps of the procurement process are initiate, solicit, award, and acquire. Security should be involved in each step of the process. CISOs should ensure that the use of third parties does not introduce vulnerabilities into the environment by implementing a third-party risk management program.

Quick Review

- In security strategic planning, it is important for each goal to be necessary, attainable, and verifiable.

- Following an enterprise architecture framework is one method for translating security business drivers to security decisions to produce an enterprise information security architecture (EISA).

- An EA model can be used to break down and document the information security program architecture and how it relates to the enterprise from a high-level business architecture perspective to low-level technical architecture processes.

- The accounting cycle is a workflow followed by the finance/accounting staff to implement the process of creating, organizing, and recording the financial transactions of the organization.

- Organization accounting systems include a data processing system used in conjunction with accounting policies and procedures following GAAP.

- An income statement is a summary of the organization's financial activity during a period of time.
- A balance sheet is a snapshot of the organization's financial position at a given point in time.
- Many CISOs use a combination of zero-based budgeting, baselining, and value-based methods to create and justify the information security budget.
- Procurement is the process of acquiring goods and services.
- The most common method for defining the scope of the work performed by a vendor is by using a document such as a statement of work, performance work statement, statement of objectives, or service-level agreement.

Questions

1. Which of the following would not be considered an essential component of the strategic planning process?

   A. Select the right people to be on the team

   B. Acquire a planning tool

   C. Select a model to follow

   D. Set a schedule

2. Which of the following techniques might a CISO use to translate security business drivers to security decisions?

   A. Informal meetings

   B. Enterprise architecture frameworks

   C. Risk management exercises

   D. All of the above

3. Which of the following are most commonly found on a balance sheet?

   A. Revenue, liabilities, and equity

   B. Revenue, liabilities, and profits

   C. Revenue, expenses, and profits

   D. Assets, liabilities, and equity

4. Which of the following are foundational pillars of procurement?

   A. Source selection, proposal, evaluation

   B. Revenue, liabilities, and profits

   C. Competition, ethics, value

   D. Accountability, ethics, source selection

5. An organization wants to purchase a turnkey inventory management system consisting of hardware and software. The organization wants to keep the price low, but its most important criteria are the experience and capabilities of the contractor. Which procurement method is best for this situation?

   A. Best value

   B. Lowest price technically acceptable (LPTA)

   C. Cost plus

   D. Time and materials

Answers

1. **B.** A planning tool is useful but is not essential. It's more important to select the right people to be involved, select an established model to follow, and choose a schedule and stick with it.

2. **D.** All of the above. A CISO may utilize informal meetings, an enterprise architecture framework, or a risk management exercise to facilitate the translation of security business drivers to security decisions.

3. **D.** A balance sheet most commonly shows the organization's assets, liabilities, and equity at a given point in time. Revenue, expenses, and profits are shown on an income statement.

4. **C.** Foundational pillars of procurement include competition, ethics, fairness, value, accountability, and reporting. Source selection, proposal, and evaluation are not pillars of procurement. Revenue, liabilities, and profits are features of accounting, not procurement.

5. **A.** The best value procurement method allows the organization to choose the vendor whose proposal best meets the requirements. LPTA would force the organization to choose the lowest price proposal as long as it meets the minimum requirements. Cost plus and time and materials are contract term methods, not procurement methods.

About the Online Content

This book comes complete with TotalTester Online customizable practice exam software with 300 practice exam questions.

System Requirements

The current and previous major versions of the following desktop browsers are recommended and supported: Chrome, Microsoft Edge, Firefox, and Safari. These browsers update frequently, and sometimes an update may cause compatibility issues with the TotalTester Online or other content hosted on the Training Hub. If you run into a problem using one of these browsers, please try using another until the problem is resolved.

Your Total Seminars Training Hub Account

To get access to the online content you will need to create an account on the Total Seminars Training Hub. Registration is free, and you will be able to track all your online content using your account. You may also opt in if you wish to receive marketing information from McGraw Hill or Total Seminars, but this is not required for you to gain access to the online content.

Privacy Notice

McGraw Hill values your privacy. Please be sure to read the Privacy Notice available during registration to see how the information you have provided will be used. You may view our Corporate Customer Privacy Policy by visiting the McGraw Hill Privacy Center. Visit the **mheducation.com** site and click **Privacy** at the bottom of the page.

Single User License Terms and Conditions

Online access to the digital content included with this book is governed by the McGraw Hill License Agreement outlined next. By using this digital content you agree to the terms of that license.

Access   To register and activate your Total Seminars Training Hub account, simply follow these easy steps.

1. Go to this URL: **hub.totalsem.com/mheclaim**

2. To register and create a new Training Hub account, enter your e-mail address, name, and password on the **Register** tab. No further information (such as credit card number) is required to create an account.

   If you already have a Total Seminars Training Hub account, enter your e-mail address and password on the **Log in** tab.

3. Enter your Product Key: `gqrz-5m5t-vdr2`

4. Click to accept the user license terms.

5. For new users, click the **Register and Claim** button to create your account. For existing users, click the **Log in and Claim** button.

   You will be taken to the Training Hub and have access to the content for this book.

Duration of License   Access to your online content through the Total Seminars Training Hub will expire one year from the date the publisher declares the book out of print.

Your purchase of this McGraw Hill product, including its access code, through a retail store is subject to the refund policy of that store.

The Content is a copyrighted work of McGraw Hill, and McGraw Hill reserves all rights in and to the Content. The Work is © 2021 by McGraw Hill.

Restrictions on Transfer   The user is receiving only a limited right to use the Content for the user's own internal and personal use, dependent on purchase and continued ownership of this book. The user may not reproduce, forward, modify, create derivative works based upon, transmit, distribute, disseminate, sell, publish, or sublicense the Content or in any way commingle the Content with other third-party content without McGraw Hill's consent.

Limited Warranty   The McGraw Hill Content is provided on an "as is" basis. Neither McGraw Hill nor its licensors make any guarantees or warranties of any kind, either express or implied, including, but not limited to, implied warranties of merchantability or fitness for a particular purpose or use as to any McGraw Hill Content or the information therein or any warranties as to the accuracy, completeness, correctness, or results to be obtained from, accessing or using the McGraw Hill Content, or any material referenced in such Content or any information entered into licensee's product by users or other persons and/or any material available on or that can be accessed through the licensee's product (including via any hyperlink or otherwise) or as to non-infringement of third-party rights. Any warranties of any kind, whether express or implied, are disclaimed. Any material or data obtained through use of the McGraw Hill Content is at your own discretion and risk and user understands that it will be solely responsible for any resulting damage to its computer system or loss of data.

Neither McGraw Hill nor its licensors shall be liable to any subscriber or to any user or anyone else for any inaccuracy, delay, interruption in service, error or omission, regardless of cause, or for any damage resulting therefrom.

In no event will McGraw Hill or its licensors be liable for any indirect, special or consequential damages, including but not limited to, lost time, lost money, lost profits or good will, whether in contract, tort, strict liability or otherwise, and whether or not such damages are foreseen or unforeseen with respect to any use of the McGraw Hill Content.

TotalTester Online

TotalTester Online provides you with a simulation of the CCISO exam. Exams can be taken in Practice Mode or Exam Mode. Practice Mode provides an assistance window with hints, references to the book, explanations of the correct and incorrect answers, and the option to check your answer as you take the test. Exam Mode provides a simulation of the actual exam. The number of questions, the types of questions, and the time allowed are intended to be an accurate representation of the exam environment. The option to customize your quiz allows you to create custom exams from selected domains or chapters, and you can further customize the number of questions and time allowed.

To take a test, follow the instructions provided in the previous section to register and activate your Total Seminars Training Hub account. When you register you will be taken to the Total Seminars Training Hub. From the Training Hub Home page, select **CCISO™ All-in-One Exam Guide TotalTester** from the Study drop-down menu at the top of the page, or from the list of Your Topics on the Home page. You can then select the option to customize your quiz and begin testing yourself in Practice Mode or Exam Mode. All exams provide an overall grade and a grade broken down by domain.

Technical Support

For questions regarding the TotalTester or operation of the Training Hub, visit **www .totalsem.com** or e-mail **support@totalsem.com**.

For questions regarding book content, visit **www.mheducation.com/customerservice**.

access   The action that a subject can impose on an object such as read, modify, delete, create, or execute.

access controls   Security features that control how users and systems communicate and interact with other systems and resources.

administrative controls   Management-oriented controls such as policies, procedures, guidelines, training, risk management, and employment practices (hiring, firing, and so on). Administrative controls are also referred to as soft controls or managerial controls.

agile   An overarching term for several development methodologies that utilize iterative and incremental development processes and encourage team-based collaboration.

Annualized Loss Expectancy (ALE)   Used to predict the potential value of a loss on an annual basis. The formula is

$$\text{Single Loss Expectancy (SLE)} \times \text{Annualized Rate of Occurrence (ARO)}$$
$$= \text{Annualized Loss Expectancy (ALE)}$$

Annualized Rate of Occurrence (ARO)   An estimate of how many times an event is estimated to occur in a given year.

asset security   The practice of identifying what assets the organization has and determining and implementing the appropriate security controls for each.

Asset Value (AV)   The value of an asset or assets that are subject to an event, when used to calculate Single Loss Expectancy (SLE). The AV can be simply the replacement cost of the asset or may include other considerations. Asset value may include expenses that may be incurred if the asset were lost, such as labor and installation costs, costs to the business due to downtime, as well as costs due to loss of business or reputation.

attribute-based access control (ABAC)   A policy-based access control that grants access rights based on technical policies that combine various attributes such as who is making the request (subject), what resource is being requested (object), environmental conditions such as time of day or location (environmental context), and what action is being requested. Access can be granted based on a variety and combination of attributes such as date, time, IP address, and so on.

audit charter   Documents the authority, scope, and responsibilities of the audit.

audit universe   Describes all the business processes and assets that are included in the audit.

authentication   The verification of a subject to confirm they are who they say they are. This is typically performed though the use of a password, passphrase, token device, smart card, cryptographic key, or biometric.

authorization   The act of granting access to an object based on predefined access management rules that establish which operations subjects are allowed to carry out on objects.

availability   The protection of systems to ensure timely access to data and resources.

balance sheet   A snapshot of the organization's financial position at a specific point in time. It lists the value of the organization's assets (what it has), the value of its liabilities (what it owes), and what it is worth (the difference between the assets and liabilities).

baseline   A starting point that serves as the basis for comparison. Commonly used in the context of configuration or change management, the baseline is the designated or official version of a document, configuration, hardware, or software item.

botnet   A group of infected systems that work together to perform an attack, with some form of centralized command and control.

business impact analysis (BIA)   A functional risk analysis for business continuity planning to determine organizational and system requirements, interdependencies, contingency requirements, and priorities in the event of a significant interruption.

Center for Internet Security (CIS)   A nonprofit organization focused on developing best practice tools, frameworks, and resources for information security.

Center for Internet Security Critical Security Controls (CIS CSC)   A voluntary framework consisting of 20 "critical" controls that focus on key fundamentals of information security. It is also known as the CIS Top 20 and previously the SANS Top 20.

change management   The practice of identifying, tracking, monitoring, and controlling changes to an environment, system, or asset.

ciphertext   Information that has been encrypted.

Clinger-Cohen Act of 1996   A US federal law that defines how the federal government acquires, uses, and disposes of information technology.

Cloud Security Alliance (CSA)   A nonprofit organization focused on promoting best practices for the use and adoption of cloud computing.

Cloud Security Alliance Cloud Controls Matrix (CSA CCM or CCM)   A control framework of security concepts and principles for cloud security developed by the Cloud Security Alliance.

collision   An occurrence when a hash algorithm creates the same hash output for two different inputs.

commercial off-the-shelf (COTS)   Software or hardware products that are for commercial sale.

compensating controls   Controls that serve as an alternate or secondary control implementation to a primary control. They are often used when the primary control is not feasible to implement due to cost, complexity, or other business constraints. Examples include implementing network isolation of business-critical applications that cannot be patched or installing fences, locks, and alarms after a determination that a full-time security guard is too expensive.

compliance   An approach to governance designed to ensure alignment with applicable laws, regulations, standards, organizational policies, ethical conduct, or other business goals.

compliance management   The processes by which an organization plans, implements, and maintains the activities that support compliance.

confidentiality   The protection of data to ensure the data is only accessible by the people authorized to see it.

configuration baseline   Specific configuration for implementations of hardware or software to ensure the correct and repeatable security implementation of assets in the enterprise. Baselines are sometimes documented along with standards.

configuration management   The management of requirements, specifications, and configurations of a product or deliverable. Sometimes includes the management of the inventory and records relating to a product or deliverable.

continuous auditing   Auditing on a more frequent basis typically through the use of technology that can rapidly collect and analyze data (such as a software agent or sensor) and provide real-time or near real-time results.

control   Something that is put into place to mitigate a potential risk. A control may be a software configuration, a hardware device, or a procedure that eliminates a vulnerability or that reduces the likelihood a threat agent will be able to exploit a vulnerability. *See also* countermeasure.

control framework   A catalog of controls used to provide a foundation to aid in the implementation of a comprehensive information security program.

Control Objectives for Information and Related Technology (COBIT)   A best practice framework for governance and management of IT developed by ISACA and the IT Governance Institute.

corrective controls   Controls that correct or compensate for adverse events that have occurred by fixing a system, process, or activity. Examples include IPSs, terminating an employee after an offense, antivirus that quarantines malicious software, using a fire extinguisher to extinguish a fire, and implementing a business continuity plan or incident response plan.

countermeasure   Something that is put into place to mitigate a potential risk. A countermeasure may be a software configuration, a hardware device, or a procedure that eliminates a vulnerability or that reduces the likelihood a threat agent will be able to exploit a vulnerability.

critical path   A single or series of events or activities that, if changed, would change the overall end date of the project.

cross-site scripting (XSS)   A type of web application attack whereby an attacker injects a malicious script into a website viewed by others. When someone visits the site, the script is executed by the victim's browser. Such scripts can access the victim's cookies, tokens, or other sensitive information.

cryptographic algorithm   A mathematical equation that can be used for encryption, decryption, or hashing.

cryptographic key   A string of values used in conjunction with cryptographic algorithms for operations such as encryption and decryption. In general, the longer the key size the more security that is provided, however, this also depends on the algorithm and the implementation used.

cryptosystem   Includes all of the necessary system components for encryption and decryption such as software, protocols, algorithms, keys, key management, and so on.

data custodian   Individual responsible for the data maintenance tasks, including implementing and maintaining controls to provide the protection level dictated by the data owner and ensuring that systems support access controls which enforce data classification. This is typically a member of the technical security staff or IT (for example, systems administrator).

data owner   Individual responsible for a particular set of data, including identifying classification level for the data to set security requirements. Data owners are typically department heads or process owners.

decryption   The process of transforming ciphertext to plaintext using cryptographic keys and algorithms.

Defense Federal Acquisition Regulation Supplement (DFARS)   A supplement to the Federal Acquisition Regulation (FAR) that provides specific acquisition regulations that US Department of Defense (DoD) agencies, contractors, and subcontractors must follow as part of the procurement process.

defense-in-depth   The coordinated use of multiple security controls in a layered approach.

Delphi technique   Technique developed by the RAND Corporation as a method to predict technological change. It is now used to facilitate discussions among subject matter experts to achieve consensus. It uses a tiered, iterative process to pose questions to the group, with each iteration delving more deeply into the topic.

detective controls   Controls that discover, detect, or identify a potential adverse activity, event, intruder, or incident. Examples include IDSs, security log review, mandatory vacations, and reviewing events captured on surveillance cameras.

deterrent controls   Controls that deter or discourage a potential adversary from performing an attack or engaging in unwanted behavior. Examples include system warning banners and warning signs.

digital signature   A hash value that is encrypted with the sender's private key. Digital signatures provide authenticity, integrity, and nonrepudiation.

directive controls   Typically administrative controls that communicate expected behavior by specifying what actions are or are not permitted. Examples include security policies, standards, and procedures.

discretionary access control (DAC)   An access control model that provides the owner, usually the creator, full control of the object (resource) to determine which subjects (users and groups) can access and share that object. Examples of DAC systems include most flavors of Unix and Linux as well as all Windows and macOS systems.

encryption   The process of transforming plaintext to ciphertext using cryptographic keys and algorithms.

engagement letter   An agreement between the entity being audited and the auditor that serves to define the terms of the engagement, set proper expectations, and prevent any misunderstandings.

enterprise architecture (EA)   The practice of diagramming and documenting the architecture of the enterprise to assist decision makers with aligning the organization's strategy around the business's people, processes, and technologies.

exposure   An instance of being exposed to a loss. A vulnerability *exposes* an organization to possible damages.

Exposure Factor (EF)   The percentage of loss that would likely occur for the subject event, used when calculating Single Loss Expectancy (SLE).

external compliance   Activities that support following external laws, regulations, standards, or other mandates that originate outside of the organization. *See also* internal compliance.

Family Educational Rights and Privacy Act of 1974 (FERPA)   A US federal law focused on protecting the privacy and confidentiality of student educational records.

Federal Information Processing Standards (FIPS)   Standards and guidelines issued by the National Institute for Standards and Technology (NIST) for the security of US federal information systems.

Federal Information Security Modernization Act of 2014 (FISMA or FISMA 2014) An amendment to the Federal Information Security Management Act of 2002 that requires US federal agencies to build, document, and implement an agency-wide information security program to support agency operations.

Federal Risk and Authorization Management Program (FedRAMP)   A US federal government program that provides a standard approach for assessing, authorizing, and continuous monitoring of cloud-based products and services. In order for a cloud service provider (CSP) to sell services to the US federal government, the CSP must be

FedRAMP authorized. FedRAMP is essentially a cybersecurity approval process for cloud-based products and services.

Gantt chart A type of chart that illustrates the project schedule and shows the dependencies of tasks. It shows which tasks must be completed for other tasks to commence and can help identify the critical path(s).

General Data Protection Regulation (GDPR) A European Union (EU) privacy law that regulates the processing of EU citizens' personal data.

governance The act of overseeing the direction of something. The something could be the organization as a whole (organization or corporate governance) or a specific part of the organization (such as, IT governance, financial governance, or security governance, and so on).

governance, risk management, and compliance (GRC) A term used to describe an integrated approach to these three practices and their associated activities. Some organizations implement GRC programs to enable a cohesive, holistic approach to organizational GRC, ensuring that the organization acts in accordance with its internal policies, external compliance requirements, and risk appetite through the alignment of strategy with organizational objectives.

Gramm-Leach-Bliley Act (GLBA) Also known as the Financial Services Modernization Act of 1999, requires financial institutions to protect individuals' nonpublic personal information.

guidelines Documents or instructions that provide general direction or recommendations without specifying a mandatory requirement.

hashing A one-way function that uses algorithms to transform information to a string of data, often used for integrity checking.

Health Information Portability and Accountability Act (HIPAA) A US federal regulation that covers the handling of protected health information (PHI) and provides a framework for protecting the security and privacy of health information.

identification The act of a subject supplying information to identify themselves as the first step in the authentication process. Such information may include a username, account number, or user ID.

income statement A summary of the organization's financial activity during a period of time. It lists all transactions including revenue and expenses and any profit or loss during the reporting period.

incremental A development life cycle model where multiple sets of development activities are carried out. Each phase of the life cycle has a predetermined timeframe and produces a complete increment of a capability. Each capability is then integrated with that of the previous phase to produce the whole product.

integrity (of data)   The accuracy, consistency, and validity of data.

internal compliance   Activities that support following internal policies or other mandates that originate within the organization. *See also* external compliance.

key performance indicator (KPI)   A metric that measures how effective the organization is at performing a specific job.

least privilege   A security principle that user permissions and access levels should be granted at the minimum level required for the job or function that needs to be performed.

malware   Malicious software that is designed to infiltrate and gain unauthorized access to computer systems in order to cause damage or disruption.

mandatory access control (MAC)   An access control model that uses a central authority that regulates access based on the *clearance* of subjects and *classification* of objects. A subject's clearance must be greater than or equal to the object's clearance. MAC models are typically utilized in specialized government and military systems or specialized OS distributions such as Security-Enhanced Linux (SELinux) developed by the US NSA and Red Hat.

message authentication code (MAC)   A type of cryptographic function that provides both integrity and authenticity using a key that is shared between the sender and recipient. MACs can be created using hash algorithms and symmetric encryption algorithms in certain modes.

need to know   A security principle that a user must have a legitimate reason for accessing specific information, such as to fulfill their role or responsibilities.

NIST Cybersecurity Framework (NIST CSF)   A risk-based cybersecurity framework developed by the US National Institute for Standards and Technology. The framework was originally designed for critical infrastructure but is applicable to any organization.

NIST Special Publication (SP)   A document published by NIST that provides detailed information in subject areas that are of interest to specific research, business, government, or industrial communities.

NIST SP 800 series   NIST publications specific to computer security.

NIST SP 800-37   Now in Rev. 2, *Risk Management Framework for Information Systems and Organizations: A System Life Cycle Approach for Security and Privacy* describes a process for managing security and privacy risk.

NIST SP 800-53   Titled *Security and Privacy Controls for Federal Information Systems and Organizations*, consists of a catalog of security and privacy controls used to assist US federal government agencies in meeting the requirements of FISMA and serves as a best practice framework for other, non-federal entities.

nonrepudiation   Prevents a sender from legitimately denying that they sent a message (for example, digital signature).

North American Electric Reliability Corporation Critical Infrastructure Protection (NERC CIP) A set of cybersecurity standards for the security of North America's power grid.

object An entity such as a network, computer, file, device, record, table, process, domain, database, or program containing information that is accessed by a subject.

Open Web Application Security Project (OWASP) An international nonprofit organization that works to improve the security of software.

organizational ethics Principles that govern the behavior of the organization, with a focus on acting with integrity, accountability, and responsibility.

Payment Card Industry Data Security Standard (PCI DSS) A standard and control framework for organizations that handle, process, and store credit card information.

phishing Obtaining sensitive information by disguising oneself as a trusted entity, usually via e-mail.

physical controls Tangible controls put in place to protect people, assets, and facilities against physical threats. Examples include fencing, lighting, locks, bollards, server room doors, alarms, and security guards.

plaintext Information in a readable format that has not been encrypted or has been decrypted.

preventive controls Controls that prevent or stop the occurrence of an adverse event or incident. Examples include mandatory background checks, firewall access control lists (ACLs), door locks, fences, bollards, and IPSs.

privacy Indicates the level of control an individual should expect to have over their own sensitive data. This is typically focused on the authorized collection, use, sharing, archival, and destruction of personal information that the organization has been entrusted with.

Privacy Act of 1974 (Privacy Act) A US federal law developed to help address privacy concerns by focusing on the balance between the government's need to collect and maintain an individual's personal information and the privacy rights of the individual.

privacy impact assessment (PIA) A risk assessment carried out to assess privacy.

Privacy Shield EU-US and Swiss-US frameworks for regulating exchanges of personal information from the European Union and Switzerland to the United States.

privilege creep When a user gradually accrues more access rights beyond what is required for their role (also known as authorization creep).

processes (or procedures) Step-by-step workflows that define how certain security functions are performed. They usually define who is responsible for the activities and how they are to be carried out.

qualitative risk analysis   A type of risk analysis that is subjective and does not use dollar amounts (although it may still involve calculations).

quality   The degree to which deliverables satisfy project requirements and customer expectations (functionality, design, price, schedule, and so on).

quality assurance (QA)   Activities that provide confidence that quality requirements are fulfilled.

quality control (QC)   Activities that detect and ensure a product or process meets established requirements.

quality management system (QMS)   A collection of processes and activities intended to ensure desired levels of quality are met, incorporating quality assurance and quality control practices.

quantitative risk analysis   A type of risk analysis used to calculate the monetary loss associated with a given threat. This is accomplished by assigning numeric values to each factor in the analysis.

ransomware   A type of malware that forces its victim to choose between paying a ransom or losing valuable assets.

recovery controls   Controls that restore an environment or operations back to regular functionality. They are similar in function to corrective controls but are thought of as having advanced capability. Examples include restoring a system from backup, removing malware from an infected system, and utilizing a watchdog process that can determine that a service has stalled and restart it.

responsibility matrix (RACI chart)   A matrix used to demarcate responsibilities for each activity or task involved in meeting project deliverables.

risk   The likelihood of a threat agent exploiting a vulnerability and the corresponding business impact.

risk acceptance   A risk treatment approach where a decision is made that the activity can proceed either because the risk is determined to be at an acceptable level or because the cost of mitigation is too high in relation to the potential impact.

risk avoidance   A risk treatment approach where a decision is made to not proceed with an activity because the risk of performing the activity is too high to be acceptable (that is, the risky activity is stopped altogether).

risk management   The process of identifying and assessing risk, reducing it to an acceptable level, and implementing the right mechanisms to maintain that level.

risk mitigation   A risk treatment approach where action is taken to reduce or minimize the impact of the risk, often by the implementation of a control (countermeasure).

risk transference   A risk treatment approach where risk is transferred to another entity. Risk transfer is most commonly accomplished by purchasing insurance or outsourcing the activity to another entity that assumes responsibility for the risk.

role-based access control (RBAC)   An access control model that enforces access based on a subject's role within the organization. Each role is assigned certain permissions and users are assigned to a role based on their function.

rootkit   Malware that enables unauthorized access to a computer and masks its existence.

Sarbanes-Oxley Act of 2002 (SOX)   A US federal law focused on holding board members and executives accountable for the accuracy of the financial statements of their organization.

scope   The definition of the boundary of the work to be performed.

scope creep   Uncontrolled growth in a project's scope.

security   The state of being secure or the freedom from potential harm.

security business drivers   Features of the business that have an impact on security.

security control   Also known as a safeguard or countermeasure, a mechanism (such as a process or technology) put into place to mitigate risk and protect the confidentiality, integrity, or availability of an asset.

security engineering   A domain of engineering that addresses security in the requirements, design, and implementation of systems.

security operations   Focuses on actively performing day-to-day functions to prevent, detect, and respond to security risks and threats.

security situational awareness   The practice of knowing what assets the organization has, where they are located, and what the security posture of each asset is.

Service Organization Controls (SOC) audit   An audit performed on a service organization (such as a cloud service provider) by a third party who assesses the internal controls of the service organization.

Single Loss Expectancy (SLE)   The potential value of a loss for a single threat event. The event can apply to a single asset or a group of assets. The formula is

Asset Value (AV) × Exposure Factor (EF) = Single Loss Expectancy (SLE)

social engineering   The use of deception to trick someone into doing something that may not be in their best interest. This technique has been used by criminals for years and is an integral part of many cyberattacks.

standard   An approved model that defines the quality or characteristics used as the basis for comparison. For instance, a *system configuration standard* establishes the approved configuration settings for a given system.

steganography   A technique used to hide secret information in plain sight, typically in innocuous looking digital files. This is accomplished through the use of special software that embeds messages inside images, videos, audio, text, or other files.

subject   An active entity such as an individual, system, process, or device that accesses an object.

SWIFT   Structured What If Technique, a structured process for group collaboration. It involves conducting brainstorming sessions using guidewords and other elements to describe systems, identify and assess risks, and propose actions to reduce risk to acceptable levels.

systems development life cycle (SDLC)   A life cycle model for developing or managing a system, product, or service. Examples of SDLCs include waterfall, agile, and incremental.

technical controls   Hardware or software implementations that provide security control functionality. Examples include encryption, password enforcement, multifactor authentication, intrusion detection systems (IDSs), intrusion prevention systems (IPSs), and firewalls. Technical controls are also referred to as *logical controls*.

threat   Any potential danger that is associated with the exploitation of a vulnerability. The threat is that someone, or something, will identify a specific vulnerability and use it against the organization or individual.

Trojan   Malware disguised as something useful.

virtual local area network (VLAN)   A logical network that may share physical medium with other networks.

virus   A program or segment of code that infects a legitimate program in order to carry out its malicious job.

vulnerability   A weakness that could potentially be exploited. It can be a software, hardware, procedural, or human weakness.

vulnerability management   The ongoing process to identify, prioritize, remediate, and mitigate vulnerabilities in the organization's environment.

warm site   An alternate data processing center that has resources at a less than full state of readiness.

waterfall   A phased development life cycle characterized by linear-sequential distinct steps, each of which must be completed before the subsequent step is started. This method is also commonly referred to as the *traditional* or *phased* approach.

work breakdown structure (WBS)   A project management tool in which a project is broken down into hierarchical work elements (tasks, subtasks, and deliverables).

work factor   The amount of time and resources required to overcome security protections and carry out a cyberattack.

worm   A virus that propagates itself to other systems.

Zachman Framework   Named for its creator, John Zachman, a framework used as a way to view and define an enterprise architecture.

INDEX

357

Made in the USA
Coppell, TX
19 December 2024